Southwestern American Literature
A Bibliography

Southwestern American Literature

A Bibliography

edited by

John Q. Anderson
Edwin W. Gaston, Jr.
James W. Lee

THE SWALLOW PRESS INC.

CHICAGO

4

Published by
The Swallow Press Incorporated
811 West Junior Terrace
Chicago, Illinois 60613

First edition
First printing

This book is printed on recycled paper

LIBRARY OF CONGRESS CATALOG CARD NUMBER: 76-3121
ISBN 0-8040-0683-0

01/14/91

To the memory of R. H. Porter, Mody C. Boatwright, John Q. Anderson, and other publishers and scholars who believed in the Southwest.

Contents

Part II   The Literature

Introduction

As a geographic region, the American Southwest is difficult to define, because, as J. Frank Dobie once said, the boundaries are themselves "fluid, expanding and contracting according to the point of view from which the Southwest is viewed and according to whatever common denominator is taken for defining it." Thus, definitions vary from Dobie's expansive vision—extending from Texas to California on the west, to Montana in the north, and to Kansas-Missouri on the east—to Lawrence Clark Powell's more restrictive view that sets the heart of the region as Arizona and New Mexico and the periphery as "the lands east of the Rio Colorado, south of the Mesa Verde, west of the Pecos, and north of the Border." For sound but finally arbitrary reasons, the editors here have designated the Southwest as the states of Arizona, New Mexico, Oklahoma, and Texas. That decision reflects, among other things, a desire to avoid unnecessary overlapping with the specific interests stated or implied by the Society for the Study of Southern Literature, which has already produced a bibliography, and the Western American Literature Association.

The Southwest, as thus defined, abounds in paradox. It is at once among the oldest and youngest regions of the nation. Prehistoric Indians gathered here in substantial numbers, and Spanish explorers brought European civilization here in the sixteenth century. But factors such as the belated arrival of the Anglo-Americans in the nineteenth century resulted in the Southwest's continuing to be one of America's last frontiers today. Similarly, the literature produced by the region partakes of paradox. The oral songs and stories of the Indians establish Southwestern literature as among the earliest in North America. Spanish travel accounts here antedate the earliest British and French writing about the American East. But the mainstream of regional writing has been

Anglo-American, and it has reflected the cultural lag characteristic of the region. From the early nineteenth century until the present, Southwestern Anglo writing has evolved slowly from the utilitarian to the belletristic, from the incipiently romantic to the realistic and naturalistic. Only since World War I has it begun to approach the stature of Eastern American writing. Non-fiction writing and folklore study dominate regional letters.

A notable list of predecessors helped prepare the way for this bibliography. Those earlier bibliographies of a general nature include Mary Tucker's *Books of the Southwest* (1937); Mabel Major, Rebecca W. Smith, and T. M. Pearce's *Southwest Heritage* (1938; revised in 1948; and revised in 1972 by Major and Pearce); J. Frank Dobie's *Guide to Life and Literature of the Southwest* (1943; revised in 1952); Jesse Lee Rader's *South of Forty* (1947); Walter S. Campbell's *The Book Lover's Southwest* (1955); Kenneth Kurtz's *Literature of the American Southwest* (1956); C. L. Sonnichsen's *The Southwest* (mimeographed in 1961; revised in mimeographed form in 1969); and Richard W. Etulain's *Western American Literature* (1972).

Earlier bibliographies devoted to single states include C. W. Raines' *A Bibliography of Texas* (1896; 1934); Goldie Capers Smith's *The Creative Arts in Texas* (1926); J. Frank Dobie and William Rogers' *Finding Literature on the Texas Plains* (1930); Thomas W. Streeter's *Bibliography of Texas, 1795-1845* (1955-60); Joseph A. Munk's *Bibliography of Arizona* (1900; 1914); Mabel Parsons' *A Courier in New Mexico* (1936); Lyle Saunders' *A Guide to Materials Bearing on Cultural Relations in New Mexico* (1944); and Mary Hays Marable and Elaine Boylan's *A Handbook of Oklahoma Writers* (1939).

Finally, earlier bibliographies devoted to literary genres and subjects include Sister M. Agatha's *Texas Prose Writings* (1936); Albert Johanssen's *The House of Beadle and Adams and Its Dime and Nickel Novels* (vols. 1-2, 1950; vol. 3, 1961); Mildred P. Harrington's *The Southwest in Children's Books* (1952); Ramon F. Adams' *Six-Guns and Saddle Leather, A Bibliography of Books and Pamphlets on Western Outlaws and Gunmen* (1954) and *The Rampaging Herd, A Bibliography of Books and Pamphlets on Men and Events in the Cattle Industry* (1959); Lawrence Clark Powell's *Heart of the Southwest: A Selected Bibliography of Novels, Stories, and Tales* (1955) and *A Southwestern Century: A Bibliography of One Hundred Books of Non-Fiction* (1958); and John Holmes Jenkins' *Cracker Barrel Chronicles, A Bibliography of Texas Town and County Histories* (1965).

But while indebted to the earlier bibliographies, this work differs in a variety of ways. Most obviously, its Part III presents the most comprehensive listing to date of individual Southwestern writers and works by and about them. In many instances it provides for the first time a detailed bibliography of writers whose works have been obscured by time and lack of availability. Then, Parts II and I, respectively, present a significant expansion and updating of works relating to the literary genres and to those dealing with the historical, social, economic, political, ethnic, and folkloric background against which the literature of the Southwest may be considered.

Admittedly, this bibliography of Southwestern American literature has been compiled from a set of deliberately mixed principles so that an *apologia* seems appropriate. On the one hand, as already suggested, the editors have sought to be as *inclusive* as possible in order to indicate directly the scope of literary activity in the entire region and, indirectly in each of the four states. Yet, perforce, they have exercised an understandable amount of *exclusivity* and even *arbitrariness* in the interest of space and other considerations. For example, for Parts I and II, the editors have worked from the conviction that both should be considerably subordinated to Part III

—that, in other words, the emphasis should be upon the individual writers rather than topics and literary genres. Dobie and Campbell have been shown earlier to have bibliographies focusing upon topics and literary genres even if they are now dated. But no previous Southwestern bibliographers have presented listings comparable to those in our Part III.

The emphasis upon individual authors has resulted in significant topics being omitted from Parts I and II. For example, local histories do not generally appear in Part I. The editors felt that Jenkins and other bibliographers had adequately covered the topic. Similarly, non-literary history is sharply limited, represented mainly by such obvious historians as Barker, Bolton, and Webb. Then, examples of photographic art appear infrequently and then usually in connection with topics for which they provide visual illustration for texts. The intention has been to deal here mostly with the arts and crafts of folk rather than professional artists.

The number of entries under a given topic in Parts I and II has been arbitrarily limited. Because of inherent intellectual difficulties and the massive number of works, for example, writing by and about Indians has been reduced to about sixty listings. Again, because of quantitative considerations, the listings of autobiographies and biographies have been held to about seventy entries. And in all three parts of the bibliography, multiple printings of a given work have been restricted to those considered to be the most important by the editors.

Designed both for general and special use, *A Bibliography of Southwestern American Literature* will be helpful to students being introduced to Southwestern literature, by instructors guiding such students, and by all other readers interested in the region. It will also serve the specialist and the collector who will find it helpful in connection with more specialized bibliographies.

The editors and the members of the Southwestern American

Literature Association wish to stimulate interest in the literature of the region, not as a separate entity but as a fascinating part of American literature in general and thereby a part of the literature of the Western World.

Unfortunately, Professor John Q. Anderson, late Emeritus Professor of English at the University of Houston, did not live to see the publication of this book. John Anderson died on February 19, 1975, and the surviving editors have keenly felt his loss in the final stages of the preparation of this work. It is to his memory that we dedicate our labors.

Edwin W. Gaston, Jr.
James W. Lee

PART I

General Topics

The
Land

Animal Life

Abernethy, Francis Edward. "Running the Fox," *The Sunny Slopes of Long Ago. Publications of the Texas Folklore Society,* 33 (1966), 146-50.

Bailey, Vernon. *Mammals of New Mexico.* Washington: U.S. Department of Agriculture, 1931.

Barclay, Lillian Elizabeth. "The Coyote: Animal and Folk-Character," *Coyote Wisdom. Publications of the Texas Folklore Society,* 14 (1938), 36-103.

Barker, Elliott S. *When the Dogs Barked 'Treed.'* Albuquerque: Univ. of New Mexico Press, 1946.

Bedichek, Roy. *Adventures with a Texas Naturalist.* Garden City, New York: Doubleday, 1947; Austin: Univ. of Texas Press, 1961.

————. "Animal Tails: Function and Folklore," *Mesquite and Willow. Publications of the Texas Folklore Society,* 27 (1957), 105-12.

————. "Folklore in Natural History," *Folk Travelers. Publications of the Texas Folklore Society,* 25 (1953), 18-39.

————. *Karánkaway Country.* Garden City, New York: Doubleday, 1950.

Brandt, Herbert. *Arizona and Its Bird Life.* Cleveland: Bird Research Foundation, 1951.

————. *Texas Bird Adventures.* Cleveland: Bird Research Foundation, 1940.

Brock, Lois. "Tarantula Lore," *The Golden Log. Publications of the Texas Folklore Society,* 31 (1962), 41-52.

Brown, Bryce C. *An Annotated Check List of the Reptiles and Amphibians of Texas.* Waco: Baylor Univ. Press, 1950.

The Caves of Texas. Ed. Charles E. Mohr. Washington: Bulletin of the National Speleological Society, 1948.

Colorado Outdoors. Denver: Department of Natural Resources and Game, Fish and Parks Division, published bi-monthly since 1951.

Combs, Joe F. *Farm Corner.* San Antonio: Naylor, 1963.

Cottam, Clarence, and James B. Trefethen. *Whitewings.* New York: Van Nostrand, 1968.

Davis, William B. *The Mammals of Texas.* Austin: Game and Fish Commission, 1960.

Dawson, Everett T. *Texas Wildlife.* Dallas: Banks Upshaw, 1955.

Dobie, J. Frank. *The Ben Lilly Legend.* Boston: Little, Brown, 1950.

————. "Do Rattlesnakes Swallow Their Young?", *Mexican Border Ballads and Other Lore. Publications of the Texas Folklore Society,* 21 (1946), 43-64.

————. *The Longhorns*. Boston: Little, Brown, 1941.

————. *The Mustangs*. Boston: Little, Brown, 1952.

————. *On the Open Range*. Dallas: Southwest Press, 1931.

————. *Rattlesnakes*. Ed. Bertha McKee Dobie. Boston: Little, Brown, 1965.

————. "The Roadrunner in Fact and Folk-Lore," *Coyote Wisdom. Publications of the Texas Folklore Society,* 14 (1938), 146-74.

————. *Tales of the Mustang*. Dallas: The Book Club of Texas, 1936.

————. *The Voice of the Coyote*. Boston: Little, Brown, 1949.

Dodge, Natt N., and Herbert S. Zim. *The American Southwest*. New York: Simon and Schuster, 1955.

Goodrum, Phil. *The Gray Squirrel in Texas*. Bulletin No. 42. Austin: Texas Parks and Wildlife Department, 1961.

Graham, R. B. Cunninghame. *The Horses of the Conquest*. Norman: Univ. of Oklahoma Press, 1949.

Graves, John. *Goodbye to a River*. New York: Knopf, 1961.

Grinnell, George B. *When Buffalo Ran*. Norman: University of Oklahoma Press, 1969.

Grizzly Bear: Portraits from Life. Ed. Bessie D. Haynes. Norman: Univ. of Oklahoma Press, 1967.

Jaeger, Edmund C. *Our Desert Neighbors*. Stanford and Palo Alto: Stanford Univ. Press, 1950.

Koster, William J. *Guide to the Fishes of New Mexico*. Albuquerque: Univ. of New Mexico Press, 1957.

Krutch, Joseph W. *Grand Canyon: Today and All Its Yesterdays*. New York: Morrow, 1958; rpt. New York: Apollo, 1968.

Lehmann, V. W. *Forgotten Legions: Sheep in the Rio Grande Plain of Texas*. Austin: Univ. of Texas Press, 1969.

McCoy, J. J. *The Hunt for the Whooping Crane*. New York: Lothrop, Lee and Shepard, 1966.

McNulty, Faith. *The Whooping Crane*. New York: Dutton, 1966.

Miles, A. L. "Wolves, Foxes, Hound Dogs, and Men," *Singers and Storytellers. Publications of the Texas Folklore Society,* 30 (1961), 194-204.

Mitchell, Robert W. "Total Number and Density Estimates of Some Species of Cavernicoles Inhabiting Fern Cave, Texas," *Annales de Spéléologie,* 23, (1968), 597-620.

Munch, T. W. *Armadillo*. Austin: Steck, 1958.

————, and M. V. DeVault. *Horned Lizards*. Austin: Steck, 1957.

————. *The Road Runner*. Austin: Steck, 1958.

Mustangs and Cow Horses. Publications of the Texas Folklore Society, 16 (1940).

Nice, Margaret Morse. *The Birds of Oklahoma.* Norman: Univ. of Oklahoma Press, 1931.

Oberholser, Harry C. *The Bird Life of Texas.* Ed. with distribution maps and additional material by Edgar B. Kincaid, Jr. Austin: Univ. of Texas Press, 1975.

Parks, H. B. "Razorbacks," *Southwestern Lore. Publications of the Texas Folklore Society,* 9 (1931), 15-26.

Peterson, Roger Tory. *A Field Guide to the Birds of Texas.* Boston: Houghton Mifflin, 1963.

Poteet, Gibbons. "Jointsnake and Hoop Snake," *Man, Bird and Beast. Publications of the Texas Folklore Society,* 8 (1931), 124-28.

Raun, Gerald C. *A Bibliography of the Recent Animals of Texas.* Austin: The Museum of the Univ. of Texas, 1962.

Roe, Frank Gilbert. *The North American Buffalo.* Toronto: Univ. of Toronto Press, 1951.

Schorger, Arlie W. *Wild Turkey, Its History and Domestication.* Norman: Univ. of Oklahoma Press, 1966.

Seton, Ernest Thompson. *The Biography of a Grizzly.* New York: Appleton-Century-Crofts, 1900.

Simmons, George Finley. *Birds of the Austin Region.* Austin: Univ. of Texas Press, 1925.

Simpson, George G. *Horses: The Story of the Horse Family in the Modern World and Through Sixty Million Years of History.* New York: Oxford Univ. Press, 1951.

The Sky Is My Tipi. Publications of the Texas Folklore Society, 22 (1949).

The Southwestern Naturalist. Dallas: The Southwestern Association of Naturalists, published quarterly since 1956.

Stebbins, Robert C. *A Field Guide to Western Reptiles and Amphibians.* Boston: Houghton Mifflin, 1966.

Strecker, John K. "On the Origins of Reptile Myths," *Publications of the Texas Folklore Society,* 5 (1926), 70-77.

————. "Reptiles of the South and Southwest in Folk-Lore," *Publications of The Texas Folklore Society,* 5 (1926), 56-69.

Sutton, George M. *Oklahoma Birds: Their Ecology and Distribution:* Norman: Univ. of Oklahoma Press, 1967.

Tales From the Big Thicket. Ed. Francis Edward Abernethy. Austin: Univ.

of Texas Press, 1966.

Texas Folk and Folklore. Publications of the Texas Folklore Society, 26 (1954).

Texas Game and Fish. Austin: Texas Game, Fish and Oyster Commission, published monthly, 1941-1965.

Texas Parks and Wildlife. Austin: Texas Parks and Wildlife Department, published monthly, 1965-date.

Underhill, Lonnie E., and Daniel F. Littlefield, Jr. "Wild Turkeys in Oklahoma," *The Chronicles of Oklahoma,* 48 (Winter 1970-71), 376-88.

Webb, R. G. *Reptiles of Oklahoma: A Stovall Museum Publication.* Norman: Univ. of Oklahoma Press, 1970.

Webb, Walter Prescott. "Wild Horse Stories of Southwest Texas," *Round the Levee. Publications of the Texas Folklore Society,* 1 (1916), 58-61.

Werler, John E. *Poisonous Snakes of Texas and First Aid Treatment of Their Bites.* Austin: Texas Parks and Wildlife Department, 1967.

Wyman, Walker D. *The Wild Horse of the West.* Caldwell, Idaho: Caxton, 1945.

Young, Stanley Paul, and Hartley H. T. Jackson. *The Clever Coyote.* Harrisburg, Pennsylvania: Stackpole; and Washington: Wildlife Management Institute, 1951.

———. *Sketches of American Wildlife.* Baltimore: Monumental Press, 1946.

———, and Edward A. Goldman. *The Wolves of North America.* Washington: American Wildlife Institute, 1944.

Francis Edward Abernethy
Stephen F. Austin State University

Plant Life

Bedichek, Roy. *Adventures with a Texas Naturalist.* Garden City, New York: Doubleday, 1947; rpt. Austin: Univ. of Texas Press, 1961.

———. "Folklore in Natural History," *Folk Travelers. Publications of the Texas Folklore Society,* 25 (1953), 18-39.

———. *Karánkaway Country.* Garden City, New York: Doubleday, 1950.

Benson, Lyman, and Robert A. Darrow. *A Manual of Southwestern Desert Trees and Shrubs.* Tucson: Univ. of Arizona Press, 1944.

Carr, William Henry. *Desert Parade: A Guide to Southwestern Desert Plants and Wildlife.* New York: Viking, 1947.

Colorado Outdoors. Denver: Department of Natural Resources and Game, Fish and Parks Division, published bi-monthly since 1951.

Combs, Joe F. *Farm Corner.* San Antonio: Naylor, 1963.

Coulter, John M. *Botany of Western Texas.* Washington: U. S. Department of Agriculture, 1891-94.

Dodge, Natt N., and Herbert S. Zim. *The American Southwest.* New York: Simon and Schuster, 1955.

Forest Trees of Texas. Eds. W. R. Matoon and C. B. Matoon. College Station: Texas Forest Service, 1963.

Geiser, Samuel Wood. *Horticulture and Horticulturists in Early Texas.* Dallas: Southern Methodist Univ. Press, 1945.

Goodman, George J. *Spring Flora of Central Oklahoma.* Norman: Univ. of Oklahoma Duplicating Service, 1958.

Gould, Frank W., and Thadis W. Box. *Grasses of the Texas Coastal Bend.* College Station: Texas A&M Univ. Press, 1965.

————. *Texas Plants: A Check List and Ecological Summary.* College Station: Texas A&M Press, 1962.

Graves, John. *Goodbye to a River.* New York: Knopf, 1961.

Hall, David. "Folk Names of Texas Cacti," *Spur of the Cock. Publications of the Texas Folklore Society,* 11 (1933), 90-93.

Hatfield, Sadie. "Folklore of Texas Plants," *Backwoods to Border. Publications of the Texas Folklore Society,* 18 (1943), 157-62.

Jaeger, Edmund C. *Desert Wild Flowers.* Stanford: Stanford Univ. Press, 1940; rev. 1947.

Kerney, Thomas H., and Robert H. Peebles. *Arizona Flora.* Berkeley: Univ. of California Press, 1964.

Krutch, Joseph W. *Grand Canyon: Today and All Its Yesterdays.* New York: Morrow, 1958; rpt. New York: Apollo, 1968.

Pasture and Range Plants. Bartlesville: Phillips Petroleum Co., 1963.

Reeves, R. G., and D. C. Bain. *Flora of South Central Texas.* College Station: Texas A&M College Press, 1947.

Rickett, Harold W. *Wildflowers of the United States.* III (Texas). New York: McGraw-Hill, 1969.

Schulz, Ellen D. *Texas Wild Flowers.* New York: Laidlaw, 1928.

Silvius, W. A. *Texas Grasses.* San Antonio: Published by the author, 1933.

The Sky Is My Tipi. Publications of the Texas Folklore Society, 22 (1949).

The Southwestern Naturalist. Dallas: The Southwestern Association of Naturalists, published quarterly since 1956.

Stockwell, William Palmer, and Lucretia Breazeale. *Arizona Cacti*. Tucson: Univ. of Arizona Press, 1933.

Tales From the Big Thicket. Ed. Francis Edward Abernethy. Austin: Univ. of Texas Press, 1966.

Texas Folk and Folklore. Publications of the Texas Folklore Society, 26 (1954).

Texas Game and Fish. Austin: Texas Game, Fish and Oyster Commission, published monthly, 1941-1965.

Texas Parks and Wildlife. Austin: Texas Parks and Wildlife Department, published monthly since 1965.

Thompson, Eloise R. *Wildflower Portraits*. Norman: Univ. of Oklahoma Press, 1964.

Thorp, Benjamin Carroll. *Texas Range Grasses*. Austin: Univ. of Texas Press, 1952.

Turner, B. L. *The Legumes of Texas*. Austin: Univ. of Texas Press, 1959.

Vines, Robert H. *Trees, Shrubs, and Woody Vines of the Southwest*. Austin: Univ. of Texas Press, 1960.

Walker, Laurence C. *Ecology and Our Forests*. New York: A. S. Barnes, 1972.

Weniger, Del. *Cacti of the Southwest: Texas, New Mexico, Oklahoma, Arkansas, and Louisiana*. Austin: Univ. of Texas Press, 1969.

Whitehouse, Eula. *Texas Flowers in Natural Colors*. Dallas: Eula Whitehouse, 1936; rpt. 1948.

Wills, Mary Motz, and Howard S. Irwin. *Roadside Flowers of Texas*. Austin: Univ. of Texas Press, 1961.

Francis Edward Abernethy
Stephen F. Austin State University

Geography and Topography

Alsberg, Henry Garfield, ed. *The American Guide: The South, The Southwest*. New York: Hastings House, 1949.

————, and others. *Arizona: The Grand Canyon State*. Rev. ed. New York: Hastings House, 1966.

————, ed. *New Mexico: A Guide to the Colorful State*. Rev. by Joseph Miller. New York: Hastings House, 1962.

Arizona and New Mexico. Rev. ed. Garden City, New York: Doubleday, 1968.

Bartlett, John Russell. *Personal Narrative of Exploration and Incidents in Texas, New Mexico, California, Sonora, and Chihuahua, Connected with The United States and Mexican Boundary Commission* [1850-1853] *during the years 1850, '51, '52 and 53.* 2 vols. New York: Appleton, 1854; Chicago: Rio Grande Press, 1965.

Beck, Warren A., and Ynez D. Haase. *Historical Atlas of New Mexico.* Norman: Univ. of Oklahoma Press, 1969.

Bonnell, George William. *Topographical Description of Texas* (1840). Waco Texian Press, 1964.

Christiansen, Page W., and Frank E. Kottlowski, eds. *Mosaic of New Mexico's Scenery, Rocks, and History: A Brief Guide for Visitors.* Socorro, New Mexico: Institute of Mining and Technology, 1964.

Day, James M., ed. *Maps of Texas, 1527-1900. The Map Collection of The Texas State Archives.* Austin: Pemberton, 1962.

Dorrah, John Hazard. *Certain Hydrologic and Climatic Characteristics of the Southwest.* Albuquerque: Univ. of New Mexico Press, 1947.

Dunbier, Roger. *The Sonoran Desert: Its Geography, Economy, and People.* Tucson: Univ. of Arizona Press, 1968.

Fergusson, Erna. *New Mexico: A Pageant of Three Peoples.* 2nd ed. New York: Knopf, 1964.

Frost, Maximilian, and Paul A. F. Walter, eds. *The Land of Sunshine: A Handbook of the Resources, Products, Industries and Climate of New Mexico* (1904). 2nd ed. Santa Fe: New Mexican Printing Company, 1906.

Galloway, Robert W. "The Full-Glacial Climate in the Southwestern United States," *Annals of the Association of American Geographers,* 60 (June 1970), 245-56.

Gibbs, H. H. "A Southwest Passage?" *U. S. Naval Institute Proceedings,* 95 (April 1969), 64-73.

Goodwyn, Larry. *South Central States.* Boston: Little, Brown, 1970.

Hastings, James Rodney, and Raymond M. Turner. *The Changing Mile.* Tucson: Univ. of Arizona Press, 1965.

Heald, Weldon F. *Sky Island.* Princeton: Van Nostrand, 1967.

Hewett, Edgar L., and Wayne L. Mawzy. *Landmarks of New Mexico.* 2nd ed. Albuquerque: Univ. of New Mexico Press, 1953.

Hill, Robert T. "Descriptive Topographic Terms of Spanish America," *National Geographic Magazine,* 7 (September 1896), 291-302.

Hine, Robert V. *Bartlett's West: Drawing the Mexican Boundary.* New Haven and London: Yale Univ. Press, 1968.

Hollon, W. Eugene. *The Great American Desert, Then and Now.* New York: Oxford Univ. Press, 1966.

Hunter, Zena M. *The Story of the Colorado River.* Garden City, New York: Doubleday, 1960; rev., 1970.

Jaeger, Edmund Carroll. *The North American Deserts.* Palo Alto: Stanford Univ. Press, 1957.

James, George Wharton, *Arizona, The Wonder Land.* Boston: Page, 1917.
———. *New Mexico: The Land of the Delight Makers.* Boston: Page, 1920.

Jett, Stephen C. "An Analysis of Navajo Place-Names," *Names,* 18 (Sept. 1970), 175-84.

Lamar, Howard Roberts. *The Far Southwest, 1842-1912: A Territorial History.* New Haven: Yale Univ. Press, 1966.

Laxalt, Robert. "New Mexico: The Golden Land," *National Geographic Magazine,* 138 (Sept. 1970), 299-345.

Lesure, Thomas Barbour. *Adventures in Arizona: An Informal Guide to the Sights, Legends, and History of the Grand Canyon State.* San Antonio: Naylor, 1956.

———. *All About Arizona—The Healthful State.* Rev. ed. Greenlawn, New York: Harian Publications, 1970.

———. *The Heart of the Southwest: Arizona, Colorado, New Mexico, Texas, Utah, Nevada.* Greenlawn, New York: Harian Publications, 1959.

Luten, Daniel B. "The Use and Misuse of a River," *American West,* 4 (May 1967), 47-53.

McGinnies, William G., and Bram J. Goldman, eds. *Arid Lands in Perspective.* Tucson: Univ. of Arizona Press, 1971.

———, and others, eds. *Deserts of the World.* Tucson: Univ. of Arizona Press, 1968.

Matthews, William Baynham. *The Settler's Map and Guide Book: Oklahoma.* Washington: W. H. Lepley, 1889.

Meinig, D. W. *Imperial Texas: An Interpretive Essay in Cultural Geography.* Austin: Univ. of Texas Press, 1969.

———. *Southwest: Three Peoples in Geographical Change, 1600-1970.* New York: Oxford Univ. Press, 1971.

Miller, Thomas Lloyd. *The Public Lands of Texas, 1519-1967.* Norman: Univ. of Oklahoma Press, 1971.

Morgan, Dale L. *Pioneer Atlas of the American West.* New York: Rand

McNally, 1969.

Morris, John W., and Edwin C. McReynolds. *Historical Atlas of Oklahoma.* Univ. of Oklahoma Press, 1971.

————. *The Southwestern United States.* New York: Van Nostrand, Reinhold, 1970.

Nash, Roderick, and others, eds. *Grand Canyon of the Living Colorado.* New York: Sierra Club, 1970.

Niklason, C. R. *Commercial Survey of the Pacific Southwest.* Washington: U. S. Department of Commerce, 1930.

Oklahoma. Oklahoma City: Industrial Development and Park Department, 1968.

Parker, Watson. "Moods, Memories and Mirages: The Desert in American Magazines," *American West,* 1 (Fall 1964), 58-63.

Paullin, Charles Oscar. *Atlas of the Historical Geography of the United States.* Ed. John K. Wright. Washington and New York: Carnegie Institution and American Geographical Society, 1932.

Pearce, T. M., and others, eds. *New Mexico Place Names: A Geographical Dictionary.* Albuquerque: Univ. of New Mexico Press, 1965.

Peyton, Green [pseud. Green Peyton Wertenbaker]. *America's Heartland: The Southwest.* Norman: Univ. of Oklahoma Press, 1948.

Richardson, Rupert Norval, and Carl Coke Rister. *The Greater Southwest.* Glendale, California: Arthur H. Clark, 1935.

Robinson, William Henry. *Under Turquoise Skies.* New York: Macmillan, 1928.

Ruth, Kent, ed. *Oklahoma: A Guide to the Sooner State.* Rev. ed. Norman: Univ. of Oklahoma Press, 1957.

Rydjord, John. *Indian Place Names: Their Origin, Evolution, and Meanings, Collected in Kansas from the Siouan, Algonquian, Shoshonean, Caddoan, Iroquoian and Other Tongues.* Norman: Univ. of Oklahoma Press, 1968.

Saunderson, Mont H. *Western Land and Water Use.* Norman: Univ. of Oklahoma Press, 1950.

Sealock, Richard B., and Pauline A. Seely. *Bibliography of Place-Name Literature: United States and Canada.* 2nd ed. Chicago: American Library Association, 1967.

Sherman, James E., and Barbar H. *Ghost Towns of Arizona.* Norman: Univ. of Oklahoma Press, 1969.

Shirk, George H. *Oklahoma Place Names.* Norman: Univ. of Oklahoma Press, 1965.

Smiley, Terah L., ed. *Climate and Man in the Southwest.* Tucson: Univ. of Arizona Press, 1958.

The Southwest: A Handbook in Pictures, Maps, and Text for the Vacationist, The Traveler, and the Stay-At-Home. Editors of *Look* in collaboration with Paul Horgan. Boston: Houghton Mifflin, 1947.

Texas: A Guide to the Lone Star State (1940). Rev. ed. New York: Hastings House, 1955.

Topographic Maps. A standard series of quadrangle maps made and issued by the U. S. Geological Survey, Department of Interior, Washington, D. C. Available on request are "Topographic Maps," a descriptive folder for how to use the maps; and a special "Index to Topographic Maps" for each state individually which shows quadrangles in print and gives ordering instructions. Quadrangles, bounded by meridians of longitude and parallels of latitude, are the most detailed and accurate maps published.

Tuan, Yi-Fu, and others. *The Climate of New Mexico.* Santa Fe: New Mexico State Planning Office, 1969.

————. "New Mexican Gullies: A Critical Review and Some Recent Observations," *Annals of the Association of American Geographers,* 56 (December 1966), 573-97.

————. *Pediments in Southeastern Arizona.* Berkeley: Univ. of California Press, 1959.

————. "Structure, Climate, and Basin Land Forms in Arizona and New Mexico," *Annals of the Association of American Geographers,* 52 (March 1962), 51-68.

Tucker, Edwin A. and George Fitzpatrick. *Men Who Matched the Mountains: The Forest Service in the Southwest.* Washington: Government Printing Office, 1972.

Ungnade, Herbert E. *Guide to the New Mexico Mountains.* Albuquerque: Univ. of New Mexico Press, 1972.

Van Dyke, John Charles. *The Desert.* New York: Scribner's, 1930.

Webb, Walter Prescott. *The Great Plains.* Boston: Ginn, 1931.

————, and others, eds. *The Handbook of Texas.* 2 vols. Austin: Texas State Historical Association, 1952. A 3rd volume appeared in 1970.

Wheeler, Lt. George M. *Annual Report Upon the Geographical Surveys West of the One Hundredth Meridian, in California, Nevada, Utah, Wyoming, New Nexico, Arizona, and Montana.* Washington: Government Printing Office, 1876.

White, C. Langdon, Edwin J. Foscue and Tom L. McKnight. *Regional*

Geography of Anglo-America. 3rd ed. Englewood Cliffs, N. J.: Prentice Hall, 1964.

John Hakac
Arizona State University

Description and Travel

Abbott, E. C., and Helena Huntington Smith. *We Pointed Them North: Recollections of a Cowpuncher.* Norman: Univ. of Oklahoma Press, 1955.

Abert, J. W. *Western American in 1846-1847; The Original Travel Diary of Lieutenant J. W. Abert, Who Mapped New Mexico for the United States Army* (1848). Ed. John Galvin. San Francisco: John Howell, 1966.

Armer, Laura. *Southwest.* New York: Longmans, 1935.

Athearn, Robert G. *Westward the Briton.* Lincoln: Univ. of Nebraska Press, 1963.

Austin, Mary. *The Land of Journey's Ending.* New York: Century, 1924.

Bandelier, Adolph F. *The Southwestern Journals of Adolph F. Bandelier, 1880-1882.* Ed. Charles H. Lange and Carroll L. Riley. Albuquerque: Univ. of New Mexico Press, 1966.

————. *The Southwestern Journals of Adolph F. Bandelier, 1883-1884.* Ed. Charles H. Lange and Carroll L. Riley. Albuquerque: Univ. of New Mexico Press, 1970.

Bennett, James A. *Forts and Forays: A Dragoon in New Mexico, 1850-1856.* Ed. Clinton E. Brooks and Frank D. Reeve. Albuquerque: Univ. of New Mexico Press, 1948.

Brewerton, George Douglas. *Overland with Kit Carson: A Narrative of the Old Spanish Trail in '48.* New York: Coward-McCann, 1930.

Briggs, L. Vernon. *Arizona and New Mexico 1882, California 1886, Mexico 1891.* New York: Argonaut, 1966.

Browne, J. Ross. *A Tour Through Arizona, 1864, or, Adventures in the Apache Country.* Tucson: Arizona Silhouettes, 1951.

Calvin, Ross. *River of the Sun.* Albuquerque: Univ. of New Mexico Press, 1946.

————. *Sky Determines: An Interpretation of the Southwest.* Rev. ed. Albuquerque: Univ. of New Mexico Press, 1965.

Conner, Daniel E. *Joseph Reddeford Walker and the Arizona Adventure.* Ed. Donald J. Berthrong and Odessa Davenport. Norman: Univ. of Oklahoma Press, 1956.

Cook, James H. *Fifty Years on the Old Frontier as Cowboy, Hunter, Guide, Scout, and Ranchman.* Norman: Univ. of Oklahoma Press, 1957.

Corle, Edwin. *The Gila, River of the Southwest.* New York: Rinehart, 1951.

Darrah, William Culp. *Powell of the Colorado.* Princeton: Princeton Univ. Press. 1951.

Davis, W. W. H. *El Gringo: or New Mexico and Her People.* Santa Fe: Rydal, 1938.

Duffus, R. L. *The Sante Fe Trail.* New York: Longmans, 1930.

Fergusson, Erna. *Our Southwest.* New York: Knopf, 1940.

Foreman, Grant. *Marcy and the Gold Seekers: The Journal of Captain R. B. Marcy, with an Account of the Gold Rush Over the Southern Route.* Norman: Univ. of Oklahoma Press, 1939.

Forrest, Earle R. *With a Camera in Old Navaholand.* Norman: Univ. of Oklahoma Press, 1970.

Fowler, Jacob. *The Journal of Jacob Fowler, Narrating an Adventure from Arkansas through the Indian Territory, Oklahoma, Kansas, Colorado, and New Mexico to the Sources of Rio Grande Del Norte 1821-1822* (1898). Ed. Elliott Coues. Lincoln: Univ. of Nebraska Press, 1970.

Gard, Wayne. *The Chisholm Trail.* Norman: Univ. of Oklahoma Press, 1954.

Garrard, Lewis H. *Wah-to-yah and the Taos Trail: or, Prairie Travel and Scalp Dances, with a Look at Los Rancheros from Muleback and the Rocky Mountain Campfire* (1850). Norman: Univ. of Oklahoma Press, 1955.

Gregg, Josiah. *Commerce of the Prairies* (1844). Ed. Max L. Moorhead. Norman: Univ. of Oklahoma Press, 1954.

————. *Diary and Letters of Josiah Gregg.* Ed. Maurice Garland Fulton. 2 vols. Norman: Univ. of Oklahoma Press, 1941, 1944.

Gregg, Kate L., ed. *The Road to Santa Fe: The Journal and Diaries of George Champlain Sibley and Others Pertaining to the Surveying and Marking of a Road from the Missouri Frontier to the Settlements of New Mexico, 1825-1827.* Albuquerque: Univ. of New Mexico Press, 1952.

Hollon, W. Eugene. *Beyond the Cross Timbers: The Travels of Randolph B. Marcy, 1812-1887.* Norman: Univ. of Oklahoma Press, 1955.

————. *The Southwest: Old and New* (1961). Lincoln: Univ. of Nebraska Press, 1968.

Horgan, Paul. *The Great River: The Rio Grande in North American History.* New York: Macmillan, 1954.

King, C. Richard, ed. *Victorian Lady on the Texas Frontier: The Journal of Ann Raney Coleman.* Norman: Univ. of Oklahoma Press, 1971.

Lane, Lydia Spencer. *I Married a Soldier*. Albuquerque: Horn and Wallace, 1964.

Loomis, Noel M. *The Texan-Santa Fe Pioneers*. Norman: Univ. of Oklahoma Press, 1958.

Lummis, Charles F. *The Land of Poco Tiempo* (1893). Albuquerque: Univ. of New Mexico Press, 1952.

——. *Mesa, Canon, and Pueblo*. New York: Century, 1925.

McWilliams, Carey. *North from Mexico*. Philadelphia: Lippincott, 1949.

Marcy, Randolph B. *Thirty Years of Army Life on the Border* (1866). Philadelphia: Lippincott, 1963.

Marion, John H. *Notes of Travel through the Territory of Arizona: Being an Account of the Trip Made by General George Stoneman and Others in the Autumn of 1870*. Ed. Donald M. Powell. Tucson: Univ. of Arizona Press, 1965.

Meline, James F. *Two Thousand Miles on Horseback. Santa Fe and Back. A Summer Tour through Kansas, Nebraska, Colorado, and New Mexico, in the Year 1866* (1869). Albuquerque: Horn and Wallace, 1966.

Meriwether, David. *My Life in the Mountains and on the Plains: The Newly Discovered Autobiography*. Ed. Robert A. Griffen. Norman: Univ. of Oklahoma Press, 1965.

Oliva, Leo E. *Soldiers on the Santa Fe Trail*. Norman: Univ. of Oklahoma Press, 1967.

Ormsby, Waterman L. *The Butterfield Overland Mail: Only Through Passenger on the First Westbound Stage*. Ed. Lyle H. Wright and Josephine M. Bynum. San Marino: Huntington Library, 1942.

Owens, William A. *Impressions of the Big Thicket*. Illustrated by Michael Frary. Austin: Univ. of Texas Press, 1973.

Seymour, Catryna Ten Eyck. *Enjoying the Southwest*. Philadelphia: Lippincott, 1973.

Sibley, Marilyn M. *Travelers in Texas, 1761-1860*. Austin: Univ. of Texas Press, 1966.

Simpson, Lieutenant James H. *Navaho Expedition: Journal of a Military Reconnaissance from Santa Fe, New Mexico to the Navaho Country* (1852). Ed. Frank McNitt. Norman: Univ. of Oklahoma Press, 1964.

Slater, John M. *El Morro, Inscription Rock, New Mexico: The Rock Itself, the Inscriptions Thereon, and the Travelers Who Made Them*. Los Angeles: Plantin Press, 1961.

Smalley, George H. *My Adventures in Arizona: Leaves from a Reporter's*

Notebook. Ed. Yndia Smalley Moore. Tucson: Arizona Pioneers' Historical Society, 1966.

Steele, James W. *Frontier Army Sketches.* Albuquerque: Univ. of New Mexico Press, 1969.

Summerhayes, Martha. *Vanished Arizona: Recollections of Army Life, 1870-1890.* Glorieta, New Mexico: Rio Grande Press, 1970.

Tilden, Freeman. *Following the Frontier: With F. Jay Haynes, Pioneer Photographer of the Old West.* New York: Knopf, 1965.

Townshend, R. B. *Last Memories of a Tenderfoot.* New York: Dodd, 1926.

Kenneth L. Donelson
Arizona State University

The
People

Indians

Aberle, S. D. "The Pueblo Indians of New Mexico," *Memoirs of the American Anthropological Association,"* 70 (1948), 1-93.

Adair, John. *Navaho and Pueblo Silversmiths.* Norman: Univ. of Oklahoma Press, 1944; rpt. 1954.

Alexander, Hartley Burr. *Pueblo Indian Painting.* Nice, France: C. Szwedzichi, 1932.

Amsden, Charles Avery. *Navaho Weaving: Its Technic & Its History.* Glorieta, New Mexico: Rio Grande Press, 1964.

Arnold, Elliott. *Blood Brothers.* New York: Meredith, 1947; rpt. 1950.

Atkinson, Mary Jordan. *Indians of the Southwest.* San Antonio: Naylor, 1963.

————. *The Texas Indians.* San Antonio: Naylor, 1935.

Bahti, Tom. *Southwestern Indian Tribes.* Flagstaff, Arizona: KC Publications, 1968.

Ball, Eve. *In the Days of Victorio: Recollections of a Warm Springs Apache.* Tucson: Univ. of Arizona Press, 1970.

Bailey, Lynn R. *Indian Slave Trade in the Southwest.* Los Angeles: Westernlore Press, 1966.

Bandelier, Adolph F. "Contributions to the History of the Southwestern Portion of the United States," *Papers of the Archaeological Institute of America, American Series,* 5 (1890), 1-206.

————. "Documentary History of the Rio Grande Pueblo," *Papers of the School of American Research,* 13 (1910), 1-27.

————. *The Delight Makers.* New York: Dodd, Mead, 1890; rpt. 1918. (Tewa)

————. *Final Report of the Investigations Among the Indians of the Southwestern United States.* 2 vols. Cambridge: J. Wilson, 1890-92.

————. *The Gilded Man.* New York: Appleton, 1893; Glorieta, New Mexico: Rio Grande Press, 1962.

————. "An Outline of the Documentary History of the Zuni Tribe," *Journal of American Ethnology and Archaeology,* 3 (1892), 1-115.

————, and Edgar L. Hewit. *Indians of the Rio Grande Valley.* Albuquerque: Univ. of New Mexico Press, 1937.

Berlandier, Jean Louis. *The Indians of Texas in 1830.* Ed. John C. Ewers. Trans. Patricia R. Leclercq. Washington: Smithsonian, 1969.

Bolton, Herbert Eugene. "Texas in the Middle of the Eighteenth Century," *Univ. of California Publications in History,* 3 (1915), 1-501. (Lipan)

Brown, Dee. *Bury My Heart at Wounded Knee: An Indian History of the American West.* New York: Holt, Rinehart, Winston, 1971.

Bunzel, R. L. "Introduction to Zuni Ceremonialism," *Annual Reports of the Bureau of American Ethnology,* 47 (1930), 467-544.

———. "The Pueblo Potter," *Columbia University Contributions to Anthropology,* 8 (1929), 1-134. (Acoma)

———. "Zuni Katcinas," *Annual Reports of the Bureau of American Ethnology,* 47 (1930), 837-1086.

———. "Zuni Ritual Poetry," *Annual Reports of the Bureau of American Ethnology,* 47 (1930), 611-835.

Colton, Harold S. *Hopi Kachina Dolls.* Albuquerque: Univ. of New Mexico Press, 1949, rpt. 1959.

Curtis, Edward S. *The North American Indian.* Ed. Frederick Webb Hodge. 20 vols. Cambridge: University Press, 1907-1930.

Curtis, Natalie, ed. *The Indians Book.* New York: Harper, 1935; rpt. New York: Dover, 1967.

Dale, E. E. *The Indians of the Southwest.* Norman: Univ. of Oklahoma Press, 1949.

Dodge, Richard I. *Our Wild Indians. Thirty Three Years' Personal Experience Among the Red Men of the Great West.* Chicago: A. G. Nettleton, 1883.

Eggan, Fred. *Social Organization of the Western Pueblos.* Chicago: Univ. of Chicago Press, 1950.

Fehrenbach, T. R. *Comanches: The Destruction of a People.* New York: Knopf, 1974.

Fergusson, Erna. *Dancing Gods.* New York: Knopf, 1931.

———. *Dancing Gods: Indian Ceremonies of New Mexico and Arizona.* Albuquerque: Univ. of New Mexico Press, 1959.

Foreman, Grant. *The Five Civilized Tribes.* Norman: Univ. of Oklahoma Press, 1934.

———. *The Last Trek of the Indians.* Chicago: Univ. of Chicago Press, 1946.

Gifford, E. W. "Apache-Pueblo," *Anthropological Records,* 4 (1940), 1-207.

Gilles, Albert S., Sr. *Comanche Days.* Dallas: Southern Methodist Univ. Press, 1973.

Hewett, Edgar L., and Bertha P. Dutton. *The Pueblo Indian World.* Albuquerque: Univ. of New Mexico Press, 1945.

Hodge, Frederick Webb. *The Early Navajo and Apache.* Washington: Judd & Detweiler, 1895.

Hooton, E. A. *The Indians of the Pecos Pueblo.* New Haven: Yale Univ. Press, 1930.

Hough, W. *The Hopi Indians.* Cedar Rapids: Univ. of Iowa Press, 1915.

Kaut, C. R. "The Western Apache Clan System," *Univ. of New Mexico Publications in Anthropology,* 9 (1957), 99 pp.

Kidder, A. V., and A. Shepard. *The Pottery of Pecos.* 2 vols. New Haven: Yale Univ. Press, 1936

Kluckhohn, Clyde. *Navaho Witchcraft.* Boston: Beacon Press, 1962.

————, and Dorothy Cross Leighton. *The Navaho.* Cambridge: Harvard Univ. Press, 1947.

Ladd, J. *The Structure of a Moral Code: A Philosophical Analysis of Ethical Discourse Applied to Ethics of the Navajo Indians.* Cambridge: Harvard Univ. Press, 1957.

LaFarge, Oliver. *The Changing Indian.* Norman: Univ. of Oklahoma Press, 1942.

————. *Laughing Boy.* Boston: Houghton Mifflin, 1929.

Lange, C. H. *Cochiti.* Austin: Univ. of Texas Press, 1960.

Leighton, Alexander H., and Dorothea C. Leighton. *The Navaho Door.* Cambridge: Harvard Univ. Press, 1944.

McNitt, Frank. *The Navajos: A Military History, 1540-1861.* Albuquerque: Univ. of New Mexico Press, 1972.

Mathews, John Joseph. *Wah-Kon-Tah. An Interpretation of the Osage Spirit, based on Notes Kept by Laban J. Miles, U. S. Agent to the Tribe.* Norman: Univ. of Oklahoma Press, 1932.

Marriott, Alice L. *Maria the Potter of Ildefonso.* Norman: Univ. of Oklahoma Press, 1958.

————. *The Ten Grandmothers.* Norman: Univ. of Oklahoma Press, 1945.

Mayhill, Mildred P. *Indian Wars of Texas.* Waco, Texas: Texian Press, 1965.

Newcomb, William W. *The Indians of Texas, from Prehistoric to Modern Times.* Austin: Univ. of Texas Press, 1961.

Nye, W. S. *Carbine and Lance: The Story of Old Fort Sill.* Norman: Univ. of Oklahoma Press, 1937.

O'Kane, Walter Collins. *Sun in the Sky.* Norman: Univ. of Oklahoma Press, 1951.

Reichard, Gladys A. *Navaho Religion: Study of Symbolism.* 2 vols. Princeton: Princeton Univ. Press, 1964.

Richardson, Rupert N. *The Comanche Barrier to the South Plains Settlements.* Glendale: A. H. Clark, 1933.

Roediger, Virginia M. *Ceremonial Costumes of the Pueblo Indians.* Berkeley: Univ. of California Press, 1941.

Russell, F. "The Pima Indians," *Annual Report of the Bureau of Ethnology,* (1908), 3-390.

Schultz (Apikun:), James Willard. *Why Gone Those Times?* Ed. Eugene Lee Silliman. Norman: Univ. of Oklahoma Press, 1974.

Sonnichsen, C. L. *The Mescalero Apaches.* Norman: Univ. of Oklahoma Press, 1958.

Stevenson, M. C. "The Zuni Indians," *Annual Report of the Bureau of American Ethnology,* 23 (1904), 13-608.

Stubbs, Stanley A. *Bird's-Eye-View of the Pueblos.* Norman: Univ. of Oklahoma Press, 1951.

Terrell, John Upton. *The Navajos: The Past and Present of a Great People.* New York: Rinehart & Winston, 1970.

Thomas, A. B. *After Coronado.* Norman: Univ. of Oklahoma Press, 1935.

Vestal, Stanley. *'Dobie Walls,' A Story of Kit Carson's Southwest.* Boston: Houghton Mifflin, 1929.

Underhill, Ruth Murray. *Ceremonial Potters in the Greater Southwest.* Seattle: Univ. of Washington Press, 1948.

———. *First Penthouse Dwellers of America.* New York: Augustin, 1938.

———. *Navajos.* Norman: Univ. of Oklahoma Press, 1956.

———. *Red Man's Religion.* Chicago: Univ. of Chicago Press, 1965.

———. "Here Come the Navaho." Indian Life and Customs Pamphlets, 8 (1953), 285 pp.

Waters, Frank. *Pumpkin Seed Point.* Chicago: Swallow, 1969 (Hopi).

Wellman, Paul I. *Death on the Prairie. The Thirty Years' Struggle for the Western Plains.* New York: Macmillan, 1934.

Wharton, Clarence. *Santanta, the Great Chief of the Kiowas and His People.* Dallas: Upshaw, 1935.

Wilbarger, J. W. *Indian Depredations in Texas* (1889). Austin: Pemberton, 1967.

Wormington, H. M. *Prehistoric Indians of the Southwest.* Denver: Museum of Natural History, 1947.

Wright, Muriel H. *A Guide to the Indian Tribes of Oklahoma.* Norman: Univ. of Oklahoma Press, 1951.

Young, R. W., and W. Morgan. *The Navaho Language*. Phoenix: Univ. of Arizona Press, 1943.

Elma Heard
Stephen F. Austin State University

Spanish

Altamira y Crevea, Raphael. *Novedades y rectificaciones en el estudio de la colonización española en América*. Madrid: Fortanet, 1917.

Babbitt, Irving. *Spanish Character and Other Essays*. Boston: Houghton Mifflin, 1940.

Bancroft, Hubert H. *California Pastoral, 1796-1848*. San Francisco: A. L. Bancroft, 1888.

Bandelier, Adolph F. A. *The Gilded Man*. New York: Appleton, 1893.

Blackmar, Frank Wilson. *Spanish Colonization in the Southwest*. Baltimore: Johns Hopkins Univ. Press, 1890.

————. *Spanish Institutions of the Southwest*. Baltimore: Johns Hopkins Univ. Press, 1891.

Bolton, Herbert E. *California*. New York: Prentice Hall, 1953.

————, ed. *Spanish Exploration in the Southwest, 1542-1706*. New York: Scribner, 1916.

————. *The Spanish Borderlands*. New Haven: Yale Univ. Press, 1921.

Bonilla, Rodrigo H. *Spanish Daily Life*. New York: Newson, 1907.

Brady, Cyrus T. *The Conquest of the Southwest*. New York: Appleton, 1905.

Brown, Vera Lee. *Anglo-Spanish Relations in America in the Closing Years of the Colonial Era (1763-1774)*. Baltimore: n. p. 1923.

Bunker, Robert, and John Adair. *First Look at Strangers*. New Brunswick, New Jersey: Rutgers Univ. Press, 1959.

Burma, John H. "The Present Status of the Spanish-Americans of New Mexico," *Social Forces,* 28 (December 1949), 133-38.

Burris, Quincy G. "Juan: A Rural Portrait," *Survey Graphic,* 33 (December 1944), 499-503.

Child, Theodore. *Spanish-American Republics*. New York: Harper, 1891.

Cornelius, E. T. "Success Among Spanish Americans," *Missionary Review of the World,* 57 (January 1934), 33-37.

Davis, William Watts Hart. *El Gringo; or, New Mexico and Her People*. New York: Harper, 1857.

————. "The Spaniard in New Mexico," *Papers,* American Historical Association, 1 (1888), 164-76.

————. *The Spanish Conquest of New Mexico.* Doylestown: n.p., 1869.

Denis, Alberta J. *Spanish Alta California.* New York: Macmillan, 1927.

Ellis, George Edward. "Las Casas, and the Relations of the Spaniards to the Indians," in Winsor, Justin, ed., *Narrative and Critical History of America,* II (1886). Boston and New York: Houghton Mifflin, 1884-89.

Fergusson, Erna. *New Mexico: A Pageant of Three Peoples.* New York: Knopf, 1952.

Forrest, Earle R. *Missions and Pueblos of the Old Southwest.* Glorieta, New Mexico: Rio Grande, 1962.

Foster, George M. *Culture and Conquest: America's Spanish Heritage.* New York: Quadrangle Books, 1960.

Gardner, Richard M. *Grito: Reyes Tijerina and the New Mexico Land Grant of 1967.* New York: Bobbs-Merrill, 1970.

Gibson, Charles. *Spain in America.* New York: Harper & Row, 1966.

————. *The Spanish Tradition in America.* New York: Harper & Row, 1968.

Gonzalez, Nancie L. *The Spanish-Americans of New Mexico.* Albuquerque: Univ. of New Mexico Press, 1969.

Hallenbeck, Cleve. *The Journey of Fray Marcos de Niza.* Illus. by Jose Cisneros and designed by Carl Hertzog. Dallas: Univ. Press, 1949.

Haring, Clarence Henry. *The Spanish Empire in America.* New York: Harcourt, Brace & World, 1963.

Hart, James D. *American Images of Spanish California.* Berkeley: Friends of the Bancroft Library, Univ. of California, 1960.

Hassaurek, Friedrich. *Four Years Among Spanish-Americans.* New York: Hurd and Houghton, 1867.

Helps, Sir Arthur. *Spanish Conquest in America.* New York: John Lane, 1900.

Henderson, Alice Corbin. *Brothers of Light.* New York: Harcourt, Brace, 1937.

Horgan, Paul. *The Heroic Triad.* New York: Holt, Rinehart & Winston, 1970.

Hughes, Anne Eugenia. *The Beginning of Spanish Settlement in the El Paso District.* Berkeley: Univ. of California Press, 1914.

Johansen, Sigurd A. *Rural Social Organization in a Spanish-American Culture Area.* Albuquerque: Univ. of New Mexico Press, 1948.

————. "The Social Organization of Spanish-American Villages," *South-*

western Social Science Quarterly, 23 (September 1942), 151-59.

Johnson, William Henry. *Pioneer Spaniards in North America.* Boston: Little, Brown, 1900-05.

Jones, Robert C. "The Latin-American Problem," *School and Society,* 58 (4 December 1943), 441-43.

Knowlton, Clark S. "Changing Spanish-American Villages of Northern New Mexico," *Sociology and Social Research,* 53 (July 1969), 455-74.

———. "Patron-Peon Pattern Among the Spanish-Americans of New Mexico," *Social Forces,* 41 (October 1962), 12-17.

———. "Spanish Americans in New Mexico," *Sociology and Social Research,* 45 (July 1961), 448-54.

Lummis, Charles Fletcher. *Flowers of Our Lost Romance.* Boston: Houghton Mifflin, 1929.

———. *The Land of Poco Tiempo.* (1893). New York: Scribner, 1893, 1925; Albuquerque: Univ. of New Mexico Press, 1952.

———. *The Spanish Pioneers.* Chicago: A. C. McClurg, 1893, 1929.

McLean, Robert M., and Grace Williams. *Old Spain in New America.* Issued by the Council of Women for Home Missions. New York: Associated Press, 1946.

Martinez, Rafael V. *My House Is Your House.* New York: Friendship Press, 1964.

Mead, Margaret, ed. *Cultural Patterns and Technical Change.* Paris: United Nations Educational, Scientific, and Cultural Organization, 1953.

Morse, Edward Leland Clark. *Spanish-American Life.* Chicago and New York: Scott Foresman, 1917.

Nabokov, Peter. *Tijerina and the Courthouse Raid.* Albuquerque: Univ. of New Mexico Press, 1969.

Nelson, Edna Deu Pree. *The California Dons.* New York: Appleton-Century-Crofts, 1962.

Ortega, Joaquin. "The Intangible Resources of New Mexico," *Papers* of the School of American Research. Santa Fe: 1945.

Otero, Nina. *Old Spain in Our Southwest.* Glorieta, New Mexico: Rio Grande, 1962.

Perrigo, Lynn I. *Our Spanish Southwest.* Dallas: Upshaw, 1960.

Pike, Zebulon M. *An Account of Expeditions to the Sources of the Mississippi.* Philadelphia: C. & A. Conrad, 1810.

Pillsbury, Dorothy L. "Adobe Village in New Mexico and Its Spanish-Speaking Folk," *Common Ground,* 4 (1944), 38-43.

———. *Roots in Adobe.* Albuquerque: Univ. of New Mexico Press, 1959.

Pitt, Leonard M. *The Decline of the Californios.* Berkeley: Univ. of California Press, 1970.

Pool, M. L. "Family in Spanishtown," *Overland,* 15 (April 1890), 199-208.

Priestly, Herbert I. *The Coming of the White Man, 1492-1848.* New York: Macmillan, 1929.

Reindorp, Reginald Carl. *Spanish-American Customs, Culture and Personality.* Macon, Georgia: Wesleyan College, 1968.

Sánchez, George I. *Forgotten People: A Study of New Mexicans.* Albuquerque: Univ. of New Mexico Press, 1940.

Sánchez, Nellie Van de Grift. *Spanish Arcadia.* Los Angeles: Powell Publishing Co., 1929.

Shepherd, William Robert. *The Spanish Heritage in America.* New York: International Telephone & Telegraph Corp., 1926.

Stowell, Jay S. *A Study of Mexicans and Spanish Americans in the United States.* New York: Home Missions Council, 1920.

Vogt, Evan Z. *People of Rimrock.* Cambridge: Harvard Univ. Press, 1966.

Wagner, Henry R. *The Spanish Southwest, 1542-1794.* New York: Arno Press, 1967.

Whitaker, A. P. *The Spanish-American Frontier: 1783-1795.* Lincoln: Univ. of Nebraska Press, 1969.

Winterburn, R. V. *The Spanish in the Southwest.* New York: American Book Co., 1903.

Charles Ramos
Midwestern University

Mexican

Altus, William David. "The American Mexican: the Survival of a Culture," *Journal of Social Psychology,* 29 (May 1949), 211-20.

Audubon, John W. *Audubon's Western Journals, 1849-1850.* Cleveland: Arthur H. Clark, 1906.

Austin, Stephen F. "The Austin Papers," ed. Eugene C. Barker, *Annual Report for the American Historical Association for the Year 1922.* Washington: Government Printing Office, 1928.

Barker, Eugene C. *Mexico and Texas.* Austin: Univ. of Texas Press, 1934.

Bartlett, John Russell. *Personal Narrative of Explorations and Incidents in Texas.* New York: Appleton, 1854.

Beals, Ralph L. "Culture Patterns of Mexican-American Life." *Proceedings, Fifth Annual Conference on the Education of Spanish-Speaking Peoples,* George Pepperdine College, Los Angeles (January 1951), 5-13.

Bean, Ellis P. *Memoir of Colonel Ellis P. Bean.* Ed. W. O. Yoakum. Houston: Book Club of Texas, 1930.

Bogardus, Emory S. *Immigration and Race Attitudes.* New York: Heath, 1928.

————. *The Mexican Immigrant.* Los Angeles: The Council on International Relations, 1929.

————. *The Mexican in the United States.* Los Angeles: Univ. of Southern California Press, 1934.

————. "Second Generation Mexicans," *Sociology and Social Research,* 13 (January 1929), 276-83.

Brenner, Anita. *Idols Behind Altars.* New York: Payson and Clarke, 1929.

Bresette, Lenna E. *Mexicans in the United States.* Washington: National Catholic Welfare Conference, 1930.

Brown, William Horace. *The Glory Seekers: Founders of the Great Southwest.* Chicago: A. C. McClurg, 1906.

Browne, J. Ross. *A Tour Through Arizona, 1864.* Tucson: Arizona Silhouettes, 1950.

Burgess, Thomas. "On the American Side of the Rio Grande," *Missionary Review of the World,* 50 (September 1927), 689-92.

Burma, John H., ed. *Mexican-Americans in the United States.* Cambridge: Schenkman Publishing Co., 1970.

————. *Spanish-Speaking Groups in the United States.* Durham: Duke Univ. Press, 1954.

Carranza, Elihu. *Pensamientos on Los Chicanos: A Cultural Revolution.* Berkeley: California Book Co., 1969.

Cerwin, Herbert. *These Are the Mexicans.* New York: Reynal and Hitchcock, 1947.

Chamberlain, Samuel E. *My Confession.* New York: Harper, 1956.

Clappe, Louise Amelia Knapp. *The Shirley Letters From the California Mines 1851-1852.* New York: Knopf, 1949.

Cline, Howard F. *The United States and Mexico.* Cambridge: Harvard Univ. Press, 1963.

Coy, Harold. *The Mexicans.* Boston: Little, Brown, 1970.

Dawson, Joseph M. "Among the Mexicans in Texas; Waco Mission," *Missionary Review of the World,* 50 (October 1927), 757-58.

De Voto, Bernard. *1846, The Year of Decision.* Boston: Little, Brown, 1943.

Dickerson, R. E. "Some Suggestive Problems in the Americanization of Mexicans," *Pedagogical Seminary* (September 1919), 288-97.

Dobie, J. Frank. *A Vaquero of the Brush Country.* Dallas: Southwest Press, 1929.

————. "The Mexican Vaquero of the Texas Border," *Southwestern Political and Social Science Quarterly,* 8 (June 1927), 15-26.

————. *Puro Mexicano.* Publications of the Texas Folklore Society, 12 (1935).

————. "Ranch Mexicans," *Survey Graphic* (May 1931), 167-70.

Evans, George W. B. *Mexican Gold Trail, the Journal of a 49er.* San Marino, California: Huntington Library Publication, 1945.

Fergusson, Erna. "New Mexico's Mexicans," *Century,* 116 (August 1928), 437-44.

Frank, Waldo. *Our America.* New York: Boni and Liveright, 1919.

Fremont, John Charles. *Memoirs of My Life.* Chicago: Belford, Clarke, 1887.

Galarza, Ernesto, and others. *Dwellers of the Sunshine Slums: Mexican Americans in the Southwest.* Santa Barbara: McNally and Loftin, 1969.

————. "Life in the United States for Mexican People," *National Conference of Social Work Proceedings of 1929.* Chicago: Univ. of Chicago Press, 1929. Pp. 399-404.

Gamio, Manuel. *Mexican Immigration to the United States.* Chicago: Univ. of Chicago Press, 1928.

————. *The Mexican Immigrant: His Life Story.* New York: Arno Press, 1969.

Garrard, Lewis H. *Wah-To-Yah and the Taos Trail.* Cincinnati: H. W. Derby and New York: A. S. Barnes, 1850; ed. Ralph P. Bieber, Glendale, California: Arthur H. Clark, 1938.

Grebler, Leo, and others. *The Mexican-American People.* New York: Free Press, 1970.

Gregg, Josiah. *Commerce of the Prairies.* New York: H. G. Langley, 1844; Philadelphia: J. W. Moore, 1851; ed. Milo Milton Quaife, Chicago: R. H. Donnelley, 1926, and rpt. Lincoln: Univ. of Nebraska Press, 1967.

Griffith, Beatrice. *American Me.* Boston: Houghton Mifflin, 1948.

Heald, J. H. "Mexicans in the Southwest," *Missionary Review of the World,* 42 (November 1919), 860-65.

Heller, Celia S. *Mexican-American Youth: Forgotten Youth at the Cross-roads.* New York: Random House, 1966.

Helm, June. *Spanish-Speaking People in the United States.* Seattle: Univ. of Washington Press, 1969.

Hollon, W. E. *The Southwest: Old and New* (1961). New York: Knopf, 1961; Lincoln: Univ. of Nebraska Press, 1968.

Horgan, Paul. *Great River, the Rio Grande in North American History.* New York: Rinehart, 1954.

Jones, Robert C. "Ethnic Family Patterns: the Mexican Family in the United States," *American Journal of Sociology,* 53 (May 1948), 450-53.

———. "The Latin-American Problem," *School and Society,* 58 (4 December 1943), 441-43.

Kendall, George Wilkins. *Narrative of the Texan Santa Fe Expedition.* London: Henry Washbourne, 1847; New York: Harper, 1884; rpt. Austin: Steck, 1935.

Kibbe, Pauline R. *Latin-Americans in Texas.* Albuquerque: Univ. of New Mexico Press, 1946.

Kluckhohn, Florence and Fred Strodtbeck. *Variation in Value Orientation.* Evanston: Row, Peterson, 1961.

Kluckhohn, Frank L. *The Mexican Challenge.* New York: Doubleday, 1939.

Kostyu, Frank A. *Shadows in the Valley.* New York: Doubleday, 1970.

McLean, Robert. *That Mexican! As He Really Is, North and South of the Rio Grande.* San Francisco: R and E Research Associates, 1971.

McNamara, Patrick H. "Mexican-Americans in the Southwest," *America,* 114 (12 March 1966), 352-54.

McWilliams, Carey. *Brothers Under the Skin.* Boston: Little, Brown, 1951.

———. "Forgotten Mexican," *Common Ground,* 3 (1943), 65-78.

———. "The Mexican Problem," *Common Ground,* 8 (1948), 3-17.

———. *North From Mexico.* New York: Monthly Review Press, 1961.

Morin, Raul. *Among the Valiant.* Alhambra, California: Borden Publishing Co., 1963.

Moore, Joan and Ralph Guzman. "The Mexican-Americans: New Wind from the Southwest," *Nation,* 202 (30 May 1966), 645-48.

Murray, Katherine M. "Mexican Community Service," *Sociology and Social Research,* 17 (July 1933), 545-50.

Nava, Julian. *Mexican Americans, Past, Present and Future.* New York: American Book Co., 1969.

Parkman, Francis. *The Oregon Trail.* Philadelphia: John C. Winston, 1931.

Pattie, James O. *The Personal Narrative of James O. Pattie of Kentucky.* Ed. Timothy Flint, Cincinnati: John H. Wood, 1831; in *Early Western Travels, 1748-1846,* ed. Reuben Gold Thwaites, Cleveland: Arthur H. Clark, 1904-07; Chicago: Lakeside Press, 1930.

Rademaker, John A. *These Are Americans.* Palo Alto, California: Pacific Books, 1951.

Rechy, John. "No Mañanas for Today's Chicanos," *Saturday Review,* 53 (14 March 1970), 31-34.

Robinson, Cecil. "Spring Water With a Taste of the Land," *American West,* 3 (Summer 1966), 6-15.

————. *With the Ears of Strangers.* Tucson: Univ. of Arizona Press, 1963.

Romano, Octavio I. "Donship in a Mexican-American Community in Texas," *American Anthropologist,* 62 (December 1960), 966-76.

Rose, Peter I. *They and We.* New York: Random House, 1964.

Rowan, Helen. "A Minority Nobody Knows," *Atlantic,* 219 (June 1967), 47-52.

Rubel, Arthur J. *Across the Tracks: Mexican-Americans in a Texas City.* Austin: Univ. of Texas Press, 1966.

Samora, Julian, ed. *La Raza: Forgotten Americans.* South Bend, Indiana: Univ. of Notre Dame Press, 1966.

————. "The Spanish-Speaking People in the United States," *Staff Paper,* U.S. Commission on Civil Rights, 1962.

Sánchez, George I. "The American of Mexican Descent," *The Chicago Jewish Forum,* 20 (Winter 1961-62).

Sánchez, José Maríe. *Viaje a Texas – en 1828-1829.* Mexico: Papeles Históricos, 1939.

Schermerhorn, R. A. *These Our People.* New York: Heath, 1949.

Shontz, Orfa J. "The Land of Poco Tiempo," *Family,* 8 (May 1927), 74-79.

Simmons, Ozzie G. "The Mutual Images and Expectations of Anglo-Americans and Mexican-Americans," *Daedalus,* 90 (Spring 1961), 286-99.

Singer, Morris. *Growth, Equality, and the Mexican Experience.* Austin: Univ. of Texas Press, 1969.

Spicer, Edward H. *Cycles of Conquest.* Tucson: Univ. of Arizona Press, 1962.

Stearns, Harold E., ed. *America Now.* New York: Literary Guild of America, 1938.

Steiner, Stan. *La Raza: The Mexican-Americans.* New York: Harper and Row, 1969.

Stowell, Jay S. *A Study of Mexicans and Spanish-Americans in the United States.* New York: Home Missions Council, 1920.

———. *The Near-Side of the Mexican Question.* New York: Home Missions Council, 1921.

Taylor, Paul S. "Mexicans North of the Rio Grande," *Survey Graphic,* 66 (1 May 1931), 135-40.

Tebbel, John, and Ramon E. Ruiz. *South by Southwest.* New York: Doubleday, 1969.

Tuck, Ruth D. *Not With the Fist.* New York: Harcourt, Brace, 1956.

Turner, Timothy G. *Bullets, Bottles and Gardenias.* Dallas: Turner, 1935.

Waugh, Julia N. *Silver Cradle.* Austin: Univ. of Texas Press, 1955.

Webb, James Josiah. *Adventures in the Santa Fe Trade 1844-1847.* Glendale, California: Arthur H. Clark, 1931.

Webb, Walter P. *The Great Plains.* New York: Grosset and Dunlap, 1931.

White, Alfred. *The Apperceptive Mass of Foreigners As Applied To Americanization, The Mexican Group.* San Francisco: R and E Research Associates, 1971.

Zea, Leopoldo. *The Latin-American Mind.* Translated from the Spanish by James H. Abbott and Lowell Dunham. Norman: Univ. of Oklahoma Press, 1963.

Charles Ramos
Midwestern University

French

Bancroft, Hubert Howe. *History of Texas and the North American States.* 2 vols. San Francisco: The History Co., 1890.

Bandelier, A. F. "The Expedition of Pedro de Villazur . . . in Search of the French and the Pawnees in the Year 1720," *Hemenway Southwestern Archaeological Expedition.* Cambridge: John Wilson, 1890. Pp. 179+.

Barker, Nancy N. "Devious Diplomat: Dubois de Saligny." *Southwestern Historical Quarterly,* 72 (1969), 324-34.

Beers, Henry Putney. *The French in North America.* Baton Rouge: Louisiana State Univ. Press, 1957.

Bieber, Ralph P., and others. *Exploring Southwestern Trails 1846–1854.* Glendale, California: Arthur H. Clark, 1938.

Blanchard, P., et A. Dauzats. *San Juan de Ulùe ou relation de l'expedition française au Mexique sous les ordres de M. Le Contre-Amiral Baudin . . . suivi de notes et documents, et d'un aperçu général sur l'état actuel du*

Texas, par M. E. Maissin . . . . Paris: Chez Gide, 1839.

Bloom, Lansing B. "The Death of Jacques D'Eglise," *New Mexico Historical Review,* 2 (1927), 369-74.

Bolton, Herbert Eugene. *Anathese de Mézières and the Louisiana-Texas Frontier, 1768-1780.* 2 vols. Cleveland: Arthur H. Clark, 1914.

————. "French Intrusions into New Mexico," *The Pacific Ocean in History.* Eds. H. M. Stephens and H. E. Bolton. New York: Macmillan, 1917.

————. "The Location of La Salle's Colony on the Gulf of Mexico," *Southwestern Historical Quarterly,* 27 (1924), 171-89.

Bonilla, Antonio. "A Brief Compendium of the events which have occurred in the Province of Texas from its conquest or reduction to the present date, 1772." Translated by Elizabeth H. West. *Quarterly of the Texas State Historical Association,* 8 (1904), 3-78.

Bugbee, Lester G. "The Real Saint Denis," *Quarterly of the Texas State Historical Association,* 1 (1897-1898), 266-81.

Castañeda, Carlos Eduardo. *Our Catholic Heritage in Texas, 1519-1936.* 7 vols. Austin: Von Boeckman-Jones, 1936. I, 279-377; VI, 149-60.

————. "Morfi's History of Texas: A Critical, Chronological Account of the Early Explorations, Attempts at Colonization, and the Final Occupation of Texas by the Spanish . . . 1673-1779." Unpubl. doctoral diss. Univ. of Texas, 1932.

Castro, Henri. *Le Texas en 1845. Castro-ville, Colonie Fondée par Henry Castro, le Septembre 1844 sur la rivière Medina, 24 milles ouest de San Antonio de Bexar.* Anvers, 1845.

Le Champ-d'Asile, au Texas, ou notice curieuse et interesante sur la formation de cette colonie, jusqu'à sa dissolution; avec des renseignments propres à eclaircir les faits, et à venger les malheureux colons des calomnies qu'on leur a prodiguées. Par C . . . D . . . A. Paris: Chez Tiger, 1820.

Chesnel, Paul. *History of Cavelier de La Salle.* Translated by Andree Chesnel Meany. New York: Putnam, 1932.

Chevrillon, André. *Louisiane et Texas.* Paris: Institut des Etudes Américaines, 1938.

Clark, Robert Carlton. "The Beginnings of Texas: Fort St. Louis and Mission San Francisco de los Tehas," *Quarterly of the Texas State Historical Association,* 5 (1902)), 171-205.

————. "Louis Juchereau de Saint-Denis and the Reestablishment of the Tejas Missions," *Quarterly of the Texas State Historical Association,* 6 (1903), 1-26.

Cleland, Robert Glass. *This Reckless Breed of Men: The Trappers and Fur Traders of the Southwest.* New York: Knopf, 1950.

Considerant, Victor Prosper. *Au Texas. Rapport à Mes Amis, bases et statuts de la Société de Colonisation Europeo-Americain au Texas.* Paris: n.f., 1854.

Cox, Isaac Joslin. *The Journeys of René Robert Cavelier, Sieur de la Salle.* 2 vols. New York, 1905.

Crocchiola, Stanley Francis Louis. *The French, New Mexico Story.* Pantex, Texas: The Author, 1962.

———. *The Odyssey of Juan Archibeque.* Pantex, Texas: The Author, 1962.

Croix, Teodoro de. *Teodoro de Croix and the Northern Frontier of New Spain, 1776-1783.* Translated by Alfred B. Thomas. Norman: Univ. of Oklahoma Press, 1941.

Dabbs, Jack Autrey. "Additional Notes on the Champ d'Asile," *Southwestern Historical Quarterly,* 54 (1951), 347-58.

Domenech, Emmanuel Henri D. *Missionary Adventures in Texas and Mexico, 1846-1852.* London: Longman, 1858.

Dunn, William Edward. *Spanish and French Rivalry in the Gulf Region of the United States, 1678-1702.* Austin, 1917. University of Texas Bulletin, No. 1705.

———. "The Spanish Search for La Salle's Colony on the Bay of Espiritu Santo, 1685-1689," *Southwestern Historical Quarterly,* 19 (1916), 323-69.

Edwards, Herbert Rook. "The Diplomatic Relations Between France and the Republic of Texas," *Southwestern Historical Quarterly,* 20 (1917), 209-41; 341-57.

Finley, John Huston. *The French in the Heart of America.* New York: Scribner's, 1915.

Folmer, Henri. "De Bellisle on the Texas Coast," *Southwestern Historical Quarterly,* 44 (1940), 204-31.

———. *Franco-Spanish Rivalry in North America, 1524-1763.* Glendale, California: Arthur H. Clark, 1953.

———. "Report on Louis de Saint Denis' Intended Raid on San Antonio in 1721," *Southwestern Historical Quarterly,* 52 (1948), 83-88.

Foreman, Grant. "Antoine Leroux, New Mexico Guide." *New Mexico Historical Review,* 31 (1956), 265-89.

Fournel, Henri. *Coup d'oeil historique et statistique sur la Texas.* Paris: Delloye, 1841.

French, B. F. *Historical Collections of Louisiana.* 5 vols. New York: Wiley and Putnam, 1846-1853.

Garrard, Lewis M. *Wah-To-Yah and the Taos Trail.* Cincinnati: H. W. Derby and New York: A. S. Barnes, 1850; ed. Ralph P. Bieber. Glendale, California: Arthur H. Clark, 1938.

Girard Just [Just Jean Etienne Roy]. *Adventures of a French captain, presently a planter in Texas, formerly a refugee from Camp Asylum.* New York: Benziger, 1876.

Goussard de Mayolle, Jeanne. *Un Voyage chez les Indiens du Nouveau-Mexique.* Rouen: Impr. de l. Gy, 1898.

Hackett, Charles Wilson. *Pichardo's Treatise on the Limits of Louisiana and Texas.* 2 vols. Austin: Univ. of Texas Press, 1931.

Hafen, LeRoy R. *The Mountain Men and the Fur Trade of the Far West.* 7 vols. Glendale, California: Arthur H. Clark, 1965.

Hammond, William J. *La Réunion, A French Settlement in Texas.* Dallas: Royal Publishing Co., 1958.

Harpe, Bernard de la. *Journal historique (1698-1723) de l'etablissement des français à la Louisiane.* New Orleans and Paris: n.p., 1831.

Harper, Elizabeth Ann. "The Taovayas Indians in Frontier Trade and Diplomacy, 1779-1835," *Panhandle Plains Historical Review,* 26 (1953), 41-73.

Hartmann and Millard. *Le Texas, ou notice historique sur Champ d'Asile, comprenant tout ce qui s'est passé depuis la formation jusqu'à la dissolution de cette colonie . . .* Paris: Brasseur Aine, 1819.

Hatcher, Mattie Austin. *The Opening of Texas to Foreign Settlement, 1801-1821.* Austin: Univ. of Texas Press, 1927.

L'Heroine du Texas, ou Voyage de Madame . . . aux États-Unis et au Mexique. Paris: Chez Plancher, 1819.

Hodge, F. W. "French Intrusion Toward New Mexico in 1695," *New Mexico Historical Review,* 4 (1929), 72-76.

Horgan, Paul. *The Centuries of Santa Fe.* New York: Dutton, 1956.

Ingraham, Joseph Holt. *Lafitte: The Pirate of the Gulf.* 2 vols. New York: Harper, 1836.

Isely, Bliss. *Blazing the Way West.* New York: Scribner's, 1939.

Joutel, Henri. *Journal historique du dernier voyage que feu M. de la Salle fit dans le golfe de Mexique . . . .* Paris: E. Robinot, 1713.

LeClerq, Chretien. *Premier établissement de la foys dans la Nouvelle France contenant la publication de l'évangile, l'histoire des colonies françaises et les fameuses découvertes depuis le fleuve St. Laurent . . . jusqu'au golphe Mexique . . .* Paris: n.p., 1691.

Lewis, Anna. "Du Tisne's Expedition into Oklahoma," *Chronicles of Oklahoma,* 2 (1924), 253-68.

Loomis, Noel M. *Pedro Vial and the Roads to Santa Fe.* Norman: Univ. of Oklahoma Press, 1967.

Maissin, Eugene. *The French in Mexico and Texas, 1838-1839.* Translated by James L. Shepherd. Salado, Texas: Anson Jones Press, 1961.

Margry, Pierre. *Découvertes et Établissements des Français dans le Sud de l'Amérique Septentrionane (1614-1754).* Paris: Maisonneuve et Leclerc, 1888.

Marryat, Frederick. *The Travels and Adventures of Monsieur Violet in California, Sonora, and Western Texas.* London: George Routledge, c. 1843.

Marshall, Thomas Maitland. *A History of the Western Boundary of the Louisiana Purchase, 1819-1841.* Berkeley: Univ. of California Press, 1914.
————. "St. Vrain's Expedition to the Gila in 1826," *Southwestern Historical Quarterly,* 19 (1915-1916), 251-60.

Miller, Edmund Thornton. "The Connection of Penalosa with the La Salle Expedition," *Quarterly of the Texas Historical Association,* 5 (1901-1902), 97-112.

Monaghan, Frank. *French Travellers in the United States, 1765-1932.* New York: Antiquarian Press, 1961.

Nasatir, Abraham P. "Jacques Clamorgan: Colonial Promoter of the Northern Border of New Spain," *New Mexico Historical Review,* 17 (1942), 101-12.

O'Rell, Max [Paul Blout]. *A Frenchman in America.* New York: Cassell, 1891.

Palmer, Frederick Alexander. *Westerners at Home: Comments of French and British Travelers on Life in the West, 1800-1840.* Ann Arbor: University Microfilms, 1949.

Parkhill, Forbes. *The Blazed Trail of Antoine Leroux.* Los Angeles: Westernlore Press, 1965.

Parkman, Francis. *La Salle and the Discovery of the Great West.* Boston: Little, Brown, 1926.

Phares, Ross. *Cavalier in the Wilderness: the Story of the Explorer and Trader, Luis Juchereau de St. Denis.* Baton Rouge: Louisiana State Univ. Press, 1952.

Ratchford, Fannie E., ed. *The Story of Champ D'Asile.* Dallas: Book Club of Texas, 1937.

Reeves, Jesse S. "The Napoleonic Exiles in America . . . 1815-1819," *Johns Hopkins University Studies in History and Political Science.* Baltimore: Johns Hopkins Univ. Press, 1905. Series 23, Nos. 9-10.

Santerre, George H. *White Cliffs of Dallas.* Dallas: Book Craft, 1955.

Shea, J. G. *The Bursting of Pierre Margry's La Salle Bubble.* New York: T. B. Sidebothan, 1879.

————. *The Expedition of Don Diego Dionisio de Peñalosa in 1662 as described by Father Nicholas de Freytas.* Chicago: Rio Grande Press, 1964.

————. *History of the Catholic Missions among the Indian Tribes of the United States.* New York: n.p., 1855.

Shelby, Charmion Clair. "Projected French Attacks upon the Northeastern Frontier of New Spain, 1719-1721," *Hispanic American Historical Review,* 13 (1933), 457-72.

————. "St. Denis's Second Expedition from Louisiana to the Rio Grande, 1716-1719," *Southwestern Historical Quarterly,* 27 (1924), 190-216.

Smith, Ralph. "The Tawehash in French, Spanish, English, and American Imperial Affairs," *West Texas Historical Association Yearbook,* 28 (1952), 18-50.

Sunder, John E. *Bill Sublette: Mountain Man.* Norman: Univ. of Oklahoma Press, 1959.

Taylor, Virginia H. *The Franco-Texas Land Co.* Austin: Univ. of Texas Press, 1969.

Thomas, Alfred B. *After Coronado.* Norman: Univ. of Oklahoma Press, 1935.

————. "Documents Bearing upon the Northern Frontier of New Mexico, 1818-1819," *New Mexico Historical Review,* 4 (1929), 149-50, 53.

————. "Governor Mendinueta's Proposals for the Defense of New Mexico, 1772-78," *New Mexico Historical Review,* 6 (1931), 21-39.

Thwaites, Reuben Gold, ed., *Early Western Travels, 1748-1846.* Cleveland: Arthur H. Clark, 1904-07.

————. *France in America, 1497-1763.* New York: Haskell, 1969.

Tonty, H. de. *Account of M. de la Salle's Last Expedition and Discoveries in North America.* London: n.p., 1698.

Vivian, Julia. *A Cavalier in Texas.* San Antonio: Naylor, 1953.

Wallace, William Swilling. *Antoine Robidoux, 1794-1860.* Los Angeles: Glen Dawson, 1953.

Waugh, Julia Nott. *Castro-Ville and Henry Castro, Empresario.* San Antonio: Standard Printing Co., 1934.
Warner, Louis H. *Archbishop Lamy, An Epoch Maker.* Santa Fe: New Mexican Publishing Corp., 1936.
Winfrey, Dorman H. "Réné Robert Cavelier La Salle," *Six Flags Over Texas.* Waco: Texian Press, 1968. Pp. 1-30.
Wright, Muriel H. "Some Geographical Names of French Origin in Oklahoma," *Chronicles of Oklahoma,* 7 (1929), 188-93.

Ernestine P. Sewell
University of Texas at Arlington

Other European Minorities

(German, Polish, Czech, Swiss, Italian, Norwegian, Swedish)

Allen, Irene Taylor. *Saga of Anderson: The Proud Story of a Historic Texas Community.* New York: Greenwich Book Publishers, 1957. (Polish)
Armbruster, Henry C. "John F. Torrey's New Braunfels' Years," *Texana,* 4 (Fall 1966), 201-12.
Arndt, Karl, ed. *Early German American Narratives.* New York: American Book Co., 1941.
Arneson, Axel. "Norwegian Settlements in Texas," *Southwestern Historical Quarterly,* 45 (October 1941), 125-35.
Banta, William, and J. W. Caldwell, Jr. *Twenty-Seven Years on the Texas Frontier.* Council Hill, Oklahoma: n.p., 1933.
Bartlett, John Russell. *Personal Narrative of Explorations and Incidents in Texas, New Mexico, California, Sonora, and Chihuahua.* 2 vols. New York: Appleton, 1854.
Benjamin, Gilbert Giddings. *The Germans in Texas: A Study in Immigration.* New York: Appleton, 1910.
Bernstein, Geneva M. "The Forgotten Wend," *West Texas Historical Association Yearbook,* 33 (1957), 127-37.
Biesele, Rudolph L. "The First German Settlement in Texas," *Southwestern Historical Quarterly,* 34 (1930-1931), 334-39.
————. *The History of the German Settlements in Texas, 1831-1861.* Austin: Von Boeckmann-Jones, 1930.

————. "Prince Solms' Trip to Texas, 1844-1845," *Southwestern Historical Quarterly,* 40 (1936-1937), 1-25.

————. "The Relations Between the German Settlers and the Indians in Texas, 1844-1860," *Southwestern Historical Quarterly,* 31 (Oct. 1927), 116-29.

————. "The San Saba Colonization," *Southwestern Historical Quarterly,* 33 (Jan. 1930), 169-83.

————. "The Texas State Convention of Germans in 1854," *Southwestern Historical Quarterly,* 33 (April 1930), 247-61.

Biggers, Don H. *German Pioneers in Texas: A Brief History of their Hardships, Struggles and Achievements.* Fredericksburg, Texas: Fredericksburg Publishing Co., 1925.

Billington, Ray Allen. *Westward Expansion: A History of the American Frontier.* 2nd ed., New York: Macmillan, 1960.

Bizzell, William Bennett. *Rural Texas.* New York: Macmillan, 1924. (Italian, Bohemian, Polish)

Blasig, Anna J. Schmidt. *The Wends of Texas.* San Antonio: Naylor, 1954.

Blegen, Theodore C., ed. *Land of their Choice.* St. Paul: Univ. of Minnesota Press, 1955. (Norwegians)

————. *Norwegian Migration to America, 1825-1860.* Northfield, Minnesota: The Norwegian-American Historical Association, 1931.

Bollaert, William. *William Bollaert's Texas.* Ed. by W. Eugene Hollon and Ruth Lapham Butler. Norman: Univ. of Oklahoma Press, 1956.

Bracht, Viktor. *Texas im Jahre 1848.* Elberfeld and Iserlohn: Julius Baedeker, 1849. Translated by Frank Schmidt. San Antonio: Naylor, 1931.

Brown, John Henry. *History of Dallas County, Texas, from 1837 to 1887.* Dallas: Milligan, Cornett and Farnham, 1887. (Swiss)

Braman, D. E. E. *Braman's Information about Texas.* Philadelphia: Lippincott, 1858.

Buck, Paul H. "The Poor Whites of the Ante-Bellum South," *American Historical Review,* 31 (1925), 41-54.

Bugbee, Lester G. "The Texas Frontier—1820-1825," *Publications of Southern History Association,* 4 (1900), 102-21.

Burke, J. *Burke's Texas Almanac and Immigrant's Handbook.* Houston: W. M. Hamilton, 1875-1885.

Caldwell, Lillian Moerbe. *Texas Wends, Their First Half Century.* Salado, Texas: Anson Jones Press, 1961.

Capek, Thomas. *The Cechs (Bohemians) in America: A Study of their Na-*

tional, Cultural, Political, Social, Economic and Religious Life. New York: Arno Press and the *New York Times,* 1969.

Chabot, Frederick C. *With the Makers of San Antonio: Genealogies of the early Latin, Anglo-American, and German Families.* San Antonio: n.p., 1937.

Cicherska, Joseph Lee. *Poles in Texas: A Report to the Lulac Council.* San Antonio, n.p., 1964.

Claghorn, Kate H. "Agricultural Distribution of Immigrants," U.S. Industrial Commission Report, 15 (1901), 492-646.

Clausen, C. A., ed. *The Lady with the Pen, Elise Waerenskjold in Texas.* Northfield, Minnesota: Norwegian-American Historical Association, 1961.

Cochran, John H. *Dallas County: A Record of its Pioneers and Progress.* Dallas: Arthur S. Mathis, Service Publishing Company, 1928. (Swiss)

Coleman, Marion Moore. "The Polish Origins of Bandera, Texas," *Polish American Studies,* 20 (January-June 1963), 21-27.

————. "Kalikst Wolski in Texas," *Texana,* 5 (Fall 1967), 203-14. (Polish)

Cranfill, J. B. *J. B. Cranfill's Chronicle: A Story of Life in Texas.* New York: Fleming H. Ravell, 1916. (Norwegian)

Daniels, R. L. "Polanders in Texas," *Lippincott's Magazine,* 31 (March 1883), 300-302.

Darst, Maury. "Six Weeks to Texas," *Texana,* 6 (Summer 1968), 140-52. (German)

Dickinson, Robert E. "Rural Settlement in the German Lands," *Annals of the Association of American Geographers,* 39 (1949), 239-63.

Dielmann, Henry B. "Emma Altgelt's Sketches of Life in Texas," *Southwestern Historical Quarterly,* 63 (1959-1960), 363-84.

Dresel, Gustav. *Houston Journal: Adventures in North America and Texas, 1837-1841.* Ed. and translated by Max Freund. Austin: Univ. of Texas Press, 1954.

Dworaczyk, Edward J. *The First Polish Colonies of America in Texas.* San Antonio: Naylor, 1936.

Ehrenberg, Hermann. *With Milam and Fannin, The Adventures of a German Boy in Texas' Revolution.* Translated by Charlotte Churchill. Austin: Pemberton, 1968.

Elliot, Claude. "Union Sentiment in Texas, 1861-1865," *Southwestern Historical Quarterly,* 50 (1946-1947), 449-77.

Engerrand, George Charles M. *The So-Called Wends of Germany and their Colonies in Texas and in Australia.* Austin: University of Texas, 1934.

Estill, Julia. "Customs among the German Descendants of Gillespie County," *Publications of the Texas Folklore Society,* 2 (1923), 67-74.

Evans, Mayme. "Sir Svante Palm's Legacy to Texas," *The American Scandinavian Review* (Spring 1949), pp. 41-45.

Ewing, Floyd F., Jr. "Origins of Unionist Sentiment on the West Texas Frontier," *West Texas Historical Association Year Book,* 32 (1956), 21-29.

Faust, Albert B. *The German Element in the United States.* 2 vols. Cambridge, Massachusetts: Riverside Press, 1909.

Fehrenbach, T. R. *A History of Texas and Texans.* New York: Macmillan, 1968.

Geiser, Samuel W. "Dr. Ernst Kapp, Early Geographer in Texas," *Field and Laboratory,* 14 (1946), 16-31.

————. *Naturalists of the Frontier.* Dallas: Southern Methodist Univ. Press, 1937.

Geue, Chester William, and Ethel Hander Geue. *A New Land Beckoned: German Immigration to Texas, 1844-1847.* Waco: Texian Press, 1966.

Geue, Ethel Hander. *New Homes in a New Land: German Immigration to Texas, 1847-1861.* Waco: Texian Press, 1970.

Greer, Richard R. "Origins of the Foreign-Born Population of New Mexico during the Territorial Period," *New Mexico Historical Review,* 17 (1942), 281-87.

Haiman, Miecislaus. *The Poles in the Early History of Texas.* Chicago: Polish R. C. U. of America, 1936.

Hatcher, Mattie Austin. *The Opening of Texas to Foreign Settlement, 1801-1820.* Austin: Univ. of Texas, 1927.

Hawgood, John A. *The Tragedy of German-America.* New York and London: Putnam, 1940.

Higham, John. *Strangers in the Land: Patterns of American Nativism, 1860-1925.* New York: Atheneum, 1965.

Hinueber, Caroline von. "Life of German Pioneers of Early Texas," *Quarterly of the Texas State Historical Association,* 2 (1899), 227-32.

Hodges, Leroy. "The Bohemian Farmers of Texas," *The Texas Magazine,* 6 (June 1912), 87-96.

————. "The Poles of Texas," *The Texas Magazine,* 16 (December 1912), 336.

Hogan, William Ransom. *The Texas Republic: A Social and Economic History.* Norman: Univ. of Oklahoma Press, 1947.

Hudson, Estelle, and Henry R. Maresh. *Czech Pioneers of the Southwest.*

42   *Southwestern American Literature*

Dallas: Southwest Press, 1934.
Jackson, John B. "Ich Bin ein Cowboy aus Texas," *Southwest Review,* 38 (Spring 1953), 158-63.
Jordan, Terry G. *German Seed in Texas Soil: Immigrant Farmers in Nineteenth-Century Texas.* Austin: Univ. of Texas Press, 1966.
————. "The Patterns and Origins of the Adelsverein German Colonists," *Texana,* 6 (Fall 1968), 245-57.
Kettner, Franz. "Letters of a German Pioneer in Texas," Ed. and translated by Terry G. Jordan and Marlis Anderson Jordan. *Southwestern Historical Quarterly,* 69 (1965-1966), 463-72.
King, Irene Marschall. *John O. Meusebach: German Colonizer in Texas.* Austin: Univ. of Texas Press, 1967.
Kleberg, Rosa. "Some Early Experiences in Texas," *Quarterly of the Texas State Historical Association,* 1 (1898), 297-302; 2 (1898), 170-73.
Lathrop, Barnes F. "Migration into East Texas, 1835-1860," *Southwestern Historical Quarterly,* 52 (July 1948), 1-31; (October 1948), 184-208; (January 1949), 325-48.
Lynch, Russell Wilford. *Czech Farmers in Oklahoma.* Stillwater, Okla.: Oklahoma A. & M. College, 1942.
Lynch, W. O. "The Westward Flow of Southern Colonists before 1861," *Journal of Southern History,* 9 (1943), 303-27.
McCampbell, Coleman. "Texas History as Revealed by Town and Community Name Origins," *Southwestern Historical Quarterly,* 58 (July 1954), 91-97.
McGrath, Sister Paul. *Political Nativism in Texas, 1825-1860.* Washington: Catholic Univ. of America, 1930.
McKay, Seth S. *Texas Politics, 1906-1944, with Special Reference to the German Counties.* Lubbock, Texas: Texas Tech Press, 1952.
Maresh, Henry R. "The Czechs in Texas," *Southwestern Historical Quarterly,* 50 (October 1946), 236-40.
Mondello, Salvatore. "America's Polish Heritage as Viewed by Miecislaus Haiman and the Periodical Press," *The Polish Review,* 4 (Winter-Spring 1959), 107-18.
Muir, Andrew Forest. "Heinrich Thuerwaechter, Colonial German Settler." *Texana,* 4 (Spring 1966), 33-40.
Neighbors, Kenneth F. "German-Comanche Treaty of 1847." *Texana,* 2 (Winter 1964), 311-22.
Norlie, Olaf Morgan. *History of the Norwegian People in America.* Minne-

apolis: Augsburg Publishing House, 1925.

Olmsted, Frederick Law. *A Journey Through Texas: or a Saddle-Trip on the Southwestern Frontier*. New York: Dix, Edwards and Co., 1857.

Owsley, Frank L. "The Pattern of Migration and Settlement on the Southern Frontier," *Journal of Southern History*, 11 (1945), 147-76.

Peterson, H. C., ed. "The Opening of Oklahoma from the European Point of View," *Chronicles of Oklahoma*, 17 (1939), 22-25.

Pochmann, Henry A., comp., and Arthur R. Schultz, ed. *Bibliography of German Culture in America to 1940*. Madison: Univ. of Wisconsin Press, 1954.

Pochmann, Henry A. *German Culture in America: Philosophical and Literary Influences, 1600-1900*. Madison: Univ. of Wisconsin Press, 1957.

Polk, Stella Gibson. *Mason and Mason County: A History*. Austin: Pemberton, 1966. (German)

Pool, William C. *Bosque County, Texas*. San Marcos, Texas: San Marcos Record Press, 1954. (Norwegian)

Przygoda, Jacek. "Poles in Texas Today," *The Quarterly Review*, 21 (October-December 1969), 1.

Qualey, Carlton C. *Norwegian Settlement in the United States*. Northfield, Minnesota: Norwegian-American Historical Association, 1938.

Ransleben, Guido E. *A Hundred Years of Comfort in Texas*. San Antonio: Naylor, 1954 (German)

Raunick, Selma Metzenthin. *Deutsche Schriften in Texas*. 2 vols. San Antonio: Freie Presse für Texas, 1935-1936.

————. "A Survey of German Literature in Texas," *Southwestern Historical Quarterly*, 33 (October 1929), 134-59.

Regenbrecht, Adalbert. "The German Settlement of Millheim (Texas) before the Civil War," *Southwestern Historical Quarterly*, 20 (1916-1917), 28-34.

Reinhardt, Louis. "The Communistic Colony of Bettina, 1846-1848," *The Quarterly of the Texas State Historical Association*, 3 (July 1899), 33-40.

Rittenhouse, Jack D. *Wendish Language Printing in Texas*. Los Angeles: Dawson's Book Shop, 1962.

Roemer, Ferdinand von. *Texas: with particular reference to German Immigration and the Physical Appearance of the Country*. Translated by Oswald Mueller. San Antonio: Standard Printing Co., 1935.

Santerre, George H. *White Cliffs of Dallas*. Dallas: Book Craft, 1955. (Belgians and Swiss)

44   *Southwestern American Literature*

Sealsfield, Charles [pseud. for Karl Postl]. *Life in the New World: or Sketches of American Society.* Translated Gustavus C. Hebbe and James MacKay. New York: J. Winchester, New World Press, 1844.

Siemering, A. "Die Lateinische Ansiedlung in Texas," *Der Deutsche Pionier,* 10 (1878), 57-62. Translated by C. W. Geue as "The Latin Settlement, in Texas," *Texana,* 5 (Summer 1967), 126-31.

Skinner, A. E., ed. "The True Effectiveness of the Mainz Society for Emigration to Texas, as Described in a Letter of Nov. 3, 1846, by Carl Blumberg," *Texana,* 7 (Winter 1969), 295-312.

Skrabanek, Robert L. "Forms of Cooperation and Mutual Aid in a Czech American Rural Community," *Southwestern Social Science Quarterly,* 30 (December 1949), 183-87.

———. "The Influence of Cultural Backgrounds on Farming Practices in a Czech American Rural Community," *Southwestern Social Science Quarterly,* 32 (March 1951), 258-66.

Smyrl, Frank H. "Unionism in Texas, 1856-1861," *Southwestern Historical Quarterly,* 68 (1964-1965), 172-95.

Starczewska, Maria. "The Historical Geography of the Oldest Polish Settlement in the United States," *The Polish Review,* 12 (Spring 1967), 11-40.

Sweet, George H. *Texas . . . or the Immigrants' Handbook of Texas.* New York: E. O'Keefe, 1871.

Tetreau, E. D. "Population Characteristics and Trends in Arizona," *Southwestern Social Science Quarterly,* 23 (1943), 331-39.

———. "Foreign Travelers in Oklahoma, 1900-1950," *Chronicles of Oklahoma,* 30 (1952), 463-67.

———. "Travel Books on Texas Published in Foreign Countries, 1900-1950," *Southwestern Historical Quarterly,* 57 (October 1953), 202-21.

Tiling, Moritz. *History of the German Element in Texas from 1820-1850.* Houston: Rein and Sons, 1913.

University of Texas Institute of Texan Cultures. *The German Texans.* San Antonio: Encino, 1970.

———. *The Norwegian Texans.* San Antonio: Encino, 1970.

Unstad, Lyder L. "Norwegian Migration to Texas: A Historic Resume with Four 'America Letters,'" *Southwestern Historical Quarterly,* 43 (Oct. 1939), 176-95.

Webb, Walter Prescott. "Christmas and New Year in Texas," *Southwestern Historical Quarterly,* 44 (1940-1941), 357-79.

Willibrand, W. A. "German in Okarche, 1892-1902," *Chronicles of Oklahoma,*

28 (1950), 284-91.

————. "In Bilingual Old Okarche," *Chronicles of Oklahoma*, 29 (1951), 337-54.

Wooster, Ralph A. "Foreigners in the Principal Towns of Ante-Bellum Texas," *Southwestern Historical Quarterly*, 66 (1962-1963), 208-20.

Wurzbach, Emil Frederick. *Life and Memoirs of Emil Frederick Wurzbach, to which Is Appended some Papers of John Meusebach.* Translated by Franz J. Dohman. San Antonio: Artes Graficas, 1937.

Wright, Muriel H., and George H. Shirk. "Artist Möllhausen in Oklahoma – 1853," *Chronicles of Oklahoma*, 31 (1953), 392-441.

Ziegler, Jesse A. *Wave of the Gulf.* San Antonio: Naylor, 1938. (German and Swedish)

Peggy Dechert Skaggs
Angelo State University

Anglo-American

Acheson, Sam. *35,000 Days in Texas.* New York: Macmillan, 1938.

Adams, Ramon F. *The Old-Time Cowhand.* New York: Macmillan, 1961.

Allen, John. *Southwest.* Philadelphia: Lippincott, 1952.

Allhands, J. L. *Gringo Builders.* Iowa City, Iowa: Privately Printed, 1931.

Athearn, Robert G. *Westward the Briton.* Lincoln: Univ. of Nebraska Press, 1963.

Austin, Mary. *The Land of Little Rain.* Boston: Houghton Mifflin, 1903.

Banta, William. *Twenty-Seven Years on the Texas Frontier.* Council Hill, Oklahoma: L. G. Park, 1934.

Bechdolt, F. R. *Tales of the Old Timers.* New York: Century, 1924.

Bracht, Viktor. *Texas in 1848.* San Antonio: Naylor, 1931.

Branch, E. Douglas. *The Cowboy and His Interpreters.* New York: Appleton, 1926.

Brown, Dee. *The Gentle Tamers: Women of the Old Wild West.* New York: Putnam, 1958.

Brown, Mark H. *Before Barbed Wire.* New York: Holt, 1956.

————.*Frontier Years.* New York: Holt, 1955.

Canton, Frank M. *Frontier Trails.* Boston: Houghton Mifflin, 1930.

Carter, Hodding, and Anthony Ragusin. *Gulf Coast Country.* New York: Duell, 1951.

46 Southwestern American Literature

Casey, Robert J. *The Texas Border*. Indianapolis: Bobbs-Merrill, 1949.
Cleaveland, Agnes M. *No Life for a Lady*. Boston: Houghton Mifflin, 1941.
———. *Satan's Paradise*. Boston: Houghton Mifflin, 1952.
Dale, E. E. *Frontier Ways*. Austin: Univ. of Texas Press, 1959.
Davis, W. W. *El Gringo, or New Mexico and Her People*. Santo Fe: Rydal, 1938.
Day, Donald. *Big Country: Texas*. New York: Duell, Sloan & Pearce, 1947.
Debo, Angie. *Oklahoma: Footloose and Fancy Free*. Norman: Univ. of Oklahoma Press, 1949.
DeShields, James. *Tall Men with Long Rifles*. San Antonio: Naylor, 1935.
Dobie, J. Frank. *Cow People*. Boston: Little, Brown, 1964.
———. *The Flavor of Texas*. Boston: Little, Brown, 1936.
Dodge, Matt N., and Herbert S. Zim. *The American Southwest*. New York: Simon and Schuster, 1955.
Duval, John C. *Early Times In Texas (1867-1892)*. Austin: H. P. N. Gammel, 1892; Austin: Steck, 1934.
Farber, James. *Those Texans*. San Antonio: Naylor, 1945.
Fergusson, Erna. *Our Southwest*. New York: Knopf, 1940.
———. *New Mexico*. New York: Knopf, 1952.
Foreman, Grant. *Pioneer Days in the Early Southwest*. Cleveland: Arthur H. Clark, 1926.
Frantz, Joe B. *The American Cowboy*. Norman: Univ. of Oklahoma Press, 1955.
Fuermann, George. *Reluctant Empire: The Mind Of Texas*. Garden City, New York: Doubleday, 1957.
Goodwyn, Frank. *Lone Star Land*. New York: Knopf, 1955.
Hafen, LeRoy. *The Mountain Men*. Glendale, California: Arthur H. Clark, 1965.
Hafen, LeRoy, and Carl Rister. *Western America*. New York: Prentice-Hall, 1941.
Haley, J. Evetts. *Men of Fiber*. El Paso: C. Hertzog, 1963.
Hogue, Wayman. *Back Yonder*. New York: Minton, Balch, 1932.
Hollon, W. Eugene. *Beyond the Cross Timbers*. Norman: Univ. of Oklahoma Press, 1955.
———. *William Bollaert's Texas*. Norman: Univ. of Oklahoma Press, 1956.
Howard, Robert. *This is the West*. New York: Rand McNally, 1957.
Jenkins, John H. *Recollections of Early Texas*. Austin: Univ. of Texas Press, 1958.

Keleher, William A. *The Fabulous Frontier*. Santa Fe: Rydal Press, 1945.
Kennedy, William. *Texas* (1841). London: R. Hastings, 1841; Ft. Worth: Molyneau, 1925.
Laswell, Mary. *I'll Take Texas*. Boston: Houghton Mifflin, 1959.
Leach, Joseph. *The Typical Texan*. Dallas: Southern Methodist Univ. Press, 1952.
Lightfoot, Roy Lander. *North of the Rio Grande*. San Antonio: Naylor, 1949.
Lockwood, Frank C. *Pioneer Days in Arizona*. New York: Macmillan, 1932.
McCambell, Coleman. *Texas Seaport*. New York: Exposition Press, 1952.
Marriott, Alice. *Hell on Horses and Women*. Norman: Univ. of Oklahoma Press, 1953.
Muir, Andrew Forest, ed. *Texas in 1837*. Austin: Univ. of Texas Press, 1958.
Nordyke, Lewis. *Cattle Empire*. New York: Morrow, 1949.
Osgood, Ernest. *The Day of the Cattlemen*. Chicago: Univ. of Chicago Press, 1957.
Perry, George S. *Texas, A World in Itself*. New York: McGraw-Hill, 1942.
Peyton, Green [pseud. for Green Peyton Wertenbaker]. *American Heartland: The Southwest*. Norman: Univ. of Oklahoma Press, 1948.
Pickrell, Annie D. *Pioneer Women in Texas*. Austin: Steck, 1929.
Richardson, Rupert. *Texas, The Lone Star State*. Englewood Cliffs, New Jersey: Prentice-Hall, 1970.
Rister, Carl Coke. *Southern Plainsmen*. Norman: Univ. of Oklahoma Press, 1938.
Rogers, John .*The Lusty Texans of Dallas*. New York: Dutton, 1951.
Sandoz, Mari. *The Buffalo Hunters*. New York: Hastings House, 1954.
———. *The Cattleman*. New York: Hastings House, 1958.
Santee, Ross. *The Cowboy*. New York: Cosmoplitan Book Corporation, 1928.
Schmitz, Joseph W. *Texas Culture*. San Antonio: Naylor, 1960.
Schmitz, J. W. *Thus They Lived*. San Antonio: Naylor, 1935.
Shipman, Daniel. *Frontier Life, 58 Years in Texas*. n.p., 1879.
Smith, E. E. *Life on the Texas Range*. Austin: Univ of Texas Press, 1952.
Sonnichsen, C. L. *Cowboys and Cattle Kings: Life on the Range Today*. Norman: Univ. of Oklahoma Press, 1950.
Sowell, A. J. *Early Settlers and Indian Fighters of Southwest Texas*. New York: Argosy-Antiquarian, 1964.
Streeter, Floyd B. *Prairie Trails and Cow Towns*. New York: Devin Adair, 1963.
Thompson, Holland, ed. *The Book of Texas*. Dallas: Grolier Society, 1929.

White, Owen P. *My Texas 'Tis of Thee.* New York: Putnam, 1930.
Winter, Nevin. *Texas, The Marvellous.* Boston: Page, 1916.

Ernest B. Speck
Sul Ross State University

Negro

Barker, E. C. "Influence of Slavery in the Colonization of Texas," *Mississippi Valley Historical Review,* 11 (June 1924), 3-36.

————. "Slave Trade in Texas," *Texas Historical Association Quarterly,* 6 (1903), 145.

Bittle, William E. and Gilbert Geis. "Racial Self-fulfillment and the Rise of an All-Negro Community in Oklahoma," *Phylon,* 18 (Fall 1957) 247-60.

Boatright, Mody C. and Donald Day, eds. *From Hell to Breakfast.* Dallas: Southern Methodist Univ. Press, 1944.

Brewer, John Mason, ed. *Heralding Dawn: an Anthology of Verse by Texas Negroes.* Dallas: June Thomason, 1936.

————. *An Historical Outline of the Negro in Travis County* [Texas]. Austin: Samuel Huston College, 1940.

————. *Negro Legislators of Texas and Their Descendants: a History of the Negro in Texas Politics from Reconstruction to Disfranchisement.* Dallas: Mathis Publishing, 1935.

————. *The Word on the Brazos.* Austin: Univ. of Texas Press, 1953.

Campbell, John Bert. *Campbell's Abstract of Creek Freedman Census Cards and Index.* Muskogee, Oklahoma: Phoenix Job Printing, 1915.

Carroll, J. M. "Baptist Work Among Negroes Prior to the Civil War," *History of Texas Baptists,* Dallas: Baptist Standard Publishing, 1923.

Cotton, Walter F. *History of Negroes in Limestone County [Texas] from 1860 to 1939.* Mexia, Texas: News Print, 1939.

Crow, John E. *Discrimination, Poverty, and the Negro; Arizona in the National Context.* Tucson: Univ. of Arizona Press, 1968.

Curlee, Abigail. "The History of a Texas Slave Plantation, 1831-63," *Southwest Historical Quarterly,* (June 1922).

Davis, William Riley. *The Development and Present Status of Negro Education in Texas.* New York: Teachers College, Columbia Univ., 1934.

Dobie, J. Frank, ed. *Texas and Southwestern Lore. Publications of the Texas Folklore Society,* 6 (1927).

DuBois, William Edward Burghardt. "The Servant in the House; Jesus Christ in Texas," in *Darkwater*. New York: Harcourt, Brace, 1920.

———. *What the Negro Has Done for the U. S. and Texas*. Washington: Government Printing Office, 1936.

Durham, Philip, and Everett L. Jones. *The Negro Cowboys*. New York: Dodd, Mead, 1965.

Flickinger, Robert Elliott. *The Choctaw Freedmen and the Story of Oak Hill Industrial Academy, Valiant, McCurtain Co., Oklahoma*. Pittsburgh, Pennsylvania: Presbyterian Board of Missions, 1914.

Gallaher, Art, Jr. *The Negro and Employment Opportunities in the South—Houston*. Atlanta: Southern Regional Council, 1961.

Graham, Katheryn Campbell. *Under the Cottonwood; a Saga of Negro Life in Which the History, Traditions and Folklore of the Negro of the Past Century Are Vividly Portrayed*. New York: W. Malliet, 1941.

Greene, Harry W. "Negro Colleges in the Southwest." *Opportunity (Journal of Negro Life)*, 5 (November 1927), 322-25.

Iles, R. Edgar. "Boley—(an Exclusive Negro Town in Oklahoma)." *Opportunity (Journal of Negro Life)*, 3 (August 1925), 231.

Kirk, W. Aston, and John T. Q. King. "Desegregation of Higher Education in Texas." *Journal of Negro Education*, 27 (Summer 1958), 318-23.

Lewis, Joseph Vance. *Out of the Ditch; a True Story of an Ex-Slave*. Houston: Rein and Sons, 1910.

Lomax, Alan. *The Rainbow Sign: a Southern Documentary*. New York: Duell, Sloan and Pearce, 1959.

McConkey, Clarence. *A Burden and an Ache*. Nashville: Abingdon Press, 1970.

Moon, F. D. "Higher Education and Desegregation in Oklahoma." *Journal of Negro Education*, 27 (Summer 1958), 300-10.

Parks, Gordon. *The Learning Tree*. New York: Harper, 1963.

Ramsdell, Charles William. *Reconstruction in Texas*. New York: Columbia Univ. Press, 1910.

St. John, Percy B. *Mary Rock or My Adventures in Texas*. London: C. H. Clarke, 1847.

Sargent, F. O. "Economic Adjustments of Negro Farmers in East Texas." *Southwestern Social Science Quarterly*, 42 (June 1961), 32-39.

Thomas, Jesse O. *Negro Participation in the Texas Centennial Exposition*. Boston: Christopher Publishing House, 1938.

Washington, Booker T. "Boley, a Negro Town in the West." *Outlook* (N.Y.),

88 (January 4, 1908), 28-31.

Webb, Walter Prescott. "Miscellany of Texas Folk-lore," *Coffee in the Gourd. Publications of the Texas Folk Lore Society,* 2 (1923), 38-49.

Jeff H. Campbell
Midwestern University

The
Work

Hunting

Alter, J. Cecil. *James Bridger*. Salt Lake City: Shepard Book Company, 1925.

Branch, C. Douglas. *The Hunting of the Buffalo* (1929). Lincoln: Univ. of Nebraska Press, 1962.

Cleland, Robert G. *This Reckless Breed of Men; the Trappers and Fur Traders of the Southwest*. New York: Knopf, 1950.

Clemens, Jeremiah. *Mustang Gray*. Philadelphia: Lippincott, 1858.

Conrad, Howard L. *"Uncle Dick" Wootton, The Pioneer Frontiersman . . . Hunter, Trapper, Guide, Scout, and Indian Fighter . . . .* Chicago: W. E. Dibble, 1890.

Cook, John R. *The Border and the Buffalo* (1907, 1938). Norman: Univ. of Oklahoma Press, 1963.

Dixon, Olive K. *The Life of Billy Dixon*. Dallas: P. L. Turner, 1927.

Dobie, J. Frank. *The Ben Lilly Legend*. Boston: Little, Brown, 1950.

————. *The Mustangs*. Boston: Little, Brown, 1952.

Dodge, Richard I. *The Hunting Grounds of the Great West*. London: Chatto and Windus, 1877.

Easton, Robert, and MacKenzie Brown. *Lord of Beasts: The Saga of Buffalo Jones*. Lincoln: Univ. of Nebraska Press, 1970.

Gard, Wayne. *The Great Buffalo Hunt*. New York: Knopf, 1959.

Garretson, Martin. *The American Bison*. New York: New York Zoological Society, 1938.

Gerstaecher, Frederick. *Wild Sports in the Far West* (1876). Durham: Duke Univ. Press, 1968.

Grant, Blanche C. *When Old Trails Were New*. New York: Press of the Pioneers, 1934.

Hamilton, W. T. *My Sixty Years on the Plains, Trapping, Trading, and Indian Fighting*. Norman: Univ. of Oklahoma Press, 1960.

Hibben, Frank C. *Hunting American Bears*. Philadelphia: Lippincott, 1950.

————. *Hunting American Lions*. New York: Crowell, 1948.

Hobbs, James. *Wild Life in the Far West*. Hartford: Wiley, Waterman and Eaton, 1873.

Inman, Henry. *Buffalo Jones' Adventures on the Plains* (1899). Lincoln: Univ. of Nebraska Press, 1970.

Jaeger, Edmund C. *Denizens of the Desert*. Boston: Houghton Mifflin, 1922.

Keene, James. *The Texas Pistol*. New York: Random House, 1955.

Mayer, Frank H., and Charles B. Roth. *The Buffalo Harvest*. Denver: Sage Books, 1958.

Mersfelder, L. C. *Cowboy — Fisherman — Hunter*. Glendale, California: Arthur H. Clark, 1962.

O'Connor, Jack. *Game in the Desert*. New York: Derrydale Press, 1939.

Sabin, Edwin L. *Kit Carson Days (1809-1869)*. New York: Press of the Pioneers, 1935.

Sandoz, Mari. *The Buffalo Hunters*. New York: Hastings House, 1954.

Strong, General William C. *Canadian River Hunt*. Norman: Univ. of Oklahoma Press, 1960.

Vasburgh, John R. *Texas Lion Hunter*. San Antonio: Naylor, 1949.

Vestal, Stanley. *Kit Carson the Happy Warrior of the Old West: A Biography*. Boston: Houghton Mifflin, 1928.

————. *Mountain Men*. Boston: Houghton Mifflin, 1937.

Webb, W. E. *Buffalo Land: An Authentic Account of the Discoveries, Adventures, and Mishaps of a Scientific and Sporting Party in the Wild West*. Cincinnati and Chicago: E. Hannaford, 1872.

Webber, Charles W. *The Hunter-Naturalist or Wild Scenes and Wild Hunters*. Philadelphia: Lippincott, 1852.

Wheeler, Homer W. *Buffalo Days*. Indianapolis: Bobbs-Merrill, 1925.

Young, Stanley, and Paul and Edward Goldman. *The Puma*. Washington: American Wildlife Institute, 1946.

John Q. Anderson
University of Houston

Exploration

Bandelier, Fanny, trans. *The Journey of Alvar Núñez Cabeza de Vaca*. New York: A. S. Barnes, 1905.

Bartlett, John R. *Personal Narrative of Explorations and Incidents in Texas, New Mexico, California, Sonora and Chihuahua, Connected with the United States and Mexican Boundary Commission during the Years 1850, '51, '52, and '53. 2 vols*. New York: Appleton, 1854; Chicago: Rio Grande Press, 1965.

Bolton, Herbert Eugene. *Coronado, Knight of Pueblos and Plains*. New York: Whittlesy House, 1927; Albuquerque: Univ. of New Mexico Press, 1949.

————. ed. *Spanish Explorations in the Southwest, 1542-1706*. New York: Scribner, 1916; New York: Barnes and Noble, 1967.

Covey, Cyclone, trans. *Cabeza de Vaca's Adventures in the Unknown Interior of America*. New York: Collier, 1961.

DeVoto, Bernard. *The Course of Empire*. Boston: Houghton Mifflin, 1952.

Emory, William H. *Report on United States and Mexican Boundary Survey, Made under the Direction of the Secretary of the Interior*. Washington: C. Wendell, 1957-1959.

Goetzmann, William H. *Army Exploration in the American West*. New Haven: Yale Univ. Press, 1959.

————. *Exploration and Empire*. New York: Knopf, 1971.

Hallenbeck, Cleve. *Alvar Núñez Cabeza de Vaca: The Journey and Route of the First European to Cross the Continent of North America*. Glendale, California: Arthur H. Clark, 1940.

————. *The Journey of Fray Marcos de Niza*. Dallas: University Press, 1949.

Hammond George P., and Agapito Rey. *Narratives of the Coronado Expedition, 1540-1542*. Albuquerque: Univ. of New Mexico Press, 1940.

Hodge, F. W. and T. H. Lewis, eds. *Spanish Explorers in the Southern United States, 1528-1543*. New York: Scribner, 1907.

Irving, Washington. *A Tour of the Prairies*. Philadelphia: Carey, Lea, & Blanchard, 1835; ed. John F. McDermott, Norman: Univ. of Oklahoma Press, 1962.

McDanield, H. F., and Nathaniel A. Taylor. *The Coming Empire, or 2000 Miles in Texas on Horseback*. Houston: N. T. Carlisle, 1936.

Pike, Zebulon M. *The Journals of Zebulon Montgomery Pike*. Ed. Donald Jackson. 2 vols. Norman: Univ. of Oklahoma Press, 1966.

Thwaites, Ruben Gold, ed. *Early Western Travels, 1748-1846*. 32 vols. Cleveland: A. H. Clark, 1904-1907.

Webb, Walter P. *The Great Plains*. New York: Ginn, 1931.

Orlan Sawey
Texas A&I University

Settlement

Bandelier, Adolph F. A. *The Gilded Man (El Dorado) and Other Pictures of the Spanish Occupancy of America*. New York: Appleton, 1893.

Barker, Eugene C., ed. *The Austin Papers*. 3 vols. Austin: Univ. of Texas Press, 1927.

Bracht, Viktor. *Texas in 1848*. Translated by Charles F. Schmidt. San Antonio: Naylor, 1931.

DeVoto, Bernard, *The Year of Decision, 1846*. Boston: Little, Brown, 1943.

Fergusson, Erna. *New Mexico: A Pageant of Three Peoples*. New York: Knopf, 1951.

Fergusson, Harvey. *Rio Grande*. New York: Knopf, 1933.

Henson, Pauline. *Founding a Wilderness Capital*. Flagstaff, Arizona: Northland, 1965.

Holley, Mary Austin. *Texas*. Austin: Steck, 1935.

————. *Mary Austin Holley: The Texas Diary*. Ed. J. P. Bryan . Austin: Univ. of Texas Press, 1965.

————. *Letters of an Early American Traveller, Mary Austin Holley: Her Life and Works, 1784-1846*. Ed. Mattie Austin Hatcher. Dallas: Southwest Press, 1933.

Jordan, Terry G. *German Seed in Texas Soil: Immigrant Farmers in Nineteenth-Century Texas*. Austin: Univ. of Texas Press, 1966.

Lamar, Mirabeau B. *The Papers of Mirabeau Buonaparte Lamar*. Ed. Charles A. Gulick, Jr. 6 vols. Austin: A. C. Baldwin, 1921.

Lathrop, Barnes F. *Migration into East Texas, 1835-1860: A Study from the United States Census*. Austin: Texas State Historical Association, 1949.

Maverick, Mary A. *Memoirs of Mary A. Maverick*. Ed. Rena Maverick Green. San Antonio: Alamo Printing, 1921.

Olmsted, Frederick Law. *A Journey Through Texas; or, A Saddle-Trip on the Southwestern Frontier*. New York: Dix, Edwards, 1857.

Porter, Eugene O. *San Elizario: A History*. Austin: Pemberton, 1973.

Roemer, Ferdinand. *Texas*. Translated by Oswald Mueller. San Antonio: Standard Printing, 1935.

Smithwick, Noah. *The Evolution of a State*. Austin: Gammel Book, 1900.

Sowell, A. J. *Rangers and Pioneers of Texas*. New York: Argosy-Antiquarian, 1964.

————. *Early Settlers and Indian Fighters of Texas*. Austin: B. C. Jones, 1900.

Webb, Walter P. *The Great Plains*. New York: Ginn, 1931.

Orlan Sawey
Texas A&I University

Early Trade

Atherton, Lewis E. "Business Techniques in the Santa Fe Trade," *Missouri Historical Review*, 34 (1940), 335-41.

Anon. "Journal of the 1st Dragoon Escort of the Santa Fe Caravan, May 21, to July 21, 1843," *Mississippi Valley Historical Review*, 12 (1925), 72-98, 235-49.

Anon. "Letters of James and Robert Aull," *Missouri Historical Society Collections*, 5 (1927-28), 267-310.

Banning, William, and G. H. Banning. *Six Horses*. New York: Century, 1930.

Barnard, Evan G. *A Rider of the Cherokee Strip*. Boston: Houghton Mifflin, 1936.

Becknell, William. "Journal of Two Expeditions from Boon's Lick to Santa Fe," *Missouri Historical Society Collections*, 2 (1906), 55-67.

Beers, Henry P. "Military Protection of the Santa Fe Trail to 1843," *New Mexico Historical Review*, 12 (1937), 113-33.

Bidwell, John. *Overland to California in '41 and '49, and Texas in '51*. Chicago: R. R. Donnelly, 1928.

Bradley, Glenn D. *The Story of the Pony Express*. 2nd ed. San Francisco: Hesperian House, 1960.

Bratt, John. *Trails of Yesterday*. Lincoln, Chicago: University Publishing, 1921.

Brewerton, G. D. *Overland with Kit Carson*. New York: Coward McCann, 1930.

Browne, J. Ross. *Adventures in the Apache Country: a Tour through Arizona and Sonora*. New York: Harper, 1869.

Chapman, Arthur. *The Pony Express: the Record of a Romantic Adventure in Business*. New York: Putnam, 1932.

Conkling, Margaret B. *The Butterfield Overland Mail, 1858-1869*. 3 vols. Glendale, California: Arthur H. Clark, 1947.

Cox, Isaac J. "Opening the Santa Fe Trail," *Missouri Historical Review*, 25 (1930), 30-66.

Culmer, Frederick A. "Marking the Santa Fe Trail," *New Mexico Historical Review*, 9 (1934), 80.

Dawson, Nicholas. *Narrative of Nicholas "Cheyenne" Dawson Overland to California in '41 and '49 and Texas in '51*. San Francisco: Grabhorn, 1933.

Denney, Arthur J. "The Pony Express Trail: Its Dramatic Story," *Nebras-*

ka History, 21 (1940), 16.

Dobie, J. Frank. "Pistols, Poker and the Petite Mademoiselle in a Stage-coach," *The Flavor of Texas.* Dallas: Dealey and Lowe, 1936.

Duffus, R. L. *The Santa Fe Trail.* New York: Longmans, Green, 1930.

Dunbar, Seymour. *History of Travel in America.* New York: Tudor, 1937.

Evans, W. B. George. *Mexican Gold Trail: the Journal of a Forty-Niner.* San Marino: n.p., 1945.

Frederick, J V. *Ben Holladay: the Stagecoach King.* Glendale, California: A. H. Clark, 1940.

Fulton, Maurice G. *Diary and Letters of Josiah Gregg.* Norman: Univ. of Oklahoma Press, 1941.

Grace, Hybernia. "The First Trip West on the Butterfield Stage," *West Texas Historical Association Year Book,* 8 (1932), 73.

Gregg, Josiah. *Commerce of The Prairies* (1844). Ed. Max L. Moorhead. Norman: Univ. of Oklahoma Press, 1954.

Gregg, Kate L. *The Road to Santa Fe.* Albuquerque: Univ. of New Mexico Press, 1952.

Hafen, LeRoy R. *The Overland Mail, 1849-1869.* Cleveland: Arthur H. Clark, 1926.

Haley, J. Evetts. "The Stage-Coach Mail," *Fort Concho and the Texas Frontier.* San Angelo: *San Angelo Standard-Times,* 1952.

Hill, Joseph J. "An Unknown Expedition to Santa Fe in 1807," *Mississippi Valley Historical Review,* 6 (1920), 560-62.

Hungerford, Edward. *Wells Fargo: Advancing the Frontier.* New York: Random House, 1949.

Inman, Henry. *The Old Santa Fe Trail: the Story of a Great Highway.* Topeka: Crane, 1899.

Jackson, W. Turrentine. *Wagon Roads West.* Berkeley: Univ. of California Press, 1952.

James, Thomas. *Three Years Among the Indians and Mexicans.* New York: Citadel Press, 1966, 1967.

Laughlin, Ruth. *Caballeros.* Caldwell, Idaho: Caxton, 1946.

Magoffin, Susan Shelby. *Down the Santa Fe Trail.* New Haven: Yale Univ. Press, 1926.

Majors, Alexander. *Seventy Years on the Frontier.* Ed. Colonel Prentiss Ingraham. Chicago: Rand, McNally, 1893.

Marriott, Alice, and Carol K. Rachlin. "Along the Borders," *American Epic.* New York: Putnam, 1969.

Morehead, Charles R., Jr. "Personal Recollections," in William E. Connelley. *Doniphan's Expedition and the Conquest of New Mexico and California.* Topeka: The Author, 1907.

Ormsby, Waterman L. *The Butterfield Overland Mail.* Eds. Lyle H. Wright and Josephine M. Bynum. San Marino: Huntington Library, 1942.

Parker, Amos Andrew. *Trip to the West and Texas.* Concord, New Hampshire: White & Fisher, 1835; 2nd ed. Boston: B. M. Massey, 1836.

Perrine, Fred S. "Military Escorts on the Santa Fe Trail," *New Mexico Historical Review,* 2 (1927), 269-85.

Robinson, Jacob S. "Sketches of the Great West," *Magazine of American History,* 32 (1927), 213-68.

Root, Frank A. and W. E. Connelley. *The Overland Stage to California.* Topeka: By Authors, 1901.

Southwest on the Turquoise Trail: the First Diaries on the Road to Santa Fe. 2 vols. Ed. Archer B. Hulbert. Denver: n.p., 1933.

Stephens, F. F. "Missouri and the Santa Fe Trade," *Missouri Historical Review,* 10 (1916), 223-62; 11 (1917), 289-312.

Settle, Raymond W., and Mary L. Settle. *Empire on Wheels.* Stanford: Stanford Univ. Press, 1949.

————. *Saddles and Spurs.* Harrisburg, Pennsylvania: Stackpole, 1955.

————. *The Pony Express Saga.* Harrisburg, Pennsylvania: Stackpole, 1955.

Tallack, William. *The California Overland Express, the Longest Stage-Ride in the World.* London, 1865.

Taylor, Benjamin F. *Short Ravelings from a Long Yarn, or Camp March Sketches of the Santa Fe Trail.* Santa Ana, California: Fine Arts Press, 1936.

Thomas, Alfred B. "The First Santa Fe Expedition, 1792-93," *Chronicles of Oklahoma,* 9 (1931), 195-208.

Thompson, Robert L. *Wiring a Continent: The History of the Telegraph Industry in the United States, 1832-1866.* Princeton: Princeton Univ. Press, 1947.

Trail to California: the Overland Journal of Vincent Geiger and Wakeman Bryarly. Ed. David M. Potter. New Haven: Yale Univ. Press, 1945.

Twitchell, R. E. *Old Santa Fe Trail.* Santa Fe: New Mexican Publishing, 1925.

Vestal, Stanley. *The Old Santa Fe Trail.* Boston: Houghton Mifflin, 1939.

Visscher, Frank J. *A Thrilling and Truthful History of the Pony Express.* Chicago: n.p., 1908.

Webb, James J. *Adventures in the Santa Fe Trade, 1844-1847*. Glendale, California: Arthur H. Clark, 1931.

Wiltsee, Ernest A. *The Pioneer Miner and the Pack Mule Express*. San Francisco, n.p., 1931.

Wyman, Walker D. "Freighting: A Big Business on the Santa Fe Trail," *Kansas Historical Quarterly*, 1 (1931), 19-21.

Young, Otis E. *The First Military Escort on the Santa Fe Trail, 1829; from the Journal and Reports of Major Bennet Riley and Lieutenant Phillip St. George Cooke*. Glendale, California: Arthur H. Clark, 1952.

"Dragoons on the Santa Fe Trail in the Autumn of 1843," *Chronicles of Oklahoma*, 32 (1954), 42-57.

Jerre A. Dulock
Arlington, Texas

Freighting and Staging

Allhands, J. L. *Railroads to the Rio*. Salado, Texas: Anson Jones Press, 1959.

Banning, William, and G. H. Banning. *Six Horses*. New York: Century, 1930.

Beebe, Lucius, and Charles Clegg. *U. S. West: The Saga of Wells Fargo*. New York: Dutton, 1939.

Bieber, Ralph D., ed. *Southern Trails to California in 1849*. Glendale, California: Arthur H. Clark, 1937.

Bloss, Roy S. *Pony Express, the Great Gamble*. Berkeley: Howell, North, 1960.

Bradley, Glenn D. *The Story of the Pony Express*. Chicago: A. C. McClurg, 1913.

Bryarly, Wakeman, and Vincent Geiger. *Trails to California*. New Haven: Yale Univ. Press, 1906.

Chapman, Arthur. *The Pony Express*. New York: Putnam, 1932.

Chrisman, Harry E. *Lost Trails of the Cimmaron*. Denver: Swallow, 1961.

Conkling, Roscoe P., and Margaret B. Conkling. *The Butterfield Overland Mail, 1857-1869*. 2 vols. Glendale, California: Arthur H. Clark, 1955.

Corle, Edwin. *The Royal Highway*. Indianapolis: Bobbs-Merrill, 1949.

Croy, Homer. *Wheels West*. New York: Hastings House, 1955.

Cox, Edward G. *A Reference Guide to the Literature of Travel*. Seattle: Univ. of Washington Press, 1959.

Day, James M., ed. *Maps of Texas, 1527-1900. The Map Collection of the Texas State Archives.* Austin: Pemberton Press, 1962.

Delano, Alonzo. *Across the Plains and Among the Diggings.* New York: Wilson-Erickson, 1936.

Dick, Everett N. *Life in the West Before the Sod-House Frontier.* Lincoln: Prairie Press, 1947.

Driggs, Howard R. *The Pony Express Goes Through.* Philadelphia: Stokes, 1935.

Duffus, R. L. *The Santa Fe Trail.* New York: Longmans, Green, 1930.

Edwards, E. J. *The Whipple Report.* Los Angeles: Westernlore Press, 1961.

Eggenhofer, Nick. *Wagons, Mules, and Men.* New York: Hastings House, 1961.

Florin, Lambert. *Western Wagon Wheels.* Seattle: Superior Publishing, 1970.

Fulton, Maurice G., and Paul Horgan, eds. *Diary and Letters of Josiah Gregg.* 2 vols. Norman: University of Oklahoma Press, 1941.

Garrard, Lewis H. *Way-toyah and the Taos Trail, 1830.* Cincinnati: H. W. Derby and New York: A. S. Barnes, 1850; Glendale, California: Arthur H. Clark, 1937.

Goetzmann, William H. *Army Exploration of the American West, 1803-1862.* New Haven: Yale Univ. Press, 1960.

———. *Exploration and Empire.* New York: Knopf, 1966.

Greeley, Horace. *An Overland Journey, From New York to San Francisco in the Summer of 1859.* Ann Arbor: University Microfilms, 1966.

Gregg, Josiah. *Commerce of the Prairies.* New York: H. G. Langley, 1844; ed. Max Moorhead. Norman: Univ. of Oklahoma Press, 1954.

Hafen, LeRoy. *The Overland Mail, 1849-1869.* Cleveland: Arthur H. Clark, 1926.

Hafen, LeRoy, and Ann W. Hafen. *The Old Spanish Trail.* Glendale, California: Arthur H. Clark, 1954.

Harris, Benjamin B. *The Gila Trail: The Texas Argonauts and the California Gold Rush.* Norman: Univ. of Oklahoma Press, 1960.

Hatch, Alden. *Wells Fargo: A Century of Service.* New York: Doubleday, 1951.

Hill, Forrest G. *Roads, Rails, and Waterways.* Norman: Univ. of Oklahoma Press, 1958.

Hough, Emerson. *The Way West.* Indianapolis: Bobbs-Merrill, 1903.

Howard, Robert West, and others. *Hoofbeats of Destiny.* New York: Signet, 1960.

Hulbert, Archer B. *Southwest on the Turquoise Trail.* Colorado Springs: Colorado College and Denver Public Library, 1933.

Hungerford, Edward. *Wells Fargo.* New York: Random House, 1946.

Inman, Henry. *The Old Santa Fe Trail.* New York: Crane, 1898.

Jackson, W. Turrentine. *Wagon Roads West.* New Haven: Yale Univ. Press, 1967.

Kendall, George W. *Narrative of the Texan Santa Fe Expedition.* New York: Harper, 1844. Austin: Steck, 1936. Facsimile ed.

Laut, Agnes. *Pilgrims of the Santa Fe.* New York: Grossett & Dunlap, 1931.

Long, Margaret. *The Santa Fe Trail.* Denver: Swallow, 1954.

Look, Editors of. *The Santa Fe Trail.* New York: Random House, 1946.

Loomis, Noel M. *Wells Fargo.* New York: Clarkson Potter, 1968.

Magoffin, Susan Shelby. *Down the Santa Fe Trail into Mexico.* Ed. Stella Drum. New Haven: Yale Univ. Press, 1926.

Majors, Alexander. *Seventy Years on the Frontier.* Ed. Prentiss Ingraham. Chicago and New York: Rand McNally, 1893. Columbus, Ohio: Long's Book Store, 1950.

Masterson, V. V. *The Katy Railroad and the Last Frontier.* Norman: Univ. of Oklahoma Press, 1952.

Moody, Ralph. *Stagecoach West.* New York: Crowell, 1967.

Moorhead, Max L. *New Mexico's Royal Road.* Norman: Univ. of Oklahoma Press, 1958.

Napton, William B. *Over the Santa Fe Trail, 1857.* Santa Fe: Stagecoach Press, 1967-68.

O'Connor, Jack. *Horse and Buggy West.* New York: Knopf, 1969.

Oliva, Leo A. *Soldiers on the Santa Fe Trail.* Norman: Univ. of Oklahoma Press, 1967.

Ormsby, Waterman L. *The Butterfield Overland Mail.* Ed. L. H. Wright and Josephine M. Bynum. Alhambra, California: Huntington Library, 1954.

Overland Narratives, Captivities, Oregon, Idaho, California, Arizona, Montana, Texas. New York: Parke-Bernet Galleries, 1941.

Porter, Clyde, and Mae Reed Porter. *Matt Field on the Santa Fe Trail.* Ed. John E. Sunder. Norman: Univ. of Oklahoma Press, 1960.

Reed, St. Clair G. *A History of Texas Railroads and of Transportation Conditions Under Spain and Mexico and the Republic and the State.* Houston: St. Clair Publishing, 1941.

Root, Frank, and W. E. Connelly. *The Overland Stage to California.* Columbus, Ohio: Long's College Book, 1950.

Rounds, Glen. *The Prairie Schooners*. New York: Holiday House, 1968.
Santleben, August. *A Texas Pioneer*. New York and Washington: Neale, 1910.
Settle, Raymond, and Mary Lind Settle. *Empire on Wheels*. Stanford: Stanford Univ. Press, 1949.
————. *War Drums and Wagon Wheels: The Story of Russell, Majors and Waddell*. Lincoln: Univ. of Nebraska Press, 1968.
Smith, Waddell F., ed. *The Story of the Pony Express*. San Francisco: Hesperian House, 1960.
Thwaites, Reuben Gold, ed. *Early Western Travels*. 32 vols. Cleveland: Arthur H. Clark, 1904-1907.
Vestal, Stanley. *The Old Santa Fe Trail*. Boston: Houghton Mifflin, 1939.
Visscher, Frank J. *A Thrilling and Truthful History of the Pony Express*. Chicago: Charles T. Powner, 1946.
Webb, James J. *Adventures in the Santa Fe Trade*. Glendale, California: A. H. Clark, 1931.
Weber, David J. *The Extranjeros: Selected Documents from the Mexican Side of the Santa Fe Trail, 1825-1828*. Santa Fe: Stagecoach Press, 1967.
Wheat, Carl I. *Mapping the American West, 1540-1857*. Worcester, Massachusetts: American Antiquarian Society, 1954.
Wilson, Neil C. *Treasure Express: Epic Days of the Wells-Fargo*. New York: Macmillan, 1936.
Young, Otis E. *The First Military Escort on the Santa Fe Trail, 1829*. Glendale, California: Arthur H. Clark, 1952.

C. L. Sonnichsen
University of Texas at El Paso

George D. Hendricks
North Texas State University

Farming and Ranching

Abbott, E. C., and Helena Huntington Smith. *We Pointed Them North: Recollections of a Cowpuncher*. Norman: Univ. of Oklahoma Press, 1955.
Adams, Ramon F. *The Old-Time Cowhand*. New York: Macmillan, 1961.
————. *The Cowman and His Philosophy*. Austin: Encino Press, 1967.

————. *The Rampaging Herd: A Bibliography of Books and Pamphlets on Men and Events in the Cattle Industry.* Norman: Univ. of Oklahoma Press, 1960.

Allen, Winnie, and Carrie Walker Allen. *Pioneering in Texas.* Dallas: Southern Publishing Company, 1935.

Allred, B. W., and J. C. Dykes. *Flat Top Ranch.* Norman: Univ. of Oklahoma Press, 1957.

Atherton, Lewis *The Cattle Kings.* Bloomington: Indiana Univ. Press, 1962.

Barnard, Evan G. *A Rider of the Cherokee Strip.* Boston: Houghton Mifflin, 1936.

Barton, H. T. *The History of the J. A. Ranch.* Austin: Von Boeckmann-Jones, 1928.

Bell, James G. *A Log of the Texas-California Cattle Trail, 1854.* Ed. J. Evetts Haley. Austin: Southwest Historical Assn., 1932.

Benton, Jesse J. *Cow By the Tail.* Boston: Houghton Mifflin, 1943.

Branch, E. Douglas. *The Cowboy and His Interpreters.* New York: Cooper Square Publishing, 1961.

Brisbin, James F. *The Beef Bonanza: Or, How to Get Rich On the Plains.* Norman: Univ. of Oklahoma Press, 1959.

Brown, Harry J. *Letters from a Texas Sheep Ranch.* Urbana: Univ. of Illinois Press, 1959.

Brown, Mark H., and W. R. Felton. *Before Barbed Wire.* New York: Holt, 1956.

Call, Hughie. *Golden Fleece.* Boston: Houghton Mifflin, 1942.

Carpenter, Will T. *Lucky 7: A Cowman's Autobiography.* Ed. Elton Miles. Austin: Univ. of Texas Press, 1957.

Carroll, John A. *Pioneering in Arizona.* Tucson: Pioneers' Historical Society, 1964.

Chase, C. M. *The Editor's Run in New Mexico and Colorado Embracing 28 Letters on Stock Raising, Agriculture.* Fort Davis, Texas: Frontier Book, 1968.

Cleaveland, Agnes Morley. *No Life for a Lady.* Boston: Houghton Mifflin, 1941.

Collings, Ellsworth. *The 101 Ranch.* Norman: Univ. of Oklahoma Press, 1937.

Coolidge, Dane. *Texas Cowboys.* Norman: Univ. of Oklahoma Press, 1957.
————. *Arizona Cowboys.* New York: Dutton, 1938.

Cox, James. *Historical and Biographical Record of the Cattle Industry and*

Cattlemen of Texas and Adjacent Territory. New York: Antiquarian Press, 1958.

Culley, John. *Cattle, Horses, and Men.* Los Angeles: Ward Ritchie Press, 1958.

Dale, Edward E. *The Range Cattle Industry.* Norman: Univ. of Oklahoma Press, 1930.

————. *Cow Country.* Norman: Univ. of Oklahoma Press, 1942.

————. *Ranching on the Great Plains from 1865 to 1925.* Norman: Univ. of Oklahoma Press, 1960.

Dobie, J. Frank. *A Vaquero of the Brush Country.* Dallas: Southwest Press, 1929.

————. *The Longhorns.* Boston: Little, Brown, 1941.

————. *Cow People.* Boston: Little, Brown, 1964.

Douglas, C. L. *Cattle Kings of Texas.* Dallas: Baugh, 1939.

Drago, Harry Sinclair. *Great American Cattle Trails.* New York: Dodd, Mead, 1965.

Duke, Cordelia S., and Joe B. Frantz. *Six Thousand Miles of Fence.* Austin: Univ. of Texas Press, 1961.

Durham, Philip, and Everett L. Jones. *The Negro Cowboys.* New York: Dodd, Mead, 1965.

Dykstra, Robert R. *The Cattle Towns.* New York: Knopf, 1968.

Ellis, Martha. *Bell Ranch Sketches.* Clarendon, Texas: Clarendon Press, 1965.

Emmett, Chris. *Shanghai Pierce.* Norman: Univ. of Oklahoma Press, 1953.

Frantz, Joe B., and J. E. Choate. *The American Cowboy: The Myth and the Reality.* Norman: Univ. of Oklahoma Press, 1955.

French, William. *Some Recollections of a Western Ranchman.* Philadelphia: Stokes, 1927.

Gann, Walter. *Tread of the Longhorns.* San Antonio: Naylor, 1949.

Gard, Wayne. *The Chisholm Trail.* Norman: Univ. of Oklahoma Press, 1954.

Gipson, Fred. *Fabulous Empire.* Boston: Houghton Mifflin, 1946.

Goodwyn, Frank. *Life on the King Ranch.* New York: Crowell, 1951.

Greer, James K. *Bois D'Arc to Barbed Wire.* Dallas: Southwest Press, 1936.

Hale, Will. *Twenty-Four Years a Cowboy and Ranchman.* Norman: Univ. of Oklahoma Press, 1959.

Haley, J. Evetts. *The XIT Ranch of Texas* (1929). Norman: Univ. of Oklahoma Press, 1953.

Halsell, H. H. *Cowboys and Cattle Land.* Lubbock, Texas: Halsell, 1937.

Hamner, Laura V. *Short Grass and Long Horns*. Norman: Univ. of Oklahoma Press, 1943.

Harrington, O'Reilly. *Fifty Years on the Trail: A True Story of Western Life*. Norman: Univ. of Oklahoma Press, 1963.

Hastings, F. S. *A Ranchman's Recollections*. Chicago: Breeder's Gazette, 1921.

Hobson, Richmond P., Jr. *The Rancher Takes a Wife*. Philadelphia: Lippincott, 1961.

Holden, W. C. *The Spur Ranch*. Boston: Christopher Publishing House, 1934.

Hough, Emerson. *The Story of the Cowboy*. New York: Appleton, 1918.

Hunt, Frazier. *Cap Mossman: Last of the Great Cowmen*. New York: Hastings House, 1951.

Hunter, J. Marvin, and George W. Saunders. *Trail Drivers of Texas*. Nashville: Cokesbury Press, 1925.

James, W. S. *Cowboy Life in Texas*. Chicago: Donahue, 1893.

Jeffers, Joe. *Ranch Wife*. New York: Doubleday, 1964.

Kennon, Bob (as told to Ramon Adams). *From the Pecos to the Powder: A Cowboy's Autobiography*. Norman: Univ. of Oklahoma Press, 1965.

Kupper, Winifred. *Texas Sheepman*. Austin: Univ. of Texas Press, 1952.

————. *The Golden Hoof*. New York: Knopf, 1945.

Lea, Tom. *The King Ranch*. 2 vols. Boston: Little, Brown, 1958.

McCauley, James E. *A Stove-Up Cowboy's Story*. Dallas: University Press, 1943.

McCoy, Joseph. *Historic Sketches of the Cattle Trade*. Glendale, California: Arthur H. Clark, 1940.

Marriott, Alice. *Hell on Horses and Women*. Norman: Univ. of Oklahoma Press, 1953.

Maudslay, Robert. *Texas Sheepman*. Ed. Winifred Kupper. Austin: Univ. of Texas Press, 1956.

Nelson, Oliver. *The Cowmen's Southwest*. Ed. Angie Debo. Glendale, California: Arthur H. Clark, 1953.

Nordyke, Lewis. *Cattle Empire*. New York: Morrow, 1949.

————. *Great Roundup*. New York: Morrow, 1955.

Osgood, E. S. *The Day of the Cattleman*. Minneapolis: Univ. of Minnesota Press, 1929.

Pelzer, Louis. *The Cattlemen's Frontier*. Glendale, Cailfornia: Arthur H. Clark, 1955.

Pearce, W. M. *The Matador Land and Cattle Company*. Norman: Univ. of Oklahoma Press, 1964.

Post, Charles C. *Ten Years a Cowboy*. Chicago: Rhodes and McClure, 1888.

Potter, Jack M. *Cattle Trails of the Old West*. Clayton, New Mexico: Leader Publishing, 1935.

Rak, Mary K. *A Cowman's Wife*. Boston: Houghton Mifflin, 1934.

Richthofen, Walter, Baron Von. *Cattle Raising on the Plains of North America*. Norman: Univ. of Oklahoma Press, 1964.

Rister, Carl Coke. *Land Hunger: David L. Payne and the Oklahoma Boomers*. Norman: Univ. of Oklahoma Press, 1942.

Rollins, Philip A. *The Cowboy*. New York: Scribner, 1957.

Sandoz, Mari. *The Cattlemen*. New York: Hastings House, 1958.

Santee, Ross. *Men and Horses*. New York: Century, 1926.

————. *Cowboy*. New York: Cosmopolitan Book Corp. 1928.

————. *Lost Pony Tracks*. New York: Scribner, 1952.

Schlebecker, John T. *Cattle Raising on the Plains, 1900-1961*. Lincoln: Univ. of Nebraska Press, 1964.

Schmitt, Martin F. *The Settler's West*. New York: Scribner, 1955.

Shaw, James C. *North from Texas*. Ed. Herbert O. Brayer. Evanston: Branding Iron Press, 1952.

Sheffy, L. F. *The Francklyn Land and Cattle Company*. Austin: Univ. of Texas Press, 1963.

Siringo, Charles A. *A Texas Cowboy* (1885). New York: William Sloane, 1950.

Smith, Erwin B., and J. Evetts Haley. *Life on the Texas Range*. Austin: Univ. of Texas Press, 1953.

Stephens, A. Ray. *The Taft Ranch: A Texas Principality*. Austin: Univ. of Texas Press, 1964.

Stewart, Edgar I., ed. *Penny-An-Acre Empire in the West*. Norman: Univ. of Oklahoma Press, 1968.

Stillwell, Hart. *Uncovered Wagon*. New York: Doubleday, 1947.

Tilghman, Zoe A. *Dugout*. Oklahoma City: Harlow, 1925.

Towne, Charles W., and Edward N. Wentworth. *Shepherd's Empire*. Norman: Univ. of Oklahoma Press, 1947.

Ward, Faye E. *The Cowboy at Work*. New York: Hastings House, 1958.

Wellman, Paul I. *The Trampling Herd*. New York: Carrick and Evans, 1939.

Westermeier, C. P. *Man, Beast, and Dust: The Story of the Rodeo*. Boulder, Colorado: Published by the Author, 1947.

Winfrey, Dorman H. *Julien Sidney Devereux and His Monte Verdi Plantation.* Waco: Texian Press, 1964.
Wise, Evelyn V. *Shepherd of the Valley.* New York: Bruce, 1949.
Wright, Solomon A. *My Rambles.* Ed. J. Frank Dobie. Austin: Texas Folklore Society, 1942.

C. L. Sonnichsen
University of Texas at El Paso

George D. Hendricks
North Texas State University

Religion

Adams, Eleanor B. "Bishop Tamarón's Visitation of New Mexico, 1760,"
New Mexico Historical Review, 28 (1953), 81-114; 29 (1954), 41-47.
Antony, Claudius. "Kit Carson, Catholic," *New Mexico Historical Review,*
10 (1935), 323-36.
Baker, William M. *The Life and Labours of the Rev. Daniel Baker, D. D.*
Philadelphia: W. S. and A. Martien, 1858.
Bayard, Ralph. *Lone Star Vanguard: the Catholic Reoccupation of Texas
(1836-48).* St. Louis: Vincentian Press, 1945.
Belknap, Helen O. *The Church on the Changing Frontier: A Study of the
Homesteader and His Church.* New York: Doran, 1922.
Bloom, Lansing B. "The Rev. Hiram Walter Reader, Baptist Missionary to
New Mexico," *New Mexico Historical Review,* 17 (1942), 113-47.
Boren, Carter E. *Religion on the Texas Frontier.* San Antonio: Naylor, 1968.
Botkin, Sam L. "Indian Missions of the Episcopal Church in Oklahoma,"
Chronicles of Oklahoma, 36 (1958), 40-47.
Boyd, E. "The Literature of Santos," *Southwest Review,* 35 (1950), 128-40.
Brown, Lawrence L. *The Episcopal Church in Texas, 1838-74.* Austin:
Church Historical Society, 1963.
Bruner, James W. *A Guide Book on Baptist Institutions in Texas.* Dallas:
Harben-Spotts, 1941.
Bryce, J. Y. "Death of Oak-Chi-Ah, a Missionary," *Chronicles of Oklahoma,*
4 (1926), 194-99.
———. "Some Notes of Interest Concerning Early Day Operations in Indian
Territory by Methodist Church South," *Chronicles of Oklahoma,* 4 (1926),
233-41.

Burleson, Georgia J., comp. *The Life and Writings of Rufus C. Burleson, D.D. LL.D.* Waco: n.p., 1901.

Burr, Nelson R. *A Critical Bibliography of Religion in America,* IV in *Religion in American Life.* Ed. James Ward Smith and A. Leland Jamison, Princeton: Princeton Univ. Press, 1961.

Callahan, Mary Generosa. *The History of the Sisters of Divine Providence, San Antonio, Texas.* Milwaukee: Bruce Press, 1954.

Carroll, James M. *A History of Texas Baptists.* Dallas: Baptist Standard Publishing, 1923.

Castañeda, Carlos E. "Earliest Catholic Activities in Texas," *Catholic Historical Review,* 17 (1932), 278-95.

———. *Our Catholic Heritage in Texas, 1519-1936.* 7 vols. Austin: Von Boeckmann-Jones, 1936.

———. *Pioneers in Sackcloth.* Austin: n. p., 1939.

Cather, Willa. *Death Comes for the Archbishop.* New York: Knopf, 1927.

Catholic Youth Organization, Diocese of Galveston, Houston District. *Diocese of Galveston Centennial, 1847-1947.* Houston: Centennial Book Committee, 1947.

Centennial Story of Texas Baptists. Dallas: Texas General Convention Executive Board, 1936.

Cohen, Anne Nathan, and Harry I. Cohen. *The Man Who Stayed in Texas: the Life of Rabbi Henry Cohen.* New York: Whittlesey House, 1941.

Cranfill, J. B. *Dr. J. B. Cranfill's Chronicle: a Story of Life in Texas.* New York: Fleming H. Revell, 1916.

Dawson, Joseph Martin. *A Thousand Months to Remember: an Autobiography.* Waco: Baylor Univ. Press, 1964.

De Escalante, Silvestre Vélez. "Letter to the Missionaries of New Mexico." *New Mexico Historical Review,* 40 (1965), 318-32.

Denison, Natalie Morrison. "Missions and Missionaries of the Presbyterian Church, U.S., Among the Choctaws, 1866-1907," *Chronicles of Oklahoma,* 24 (1946), 426-48.

Domenech, Emanuel H. D. *Missionary Adventures in Texas and Mexico: A Personal Narrative of Six Years' Sojourn in those Regions.* London: Longmans, 1858.

Doyon, Bernard. *The Cavalry of Christ on the Rio Grande, 1849-83.* Milwaukee: Bruce Press, 1956.

Drake, Florence. "Mary Bourbonnais Organized a Sunday School," *Chronicles of Oklahoma,* 40 (1962), 386-89.

Dreyfus, A. Stanley, comp. *Henry Cohen: Messenger of the Lord.* New York: Bloch, 1963.

Eckstein, Stephen Daniel. *History of the Churches of Christ in Texas. 1824-1950.* Austin: Firm Foundation Publishing House, 1963.

Ellis, Florence Hawley, and Edwin Baca. "The Apuntos of Father J. B. Ralliere," *New Mexico Historical Review,* 32 (1957), 10-35; 259-73.

Ellis, Florence Hawley. "Tomé and Father J. B. R.", *New Mexico Historical Review,* 30 (1955), 89-114; 195-220.

Evans, William F. *Border Skylines.* Dallas: For the Bloys Camp Meeting Association, Fort Davis, Texas, 1940.

Fitzmorris, Mary Angela. *Four Decades of Catholicism in Texas, 1820-60.* Washington: Catholic Univ., 1926.

Foreman, Carolyn Thomas. "Fairfield Mission," *Chronicles of Oklahoma,* 27 (1949), 373-88.

Foreman, Grant. "Notes of a Missionary among the Cherokees," *Chronicles of Oklahoma,* 16 (1938), 171-89.

Foreman, Minta Ross. "Reverend Stephen Foreman, Cherokee Missionary," *Chronicles of Oklahoma,* 18 (1940), 229-42.

Garrison, Winfred E., and Albert T. DeGroot. *The Disciples of Christ: A History.* St. Louis: n.p., 1950.

Gaustad, Edwin Scott. *Historical Atlas of Religion in America.* New York: Harper and Row, 1962.

Gilbert, M. H., comp. *Archdiocese of San Antonio, 1874-1949.* San Antonio: n.p., 1949.

Graves, H. A. *Andrew Jackson Potter: the Fighting Parson of the Texan Frontier.* Nashville: Southern Methodist Publishing House, 1881.

Gravis, Peter W. *Twenty-five Years on the Outside Row of the Northwest Texas Annual Conference.* 1892.

Habig, Marion A. "Mission San José y San Miguel de Aguayo, 1720-1824," *Southwestern Historical Quarterly,* 71 (1968), 496-516.

Harper, Richard H. "The Missionary Work of the Reformed (Dutch) Church in America in Oklahoma," *Chronicles of Oklahoma,* 18 (1940), 252-65; and 19 (1941), 170-79.

Havins, T. R. "Frontier Mission Difficulties," *West Texas Historical Association Yearbook,* 15 (1939), 54-74.

Haymes, Joseph O. *History of the Northwest Texas Conference, the Methodist Church: First Fifty Years, 1910-60.* Nashville: Printed for the Conference, 1962.

Hazelrigg, Charles. "The Christian Church of Sheridan, Oklahoma," *Chronicles of Oklahoma,* 20 (1942), 398-401.

Hiemstra, William L. "Presbyterian Missionaries and Mission Churches among the Choctaw and Chickasaw Indians, (1852-65)," *Chronicles of Oklahoma,* 26 (1948), 459-67.

Hinds, Roland. "Early Creek Missions," *Chronicles of Oklahoma,* 17 (1939), 48-61.

Holway, Hope. "Union Mission, 1826-37," *Chronicles of Oklahoma,* 40 (1962), 355-78.

House, R. Martin. " 'The Only Way Church' and the Sac and Fox Indians," *Chronicles of Oklahoma,* 43 (1965), 443-66.

Howlett, William J. *Life of the Rt. Reverend Joseph P. Machebeuf.* Pueblo, Colorado: Franklin Press, 1908.

Jeter, Jerry B. "Pioneer Preacher," *Chronicles of Oklahoma,* 23 (1945), 358-68.

Kaufman, Edmund G. "Mennonite Missions among the Oklahoma Indians," *Chronicles of Oklahoma,* 40 (1962), 41-54.

Kelly, Henry W. "Franciscan Missions of New Mexico, 1740-60," *New Mexico Historical Review,* 25 (1940), 345-68; and 26 (1941), 148-83.

Kessell, John L. "The Making of a Martyr: the Young Franciscan Garcés," *New Mexico Historical Review,* 45 (1970), 181-96.

Kinsolving, Arthur B. *Texas George: the Life of George Herbert Kinsolving, Bishop of Texas, 1892-1928.* Milwaukee: Morehouse Publishing, 1932.

Kjaer, Jens Christian. "The Lutheran Mission at Oaks, Oklahoma," *Chronicles of Oklahoma,* 28 (1950), 42-51.

Kress, Margaret K., trans. "Diary of a Visit of Inspection of the Texas Missions Made by Fray José de Solís in the Year 1767-68," *Southwestern Historical Quarterly,* 35 (1931), 28-76.

Lauderdale, Virginia E. "Tullahassee Mission," *Chronicles of Oklahoma,* 26 (1948), 285-300.

Lewis, Anne. "Letters Regarding Choctaw Missions and Missionaries," *Chronicles of Oklahoma,* 17 (1939), 275-85.

Lide, Anne A. *Robert Alexander and the Early Methodist Church in Texas.* La Grange, Texas: *La Grange Journal,* 1935.

McCullough, William Wallace, Jr. *John McCullough: Pioneer Presbyterian Missionary and Teacher in the Republic of Texas.* Austin: Pemberton Press, 1966.

McLean, John H. *Reminiscences of Rev. Jno. H. McLean, A.M., D.D.*

Nashville: Smith and Lamar, 1918.

Mackey, Alice Hurley. "Father Murrow: Civil War Period," *Chronicles of Oklahoma,* 12 (1934), 55-65.

Mason, Zane Allen. *Frontiersmen of the Faith: A History of Baptist Pioneer Work in Texas, 1865-85.* San Antonio: Naylor, 1970.

————. "Some Experiences of Baptists on the Texas Frontier," *West Texas Historical Association Yearbook,* 36 (1960), 51-62.

Mayer, Frederick Emanuel. *The Religious Bodies of America.* St. Louis: Concordia Publishing House, 1956.

Morrell, Z. N. *Flowers and Fruits from the Wilderness.* Boston: Gould and Lincoln, 1872.

Morrison, W. B. "The Choctaw Mission of the American Board of Commissioners for Foreign Missions," *Chronicles of Oklahoma,* 4 (1926), 166-83.

Muir, Andrew Forest. "No Sabbath in West Texas: Missionary Appeals from Boerne, 1867-68," *West Texas Historical Association Yearbook,* 31 (1955), 114-21.

Murphy, Dubose. "Early Days of the Protestant Episcopal Church in Texas," *Southwestern Historical Quarterly,* 34 (1931), 293-316.

Nail, Olin W. *History of Texas Methodism, 1900-60.* Austin: Capital Printing, 1961.

Nieberding, Velma. "Chief Splitlog and the Cayuga Mission Church," *Chronicles of Oklahoma,* 32 (1954), 18-28.

————. "The Very Reverend Urban de Hasque, S. T. D., L. L. D.: Pioneer Priest of Indian Territory," *Chronicles of Oklahoma,* 38 (1960), 35-42.

————. "Sacred Heart Academy at Vinita Established 1897," *Chronicles of Oklahoma,* 40 (1962), 379-85.

Norton, Wesley. "The Methodist Episcopal Church and the Civil Disturbances in North Texas in 1859 and 1860," *Southwestern Historical Quarterly,* 68 (1965), 317-41.

O'Connor, Kathryn S. *The Presidio La Bahia del Espritu (Espirtu) santo de Zuniga, 1721 to 1846.* Austin: Von Boeckmann-Jones, 1966.

Paap, Opal Leigh. *Pioneer Preacher.* New York: Crowell, 1948.

Parisot, P. F. *The Reminiscences of a Texas Missionary.* San Antonio: St. Mary's Church, 1899.

Paschal, George H., Jr., and Judith A. Benner. *One Hundred Years of Challenge and Change: a History of the Synod of Texas of the United Presbyterian Church in the U.S.A.* San Antonio: Trinity Univ. Press, 1968.

Peyton, Green [pseud. for Green Peyton Wertenbaker]. *For God and Texas: the Life of P. B. Hill.* New York: Whittlesey House, 1947.

Phelan, Macum. *A History of Early Methodism in Texas, 1817-66.* Nashville: Cokesbury, 1924.

————. *A History of the Expansion of Methodism in Texas, 1867-1902.* Dallas: Mathis, Van Nort, 1937.

Puckett, Fidelia Miller. "Ramon Ortiz: Priest and Patriot," *New Mexico Historical Review,* 25 (1950), 264-95.

Rael, Juan B. *The Sources and Diffusion of the Mexican Shepherds' Plays.* Guadalajara, Mexico: Librera La Joyita, 1965.

Rankin, George C. *The Story of My Life: or more than a Half Century as I have Lived It and Seen It.* Nashville: Smith and Lamar, 1912.

Ray, Georgia Miller. *The Jeff Ray I Knew: a Pioneer Preacher in Texas.* San Antonio: Naylor, 1952.

Red, William Stuart. *A History of the Presbyterian Church in Texas.* Austin: Steck, 1936.

————. "Allen's Reminiscences of Texas, 1838-42," *Southwestern Historical Quarterly,* 17 (1913), 283-305.

————. *The Texas Colonists and Religion, 1821-36.* Austin: E. L. Shettles, 1924.

Reed, Ora Eddleman. "The Robe Family—Missionaries," *Chronicles of Oklahoma,* 26 (1948), 301-12.

Rey, Agapito. "Missionary Aspects of the Founding of New Mexico," *New Mexico Historical Review,* 23 (1948), 22-31.

Riley, Benjamin, F. *History of the Baptists of Texas.* Dallas: n.p., 1907.

Roberts, Bruce. *Springs from the Parched Ground.* Uvalde, Texas: Hornby Press, 1950.

Routh, E. C. "Early Missionaries to the Cherokees," *Chronicles of Oklahoma,* 15 (1937), 449-65.

Sallee, Annie Jenkin. *A Friend of God: Highlights in the Life of Judge W. H. Jenkin, Outstanding Christian Layman of Texas.* San Antonio: Naylor, 1952.

Salpointe, Jean Baptist. *Soldiers of the Cross: Notes on the Ecclesiastical History of New Mexico, Arizona and Colorado.* Banning, California: St. Boniface's School, 1898.

Scholes, France V. "Church and State in New Mexico, 1610-1650," *New Mexico Historical Review,* 11 (1936), 9-76; and 12 (1937), 78-106.

————. "Documents for the History of New Mexican Missions in the Seventeenth Century," *New Mexico Historical Review,* 4 (1929), 45-58; 195-201.

————. "The First Decade of the Inquisition in New Mexico," *New Mexico Historical Review,* 10 (1935), 195-241.

————. "Problems in the Early Ecclesiastical History of New Mexico," *New Mexico Historical Review,* 7 (1932), 32-74.

————, and Lancing B. Bloom. "Friar Personnel and Mission Chronology, 1598-1629," *New Mexico Historical Review,* 19 (1944), 319-36; and 20 (1945), 58-82.

Seno, José D. "The Chapel of Don Antonio José Ortiz," *New Mexico Historical Review,* 13 (1938), 347-59.

Spindler, Frank MacD. "Concerning Hempstead and Waller County: III. Religious Expression," *Southwestern Historical Quarterly,* 59 (1956), 466-69.

————. "Concerning Hempstead and Waller County: IV. Saint Bartholomew's Episcopal Church," *Southwestern Historical Quarterly,* 59 (1956) 469-72.

Stewart, Martha. "The Indian Mission Conference of Oklahoma," *Chronicles of Oklahoma,* 40 (1962), 330-36.

Thomason, John W. *Lone Star Preacher.* New York: Scribner, 1941.

Thrall, Homer S. *A Brief History of Methodism in Texas.* Nashville: M. E. Church, South, 1889.

Vernon, Walter N. *Methodism Moves Across North Texas.* Dallas: Historical Society of North Texas Conference, The Methodist Church, 1967.

————. *William Stevenson: Riding Preacher.* Dallas: Southern Methodist Univ. Press, 1964.

Wardell, M. L. "Protestant Missions among the Osages, 1820-38," *Chronicles of Oklahoma,* 2 (1924), 285-97.

Warner, Louis H. *Archbishop Lamy: an Epoch Maker.* Santa Fé: New Mexican Publishing, 1936.

Warner, Michael J. "Protestant Missionary Activity among the Navajo, 1890-1912," *New Mexico Historical Review,* 45 (1970), 209-32.

Webb, Murl L. "Religious and Educational Efforts among Texas Indians in the 1850's," *Southwestern Historical Quarterly,* 69 (1965), 22-37.

Weddle, Robert S. "San Juan Bautista: Mother of Texas Missions," *Southwestern Historical Quarterly,* 71 (1968), 542-63.

White, Charley C., and Ada Morehead Holland. *No Quittin' Sense.* Austin: Univ. of Texas Press, 1969.

Woolworth, Laura Fowler. *Littleton Fowler, 1803-46: A Missionary to the Republic of Texas, 1837-46.* Shreveport: n.p., 1936.

Wuthenau, A. von. "The Spanish Military Chapels in Santa Fé and the Reredos of Our Lady of Light," *New Mexico Historical Review,* 10 (1935), 175-94.

Henry L. Alsmeyer, Jr.,
David Alsmeyer
Texas A&M University

Politics

Alexander, Charles C. *The Ku Klux Klan in the Southwest.* Lexington: Univ. of Kentucky Press, 1965.

Ashurst, Henry F. *A Many Colored Toga: The Diary of Henry Fountain Ashurst.* Tucson: Univ. of Arizona Press, 1962.

Athearn, Robert G. *Rebel of the Rockies: A History of the Denver And Rio Grande Western Railroad.* New Haven: Yale Univ. Press, 1962.

Atherton, Lewis E. *The Cattle Kings.* Bloomington: Indiana Univ. Press, 1961.

Bailey, Lynn R. *The Indian Slave Trade in the Southwest.* Los Angeles: Westernlore, 1966.

Bailey, Ralph E. *Indian Fighter: The Story of Nelson A. Miles.* New York: Morrow, 1965.

Bainbridge, John. *The Super Americans.* New York: Doubleday, 1961.

Bancroft, Hubert Howe. *The Works of Hubert Howe Bancroft.* 39 vols. San Francisco: A. L. Bancroft, 1882-1890. Vols. 15-16, *History of the North Mexican States and Texas.* Vol. 17, *History of Arizona and New Mexico.*

————. *History of Arizona and New Mexico, 1530-1888.* Albuquerque: Horn and Wallace, 1962. Facsimile of the 1889 edition.

Barker, Eugene C. *The Life of Stephen F. Austin, Founder of Texas, 1793-1836.* Nashville: Cokesbury, 1925. Austin: Univ. of Texas Press, 1949.

————. *Mexico and Texas, 1821-1835.* Dallas: P. L. Turner, 1928.

Bill, Alfred H. *Rehearsal for Conflict: The War with Mexico, 1846-1848.* New York: Knopf, 1947.

Binkley, W. C. *The Texas Revolution.* Baton Rouge: Louisiana State Univ. Press, 1952.

Bryant, Keith L., Jr. *Alfalfa Bill Murray.* Norman: Univ. of Oklahoma Press, 1968.

Buck, Solon J. *The Agrarian Crusade.* New Haven: Yale Univ. Press. 1920.

Carsdorph, Paul. *The Republican Party in Texas, 1865-1965.* Austin: Univ. of Texas Press, 1965.

Clark, Ira G. *Then Came the Railroad: The Century from Steam to Diesel in the Southwest.* Norman: Univ. of Oklahoma Press, 1958.

Clark, James A. *The Tactful Texan: A Biography of Governor Will Hobby.* New York: Random House, 1958.

Clarke, Dwight L. *Stephen Watts Kearny: Soldier of the West.* Norman: Univ. of Oklahoma Press, 1961.

Clarke, Mary W. *David G. Burnet.* Austin: Univ. of Texas Press, 1969.

Colton, Ray G. *The Civil War in the Western Territories.* Norman: Univ. of Oklahoma Press, 1959.

Connor, Seymour V., and others. *The Saga of Texas.* 6 vols. Austin: Steck-Vaughn, 1965.

Dale, E. E. *The Indians of the Southwest.* Norman: Univ. of Oklahoma Press, 1930.

————, and Morris L. Wardell. *History of Oklahoma.* New York: Prentice-Hall, 1948.

De Shields, James T. *They Sat in High Places: The Presidents and Governors of Texas.* San Antonio: Naylor, 1940.

De Voto, Bernard. *The Year of Decision, 1846.* Boston: Houghton Mifflin, 1950.

Dorough, Dwight. *Mr. Sam.* New York: Random House, 1962.

Faulk, Odie B. *Arizona: A Short History.* Norman: University of Oklahoma Press, 1970.

————. *Too Far North—Too Far South.* Los Angeles: Westernlore, 1967.

————. *Land of Many Frontiers: A History of the American Southwest.* New York: Oxford Univ. Press, 1968.

Fite, Gilbert C. *The Farmer's Frontier, 1865-1900.* Norman: Univ. of Oklahoma Press, 1966.

Forbes, Gerald. *Flush Production: The Epic of Oil in the Gulf Southwest.* Norman: Univ. of Oklahoma Press, 1942.

Foreman, Grant. *The Five Civilized Tribes.* Norman: Univ. of Oklahoma Press, 1970.

Friend, Llerena B. *Sam Houston: The Great Designer.* Austin: Univ. of Texas Press, 1951.

Fritz, Henry E. *The Movement for Indian Assimilation, 1860-1890.* Philadelphia: Univ. of Pennsylvania Press, 1963.

Fuermann, George. *Reluctant Empire: The Mind of Texas.* New York: Doubleday, 1957.

Gambrell, Herbert. *Anson Jones, Last President of Texas.* Garden City, New York: Doubleday, 1948. Austin: Univ. of Texas Press, 1964.

———. *Mirabeau Buonaparte Lamar: Troubadour and Crusader.* Dallas: Southwest Press, 1934.

Garber, Paul N. *The Gadsden Treaty.* Gloucester, Massachusetts: Peter Smith, 1959.

Garrett, Julia K. *Green Flag Over Texas.* New York and Dallas: Cordova Press, 1939.

Gibson, Arrell M. *The Life and Death of Colonel Albert Jenkins Fountain.* Norman: Univ. of Oklahoma Press, 1965.

Gittinger, Roy. *The Formation of the State of Oklahoma.* Norman: Univ. of Oklahoma Press, 1939.

Goodwyn, Frank. *Lone-Star Land: Twentieth Century Texas in Perspective.* New York: Knopf, 1955.

Greer, James K. *Colonel Jack Hays: Texas Frontier Leader and California Builder.* New York: Dutton, 1952.

Greever, William S. *Arid Domain: The Santa Fe and Its Western Grant.* Palo Alto: Stanford Univ. Press, 1954.

———. *The Bonanza West: The Story of the Western Mining Rushes, 1848-1900.* Norman: Univ. of Oklahoma Press, 1963.

Groves, Leslie R. *Now It Can Be Told: The Story of the Manhattan Project.* New York: Harper, 1962.

Hagen, William T. *Indian Police and Judges: Experiments in Acculturation and Control.* New Haven: Yale Univ. Press, 1966.

Haley, J. Evetts. *George W. Littlefield, Texan.* Norman: Univ. of Oklahoma Press, 1943.

———. *Men of Fiber.* El Paso: Carl Hartzog, 1963.

———. *The XIT Ranch of Texas and the Early Days of the Llano Escatado.* Chicago: Lakeside Press, 1929; Norman: Univ. of Oklahoma Press, 1967.

———. *Fort Concho and the Texas Frontier.* San Angelo, Texas: *San Angelo Standard-Times,* 1952.

Hall, Martin H. *Sibley's New Mexico Campaign.* Austin: Univ. of Texas, 1960.

Henderson, Richard B. *Maury Maverick: A Political Biography.* Austin:

Univ. of Texas Press, 1970.

Herner, Charles. *The Arizona Rough Riders*. Tucson: Univ. of Arizona Press, 1970.

Hicks, John D. *The Populist Revolt*. Minneapolis: Univ. of Minnesota Press, 1931.

Holbrook, Stewart H. *Davy Crockett*. New York: Random House, 1955.

Holden, W. C. *The Spur Ranch*. North Quincy, Massachusetts: Christopher Publishing House, 1934.

Hollon, W. Eugene. *The Southwest: Old and New*. New York: Knopf, 1961; Lincoln: Univ. of Nebraska Press, 1968.

Holmes, Jack E. *Politics in New Mexico*. Albuquerque: Univ. of New Mexico, 1967.

Horgan, Paul. *Great River: The Rio Grande in North American History*. 2 vols. New York: Dutton, 1954.

Horn, Calvin. *New Mexico's Troubled Years*. Albuquerque: Horn and Wallace, 1963.

Hunt, Aurora. *Kirby Benedict, Frontier Judge*. Glendale, California: Arthur H. Clark, 1961.

Jackson, W. Turrentine. *Wagon Roads West*. Berkeley: Univ. of California Press, 1952.

James, Marquis. *The Raven: A Biography of Sam Houston*. Indianapolis: Bobbs-Merrill, 1929.

Jenkins, John, ed. *The Papers of the Texas Revolution*. 10 vols. Austin: Presidial Press, 1973.

Jonas, Frank H. *Politics in the American West*. Salt Lake City: Univ. of Utah Press, 1969.

Jones, Billy Mac. *Health Seekers in the Southwest, 1817-1900*. Norman: Univ. of Oklahoma Press, 1967.

Judah, Charles B. *The Republican Party in New Mexico: A Challenge to Constructive Leadership*. Albuquerque: Univ. of New Mexico Press, 1959.

———. *Governor Richard C. Dillon: A Study in New Mexico Politics*. Albuquerque: Univ. of New Mexico Press, 1948.

Keleher, William A. *The Maxwell Land Grant: A New Mexico Item*. Santa Fe: Rydal Press, 1942.

———. *Turmoil in New Mexico, 1846-1868*. Santa Fe: Rydal Press, 1951.

———. *Violence in Lincoln County, 1869-1881*. Albuquerque: Univ. of New Mexico Press, 1957.

King, Alvy L. *Louis T. Wigfall: Southern Fire-Eater*. Baton Rouge: Louisiana State Univ. Press, 1970.
King, Charles. *Campaigning with Crook*. New York: Harper, 1890. Norman: Univ. of Oklahoma Press, 1964.
Lamar, Howard R. *The Far Southwest, 1846-1912: A Territorial History*. New Haven: Yale Univ. Press, 1966.
Larson, Robert W. *New Mexico's Quest for Statehood, 1846-1912*. Albuquerque: Univ. of New Mexico Press, 1968.
Lathrop, Barnes F. *Migration in East Texas, 1835-1860*. Austin: Steck, 1949.
Lea, Tom. *The King Ranch*. 2 vols. Boston: Little, Brown, 1957.
Lindheim, Milton. *The Republic of the Rio Grande: Texans in Mexico*. Waco: W. M. Morrison, 1964.
Lohbeck, Don. *Patrick J. Hurley*. Chicago: Henry Regnery, 1957.
McClintock, James H. *Arizona, Prehistoric, Aboriginal, Pioneer, Modern; the Nation's Youngest Commonwealth within a Land of Ancient Culture*. 3 vols. Chicago: S. J. Clarke, 1916.
McKay, Seth S. *Seven Decades of the Texas Constitution of 1876*. Lubbock: Texas Tech Univ., 1942.
———. *W. Lee O'Daniel and Texas Politics, 1838-1942*. Lubbock: Texas Tech. Univ., 1944.
McKee, Irving. *"Ben Hur" Wallace: The Life of General Lew Wallace*. Berkeley: Univ. of California Press, 1947.
McReynolds, Edwin C. *Oklahoma: A History of the Sooner State*. Norman: Univ. of Oklahoma Press, 1964.
Martin, Roscoe. *The People's Party in Texas: A Study of Third Party Politics*. Austin: Univ. of Texas Press, 1970.
Masterson, V. V. *The Katy Railroad and the Last Frontier*. Norman: Univ. of Oklahoma Press, 1952.
Maxwell, Robert S. *Whistle in the Piney Woods: Paul Bremond and the Houston, East and West Texas Railway*. Houston: Texas Gulf Coast Historical Association, 1963.
Nalle, Ouida Ferguson. *The Fergusons of Texas*. San Antonio: Naylor, 1946.
Nance, J. Milton. *After San Jacinto: The Texas-Mexican Frontier, 1836-1841*. Austin: Univ. of Texas Press, 1963.
———. *Attack and Counterattack: The Texas-Mexican Frontier, 1842*. Austin: Univ. of Texas Press, 1964.
Nye, Wilbur S. *Carbine and Lance: The Story of Old Fort Sill*. Norman: Univ. of Oklahoma Press, 1937.

Nunn, W. C. *Texas Under the Carpetbaggers.* Austin: Univ. of Texas Press, 1962.

Oberste, W. H. *Texas Irish Empressarios and Their Colonies: Power and Hewitson, McMullen and McGloin.* Austin: Von Boeckmann-Jones, 1953.

Otero, Miguel Antonio. *My Nine Years as the Governor of the Territory of New Mexico, 1897-1906.* Albuquerque: Univ. of New Mexico Press, 1940.

Paré, Madeline F., and Bert M. Fireman. *Arizona Pageant.* Phoenix: Arizona Historical Foundation, 1965.

Paul, Rodman W. *Mining Frontiers of the Far West, 1848-1880.* New York: Holt, Rinehart & Winston, 1963.

Pearce, William M. *The Matador Land and Cattle Company.* Norman: Univ. of Oklahoma Press, 1964.

Perrigo, Lynn. *The American Southwest: Its People and Culture.* New York: Holt, Rinehart & Winston, 1971.

Pomeroy, Earl. *In Search of the Golden West. The Tourist in Western America.* New York: Knopf, 1957.

Pool, William C., and others. *Lyndon Baines Johnson: The Formative Years.* San Marcos: Southwest Texas State College, 1965.

―――, and others. *Texas: Wilderness to Space Age.* San Antonio: Naylor, 1962.

Powell, Donald M. *The Peralta Grant. James Addison Reavis and Barony of Arizona.* Norman: Univ. of Oklahoma Press, 1960.

Procter, Ben H. *Not Without Honor: The Life of John H. Reagan.* Austin: Univ. of Texas Press, 1964.

Ramsdell, Charles W. *Reconstruction in Texas.* New York: Columbia Univ. and Longmans, Green, 1910.

Reeve, Frank. *History of New Mexico.* 3 vols. New York: Lewis Historical Publishing, 1961.

Richardson, Rupert N. *Texas, the Lone Star State.* Englewood Cliffs: Prentice-Hall, 1958.

―――, and Carl C. Rister. *The Greater Southwest.* Glendale, California: Arthur H. Clark, 1937.

Richardson, Rupert N. *The Comanche Barrier to South Plains Settlement: A Century and a Half of Savage Resistance to the Advancing White Frontier.* Glendale, California: Arthur H. Clark, 1933.

―――. *The Frontier of Northwest Texas, 1846-1876.* Glendale, California: Arthur H. Clark, 1963.

Rister, Carl C. *Fort Griffin on the Texas Frontier.* Norman: Univ. of Oklahoma Press, 1956.

———. *Oil! Titan of the Southwest*. Norman: Univ. of Oklahoma Press, 1949.

Roland, Charles P. *Albert Sidney Johnston: Soldier of Three Republics*. Austin: Univ. of Texas Press, 1964.

Rolle, Andrew. *The Lost Cause: The Confederate Exodus to Mexico*. Norman: Univ. of Oklahoma Press, 1965.

Sacks, B. *Be It Enacted: The Creation of the Territory of Arizona*. Phoenix: Arizona Historical Foundation, 1964.

Santa Anna, Antonio Lopez de. *The Mexican Side of the Texas Revolution*. Translated by Carlos E. Castañeda. Dallas: P. L. Turner, 1928.

Schmitz, Joseph W. *Texas Statecraft, 1836-1845*. San Antonio: Naylor, 1941.

Shackford, James A. *Davy Crockett: The Man and the Legend*. Chapel Hill: Univ. of North Carolina Press, 1956.

Sheffy, Lester F. *The Francklyn Land and Cattle Co.: A Panhandle Enterprise, 1882-1957*. Austin: Univ. of Texas Press, 1963.

Shirley, Emma. *The Administration of Pat N. Neff, Governor of Texas, 1921-1925*. Waco: Baylor University, 1938.

Siegel, Stanley. *A Political History of the Republic of Texas*. Austin: Univ. of Texas Press, 1956.

Singletary, Otis A. *The Mexican War*. Chicago: Univ. of Chicago Press, 1960.

Smith, Cornelius C., Jr. *William Sanders Oury: History-maker of the Southwest*. Tucson: Univ. of Arizona Press, 1967.

Smith, Justin H. *The Annexation of Texas*. New York: Baker and Taylor, 1911.

———. *The War with Mexico*. 2 vols. New York: Macmillan, 1919.

Smithwick, Noah. *The Evolution of a State*. Austin: Gammel Book, 1900. Austin: Steck, 1935.

Sonnichsen, C. L. *Roy Bean: Law West of the Pecos*. New York: Macmillan, 1943.

Spratt, John S. *The Road to Spindletop: Economic Changes in Texas, 1875-1901*. Dallas: Southern Methodist Univ. Press, 1955.

Standage, Henry. *The March of the Mormon Battalion*. New York: Century, 1928.

Steen, Ralph W. *Twentieth Century Texas: An Economic and Social History*. Austin: Steck, 1942.

Stephens, A. Ray. *The Taft Ranch: A Texas Principality*. Austin: Univ. of

Texas Press, 1966.

Sterling, William W. *Trails and Trials of a Texas Ranger.* Norman: Univ. of Oklahoma Press, 1969.

Terrell, John U. *War for the Colorado River.* 2 vols. Glendale, California: Arthur H. Clark, 1965.

Twitchell, Ralph E. *Leading Facts of New Mexican History.* 5 vols. Cedar Rapids, Iowa: Torch Press, 1911-1917.

Utley, Robert M. *Frontiersman in Blue: The United States Army and the Indian, 1848-1865.* New York: Macmillan, 1967.

Wagoner, Jay J. *Arizona Territory, 1863-1912: A Political History.* Tucson: Univ. of Arizona Press, 1970.

Wallace, Edward S. *Destiny and Glory.* New York: Coward McCann, 1957.

Webb, Walter Prescott. *Divided We Stand: The Crisis of a Frontierless Democracy.* New York: Farrar and Rinehart, 1937.

————. *The Texas Rangers: A Century of Frontier Defense.* Boston: Houghton Mifflin, 1935. Austin: Univ. of Texas Press, 1965.

Weeks, Oliver D. *Texas Presidential Politics in 1952.* Austin: Univ. of Texas Press, 1953.

Weinberg, Albert K. *Manifest Destiny: A Study of Nationalist Expansionism in American History.* Baltimore: Johns Hopkins Univ. Press, 1935.

Westphall, Vic. *The Public Domain in New Mexico, 1854-1891.* Albuquerque: Univ. of New Mexico Press, 1965.

White, Gerald Taylor. *Formative Years in the Far West: A History of Standard Oil Company of California and Predecessors through 1919.* New York: Appleton, 1962.

Wilson, Neill C. *Southern Pacific: The Roaring Story of a Fighting Railroad.* New York: McGraw-Hill, 1952.

Wyllys, Rufus K. *Arizona: The History of a Frontier State.* Phoenix: Hobson & Herr, 1955.

Yoakum, Henderson. *History of Texas from its First Settlement in 1685 to its Annexation in 1846.* 2 vols. New York: Redfield, 1856.

Young, Otis E. *The West of Philip St. George Cooke, 1809-1895.* Glendale, California: Arthur H. Clark, 1955.

J. A. Carroll
Texas Christian University

M. E. Bradford
University of Dallas

Justice

Adams, Ramon F. *A Fitting Death for Billy the Kid.* Norman: Univ. of Oklahoma Press, 1960.
———. *Six-Guns and Saddle Leather.* Norman: Univ. of Oklahoma Press, 1954.
Adams, Verdon R. *Tom White: The Life of a Lawman.* El Paso: Texas Western Press, 1972.
Aikman, Duncan. *Calamity Jane and the Lady Wildcats.* New York: Holt, 1927.
Anonymous. *The Dalton Brothers, by an Eye Witness.* New York: Fell, 1955.
Appell, George C. *The Man Who Shot Quantrill.* New York: Doubleday, 1957.
Appler, Augustus C. *The True Life, Character and Daring Exploits of the Younger Brothers.* Chicago: Belford Clark, 1884.
———. *The Younger Brothers.* New York: F. Fell, 1955.
Baker, Pearl. *The Wild Bunch at Robbers' Roost.* Los Angeles: Westernlore Press, 1965.
Balcourt, Edgar D. *The Dalton Brothers and Their Astounding Career of of Crime.* New York: Fell, 1955.
Bartholomew, Ed. *The Biographical Album of Western Gunmen.* Ruidoso, New Mexico: Frontier Book, 1958.
———. *Wyatt Earp.* 2 vols. Toyahvale, Texas: Frontier Book, 1963-64.
Bearss, Edwin C., and A. M. Gibson. *Fort Smith.* Norman: Univ. of Oklahoma Press, 1968.
Bechdoldt, Fred R. *When the West Was Young.* New York: Century, 1922.
Block, Eugene B. *Great Train Robberies of the West.* New York: Coward McCann, 1959.
———. *Great Stagecoach Robbers of the West.* New York: Doubleday, 1962.
Breakenridge, William. *Helldorado.* New York: Houghton Mifflin, 1928.
Brent, William. *The Complete and Factual Life of Billy the Kid.* New York: Fell, 1944.
Breihan, Carl W. *Badmen of the Frontier Days.* New York: Robert M. McBride, 1957.
———. *Great Lawmen of the West.* New York: Bonanza, 1968.
———. *Younger Brothers.* San Antonio: Naylor, 1961.
Bronson, Edgar B. *The Red Blooded Heroes of the Frontier.* Chicago: A. C. McClurg, 1910.

Brown, Will C. *Sam Bass and Company.* New York: Signet, 1960.

Burns, Walter Noble. *The Saga of Billy the Kid.* New York: Grosset and Dunlap, 1926.

————. *Tombstone.* Garden City, New York: Garden City Publishing, 1927.

Canton, Frank M. *Frontier Trails.* New York: Houghton Mifflin, 1930.

Castleman, Harvey N. *Sam Bass, the Train Robber.* Girard, Kansas: Haldeman-Julius, 1944.

Charnley, Mitchell. *Jean Lafitte, Gentleman Smuggler.* New York: Viking, 1934.

Clairmonte, Glenn. *Calamity Was the Name for Jane.* Denver: Swallow, 1961.

Coe, Geroge. *Frontier Fighter.* New York: Houghton Mifflin, 1934.

Connelley, W. E. *Wild Bill and His Era.* New York: Press of the Pioneers, 1933.

Cook, D. J. *Hands Up, or Twenty Years of Detective Life in the Mountains and the Plains.* Norman: Univ. of Oklahoma Press, 1959.

Coolidge, Dane. *Fighting Men of the West.* New York: Dutton, 1932.

Corle, Edwin. *Billy the Kid.* New York: Duell, Sloan & Pearce, 1953.

Crichton, Kyle S. *Law and Order, Ltd.* Santa Fe: New Mexican, 1928.

Croy, Homer. *He Hanged Them High.* New York: Duell, Sloan & Pearce, 1952.

————. *Trigger Marshal: The Story of Chris Madsen.* New York: Duell, Sloan & Pearce, 1958.

Cunningham, Eugene. *Triggernometry.* Caldwell, Idaho: Caxton, 1940.

Dalton, Emmett. *When the Daltons Rode.* New York: Doubleday, Doran, 1931.

Davis, Britton. *The Truth About Geronimo.* New Haven: Yale Univ. Press, 1929.

Dillon, Richard. *Wells Fargo Detective: The Biography of James B. Hume.* New York: Coward McCann, 1969.

Dodge, Fred. *Under Cover for Wells Fargo. The Unvarnished Recollections of Fred Dodge.* Boston: Houghton Mifflin, 1969.

Douglas, C. L. *Gentlemen in White Hats.* Dallas: Southwest Press, 1934.

Drago, Harry Sinclair. *Outlaws on Horseback.* New York: Dodd, Mead, 1964.

Dykes, J. C. *Billy the Kid: The Bibliography of a Legend.* Albuquerque: Univ. of New Mexico Press, 1952.

————, ed. *The West of the Texas Kid, 1881-1910: Recollections of Thomas Edgar Crawford.* Norman: Univ. of Oklahoma Press, 1962.

Erwin, Allen A. *The Southwest of John H. Slaughter, 1841-1922.* Glendale,

California: Arthur H. Clark, 1968.

Fisher, Clark. *King Fisher: His Life and Times.* Norman: Univ. of Oklahoma Press, 1966.

Ford, John S. *Rip Ford's Texas.* Austin: Univ. of Texas Press, 1964.

Forrest, Earl R. *Arizona's Dark and Bloody Ground.* Caldwell, Idaho: Caxton, 1936.

Fuller, Henry C. *A Texas Sheriff.* Nacogdoches, Texas: Baker Printing, 1931.

Ganzhorn, Jack. *I've Killed Men: An Epic of Early Arizona.* New York: Devon-Adair, 1959.

Gard, Wayne. *Frontier Justice.* Norman: Univ. of Oklahoma Press, 1936.

Garrett, Pat F. *Pat F. Garrett's Authentic Life of Billy the Kid.* Albuquerque: Horn and Wallace, 1964.

Greene, Jonathan H. *A Desperado in Arizona, 1858-1860; Or, the Life, Trial, Death, and Confession of Samuel H. Calhoun, the Soldier-Murderer.* Santa Fe: Stagecoach Press, 1964.

Greer, James K. *Colonel Jack Hays.* New York: Dutton, 1952.

Gresham, Noel. *Tame the Restless Wind: The Life and Legends of Sam Bass.* New York: Random House, 1968.

Guzman, Martin Luis. *Memoirs of Pancho Villa.* Austin: Univ. of Texas Press, 1967.

Haley, J. Evetts. *Jeff Milton, A Good Man with a Gun.* Norman: Univ. of Oklahoma Press, 1948.

Hanes, Bailey C. *Bill Doolin, Outlaw.* Norman: Univ. of Oklahoma Press, 1968.

Hardin, John Wesley. *Life of John Wesley Hardin, Written by Himself.* Seguin, Texas: Smith & Moore, 1896; Norman: Univ. of Oklahoma Press, 1961.

Harman, S. W. *Hell on the Border.* Fort Smith, Arkansas: Hell on the Border Publishing, 1953.

Hayes, Jess G. *Boots and Bullets: The Life and Times of John W. Wentworth.* Tucson: Univ. of Arizona Press, 1967.

Hendricks, George D. *The Bad Man of the West.* San Antonio: Naylor, 1970.

Hertzog, Peter, comp. *A Directory of New Mexico Desperados.* Santa Fe: Press of the Territorian, 1965.

Holloway, Carroll C. *Texas Gun Lore.* San Antonio: Naylor, 1952.

Horan, James D. *Across the Cimarron.* New York: Crown, 1956.

———. *Desperate Men.* New York: Putnam, 1949; Garden City, New York: Doubleday, 1962.

────. *Desperate Women.* New York: Putnam, 1952.

Horn, Tom. *Life of Tom Horn, Government Scout and Interpreter.* Norman: Univ. of Oklahoma Press, 1964.

Hughes, W. J. *Rebellious Ranger: Rip Ford and the Old Southwest.* Norman: Univ. of Oklahoma Press, 1964.

Hunt, Frazier. *The Tragic Days of Billy the Kid.* New York: Hastings House, 1956.

Jackson, Joseph H. *Bad Company.* New York: Harcourt Brace, 1949.

────. *Tintypes in Gold.* New York: Macmillan, 1939.

Jenkins, John H., and H. Gordon Frost. *"I'm Frank Hamer": The Life of a Texas Peace Officer.* Austin: Pemberton Press, 1968.

Jennings, N. A. *Texas Ranger.* New York: Scribner, 1899. Dallas: Southwest Press, 1930.

Keleher, William A. *The Fabulous Frontier.* Albuquerque: Univ. of New Mexico Press, 1965.

Kelly, Charles. *The Outlaw Trail. The Story of Butch Cassidy.* New York: Devon-Adair, 1959.

Lake, Stuart N. *Wyatt Earp, Frontier Marshal.* New York: Houghton Mifflin, 1931.

Martin, Charles L. *A Sketch of Sam Bass, the Bandit.* Norman: Univ. of Oklahoma Press, 1956.

Martin, Douglas D. *Tombstone's Epitaph.* Albuquerque: Univ. of New Mexico Press, 1951.

Masterson, W. B. (Bat). *Famous Gunfighters of the Western Frontier.* Houston: Frontier Press of Texas, 1957; Fort Davis, Texas: Frontier Book, 1968. First published in 1907 in *Human Life* magazine.

Miller, F. D. *Shady Ladies of the West.* Los Angeles: Westernlore Press, 1964.

Metz, Leon C. *Dallas Stoudemire: The Man Who Tamed El Paso.* Austin: Pemberton Press, 1968.

Mullin, Robert N., ed. *Maurice G. Fulton's History of the Lincoln County War.* Tucson: Univ. of Arizona Press, 1968.

Mumey, Nolie. *Calamity Jane, 1852-1903.* Denver: Range Press, 1950.

────. *Poker Alice.* Denver: Artcraft Press, 1951.

Myers, John Myers. *The Last Chance: Tombstone's Early Years.* New York: Dutton, 1950.

Nordyke, Lewis. *John Wesley Hardin, Texas Gunman.* New York: Morrow, 1957.

O'Connor, Richard. *Bat Masterson.* New York: Doubleday, 1957.

———. *Wild Bill Hickok.* New York: Doubleday, 1959.

———. *Pat Garrett.* New York: Doubleday, 1960.

Otero, Miguel. *The Real Billy the Kid.* Elmira, New York: Wilson-Erickson, 1936.

Paine, Albert B. *Captain Bill McDonald.* Boston: Little, Brown, 1909.

Plenn, J. H. and C. J. LaRoche. *The Fastest Gun in Texas.* New York: New American Library, 1956.

Poe, John W. *The Death of Billy the Kid.* New York: Houghton Mifflin, 1933.

Raine, William M. *Famous Sheriffs and Western Outlaws.* Garden City, New York: Garden City Publishing, 1928.

———. *Guns of the Frontier.* New York: Houghton Mifflin, 1940.

Rascoe, Burton. *Belle Starr.* New York: Random House, 1941.

———. *The Dalton Brothers.* New York: Fell, 1954.

Raymond, Dora N. *Captain Lee Hall of Texas.* Norman: Univ. of Oklahoma Press, 1940.

Richards, Colin. *Buckskin Frank Leslie: Gunman of Tombstone.* El Paso: Texas Western Press, 1964.

———. *How Pat Garrett Died.* Santa Fe: Palomino Press, 1970.

Ripley, Thomas. *They Died With Their Boots On.* New York: Sun Dial Press, 1937.

Rosa, Joseph G. *The Gunfighter: Man or Myth?* Norman: Univ. of Oklahoma Press, 1969.

———. *They Called Him Wild Bill.* Norman: Univ. of Oklahoma Press, 1964.

Sabin, E. L. *Wild Men of the Wild West.* New York: Crowell, 1929.

Saxon, Lyle. *Lafitte The Pirate.* New York: Appleton, 1931.

Settle, William A., Jr. *Jesse James Was His Name, or, Fact and Fiction Concerning the Careers of the Notorious James Brothers of Missouri.* Columbia: Univ. of Missouri Press, 1966.

Shirley, Glenn. *Buckskin and Spurs: A Gallery of Frontier Rogues and Heroes.* New York: Hastings House, 1962.

———. *Law West of Fort Smith.* New York: Holt, 1957.

———. *Six-Gun and Silver Star.* Albuquerque: Univ. of New Mexico Press, 1965.

———. *Toughest of Them All.* Albuquerque: Univ. of New Mexico Press, 1965.

Sonnichsen, C. L. *Billy King's Tombstone.* Caldwell, Idaho: Caxton, 1942.

————. *Ten Texas Feuds*. Albuquerque: Univ. of New Mexico Press, 1957.
Stanley, F. *Desperadoes of New Mexico*. Canadian, Texas: Privately Printed, 1953.
Tilghman, Zoe A. *Marshal of the Last Frontier*. Glendale, California: Arthur H. Clark, 1949.
Vestal, Stanley. *Queen of Cow Towns, Dodge City*. New York: Harper, 1952.
Waters, Frank. *The Earp Brothers of Tombstone*. New York: C. N. Potter, 1960.
Webb, Walter Prescott. *The Texas Rangers*. Boston: Houghton Mifflin, 1935. Austin: Univ. of Texas Press, 1965.
Wellman, Paul I. *A Dynasty of Western Outlaws*. New York: Doubleday, 1961.
White, Owen P. *Trigger Fingers*. New York: Putnam, 1937.
Wilstach, Frank J. *Wild Bill Hickok, the Prince of Pistoleers*. New York: Doubleday, 1926.
Younger, Cole. *Cole Younger*. Toyahvale, Texas: Frontier Book, 1955.

George D. Hendricks
North Texas State University

Commerce and Transportation

Allhands, James L. *Gringo Builders*. Iowa City: Privately Printed, 1931.
————. *Railroads to the Rio*. Salado, Texas: Anson Jones Press, 1960.
Beebe, Lucius. *The Central Pacific & The Southern Pacific Railroads*. Berkeley: Howell-North, 1963.
Clark, Ira G. *Then Came the Railroads: The Century from Steam to Diesel in the Southwest*. Norman: Univ. of Oklahoma Press, 1958.
Donovan, Frank P. *The Railroad in Literature*. Boston: The Railway and Locomotive Historical Society, 1940.
Duke, Donald, and Stan Kistler. *Santa Fe: Steel Trails Through California*. San Marino: Pacific Railroad Publishers, 1963.
Farrington, S. Kip, Jr. *Railroading: The Modern Way*. New York: Coward McCann, 1951.
Hayes, William Edward. *Iron Road to Empire: The History of 100 Years of the Progress and Achievements of the Rock Island Lines*. New York: Simmons-Boardman, 1953.

Holbrook, Stewart H. *The Story of American Railroads*. New York: Crown, 1947.

Kerr, John Leeds. *Destination Topolobampo: The Kansas City, Mexico & Orient Railway*. San Marino: Golden West Books, 1968.

Marshall, James. *Santa Fe: The Railroad That Built an Empire*. New York: Random House, 1945.

Masterson, Vincent V. *The Katy Railroad and the Last Frontier*. Norman: Univ. of Oklahoma Press, 1952.

Potts, Charles Shirley. *Railroad Transportation in Texas*. Austin: Univ. of Texas Press, 1909.

Waters, L. L. *Steel Trails to Santa Fe*. Lawrence: Univ. of Kansas Press, 1950.

Wilson, Neill C., and Frank J. Taylor. *Southern Pacific: The Roaring Story of a Fighting Railroad*. New York: McGraw-Hill, 1952.

John T. Smith
North Texas State University

Mining and Oil

Altsheler, Joseph. *Apache Gold; a Story of the Strange Southwest*. New York: Appleton, 1913.

Ball, Max W. *This Fascinating Oil Business*. New York: Bobbs-Merrill, 1940.

Boatright, Mody C. *Gib Morgan: Minstrel of the Oil Fields*. Austin: Texas Folklore Society, 1945.

Boone, Lalia Phipps. *The Petroleum Dictionary*. Norman: Univ. of Oklahoma Press, 1952.

Box, Michael James. *Captain James Box's Adventures and Explorations in New and Old Mexico; being the record of ten years travel and research and a guide to the mineral treasures of Durango, Chihuahua, the Sierra Nevada . . . and the Southern part of Arizona*. New York: J. Miller, 1869.

Browne, J. Ross. *Adventures in the Apache Country: A Tour Through Arizona and Sonora, With Notes on the Silver Regions of Nevada*. New York: Harper, 1869.

Canfield, Chauncey de Leon. *The Diary of a Forty-Niner*. New York: Morgan Shepard, 1906.

Caughey, John Walton. *Gold is the Cornerstone.* Berkeley: Univ. of California Press, 1948.

————, ed. *Rushing for Gold.* Berkeley: Univ. of California Press, 1949.

Clark, James A., and Michel T. Halbouty. *Spindletop.* New York: Random House, 1952.

Clemens, Samuel Langhorne [Mark Twain]. *Roughing It.* Chicago: F. G. Gilman, 1872.

Cloud, Wilbur F. *Petroleum Production.* Norman: Univ. of Oklahoma Press, 1937.

Connelly, W. L. *The Oil Business as I Saw It.* Norman: Univ. of Oklahoma Press, 1954.

Coolidge, Dane. *Death Valley Prospectors.* New York: Dutton, 1936.

Cronyn, George W. *'49, A Novel of Gold.* Philadelphia: Dorrance, 1925.

Dobie, J. Frank. *Apache Gold and Yaqui Silver.* Boston: Little, Brown, 1939.

————. *Coronado's Children; Tales of Lost Mines and Buried Treasures of the Southwest.* Dallas: Southwest Press, 1930.

————, Ed. *Legends of Texas.* Austin: *Publications of the Texas Folklore Society* 3 (1924).

————, Ed. *Southwestern Lore.* Dallas: *Publications of the Texas Folklore Society,* 9 (1931).

————. *Tales of Old-Time Texas.* Boston: Little, Brown, 1955.

Emrich, Duncan, ed. *Comstock Bonanza.* New York: Vanguard, 1950.

Foote, Mary Hallock. *The Led-Horse Claim: A Romance of a Mining Camp.* Boston: J. R. Osgood, 1883.

Forbes, Gerald. *Flush Production: The Epic of Oil in the Gulf-Southwest.* Norman: Univ. of Oklahoma Press, 1942.

Gillis, William R. *Goldrush Days with Mark Twain.* New York: Boni, 1930.

Glasscock, Carl B. *Here's Death Valley.* New York: Bobbs-Merrill, 1940.

————. *Then Came Oil.* Indianapolis: Bobbs-Merrill, 1938.

Glasscock, Lucille. *A Texas Wildcatter.* San Antonio: Naylor, 1952.

Hinton, Richard J. *The Handbook to Arizona: Its Resources, History, Towns, Mines, Ruins, and Scenery.* San Francisco: Payor, Upham, 1878; New York: American News, 1878. Facsimile rpt. by George W. Chambers. Tucson: Arizona Silhouettes, 1954.

Hollister, Ovando J. *The Mines of Colorado.* Springfield, Massachusetts: S. Bowles, 1867.

House, Boyce. *Oil Boom: The Story of Spindletop, Burkburnett, Mexia, Smackover, Desdemona, and Ranger.* Caldwell, Idaho: Caxton, 1941.

90   *Southwestern American Literature*

Ingham, George Thomas. *Digging Gold Among the Rockies*. Philadelphia: Hubbard, 1888.

Jaeger, Edmund C. *The North American Deserts*. Stanford: Stanford Univ. Press, 1957.

Karsner, David. *Silver Dollar: The Story of the Tabors*. New York: Covici-Friede, 1932.

Lyman, George T. *The Saga of the Comstock Lode*. New York: Scribner, 1934.

Manley, William Lewis. *Death Valley in '49; Important Chapter of a California Pioneer History; The Autobiography of a Pioneer, Detailing His Life from a Humble Home in the Green Mountains to the Gold Mines of California; and Particularly Reciting the Sufferings of the Band of Men, Women and Children Who Gave "Death Valley" Its Name*. San Jose: Pacific Tree and Vine, 1894.

Mathews, John Joseph. *Life and Death of an Oilman: The Career of E. W. Marland*. Norman: Univ. of Oklahoma Press, 1951.

Mitchell, John Donald. *Lost Mines of the Great Southwest, Including Stories of Hidden Treasures*. Phoenix: Journal, 1933.

Northrop, Stuart A. *Mining Districts of New Mexico*. Albuquerque: Univ. of New Mexico Press, 1942.

Phillips, John Arthur. *The Mining and Metallurgy of Gold and Silver*. London: E. and F. N. Spon, 1867.

Rister, Carl Coke. *Oil! Titan of the Southwest*. Norman: Univ. of Oklahoma Press, 1949.

Shinn, Charles Howard. *The Story of the Mine as Illustrated by the Great Comstock Lode of Nevada*. New York: Appleton, 1896.

———. *Mining Camps, 1885*. New York: Knopf, 1948.

Stuart, Granville, and Paul C. Phillips, eds. *Forty Years on the Frontier*. 2 vols. Cleveland: Arthur H. Clark, 1925.

Tait, Samuel W. *Wildcatters: An Informal History of Oil-Hunting in America*. Princeton: Princeton Univ. Press, 1946.

Waters, Frank. *Midas of the Rockies*. Denver: Swallow, 1937.

Webber, Charles Wilkins. *Gold Mines of the Gila: A Sequel to Old Hicks the Guide*. New York: De Witt and Davenport, 1849.

Willison, George Finlay. *Here They Dug the Gold*. New York: Brentano's, 1931.

Wright, William. [pseud. Dan de Quille]. *History of the Big Bonanza*. San Francisco: Bancroft, 1876.

Wynn, Marcia Rittenhouse. *Desert Bonanza: Story of Early Randsburg, Mojave Desert Mining Camp.* Culver City, California: Murray and Gee, 1949.

Jo Wilkinson Lyday
San Jacinto College

Industry

Adams, Ramon F. *The Rampaging Herd: A Bibliography of Books and Pamphlets on Men and Events in the Cattle Industry.* Norman: Univ. of Oklahoma Press, 1959.

Clark, James A., and Michel Halbouty. *Spindletop.* New York: Random House, 1952.

Connelly, W. L. *The Oil Business As I Saw It.* Norman: Univ. of Oklahoma Press, 1954.

Dunning, Charles H., and Edward H. Perlow, Jr. *Silver, From Spanish Missions to Space Age Missiles.* Pasadena, Texas: Hicks Publishing Corp. 1966.

Fisher, Vardis, and Opal L. Holmes, *Gold Rushes and Mining Camps of the Early American West.* Caldwell, Idaho: Caxton, 1968.

Forbes, Gerald. *Flush Production: The Epic of Oil in the Gulf Southwest.* Norman: Univ. of Oklahoma Press, 1952.

Fornell, Earl. *The Galveston Era.* Austin: Univ. of Texas Press, 1961.

Frantz, Joe B. *Gail Borden, Dairyman to a Nation.* Norman: Univ. of Oklahoma Press, 1951.

Frederick, James V. *Ben Holladay, the Stagecoach King. A Chapter in the Development of Transcontinental Transportation.* Glendale, California: Arthur H. Clark, 1940.

Fuermann, George. *Houston: Land of the Big Rich.* New York: Doubleday, 1952.

Glasscock, Lucille. *A Texas Wildcatter.* San Antonio: Naylor, 1952.

Gregg, Josiah. *Commerce on the Prairie.* New York: H. G. Langley, 1844. Ed. Max L. Moorhead. Norman: Univ of Oklahoma Press, 1954.

Immigrants in Industry: Recent Immigrants in Agriculture. Washington: Government Printing Office, 1911.

Knight, Oliver. *Fort Worth.* Norman: Univ. of Oklahoma Press, 1953.

Lewis, Marvin, ed. *The Mining Frontier.* Norman: Univ. of Oklahoma Press, 1967.

McCampbell, Coleman. *Saga of a Frontier Seaport.* Dallas: Southwest Press, 1954.

Mathews, John J. *Life and Death of an Oilman: The Career of E. W. Marland.* Norman: Univ. of Oklahoma Press, 1951.

Rogers, John W. *The Lusty Texans of Dallas.* New York: Dutton, 1951.

Sonnichsen, C. L. *Pass of the North.* El Paso: Texas Western College Press, 1968.

Walker, Stanley. *The Dallas Story.* New York: Harper, 1956.

John Q. Anderson
University of Houston

Military

Albert, James W. *Report of an Expedition . . . On the Upper Arkansas & Through the Country of the Comanche Indians.* Canyon, Texas: Panhandle-Plains Historical Society, 1941.

Bandel, Eugene. *Frontier Life in the Army.* Glendale, California: Arthur H. Clark, 1932.

Bigelow, Lt. John Jr. *On the Bloody Trail of Geronimo.* Los Angeles: Westernlore Press, 1968.

Bourke, John G. *An Apache Campaign in the Sierra Madre.* New York: Scribner, 1958.

————. *With General Crook in the Indian Wars.* Palo Alto: The American West, 1968.

Braddy, Haldeen. *Pershing's Mission in Mexico.* El Paso: Texas Western Press, 1966.

Butterworth, William E. *Soldiers on Horseback.* New York: Norton, 1967.

Byrne, P. E. *Soldiers of the Plains.* New York: Minton, Balch, 1926.

Carter, Capt. Robert G. *On the Border with MacKenzie.* Washington: Eynon, 1935.

Chabot, Frederick C. *The Perote Prisoners.* San Antonio: Naylor, 1934.

Clarke, Dwight L. *Stephen Watts Kearney: Soldier of the West.* Norman: Univ. of Oklahoma Press, 1961.

Cooke, Philip St. George. *The Conquest of New Mexico and California in 1846-1848.* New York: Putnam, 1878. Albuquerque: Horn & Wallace, 1964.

Copeland, Fayette. *Kendall of the Picayune.* Norman: Univ. of Oklahoma Press, 1943.

Craig, Reginald S. *The Fighting Parson.* Los Angeles: Westernlore Press, 1964.

Croghan, Colonel George. *Army Life on the Western Frontier.* Norman: Univ. of Oklahoma Press, 1959.

Custer, Elizabeth B. *Following the Guidon.* New York: Harper, 1890. Norman: Univ. of Oklahoma Press, 1966.

Custer, George A. *My Life on the Plains.* New York: Sheldon, 1874. New York: Citadel, 1962.

Davis, Bob. *Frontier Forts of Texas.* Waco: Texian Press, 1966.

Dellenbaugh, Frederick S. *George Armstrong Custer.* New York: Putnam, 1914.

Downey, Fairfax. *General Crook: Indian Fighter.* Philadelphia: Westminster Press, 1957.

Dyer, Brainerd. *Zachary Taylor.* New York: Barnes & Noble, 1967.

Emory, William H. *Lieutenant Emory Reports (1811-1887).* Albuquerque: Univ. of New Mexico Press, 1951.

Farmer, James E. *My Life with the Army in the West.* Santa Fe: Stagecoach Press, 1967.

Foreman, Grant. *Advancing the Frontier, 1830-1860.* Norman: Univ. of Oklahoma Press, 1933.

Frazer, Robert W. *Forts of the West.* Norman: Univ. of Oklahoma Press, 1965.

Fremont, J. C. *Memoirs of My Life.* Chicago and New York: Belford, Clarke & Co., 1887.

Frink, Maurice, and Casey E. Barthelmess. *Photographer on An Army Mule.* Norman: Univ. of Oklahoma Press, 1965.

Frost, Lawrence A. *The Court Martial of General George Armstrong Custer.* Norman: Univ. of Oklahoma Press, 1968.

Giese, Dale F. *My Life with the Army in the West: Memoirs of J. E. Farmer.* Santa Fe: Stagecoach Press, 1968.

Goetzmann, William H. *Army Exploration of the American West, 1803-1862.* New Haven: Yale Univ. Press, 1960.

———. *Exploration and Empire.* New York: Knopf, 1966.

Graham, Col. W. A. *The Custer Myth.* Harrisburg, Pennsylvania: Stackpole Books, 1953.

Hart, Herbert M. *Old Forts of the Southwest.* Seattle: Superior Publishing, 1968.

Herr, Maj. Gen. John K., and Edward S. Wallace. *The Story of the U. S.*

94   *Southwestern American Literature*

Cavalry. Boston: Little, Brown, 1954
Hollon, W. Eugene. *Beyond the Cross Timbers, the Travels of Randolph B. Marcy, 1812-1887.* Norman: Univ. of Oklahoma Press, 1955.
Hughes, J. *Doniphan's Expedition, Containing an Account of the Conquest of New Mexico . . . with a Sketch of the Life of Col. Doniphan.* Cincinnati: J. A. and U. P. James, 1847; Topeka, Kansas: Published by the Author, 1907.
James, Edwin. *Account of An Expedition* [Major Stephen F. Long] in *Early Western Travels,* ed. Reuben Gold Thwaites, 32 vols., Philadelphia: Carey and Lea, 1823; Cleveland: Arthur H. Clark, 1904-7. Vol. I.
Kendall, George W. *Narrative of the Texan Santa Fe Expedition.* New York: Harper, 1844. Austin: Steck, 1936.
King, Charles. *Campaigning with Crook.* New York: Harper, 1890; Norman: Univ. of Oklahoma Press, 1964.
———. *Starlight Ranch and Other Stories of Army Life On the Frontier.* Philadelphia: Lippincott, 1905.
Leckie, William H. *The Buffalo Soldiers: A Narrative of the Negro Calvary in the West.* Norman: Univ. of Oklahoma Press, 1967.
———. *The Military Conquest of the Southern Plains.* Norman: Univ. of Oklahoma Press, 1963.
Loomis, Noel M. *The Texan-Santa Fe Pioneers.* Norman: Univ. of Oklahoma Press, 1958.
Lowe, Percival G. *Five Years a Dragoon ('49 to '54) and Other Adventures on the Great Plains.* Kansas City, Missouri: F. Hudson, 1906. Norman: Univ. of Oklahoma Press, 1965.
Lummis, Charles F. *General Crook and the Apache Wars.* Flagstaff, Arizona: Northland Press, 1966.
McKee, Irving: *"Ben Hur" Wallace, the Life of General Lew Wallace.* Berkeley: Univ. of California Press, 1947.
Marcy, Capt. Randolph B. *Border Reminiscences.* New York: Harper, 1872.
———. *Thirty Years of Army Life on the Border.* New York: Harper, 1866. Philadelphia: Lippincott, 1963.
———, and G. B. McClellan. *Adventures on Red River.* Norman: Univ. of Oklahoma Press, 1937.
Marion, J. H. *Notes of Travel Through the Territory of Arizona.* Tucson: Univ. of Arizona Press, 1965.
Mazzanovich, Anton. *Trailing Geronimo.* Los Angeles: Gem Publishing, 1926.

Merrill, James M. *Spurs to Glory: The Story of the United States Cavalry.* New York: Rand McNally, 1966.

Monoghan, Jay. *Custer: The Life of Gen. George Armstrong Custer.* Lincoln: Univ. of Nebraska Press, 1971.

Nye, Capt. W. S. *Carbine and Lance: The Story of Old Fort Sill.* Norman: Univ. of Oklahoma Press, 1937.

O'Flaherty, Liam. *General Jo Shelby: Undefeated Rebel.* Chapel Hill: Univ. of North Carolina Press, 1954.

Oliva, Leo A. *Soldiers on the Santa Fe Trail.* Norman: Univ. of Oklahoma Press, 1967.

Pierce, Gerald S. *Texas Under Arms: The Camps, Posts, Forts, and Military Towns of the Republic of Texas, 1836-1846.* Austin: Encino Press, 1969.

Price, George F. *Across the Continent with the Fifth Cavalry.* New York: Antiquarian Press, 1959.

Pike, Major Z. M. *Account of Expeditions.* Baltimore: John Binns, 1810.

Prucha, Francis Paul, ed. *Army Life on the Western Frontier.* Norman: Univ. of Oklahoma Press, 1959.

———. *The Sword of the Republic: The United States Army on the Frontier, 1783-1846.* New York: Macmillan, 1969.

Rickey, Don, Jr. *Forty Miles a Day on Beans and Hay.* Norman: Univ. of Oklahoma Press, 1963.

Rister, Carl Coke. *Border Command.* Norman: Univ. of Oklahoma Press, 1944.

Schmitt, Martin F., ed. *General George Crook: His Autobiography.* Norman: Univ. of Oklahoma Press, 1960.

Scobee, Barry. *The Story of Fort Davis.* San Antonio: Naylor, 1947.

Simpson, James H. *Navaho Expedition.* Norman: Univ. of Oklahoma Press, 1964.

Stapp, William Preston. *The Prisoners of Perote.* Austin: Steck, 1935.

Toulmin, Harry A. *With Pershing in Mexico.* Harrisburg, Pennsylvania: Military Service Publishing, 1935.

Utley, Robert M. *Custer and the Great Controversy. The Origin and Development of a Legend.* Los Angeles: Westernlore Press, 1963.

———. *Frontiersmen in Blue: The United States Army and the Indian.* New York: Macmillan, 1967.

Wetmore, Helen Cody. *Last of the Great Scouts: The Life Story of Colonel William F. Cody.* Lincoln: Univ. of Nebraska Press, 1918.

Wormser, Richard. *The Yellowlegs. The Story of the United States Cavalry.*

Garden City, New York: Doubleday, 1966.
Wright, Arthur. *The Civil War in the Southwest.* Denver: Swallow, 1964.
Young, Otis E. *The West of Philip St. George Cooke.* Glendale, California: Arthur H. Clark, 1956.

George D. Hendricks
North Texas State University

The
Art

Folklore

Abernethy, Francis E., ed. *Folklore of Texan Culture. Publications of the Texas Folklore Society,* 38 (1974).

———. *J. Frank Dobie.* Austin: Steck-Vaughn, 1967.

———, ed. *Observations and Reflections on Texas Folklore. Publications of the Texas Folklore Society,* 37 (1972).

———, ed. *Tales from the Big Thicket.* Austin: Univ. of Texas Press, 1966.

Adams, Ramon F., comp. *Six-Guns and Saddle Leather. A Bibliography of Books and Pamphlets on Western Outlaws and Gunmen.* Norman: Univ. of Oklahoma Press, 1954.

———. *Cowboy Lingo.* Boston: Houghton Mifflin, 1927.

Allen, Jules Verne. *Cowboy Lore.* San Antonio: Naylor, 1933.

Anderson, John Q. *Tales of Frontier Texas, 1830-1860.* Dallas: Southern Methodist Univ. Press, 1967.

———. *Texas Folk Medicine; 1,333 Cures, Remedies, Preventives, and Health Practices.* Austin: Encino Press, 1970.

Applegate, Frank G. *Native Tales of New Mexico.* London and Philadelphia: Lippincott, 1932.

Barnes, Will C. *Arizona Place Names.* Tucson: Univ. of Arizona Press, 1935.

Benedict, Carl P. *A Tenderfoot Kid on Gyp Water.* Dallas: Univ. Press for the Texas Folklore Society, 1943.

Benedict, Ruth. *Tales of the Cochiti Indians.* Washington: Government Printing Office, 1931.

Bickley, J. H. T. *The Ghosts of the Chisos.* San Antonio: Naylor, 1950.

Boatright, Mody C. *Folk Laughter on the American Frontier.* New York: Macmillan, 1949.

———. *Folklore of the Oil Industry.* Dallas: Southern Methodist Univ. Press, 1963.

———. *Gib Morgan, Minstrel of the Oil Fields.* El Paso: Texas Folklore Society, 1945.

———. *Tall Tales from Texas Cow Camps.* Dallas: Southwest Press, 1934.

Boggs, Ralph Steele. *Bibliography of Latin American Folklore.* New York: H. W. Wilson, 1940.

———. *Index of Spanish Folktales.* Chicago: Univ. of Chicago Press, 1930.

Botkin, Benjamin A. *The American Play-Party Song, with a Collection of Oklahoma Texts and Tunes.* Lincoln: Univ. of Nebraska Press, 1937.

————. *Folk Say: A Regional Miscellany.* 4 vols. Norman: Univ. of Oklahoma Press, 1929-1932.

————. *Lay My Burdens Down.* Chicago: Univ. of Chicago Press, 1945.

————. *A Treasury of Western Folklore.* New York: Crown, 1951.

Bowyer, John W., and C. H. Thurman, eds. *The Annals of Elder Horn.* New York: Richard R. Smith, 1930. (Texas).

Braddy, Haldeen *Cock of the Walk. Legend of Pancho Villa.* Albuquerque: Univ. of New Mexico Press, 1955.

Brewer, J. Mason. *Dog Ghosts and Other Texas Negro Folk Tales.* Austin: Univ. of Texas Press, 1958.

————. *The Word on the Brazos.* Austin: Univ. of Texas Press, 1953.

Byrd, James W. *J. Mason Brewer, Negro Folklorist.* Austin: Steck-Vaughn, 1967.

Calvin, Ross. *Rivers of the Sun; Stories of the Storied Gila.* Albuquerque: Univ. of New Mexico Press, 1946.

————. *Sky Determines.* New York: Macmillan, 1934.

Campa, Arthur L. *A Bibliography of Spanish Folk-Lore in New Mexico.* Albuquerque: Univ. of New Mexico Press, 1930.

————. *New Mexico Folk Tales.* Albuquerque: Univ. of New Mexico Press, 1930.

————. *Sayings and Riddles in New Mexico.* Albuquerque: Univ. of New Mexico Press, 1937.

Chapman, Iva. *Twelve Legendary Stories of Texas.* San Antonio: Naylor, 1940.

Chavez, Angelico. *From an Altar Screen; El Ritablo: Tales from New Mexico.* New York: Farrar, Straus & Giroux, 1957.

Clark, LaVerne Harrell. *They Sang for Horses: The Impact of the Horse On the Navajo and Apache.* Tucson: Arizona Univ. Press, 1966.

Coolidge, Mary Roberts. *The Rainmakers.* Boston: Houghton Mifflin, 1929. (Zuni).

Corle, Edwin. *Desert Country.* New York: Duell, Sloan & Pearce, 1941.

Cushing, Frank Hamilton. *Zuni Tales.* New York: Knopf, 1931.

Cutbirth, Ruby Nichols. *Ed Nichols Rode a Horse.* Dallas: Univ. Press for the Texas Folklore Society, 1943.

Dale, E. E. *Cow Country.* Norman: Univ. of Oklahoma Press, 1942.

————. *Frontier Ways.* Austin: Univ. of Texas Press, 1959

Day, Donald. *Big Country: Texas.* New York: Duell, Sloan & Pearce, 1947.

DeAngulo, Jaime. *Indian Tales.* New York: Winn, 1953.

Debo, Angie. *And Still the Waters Run.* New York: Gordian Press, 1968. (Oklahoma, Indian).

DeHuff, Elizabeth. *Taytay's Tales.* New York: Harcourt, Brace, 1922.

Dick, Everett. *The Sod House Frontier.* New York: Appleton, 1937.

Dobie, J. Frank. *Apache Gold and Yaqui Silver.* Boston: Little, Brown, 1939.

———. *The Ben Lilly Legend.* Boston: Little, Brown, 1950.

———. *Coronado's Children. Tales of Lost Mines and Buried Treasure of the Southwest.* Garden City, New York: Garden City Publishing, 1934.

———. *The Flavor of Texas.* Dallas: Dealey & Lowe, 1936.

———. *Guide to Life and Literature of the Southwest.* Austin: Univ. of Texas Press, 1943; revised ed., Dallas: Southern Methodist Univ. Press, 1952

———. *I'll Tell You a Tale.* Boston: Little, Brown, 1960.

———. *The Longhorns.* Boston: Little, Brown, 1941.

———. *The Mustangs.* Boston: Little, Brown, 1952.

———. *On the Open Range.* Dallas: Southwest Press, 1931.

———. *Rattlesnakes.* Boston: Little, Brown, 1965.

———. *Tales of Old-Time Texas.* Boston: Little, Brown, 1955.

———. *Tongues of the Monte.* Garden City, New York: Doubleday, Doran, 1935; rpt. as *The Mexico I Like.* Dallas: Univ. Press, 1942.

———. *Vaquero of the Brush Country.* Dallas: Southwest Press, 1929.

Dorsey, George A. *The Mythology of the Wichita.* Washington: Carnegie Institution, 1904.

———. *Pawnee Hero Stories and Folk Tales.* New York: Scribner, 1904.

———. *Traditions of the Caddo.* Washington: Carnegie Institution, 1905.

———, and Alfred L. Kroeber. *Traditions of the Arapaho.* Chicago: American Museum of Natural History, 1903.

———. *Traditions of the Osage.* Washington: Carnegie Institution, 1904.

Earle, Edwin, *Hopi Kachinas.* New York: J. J. Augustin, 1938.

Emery, Emma Wilson. *Aunt Puss and Others. Old Days in the Piney Woods.* Austin: Encino Press, 1969.

Emmons, Martha. *Deep Like the Rivers: Stories by My Negro Friends.* Austin: Encino Press, 1969.

Espinosa, Jose Manuel. *Spanish Folk-Tales from New Mexico.* Philadelphia: American Folklore Society, 1937.

Fergusson, Erna. *Dancing Gods. Indian Ceremonials of New Mexico and Arizona.* New York: Knopf, 1931.

Fife, Austin E., and Alta S. Fife. *Cowboy and Western Songs. A Comprehensive Anthology.* New York: Clarkson N. Potter, 1969.

Fisher, Stanley A. *In the Beginning: A Navajo Creation Myth.* Chicago: Univ. of Chicago Press, 1953.

Folsom-Dickerson, W. E. S. *The White Path.* San Antonio: Naylor, 1965. (Alabama Koasati).

Fulcher, Walter. *The Way I Heard It: Tales of the Big Bend.* Austin: Univ. of Texas Press, 1959.

Giddings, Ruth Warner. *Yaqui Myths and Legends.* Tucson: Univ. of Arizona Press, 1968.

Gillmor, Frances. *Windsinger, Story of a Navajo Medicine Man.* New York: Minton, Balch, 1930.

Goddard, Pliny E. *Myths and Tales from the San Carlos Apaches.* New York: American Museum of Natural History, 1919.

Goodwin, Grenville. *Myths and Tales of the White Mountain Apaches.* Philadelphia: American Folklore Society, 1939.

Goodwyn, Frank. *The Devil in Texas.* Dallas: Dealey and Lowe, 1936.

Hallenbeck, Cleve, and Juanita Williams. *Legends of the Spanish Southwest.* Glendale, California: Arthur H. Clark, 1928.

Hammer, Laura V. *Light N' Hitch.* Dallas: American Guild Press, 1958.

Hand, Wayland D. *Eyes on Texas: 50 Years of Folklore in the Southwest.* Austin: Texas Folklore Society, 1967.

Hart, John A. *Pioneer Days in the Southwest from 1850-1879.* Guthrie, Oklahoma: State Capitol, 1909.

Hatcher, Mattie Austin. *Myths and Legends of the Texas Indians.* Austin: Texas Folklore Society, 1927.

Haywood, Charles. *A Bibliography of North American Folklore and Folksongs.* 2 vols. New York: Dover, 1961.

Hendricks, George D. *The Bad Man of the West.* San Antonio: Naylor, 1971.

————. *Mirrors, Mice, and Mustaches: A Sampling of Superstitions and Popular Beliefs in Texas.* Austin: Texas Folklore Society, 1966.

House, Boyce. *Tall Tales from Texas.* San Antonio: Naylor, 1945.

Hughs, Fannie M. B. *Legends of Texas Rivers.* Dallas: Mathis, Van Nort, 1937.

James, Ahlee. *Tewa Firelight Tales.* New York: Longmans, Green, 1927.

Kilpatrick, Jack F., and Anna G. Kilpatrick. *Folktales of the Oklahoma Cherokees.* Dallas: Southern Methodist Univ. Press, 1964.

————. *Friends of Thunder: Folktales of the Oklahoma Cherokees.* Dallas: Southern Methodist Univ. Press, 1964.

————. *New Echota Letters.* Dallas: Southern Methodist Univ. Press, 1968. (Cherokee).

————. *Run Toward the Nightland: Magic of the Oklahoma Cherokees.* Dallas: Southern Methodist Univ. Press, 1967.

Kluckhohn, Clyde. *Navajo Witchcraft.* Cambridge: Harvard Univ. Press, 1944.

LaBarre, Weston. *The Peyote Cult.* New Haven: Yale Univ. Press, 1938.

Laski, Vera. *Seeking Life.* Philadelphia: American Folklore Society, 1958. (Pueblo)

Leach, Joseph. *The Typical Texan, Biography of an American Myth.* Dallas: Southern Methodist Univ. Press, 1952.

Lewis, Willy Newbury. *Between Sun and Sod.* Clarendon, Texas: Clarendon Press, 1938.

Link, Margaret S. *The Pollen Path: A Collection of Navajo Myths.* Stanford: Stanford Univ. Press, 1956.

Lockwood, Francis Cummings. *Pioneer Days in Arizona, From the Spanish Occupation to Statehood.* New York: Macmillan, 1932.

Lomax, Alan, and Sidney R. Cowell. *American Folk Songs and Folk Lore. A Regional Bibliography.* New York: Progressive Education Association, 1942.

Lomax, John Avery. *Adventures of a Ballad Hunter.* New York: Macmillan, 1947.

————, and Alan Lomax. *American Ballads and Songs.* New York: Macmillan, 1934.

————. *Cowboy Songs and Other Frontier Ballads.* New York: Macmillan, 1938.

————, and Alan Lomax. *Negro Folk Songs as Sung by Leadbelly.* New York: Macmillan, 1936.

————. *Songs of the Cattle Trail and Cow Camps.* New York: Macmillan, 1950.

————. *Cow Camps and Cattle Herds.* Intro. John A. Lomax, Jr. Austin: Encino Press, 1967.

Long, Haniel. *Pinon Country.* New York: Duell, Sloan & Pearce, 1941.

Lummis, Charles F. *The Land of Poco Tiempo.* New York: Scribner, 1925.

————.*Pueblo Indian Folk Tales.* New York: Century, 1910.

Lucero-White, Aurora, comp. and ed. *The Folklore of New Mexico.* Santa Fe: Seton Village Press, 1941.

Madison, Virginia, and Hallie Stillwell. *How Come It's Called That.* Albuquerque: Univ. of New Mexico Press, 1958. (Texas).

Malone, Bill C. *Country Music U. S. A.: A Fifty-Year History*. Austin: Univ. of Texas Press, 1968.

Marriott, Alice L. *The Ten Grandmothers*. Norman: Univ. of Oklahoma Press, 1945.

——. *Winter-Telling Tales*. New York: William Sloan, 1947. (Kiowa).

Mathews, John Joseph. *The Osages: Children of the Middle Waters*. Norman: Univ. of Oklahoma Press, 1961.

Matthews, Washington. *Navaho Legends*. Boston: Houghton Mifflin, 1897.

Mitchell, John D. *Lost Mines of the Southwest*. Phoenix: Journal Company, 1933.

Mooney, James. *Myths of the Cherokees*. Washington: Bureau of American Ethnology, 1902.

Moore, Chauncey O., and Ethel Moore. *Ballads and Folksongs of the Southwest*. Norman: Univ. of Oklahoma Press, 1964.

Moorman, Lewis J. *Pioneer Doctor*. Norman: Univ. of Oklahoma Press, 1951.

Morrell, Z. N. *Flowers and Fruits from the Wilderness*. Boston: Gould and Lincoln, 1872, 1873. (Pioneer Folkways).

Mourning, Dove. *Coyote Stories*. Caldwell, Idaho: Caxton, 1934.

Niggli, Josephine. *Mexican Folk Plays*. Chapel Hill: Univ. of North Carolina Press, 1938.

Norquest, Carrol. *Rio Grande Wetbacks*. Albuquerque: Univ. of New Mexico Press, 1972.

Nye, Wilbur S. *Bad Medicine and Good: Tales of the Kiowas*. Norman: Univ. of Oklahoma Press, 1962.

Opler, Morris E. *Myths and Legends of the Lipan Apache Indians*. Philadelphia: American Folklore Society, 1940.

——. *Myths and Tales of the Chiracahua Apache Indians*. Philadelphia: American Folklore Society, 1942.

——. *Myths and Tales of the Jicarilla Apache Indians*. Philadelphia: American Folklore Society, 1938.

Owens, William A. *Swing and Turn: Texas Play Party Games*. Dallas: Tardy, 1936.

——. *Texas Folk Songs*. Dallas: Southern Methodist Univ. Press, 1950.

Paredes, Americo. *"With His Pistol in His Hand": A Border Ballad and Its Hero*. Austin: Univ. of Texas Press, 1958.

Parsons, Elsie Clews. *Kiowa Tales*. Philadelphia: American Folklore Society, 1929.

Patterson, Paul. *Pecos Tales*. Austin: Encino Press, 1967.

Pearce, James E. *Tales That Dead Men Tell.* Austin: Univ. of Texas Press, 1935.

Pearce, T. M. *New Mexico Place Names.* Albuquerque: Univ. of New Mexico Press, 1965.

Publications of the Texas Folklore Society. Round the Levee. Ed. Stith Thompson. Austin: TFS, 1916; rpt. 1935, No. 1.

Radin, Paul. *The Trickster: A Study in American Indian Mythology.* London: Routledge and Kegan Paul, 1956.

Rael, Juan B. *The New Mexico Alabado.* Stanford: Stanford Univ. Press, 1951.

———. *The Sources and Diffusion of the Mexican Shepherd's Play.* Guadalajara, Mexico: Librera La Joyita, 1965.

Ransom, Nancy R. *Texas Wild Flower Legends.* Dallas: Kaleidograph Press, 1933.

Rosa, Joseph G. *The Gunfighter: Man or Myth.* Norman: Univ. of Oklahoma Press, 1968.

Saxon, Lyle. *Lafitte the Pirate.* New York: Appleton, 1931.

Scarborough, Dorothy. *On the Trail of Negro Folk-Songs.* Cambridge: Harvard Univ. Press, 1925.

Schmitz, Joseph. *Thus They Lived: Social Life in the Republic of Texas.* San Antonio: Naylor, 1935.

Shaw, Anna Moore. *Pima Indian Legends.* Tucson: Univ. of Arizona Press, 1968.

Shaw, Loyd. *Cowboy Dances.* Caldwell, Idaho: Caxton, 1939.

Sherman, James E., and Barbara H. Sherman. *Ghost Towns of Arizona.* Norman: Univ. of Oklahoma Press, 1968.

Shirk, George H. *Oklahoma Place Names.* Norman: Univ. of Oklahoma Press, 1965.

Simmons, Merle. *The Mexican Corrido as a Source for Interpretive Study of Modern Mexico.* Bloomington: Indiana Univ. Press. 1957.

Smith, Walter V. *Tales of the Spanish Southwest, Stories of the Spanish Rule in California, New Mexico, Arizona, and Texas.* New York: Holt, 1934.

Songs of the American West. Ed. Richard E. Lingenfelter, Richard A. Dwyer, and David Cohen. Berkeley and Los Angeles: Univ. of California Press, 1968.

Speck, Ernest, ed. *Mody Boatright, Folklorist.* Austin: Univ. of Texas Press, 1973.

———. *Mody C. Boatright.* Austin: Steck-Vaughn, 1970.

Steckmesser, Kent L. *The Western Hero in History and Legend*. Norman: Univ. of Oklahoma Press, 1965.

Storm, Barry. *Trail of the Lost Dutchman. An Authentic Story of the Fabulous Lost Dutchman and of Other Originally Spanish Mines in the Superstition Mountains of Arizona*. Phoenix: Goldwaters, 1939.

———. *Coffee in the Gourd*. Ed. J. Frank Dobie. Austin: TFS, 1923; rpt. 1935. No. 2

——— *Legends of Texas*. Ed. J. Frank Dobie. Austin: TFS, 1924; rpt. Philadelphia: Folklore Associates, 1964. No. 3.

———. *Publications of the Texas Folklore Society*. Ed. J. Frank Dobie. Austin: TFS, 1925; rpt. as *Happy Hunting Ground*. Philadelphia: Folklore Associates, 1964. No. 4.

———. *Publications of the Texas Folklore Society*. Ed. J. Frank Dobie. Austin: TFS, 1925. Rpt. as *Rainbow in the Morning*. Philadelphia: Folklore Associates, 1964. No. 5.

———. *Texas and Southwestern Lore*. Ed. J. Frank Dobie. Austin: TFS, 1927; 1934. No. 6.

———. *Follow de Drinkin' Gou'd*. Ed. J. Frank Dobie. Austin: TFS, 1928. No. 7.

———. *Man, Bird, and Beast*. Ed. J. Frank Dobie. Austin: TFS, 1930. No. 8.

———. *Southwestern Lore*. Ed. J. Frank Dobie. Austin: TFS, 1931; rpt. Philadelphia: Folklore Associates, 1964. No. 9.

———. *Tone the Bell Easy*. Ed. J. Frank Dobie. Austin: TFS, 1932. No. 10.

———. *Spur-of-the-Cock*. Ed. J. Frank Dobie. Austin: TFS, 1933. No. 11.

———. *Puro Mexicano*. Ed. J. Frank Dobie. Austin: TFS, 1935; rpt. Dallas: Southern Methodist Univ. Press, 1969. No. 12.

———. *Straight Texas*. Ed. J. Frank Dobie. Austin: TFS, 1937; rpt. Philadelphia: Folklore Associates, 1964. No. 13.

———.*Coyote Wisdom*. Ed. J. Frank Dobie, Mody C. Boatright, and Harry H. Ransom. Austin: TFS, 1938. No. 14.

———. *In the Shadow of History*. Ed. J Frank Dobie, Mody C. Boatright, and Harry H. Ransom. Austin: TFS, 1939. No. 15.

———. *Mustangs and Cow Horses*. Ed. J. Frank Dobie, Mody C. Boatright, and Harry H. Ransom. Austin: TFS, 1942; 2nd ed. Dallas: Southern Methodist Univ. Press, 1965. No. 16.

———. *Texian Stomping Grounds*. Ed. J. Frank Dobie, Mody C. Boatright, and Harry H. Ransom. Austin: TFS, 1941. No. 17

———. *Backwoods to Border*. Ed. Mody C. Boatright and Donald Day. Austin and Dallas: Univ. Press, 1943. No. 18.

————. *From Hell to Breakfast*. Ed. Mody C. Boatright and Donald Day. Austin and Dallas: Univ. Press, 1944. No. 19.

————. *Gib Morgan, Minstrel of the Oil Fields*. By Mody C. Boatright. Dallas: Southern Methodist Univ. Press, 1945. No. 20.

————. *Mexican Border Ballads and Other Lore*. Ed. Mody C. Boatright. Austin: TFS, 1946. No. 21.

————. *The Sky Is My Tipi*. Ed. Mody C. Boatright. Austin and Dallas: Univ. Press, 1949. No. 22.

————. *Texas Folk Songs*. By William A. Owens. Austin and Dallas: Univ. Press, 1950. No. 23.

————. *The Healer of Los Olmos and Other Mexican Lore*. Ed. Wilson M. Hudson. Dallas: Southern Methodist Univ. Press, 1951. No. 24.

————. *Folk Travelers: Ballads, Tales, and Talk*. Ed. Mody C. Boatright, Wilson M. Hudson, and Allen Maxwell. Dallas: Southern Methodist Univ. Press, 1953. No. 25.

————. *Texas Folk and Folklore*. Ed. Mody C. Boatright, Wilson M. Hudson, and Allen Maxwell. Dallas: Southern Methodist Univ. Press, 1954. No. 26.

————. *Mesquite and Willow*. Ed. Mody C. Boatright, Wilson M. Hudson, and Allen Maxwell. Dallas: Southern Methodist Univ. Press, 1957. No. 27.

————. *Madstones and Twisters*. Ed. Mody C. Boatright, Wilson M. Hudson, and Allen Maxwell. Dallas: Southern Methodist Univ. Press, 1958. No. 28.

————. *And Horns on the Toads*. Ed. Mody C. Boatright, Wilson M. Hudson, and Allen Maxwell. Dallas: Southern Methodist Univ. Press, 1959. No. 29.

————. *Singers and Storytellers*. Ed. Mody C. Boatright, Wilson M. Hudson, and Allen Maxwell. Dallas: Southern Methodist Univ. Press, 1961. No. 30.

————. *The Golden Log*. Ed. Mody C. Boatright, Wilson M. Hudson, and Allen Maxwell. Dallas: Southern Methodist Univ. Press, 1962. No. 31.

————. *A Good Tale and a Bonnie Tune*. Ed. Mody C. Boatright, Wilson M. Hudson, and Allen Maxwell. Dallas: Southern Methodist Univ. Press, 1964. No. 32.

————. *The Sunny Slopes of Long Ago*. Ed. Wilson M. Hudson and Allen Maxwell. Dallas: Southern Methodist Univ. Press, 1966. No. 33

————. *Tire Shrinker to Dragster*. Ed. Wilson M. Hudson. Austin: Encino Press, 1968. No. 34.

————. *Hunters and Healers*. Ed. Wilson M. Hudson. Austin: Encino Press, 1971. No. 35.

————. *Diamond Bessie and the Shepherds*. Ed. Wilson M. Hudson. Austin: Encino, 1972. No. 36.

————. *Observations and Reflections on Texas Folklore.* Ed. Francis Edward Abernethy. Austin: Encino, 1972. No. 37.

————. *The Folklore of Texan Cultures.* Ed. Francis Edward Abernethy. Austin: Encino, 1974. No. 38.

Thane, Eric. *High Border Country.* New York: Duell, Sloan & Pearce, 1942.

Thompson, Stith. *Tales of the North American Indians.* Chicago: Univ. of Chicago Press, 1945.

Thorp, N. Howard. *Songs of the Cowboys.* Boston: Houghton Mifflin, 1921.

Tully, Marjorie F., and Juan B. Real. *An Annotated Bibliography of Spanish Folklore in New Mexico and Southern Colorado.* Albuquerque: Univ. of New Mexico Press, 1950.

Turner, Martha Anne. *The Yellow Rose of Texas: The Story of a Song.* Southwestern Studies Monograph No. 31. El Paso: Texas Western Press, 1971.

Tyler, Hamilton A. *Pueblo Gods and Myths.* Norman: Univ. of Oklahoma Press, 1964.

Underhill, Ruth M. *Papago Indian Religion.* New York: Columbia Univ. Press, 1946.

————. *Red Man's Religion: Beliefs and Practices of the Indians North of Mexico.* Chicago: Univ. of Chicago Press, 1965.

————. *Singing for Power: The Song Magic of the Papago Indians of Southern Arizona.* Berkeley: Univ. of California Press, 1938.

Van Stone, Mary R. *Spanish Folk Songs of New Mexico.* Chicago: Seymour, 1926.

Waters, Frank. *Masked Gods: Navajo and Pueblo Ceremonialism.* Albuquerque: Univ. of New Mexico Press, 1951.

Weight, Harold O. *Lost Ship of the Desert: A Legend of the Southwest.* Twentynine Palms, California: Calico Press, 1959.

Wheelwright, Mary. *The Myths and Prayers of the Great Star Chant and the Myth of the Coyote Chant.* Santa Fe: New Mexico Museum of Navajo Ceremonial Art, 1956.

Wylder, Meldrum K. *Rio Grande Medicine Man.* Santa Fe: Rydal Press, 1958.

Zavala, Adina de. *History and Legends of the Alamo and Other Missions.* San Antonio: Published by the author, 1917.

John Q. Anderson
University of Houston

Arts

Adair, John. *The Navajo and Pueblo Silversmiths*. Norman: Univ. of Oklahoma Press, 1944.

Adams, Ramon F., and Homer E. Britzman, eds. *Charles M. Russell: The Cowboy Artist*. 2 vols. Pasadena, California: Trail's End Publishing, 1949.

Alexander, Hartley B. *Pueblo Indian Painting*. Nice, France: C. Czwedzicki, 1932.

Amsden, Charles A. *Navaho Weaving*. Albuquerque: Univ. of New Mexico Press, 1952.

Bahti, Tom. *Southwestern Indian Arts and Crafts*. Flagstaff, Arizona: KC Publications, 1968.

Boyd, E. *Saints and Saint Makers of New Mexico*. Santa Fe: Laboratory of Anthropology, 1946.

Chapman, Kenneth M., ed. *Pueblo Indian Pottery*. Nice, France: C. Czwedzicki, 1933.

Cisneros, José. *Riders of the Border; A Selection of 30 Drawings*. El Paso: Texas Western Press, 1971.

Coke, Van Deren. *Taos and Santa Fe: The Artist's Environment, 1882-1942*. Albuquerque: Univ. of New Mexico Press, 1963.

Dawdy, Doris Ostander, comp. *Annotated Bibliography of American Indian Painting*. New York: Museum of the American Indian, Heye Foundation, 1968.

Densmore, Frances. *Cheyenne and Arapaho Music*. Los Angeles: Southwest Museum, 1936.

Dickey, Roland. *New Mexico Village Art*. Albuquerque: Univ. of New Mexico Press, 1952.

Douglas, Frederic H., and René d'Harnancourt. *Indian Art of the United States*. New York: Museum of Modern Art, 1941.

Ewers, John C. *Plains Indian Painting: A Description of Aboriginal American Art*. Stanford: Stanford Univ. Press, 1939.

Gentilz: Artist of the Old Southwest. Drawings and paintings by Theodore Gentilz. Text by Dorothy Steinbomer Kendall. Archival research by Carmen Perry. Austin: Univ. of Texas Press, 1974.

Guthe, Carl E. *Pueblo Pottery Making: A Study at the Village of San Ildefonso*. New Haven: Yale Univ. Press, 1925.

Hotz, Gottfried. *Indian Skin Paintings from the American Southwest*. Norman: Univ. of Oklahoma Press, 1976.

Luhan, Mabel Dodge. *Taos and Its Artists.* New York: Duell, Sloan and Pearce, 1947.

McCracken, Harold. *Frederic Remington: Artist of the Old West.* Philadelphia: Lippincott, 1947.

Marriott, Alice. *María: The Potter of San Ildefonso.* Norman: Univ. of Oklahoma Press, 1948.

Mason, Bernard S. *Book of Indian Crafts and Costumes.* New York: Barnes, 1946.

Mera, H. P. *Pueblo Indian Embroidery.* Albuquerque: Univ. of New Mexico Press, 1943.

Russell, Charles M. *Trails Plowed Under.* Garden City, New York: Doubleday, 1946.

Sides, Dorothy Smith. *Decorative Art of the Southwestern Indians.* New York: Dover, 1961.

Smith, Goldie C. *The Creative Arts in Texas: A Handbook of Biography.* Nashville: Cokesbury, 1926.

Snodgrass, Jeanne O. *American Indian Painters: A Biographical Directory.* New York: Museum of the American Indian, 1968.

Taft, Robert. *Artists and Illustrators of the Old West, 1850-1900.* New York: Scribner, 1953.

Wissley, Clark. *Costumes of the Plains Indians.* New York: Museum of Natural History, 1915.

John Q. Anderson
University of Houston

Dictionaries & Lexicons

Adams, Ramon F. *Cowboy Lingo.* Boston: Houghton Mifflin, 1936.

————. *Western Words.* Norman: Univ. of Oklahoma Press, 1944.

————. *Western Words: A Dictionary of the American West.* Norman: Univ. of Oklahoma Press, 1966.

————. *Western Words: A Dictionary of the Range, Cow Camp, and Trail.* Norman: Univ. of Oklahoma Press, 1956.

Anderson, John Q. "From Flygap to Whybark: Some Unusual Texas Place Names." *The Golden Log. Publications of the Texas Folklore Society,* 31 (1962).

————. "Texas Stream Names," *A Good Tale and a Bonnie Tune. Publica-*

tions of the Texas Folklore Society, 33 (1964).

Ashbacker, Frances M. *Pronouncing Directory of Cities, Towns, and Counties in Texas.* San Antonio: n.p., 1953.

Atwood, Bagby. *The Regional Vocabulary of Texas.* Austin: Univ. of Texas Press, 1962.

Austin, Mary. "Geographical Terms from the Spanish," *American Speech,* 8 (October 1933), 7-10.

Caffee, N. M. "Southern 'L' Plus a Consonant," *American Speech,* 15 (October 1940), 259-61.

Carlisle, Mrs. George F. *The Origin of Some of the Dallas Street Names.* Dallas: Local History and Genealogical Society, 1957.

Clifton, Ernest. "For the DAE Supplement: The Vocabulary of 'Sam Slick' in Texas," *American Speech,* 20 (April 1945), 111-13.

————. "Some [u]—[ju] Variations in Texas," *American Speech,* 34 (October 1959), 190-93.

Dignowity, Hartman. "Nicknames in the Texas Oil Fields." *Texas and Southwestern Lore. Publications of the Texas Folklore Society,* 26, (1954).

Edgarton, William. "A Note on 'Spigot' and 'Spicket,' " *American Speech,* 23 (February 1948), 33-35.

Eikel, Fred. "New Braunfels German: Part I," *American Speech,* 41 (February 1966), 5-16.

————. "New Braunfels German: Part II," *American Speech,* 41 (December 1966), 254-60.

————. "New Braunfels German: Part III," *American Speech,* 41 (May 1967), 83-104.

————. "The Use of Cases in New Braunfels German," *American Speech,* 24 (December 1949), 278-81.

Evans, Medford. "Southern Long 'I,' " *American Speech,* 10 (October 1935), 188-90.

Feagles, Elizabeth. *Walk Like a Cowboy.* San Antonio: Naylor, 1953.

Gilbert, Glenn. "English Loan Words in the German of Fredericksburg, Texas," *American Speech,* 40 (May 1965), 102-12.

————. *The German Dialect Spoken in Kendall and Gillespie Counties, Texas.* Unpubl. doctoral diss. Cambridge: Harvard Univ., 1963.

Hall, David. "Folk Names of Texas Cacti," *Spur-of-the-Cock. Publications of the Texas Folklore Society,* 11 (1933).

Haslam, Gerald H. "The Language of Oil Fields," *American Speech,* 24 (June 1967), 191-201.

Heflin, Woodford A. *Characteristic Features of New Mexico English Between 1805 and 1890*. Unpubl. doctoral diss. Chicago: Univ. of Chicago, 1942.

Hendricks, George D. "The Names of Western Wild Animals," *Folk Travelers. Publications of the Texas Folklore Society*, 25 (1953).

Hogan, Charles. "A Yankee Comments on Texas Speech," *American Speech*, 20 (April 1945), 81-84.

Holmer, N. M. *Indian Place Names in North America*. Cambridge: Harvard Univ. Press, 1948.

Hymes, Dell H., and William E. Bittle. *Studies in Southwestern Ethnolinguistics*. New York: Humanities Press, 1967.

Jenkins, Thelma A. *Study of Cowboy Diction*. Detroit, Michigan: Gale Research, 1931.

Jourdan, Mary. "Familiar Sayings of Old Time Texans," *Rainbow in the Morning. Publications of the Texas Folklore Society*, 5 (1925).

Kany, Charles E. *American-Spanish Semantics*. Berkeley: Univ. of California Press, 1960.

Krumpelmann, John T. "More Words From Mexico," *American Speech*, 32 (October 1957), 176-79.

Law, Robert A. "A Note on Four Negro Words." *Texas and Southwestern Lore. Publications of the Texas Folklore Society*, 6 (1934).

Lomax, Ruby T. "Negro Nicknames," *Backwoods to Border. Publications of the Texas Folklore Society*, 18 (1943).

Madison, Virginia, and Hallie Stillwell. *How Come It's Called That? Big Bend Place Names*. Albuquerque: Univ. of New Mexico Press, 1958.

Martin, Elizabeth Kathryn. *Lexicon of the Texas Oil Fields*. Unpubl. doctoral diss. Commerce: East Texas State Univ., 1969.

Martin, George C. *Some Texas Streams and Place Names*. San Antonio: Norman Brock, 1947.

Mason, Julian. "The Etymology of 'Buckaroo,'" *American Speech*, 35 (February 1960), 51-55.

Massengill, Fred I. *Texas Towns*. Terrell, Texas: Fred I. Massengill, 1936.

Meredith, M. J. *"Poorboy,* a Verb Used in the Texas Oil Fields," *American Speech*, 30 (February 1955), 71.

Norman, A. M. Z. "Migration to Southeast Texas: People and Words," *Southwest Social Science Quarterly*, 37 (September 1956), 149-58.

Norman, Arthur. "A Southeast Texas Dialect Study." *Orbis*, 5 (1956), 61-79.

Osborne, Walter D. "The Origin of Cow Savvy," *The Quarter Horse Journal*, 19 (July 1967), 20-48.

Pearce, T. M. *New Mexico Place Names.* Albuquerque: Univ. of New Mexico Press, 1965.

———. "Trader Terms in Southwestern English," *American Speech,* 16 (October 1941), 179-86.

Pyles, Thomas. "Onomastic Individualism in Oklahoma," *American Speech,* 22 (December 1947), 257-64.

Ringe, D. A. "Pike: To be Nosy, to Pry," *American Speech,* 34 (December 1959), 306-7.

Rudjord, John. *Indian Place Names: Their Origin, Evolution, and Meanings.* Norman: Univ. of Oklahoma Press, 1968.

Sawyer, Janet B. "Social Aspects of Bilingualism in San Antonio, Texas," *Publications of the American Dialect Society,* 41 (April 1964), 7-15.

Shrink, George, H. *Oklahoma Place Names.* Norman: Univ. of Oklahoma Press, 1965.

Sorving, Ralph. "Southwestern Plant Names From Spanish," *American Speech,* 27 (May 1953), 97-105.

Stanley, Oma. "Negro Speech of East Texas," *American Speech,* 16 (February 1941), 3-16.

———. "The Speech of East Texas," *American Speech,* 11 (February 1936), 3-36.

———. "The Speech of East Texas (II)," *American Speech,* 11 (April 1936), 145-66.

———. "The Speech of East Texas (III)," *American Speech,* 11 (October 1936), 232-51.

———. "The Speech of East Texas (IV)," *American Speech,* 11 (December 1936), 327-55.

Swinburne, L. "American Dialect of the Plains: Bucolic," *Scribner's Magazine,* 2 (1887), 505.

Tarpley, Fred. *From Blinky to Blue-John: A Word Atlas of Northeast Texas.* Wolfe City, Texas: University Press, 1970.

———. *Place Names of Northeast Texas.* Commerce: East Texas State University, 1969.

Thomas, C. K. "Notes on the Pronunciation of 'On,'" *American Speech,* 22 (April 1947), 104-7.

Van Emden, Frieda. *Sure Enough, How Come?* San Antonio: Naylor, 1952.

Wheatley, Katherine E. "Southern Standards," *American Speech,* 9 (February 1934), 36-45.

Wheatley, Katherine and Oma Stanley. "Three Generations of East Texas

Speech," *American Speech,* 34 (May 1959), 83-94.

Wood, Gordon R. "Word Distribution in the Interior South," *Publication of the American Dialect Society,* 35 (1961), 1-16.

Woodbridge, H. C. "Handful of Western Americanisms," *American Speech,* 33 (May 1958), 140-42.

Young, Della I. "Names in the Old Cheyenne and Arapahoe Territory and the Texas Panhandle," *Texas and Southwestern Lore. Publications of the Texas Folklore Society,* 6 (1934).

Fred Tarpley
East Texas State University

The
Ethos

Armer, Laura A. *Southwest.* New York: Longmans, Green, 1935.

Austin, Mary. *The American Rhythm.* New York: Harcourt, Brace, 1925.

——. *Land of Journey's Ending.* New York: Century, 1924.

Bainbridge, John. *The Super Americans.* New York: Doubleday, 1961.

Bolton, Herbert E. *The Spanish Borderlands.* New Haven: Yale Univ. Press, 1921.

Calvin, Ross, *Sky Determines; an Interpretation of the Southwest.* New York: Macmillan, 1934.

——. *Rivers of the Sun; Stories of the Storied Gila.* Albuquerque: Univ. of New Mexico Press, 1946.

Corle, Edwin. *Desert Country.* New York: Duell, Sloan and Pearce, 1941.

Faulk, Odie B. *Land of Many Frontiers; A History of the American Southwest.* New York: Oxford Univ. Press, 1968.

Fergusson, Erna. *Our Southwest.* New York: Knopf, 1940.

Fergusson, Harvey. *Rio Grande.* New York: Knopf, 1933.

Foreman, Grant. *The Five Civilized Tribes.* Norman: Univ. of Oklahoma Press, 1934.

——. *Indians and Pioneers; The Story of the American Southwest before 1830.* New Haven: Yale Univ. Press, 1930.

——. *Pioneer Days in the Early Southwest.* Cleveland: Arthur H. Clark, 1926.

Hall, D. J. *Enchanted Sand.* New York: Morrow, 1933.

Holden, W. C. *Alkali Trails.* Dallas: Southwest Press, 1930.

Hollon, William E. *The Southwest: Old and New.* New York: Knopf, 1961.

James, George W. *Arizona, the Wonderland.* Boston: Page, 1917.

Kluckhohn, Clyde. *To the Foot of the Rainbow.* New York: Century, 1927.

Lamar, Howard R. *The Far Southwest, 1846-1912: A Territorial History.* New Haven: Yale Univ. Press, 1966.

Landes, Ruth. *Latin Americans of the Southwest.* St. Louis: McGraw-Hill, 1965.

Lummis, Charles F. *The Land of Poco Tiempo.* New York: Scribner, 1925.

——. *Mesa, Canyon and Pueblo.* New York: Century, 1925.

Perrigo, Lynn I. *The American Southwest: Its Peoples and Cultures.* New York: Holt, Rinehart and Winston, 1971.

Richardson, R. N. *The Greater Southwest.* Glendale, California: Arthur H. Clark, 1934.

Rister, Carl C. *The Southwestern Frontier—1865-1881.* Cleveland: Arthur H. Clark, 1928.

Roder, Jesse Lee. *South of 40, from the Mississippi to the Rio Grande.* Norman: Univ. of Oklahoma Press, 1947.

Sears, Paul B. *Deserts on the March.* Norman: Univ. of Oklahoma Press, 1935.

Smith, Henry Nash. "A Note on the Southwest," *Southwest Review,* 14 (Spring 1929), 268-69.

Vestal, Stanley. *Short Grass Country.* New York: Duell, Sloan and Pearce, 1941.

Waters, Frank. *The Colorado.* New York: Holt, Rinehart, Winston, 1946.

Webb, Walter P. *Divided We Stand.* Boston: Houghton Mifflin, 1937.

———. *The Great Plains.* Boston: Ginn, 1931.

John Q. Anderson
University of Houston

PART II

The Literature

The
Genres

Bibliographies

Adams, Ramon F. *Six-Guns and Saddle Leather, A Bibliography of Books and Pamphlets on Western Outlaws and Gunmen*. Norman: Univ. of Oklahoma Press, 1954.

————. *The Rampaging Herd, A Bibliography of Books and Pamphlets on Men and Events in the Cattle Industry*. Norman: Univ. of Oklahoma Press, 1959.

————. *Burs Under the Saddle: A Second Look at Books and Histories of the West*. Norman: Univ. of Oklahoma Press, 1964.

Agatha [Sheehan], Sister M. *Texas Prose Writings*. Dallas: Banks Upshaw, 1936.

Barns, Florence E. *Texas Writers of Today*. Dallas: Tardy, 1935.

Bloom, L. B. "Bourke on the Southwest," *New Mexico Historical Review,* 8 (January 1933), 1-30.

Bratcher, James T. *Analytical Index to Publications of the Texas Folklore Society,* Volumes 1-36. Foreword by Wilson M. Hudson; historical note on the Texas Folklore Society by Francis E. Abernethy. Dallas: Southern Methodist Univ. Press, 1973.

Campbell, Walter S. *The Booklover's Southwest: A Guide to Good Reading*. Norman: Univ. of Oklahoma Press, 1955.

Cohen, Hennig, and William B. Dillingham, eds. *Humor of the Old Southwest*. Boston: Houghton Mifflin, 1964.

Colville, Derek. "Checklist to Travel Essays Relating to the Southwest Which Appeared in the New Orleans *Daily Picayune,* 1819-1941," *New Mexico Historical Review,* 33 (July 1958), 232-35.

Dobie, J. Frank. *Guide to Life and Literature of the Southwest*. Rev. ed. Dallas: Southern Methodist Univ. Press, 1952.

————, and John William Rogers. *Finding Literature on the Texas Plains*. Dallas: Southwest Press, 1930.

Dykes, J. C. *Billy the Kid, The Bibliography of A Legend*. Albuquerque: Univ. of New Mexico Press, 1952.

Etulain, Richard W. *Western American Literature*. Vermillion: Univ. of South Dakota Press, 1972.

Gerstenberger, Donna and George Hendrick. *The American Novel*. Chicago: Swallow, 1961.

Gohdes, Clarence. *Literature and Theater of the States and Regions of the U.S.A.: An Historical Bibliography*. Durham: Duke Univ. Press, 1967.

Harrington, Mildred Priscilla. *The Southwest in Children's Books: A Bibliography*. Baton Rouge: Louisiana State Univ. Press, 1952.

Jenkins, John Holmes. *Cracker Barrel Chronicles, A Bibliography of Texas Town and County Histories*. Austin: Pemberton Press, 1965.

Johanssen, Albert. *The House of Beadle and Adams And Its Dime and Nickel Novels: The Story of A Vanished Literature*. 3 vols. Norman: Univ. of Oklahoma Press, 1950 (Vols. 1-2) and 1961 (Vol. 3).

Kurtz, Kenneth. *Literature of the American Southwest: A Selective Bibliography*. Los Angeles: Occidental College, 1956.

Major, Mabel, and T. M. Pearce. *Southwest Heritage:A Literary History with Bibliography*. Third ed., revised and enlarged. Albuquerque: Univ. of New Mexico Press, 1972. First edition (1938) and second edition, revised and enlarged (1948), by Mabel Major, Rebecca W. Smith, and T. M. Pearce.

Marable, Mary Hays, and Elaine Boylan. *A Handbook of Oklahoma Writers*. Norman: Univ. of Oklahoma Press, 1939.

Munk, Joseph A. *Bibliography of Arizona*. Los Angeles: Southwest Museum, 1900. Rpt., 1914.

Nilon, Charles H., comp. *Bibliography of Bibliographies in American Literature*. New York: R. R. Bowker, 1970.

Parsons, Mabel. *A Courier in New Mexico*. Tesuque, New Mexico: Tesuque Printers, 1936.

Powell, Lawrence Clark. *Heart of the Southwest: A Selected Bibliography of Novels, Stories, and Tales Laid in Arizona and New Mexico and Adjacent Lands*. Los Angeles: Dawson's Book Shop, 1955.

—————. *A Southwestern Century: A Bibliography of One Hundred Books of Non-Fiction about the Southwest*. Van Nuys, California: J. E. Reynolds, 1958.

—————. *Southwestern Book Trails: A Reader's Guide to the Heartland of New Mexico and Arizona*. Albuquerque: Horn and Wallace, 1963.

Rader, Jesse Lee. *South of Forty, from the Mississippi to the Rio Grande: A Bibliography*. Norman: Univ. of Oklahoma Press, 1947.

Raines, C. W. *A Bibliography of Texas*. Austin: Gammel, 1896. Rpt., 1934.

Rittenhouse, Jack D. *The Santa Fe Trail: A Historical Bibliography*. Albuquerque: Univ. of New Mexico Press, 1971.

Saunders, Lyle. *A Guide to Materials Bearing on Cultural Relations in New Mexico*. Albuquerque: Univ. of New Mexico Press, 1944.

—————. "A Guide to the Literature of the Southwest," *New Mexico Quarterly*, 13-24 (1942-1954).

Smith, Goldie Capers. *The Creative Arts in Texas: A Handbook of Biography*. Nashville: Cokesbury, 1926.

Streeter, Thomas W. *Bibliography of Texas, 1795-1845*. 5 vols. Cambridge: Harvard Univ. Press, 1955-1960.

Tucker, Mary. *Books of the Southwest: A General Bibliography*. New York: J. J. Augustin, 1937.

Wagner, Henry Raup. *The Spanish Southwest, 1542-1794: An Annotated Bibliography*. 2 vols. Albuquerque: Quivira Society, 1937.

Winkler, E. W., and L. B. Friend, eds. *Check List of Texas Imprints 1861-1876*. Austin: Texas State Historical Association, 1964.

James T. F. Tanner
North Texas State University

Anthologies

(Anthologies listed here are general—either of prose or of prose and poetry combined. For anthologies of poetry only, see Poetry.)

Banks, C. Stanley, and Grace Taylor McMillan, eds. *The Texas Reader: An Anthology of Romantic History, Biography, Legends, Folklore, and Epic Stories of the Lone Star State*. San Antonio: Naylor, 1947.

Barns, Florence Elberta. *Texas Writers of Today*. Dallas: Tardy, 1935.

Barton, Marion Harges, ed. *Fiesta*. Albuquerque: Valiant Press, 1952.

Becker, May Lamberton, ed. *Golden Tales of the Southwest*. New York: Dodd, Mead, 1939.

Boyer, Mary G., ed. *Arizona in Literature, A Collection of the Best Writings of Arizona Authors from Early Spanish Days to the Present Time*. Glendale: Arthur H. Clark, 1934.

Bradley, Ann and Lawrence A. Sharp, eds. *Echoes of the Southland. Literature of the South and Southwest*. 2 vols. Austin: Steck, 1941.

Eagleton, Davis Foute, ed. *Writers and Writings of Texas*. New York: Broadway, 1913.

———. *Texas Literature Reader*. Dallas: Southern Publishing, 1916.

Greer, Hilton Ross, ed. *Best Short Stories from the Southwest*. Dallas: Southwest Press, 1928.

———, ed. *Best Short Stories from the Southwest, Second Series*. Dallas: Southwest Press, 1931.

Kyger, John Charles Fremont. *Texas Gems: A Collection of Prose and Poetry.* Denison, Texas: Murray's Steam Printing House, 1885.

Major, Mabel, and Rebecca W. Smith, eds. *The Southwest in Literature: An Anthology for High Schools.* New York: Macmillan, 1929.

Mohle, Eula Phares, ed. *Texas Sampler.* New York: Oxford Book Company, 1955.

Pearce, T. M., and Telfair Hendon, eds. *America in the Southwest.* Albuquerque: Univ. of New Mexico Press, 1933.

———— and A. P. Thomason, eds. *Southwesterners Write.* Albuquerque: Univ. of New Mexico Press, 1947.

Peery, William, ed. *21 Texas Short Stories.* Austin: Univ. of Texas Press, 1954.

Perry, George Sessions, ed. *Roundup Time: A Collection of Southwestern Writing.* New York: Whittlesey House, McGraw-Hill, 1943.

Pickrell, Annie Doom. *True Stories in Texas.* San Antonio: Naylor, 1936.

Shockley, Martin, ed. *Southwest Writers Anthology.* Austin: Steck-Vaughn, 1967.

Sonnichsen, C. L., ed. *The Southwest in Life and Literature.* New York: Devin-Adair, 1962.

Stover, Elizabeth Matchett, ed. *Son-of-a-Gun Stew: A Sampling of the Southwest.* Dallas: Southern Methodist Univ. Press, 1945.

Taylor, J. Golden, ed. *The Literature of the American West.* Boston: Houghton Mifflin, 1971.

Tinkle, Lon, and Allen Maxwell, eds. *The Cowboy Reader.* New York: Longmans, Green, 1959.

White, James P., ed. *The Bicentennial Collection of Texas Short Stories.* Fort Worth and Dallas: Texas Center for Writers Press, 1974.

Arthur M. Sampley
North Texas State University

Biographies, Autobiographies, Memiors

Biographies

Adams, Vernon R. *Tom White: The Life of a Lawman.* El Paso: Texas Western Press, 1972.

Arnold, Oren. *Savage Son*. Albuquerque: Univ. of New Mexico Press, 1951.

Ball, Eve. *Ma'am Jones of the Pecos*. Tucson: Univ. of Arizona Press, 1969.

————. *In the Days of Victoria: Recollections of a Warm Springs Apache.* Tucson: Univ. of Arizona Press, 1970.

Barker, Eugene C. *The Life of Stephen F. Austin.* Nashville: Cokesbury, 1925.

Bolton, Herbert E. *Coronado: Knight of Pueblos and Plains.* New York: Whittlesey House, 1949; also published as *Coronado on the Turquoise Trail: Knight of Pueblos and Plains.* Albuquerque: Univ. of New Mexico Press, 1949; rpt. 1964.

Burns, Walter Noble. *The Saga of Billy the Kid.* Garden City, Doubleday, Page, 1926.

Clum, Woodworth. *Apache Agent: The Story of John P. Clum.* Boston: Houghton Mifflin, 1936.

Coe, Wilbur. *Ranch on the Ruidoso: The Story of a Pioneer Family in New Mexico, 1871-1968.* New York: Knopf, 1968.

Cookridge, E. H. *The Baron of Arizona: The Great Twelve-Million-Acre Swindle.* New York: John Day, 1967.

Cotner, Robert C. *James Stephen Hogg: A Biography.* Austin: Univ. of Texas Press, 1959.

Crichton, Kyle S. *Law and Order Limited: The Life of Elfego Baca.* Santa Fe: New Mexican Publishing Co., 1928.

Crosby, Thelma, and Eve Ball. *Bob Crosby: World Champion Cowboy.* Clarendon: Clarendon Press, 1966.

Croy, Homer. *Trigger Marshal: The Story of Chris Madsen.* New York: Duell, Sloan and Pearce, 1958.

Dobie, J. Frank. *A Vaquero of the Brush Country.* Boston: Little, Brown, 1929.

Emmett, Chris. *Shanghai Pierce: A Fair Likeness.* Norman: Univ. of Oklahoma Press, 1953.

Frantz, Joe B. *Gail Borden, Dairyman to a Nation.* Norman: Univ. of Oklahoma Press, 1951.

Gambrell, Herbert P. *Mirabeau Buonaparte Lamar, Troubadour and Crusader.* Dallas: Southwest Press, 1934.

Gard, Wayne. *Sam Bass.* Boston: Houghton Mifflin, 1936.

Gentilz: Artist of the Old Southwest. Drawings and paintings by Theodore Gentilz. Text by Dorothy Steinbomer Kendall. Archival research by Carmen Perry. Austin: Univ. of Texas Press, 1974.

Gillmor, Frances. *Traders to the Navajos: The Story of the Weatherills of Kayenta.* Boston: Houghton Mifflin, 1934.

Glasscock, Lucille. *A Texas Wildcatter.* San Antonio: Naylor, 1952.

Haley, J. Evetts. *Charles Goodnight: Cowman and Plainsman.* Boston: Houghton Mifflin, 1936.

———. *Jeff Milton: A Good Man with a Gun.* Norman: Univ. of Oklahoma Press, 1948.

———. *Men of Fiber.* El Paso: Carl Hertzog, 1963.

———, ed. *Bill Oden: Early Days on the Texas-New Mexico Plains.* Canyon, Texas: Palo Dura Press, 1965.

Hallenbeck, Cleve. *The Journey of Fray Marcos de Niza.* Dallas: Univ. Press, 1949.

Hammond, George P. *Don Juan de Oñate and the Founding of New Mexico.* Santa Fe: El Palacio Press, 1927.

James, Marquis. *The Raven, The Life Story of Sam Houston.* Indianapolis: Bobbs, Merrill, 1929.

Klasner, Lily. *My Girlhood Among Outlaws.* Ed. Eve Ball. Tucson: Univ. of Arizona Press, 1972.

Krakel, Dean Fenton. *James Boren: A Study in Discipline.* Flagstaff, Arizona: Northland Press, 1968.

Lake, Stuart N. *Wyatt Earp, Frontier Marshal.* Boston: Houghton Mifflin, 1931.

Lee, Rebecca Smith. *Mary Austin Holley.* Austin: Univ. of Texas Press, 1962.

Lister, Florence C. and Robert H. Lister. *Earl Morris and Southwestern Archaeology.* Albuquerque: Univ. of New Mexico Press, 1968.

Marriott, Alice. *María: The Potter of San Ildefonso.* Norman: Univ. of Oklahoma Press, 1948.

Mathews, John J. *Life and Death of an Oilman: The Career of E. W. Marland.* Norman: Univ. of Oklahoma Press, 1951.

Means, Florence C. *Sagebrush Surgeon.* New York: Friendship Press, 1955.

Raymond, Dora N. *Captain Lee Hall of Texas.* Norman: Univ. of Oklahoma Press, 1940.

Richards, Colin. *Buckskin Frank Leslie: Gunman of Tombstone.* El Paso: Texas Western Press, 1964.

———. *How Pat Garrett Died.* Santa Fe: Palomino Press, 1970.

Scobee, Barry. *Nick Mersfelder: A Remarkable Man.* Fort Davis, Texas: Fort Davis Historical Society, 1969.

Seale, William. *Texas Riverman: The Life of Captain Andrew Smyth.* Austin: Univ. of Texas Press, 1966.

————. *Sam Houston's Wife: A Biography of Margaret Lea Houston.* Norman: Univ. of Oklahoma Press, 1970.

Simmons, Marc. *The Little Lion of the Southwest: A Life of Manuel Antonio Chaves.* Chicago: Swallow, 1973.

Sonnichsen, Charles L. *Roy Bean, Law West of the Pecos.* New York: Macmillan, 1943.

Thrapp, Dan L. *Al Sieber: Chief of Scouts.* Norman: Univ. of Oklahoma Press, 1964.

Tilghman, Zoe A. *Marshal of the Last Frontier.* Glendale: Arthur H. Clark, 1949.

————. *Quanah, The Eagle of the Comanches.* Oklahoma City: Harlow, 1938.

Tinkle, Lon. *Mr. De, a Biography of Everette Lee De Golyer.* New York: Little, Brown, 1970.

Udall, Louise. *Me and Mine: The Life Story of Helen Sekaquaptewa.* Tucson: Univ. of Arizona Press, 1969.

Warner, Louis H. *Archbishop Lamy: An Epoch Maker.* Santa Fe: New Mexican Publishing Co., 1936.

Waters, Frank. *The Earp Brothers of Tombstone.* New York: Clarkson N. Potter, 1960.

————. *To Possess the Land: A Biography of Arthur Rochford Manby.* Chicago: Swallow, 1973.

Autobiographies

Abbott, E. C., and Helena H. Smith. *We Pointed Them North.* New York: Farrar and Rinehart, 1939.

Banta, Albert F. *Albert F. Banta, Arizona Pioneer.* Albuquerque: Historical Society of New Mexico, 1953.

Barrett, S. M., ed. *Geronimo's Story of His Life.* New York: Duffield, 1906.

Bourke, John G. *On the Border with Crook.* New York: Scribner's 1891.

Bourne, Eulalia. *Woman in Levi's.* Tucson: Univ. of Arizona Press, 1967.

Briggs, L. Vernon. *Arizona and New Mexico 1882, California 1886, Mexico 1891.* New York: Argonaut, 1966.

Chrisman, Harry E. *Fifty Years on the Owl Hoot Trail: Jim Herron, The First Sheriff of No Man's Land, Oklahoma Territory.* Chicago: Swallow, 1969.

Cleaveland, Agnes M. *No Life for a Lady.* Boston: Houghton Mifflin, 1941.

Collins, Hubert E. *Warpath and Cattle Trail.* New York: Morrow, 1928.

Cook, James H. *Fifty Years on the Old Frontier.* New Haven: Yale Univ. Press, 1923.

Curry, George. *An Autobiography, 1861-1947.* ed. H. B. Hening. Albuquerque: Univ. of New Mexico Press, 1958.

Dixon, Olive K., ed. *Life and Adventures of Billy Dixon.* Dallas: P. L. Turner, 1927.

Dyk, Walter, ed. *Son of Old Man Hat: A Navajo Autobiography.* New York: Harcourt, Brace, 1938.

Fergusson, Harvey. *Home in the West: An Inquiry into My Origins.* New York: Duell, Sloan and Pearce, 1945.

French, William. *Some Recollections of a Western Ranchman.* London: Methuen, 1927.

Garrard, Lewis H. *Wah-to-Yah, and the Taos Trail.* Norman: Univ. of Oklahoma Press, 1950. First published Cincinnati: H. W. Derby, 1850.

Gustafson, A. M., ed. *John Spring's Arizona.* Tucson: Univ. of Arizona Press, 1966.

Hallenbeck, Cleve. *The Journey of Fray Marcos de Niza.* Dallas: University Press, 1949.

Hardin, John Wesley. *The Life of John Wesley Hardin.* Seguin, Texas: Smith and Moore, 1896.

Harkey, Daniel R. *Mean as Hell.* Albuquerque: Univ. of New Mexico Press, 1948.

Hoyt, Henry F. *A Frontier Doctor.* Boston: Houghton Mifflin, 1929.

Jackson, Ralph S. *Home on the Double Bayou: Memories of an East Texas Ranch.* Austin: Univ. of Texas Press, 1961.

James, Marquis. *The Cherokee Strip.* New York: Viking, 1945.

Jenkins, John H., ed. *Recollections of Early Texas: The Memoirs of John Holland Jenkins.* Austin: Univ. of Texas Press, 1958.

Jennings, Napoleon A. *A Texas Ranger.* Dallas: Southwest Press, 1930.

Linn, John J. *Reminiscences of Fifty Years in Texas.* Austin: Steck, 1936.

Luhan, Mabel D. *Edge of the Taos Desert: An Escape to Reality.* New York: Harcourt, Brace, 1937.

Magoffin, Susan Shelby. *Down the Santa Fe Trail and into Mexico.* New Haven: Yale Univ. Press, 1926.

Marcy, Randolph B. *Thirty Years of Army Life on the Border.* New York: Harper, 1866.

Mathews, John J. *Wah' Kon-Tah: The Osage and the White Man's Road.* Norman: Univ. of Oklahoma Press, 1932.

Matthews, Sallie Reynolds. *Interwoven: A Pioneer Chronicle.* Houston: Anson Jones, 1936. Rpt. El Paso: Carl Hertzog, 1958.

Maudsley, Robert. *Texas Sheepman.* Austin: Univ. of Texas Press, 1951.

Moore, Daniel G. *Log of a Twentieth Century Cowboy.* Tucson: Univ. of Arizona Press, 1965.

Moorman, Lewis J. *Pioneer Doctor.* Norman: Univ. of Oklahoma Press, 1951.

Myres, S. D., ed. *Pioneer Surveyor, Frontier Lawyer: The Personal Narrative of O. W. Williams.* El Paso: Texas Western Press, 1966.

Otero, Miguel A. *My Life on the Frontier.* In 2 vols. Vol. 1, New York: Press of the Pioneers, Inc., 1935. Vol. 2, Albuquerque: Univ. of New Mexico Press, 1939.

————. *My Nine Years As Governor of the Territory of New Mexico, 1897-1906.* Albuquerque: Univ. of New Mexico Press, 1940.

Owens, William A. *This Stubborn Soil.* New York: Scribner's, 1966.

————. *A Season of Weathering.* New York: Scribner's, 1973.

Rak, Mary K. *A Cowman's Wife.* Boston: Houghton Mifflin, 1934.

Simmons, Leo W., ed. *Sun Chief: Autobiography of a Hopi Indian.* New Haven: Yale Univ. Press, 1942.

Siringo, Charles A. *A Texas Cowboy.* New York: Sloan, 1950. First published Chicago: M. Umbdenstock, 1885.

Sloan, Richard E. *Memoirs of an Arizona Judge.* Stanford: Stanford Univ. Press, 1932.

Wallis, Jonnie Lockhart, comp. *Sixty Years on the Brazos; the Life and Letters of Dr. John Washington Lockhart 1824-1900.* Waco: Texian Press, 1967.

Wheeler, Homer W. *Buffalo Days: Forty Years in the Old West.* Indianapolis: Bobbs-Merrill, 1925.

White, Owen P. *The Autobiography of a Durable Sinner.* New York: Putnam, 1942.

Zuber, William Physick. *My Eighty Years in Texas.* Ed. Janis Boyle Mayfield. Notes and introduction by Llerena Friend. Austin: Univ. of Texas Press, 1971.

Robert J. Barnes
Lamar University

Literary History and Criticism

Arizona: A State Guide. New York: Hastings House, 1940.

Barns, Florence Elberta. *Texas Writers of Today.* Foreword by Robert Adger Law. Dallas: Tardy, 1935.

Bolton, Herbert E. *The Spanish Borderlands.* New Haven: Yale Univ. Press, 1921.

Boynton, Percy Holmes. *The Rediscovery of the Frontier.* Chicago: Univ. of Chicago Press, 1931.

Branch, Edward Douglas. *The Cowboy and His Interpreters.* New York: Appleton, 1926.

Burke, W. J., and Will D. Howe. *American Authors and Books.* New York: Grammercy, 1943.

Campbell, Walter S. *The Book Lovers' Southwest.* Norman: Univ. of Oklahoma Press, 1955.

Dobie, J. Frank. *Guide to Life and Literature of the Southwest.* Dallas: Southern Methodist Univ. Press, 1952.

Eagleton, Davis F. *Writers and Writings of Texas.* New York: Broadway Publishing Co., 1913.

Fergusson, Erna. *New Mexico.* New York: Knopf, 1951.

Gaston, Edwin W., Jr. *The Early Novel of the Southwest.* Albuquerque: Univ. of New Mexico Press, 1961.

Haslam, Gerald W., ed. *Western Writing.* Albuquerque: Univ. of New Mexico Press, 1974.

Johannsen, Albert. *The House of Beadle and Adams and Its Dime and Nickel Novels: The Story of a Vanished Literature.* Foreword by John T. McIntyre. 2 vols. Norman: Univ. of Oklahoma Press, 1950. Vol. 3, 1961.

Kazin, Alfred. *Bright Book of Life: American Novelists and Storytellers from Hemingway to Mailer.* Boston: Little, Brown, 1973.

Knickerbocker, K. L., and H. Willard Reninger. *Interpreting Literature.* New York: Holt, 1955.

Leisy, Ernest E. *The American Historical Novel.* Norman: Univ. of Oklahoma Press, 1950.

Major, Mabel, and T. M. Pearce. *Southwest Heritage.* Third ed., revised and enlarged. Albuquerque: Univ. of New Mexico Press, 1972. First edition (1938) and second revised and enlarged (1948) by Mabel Major, Rebecca W. Smith, and T. M. Pearce.

Marable, Mary, and Elaine Boylan. *A Handbook of Oklahoma Writers.* Norman: Univ. of Oklahoma Press, 1939.

New Mexico: A Guide to the Colorful State. New York: Hastings House, 1940.

Oklahoma: A Guide to the Sooner State. Norman: Univ. of Oklahoma Press, 1941.

Parrington, Vernon Louis. *Main Currents in American Thought.* 3 vols. in one. New York: Harcourt, Brace, 1930.

Payne, Leonidas Warren, Jr. *A Survey of Texas Literature.* New York: Rand McNally, 1928.

Pilkington, William T. *My Blood's Country: Studies in Southwestern Literature.* Fort Worth: Texas Christian Univ. Press, 1973.

Powell, Lawrence Clark. *Heart of the Southwest.* Los Angeles: Dawson's Book Shop, 1955.

————. *Books West Southwest.* Los Angeles: Ward Ritchie Press, 1957.

————. *Southwest Classics.* Los Angeles: Ward Ritchie Press, 1974.

Quinn, Arthur Hobson. *American Fiction: An Historical and Critical Survey.* New York: Appleton-Century, 1936.

————. *The Literature of the American People.* New York: Appleton-Century-Crofts, 1951.

Raines, Lester Courtney. *Writers and Writings of New Mexico.* Las Vegas: New Mexico Normal University, 1934. Mimeographed.

Richardson, Rupert Norval, and Carl Coke Rister. *The Greater Southwest.* Glendale: Arthur H. Clark, 1935.

Richardson, Rupert Norval. *Texas: The Lone Star State.* 2nd ed. Englewood Cliffs: Prentice-Hall, 1958.

Rogers, John Williams and J. Frank Dobie. *Finding Literature on the Texas Plains.* Dallas: Southwest Press, 1931.

Spiller, Robert E. and others, eds. *Literary History of the United States.* Rev. ed. in one vol. New York: Macmillan, 1953.

Texas: A Guide to the Lone Star State. New York: Hastings House, 1940.

Trent, William P. and others. *Cambridge History of American Literature.* Vol. 3. New York: Macmillan, 1933.

Tucker, Mary. *Books of the Southwest.* New York: J. J. Augustin, 1937.

Vestal, Stanley. *Short Grass Country.* New York: Duell Sloan and Pearce, 1941.

E. Hudson Long
Baylor University

Drama

Folk

Altman, George J. "The Yaqui Easter Play of Guadalupe, Arizona," *Masterkey*, 20 (1946), 181-89; 21 (1947), 19-23, 67-72.

Austin, Mary. "Native Drama in New Mexico," *Theatre Arts Monthly*, 13 (August 1929), 561-67.

————. "Folk Plays of the Southwest," *Theatre Arts Monthly*, 17 (August 1933), 599-610.

————. "Spanish Manuscripts of the Southwest," *Southwest Review*, 19 (July 1934), 402-09.

Bach, Marcus. "Los Pastores," *Theatre Arts Monthly*, 24 (April 1940), 283-88.

Barker, George C. "Some Aspects of Penitential Processions in Spain and in the American Southwest," *Journal of American Folk-Lore*, 70 (1957), 137-42.

————. *The Shepherds' Play of the Prodigal Son (Coloquio de pastores del hijo pródigo): A Folk Drama of Old Mexico*. Berkeley: Univ. of California Press, 1953. Folklore Studies, No. 2.

Bourke, John Gregory. "The Miracle Play of the Rio Grande," *Journal of American Folk-Lore*, 6 (1893), 89-95.

Brewer, Fred Meza. "Los Pastores, a Problem in Sources, Language, and Folk Theatre," *New Mexico Folklore Record*, 2 (1947-48), 46-57.

Campa, Arthur L. "Religious Spanish Folk Drama in New Mexico," *New Mexico Quarterly*, 2 (1932), 3-13.

————. "Spanish Religious Folktheatre in the Spanish Southwest (First Cycle)" *University of New Mexico Bulletin*, 5 (1934), 5-69.

————. "Spanish Religious Folktheatre in the Spanish Southwest (Second Cycle)," *University of New Mexico Bulletin*, 5 (1934), 5-155.

————. "The New Mexican Spanish Folktheater," *Southern Folklore Quarterly*, 5 (1941), 127-31.

Cole, M. R. *Los Pastores, A Mexican Play of the Nativity*. New York: Memoirs of the American Folk-Lore Society, Vol. IX, 1907.

Deering, Ivah E. "Los Pastores," *The Survey*, 67 (1931), 264-65.

Dorson, Richard M. *American Folklore*. Chicago: Univ. of Chicago Press, 1959.

————. *Buying the Wind: Regional Folklore in the United States*. Chicago:

Univ. of Chicago Press, 1964. Excerpt from *Pastorela,* pp. 466-79.

Ellis, Florence Hawley. "Passion Play in New Mexico," *New Mexico Quarterly,* 22 (1952), 200-12.

Englekirk, John E. "Notes on the Repertoire of the New Mexican Spanish Folktheater," *Southern Folklore Quarterly,* 4 (1940), 227-37.

———. "The Source and Dating of New Mexican Spanish Folk Plays," *Western Folklore,* 16 (1957), 232-55.

———. "The Passion Play in New Mexico," *Western Folklore,* 25 (1966) 17-33, 105-21.

Espinosa, Aurelio M., Jr. "The Fields of Spanish Folklore in America," *Southern Folklore Quarterly,* 5 (1941), 29-35.

Gillet, Joseph E. "Valencian 'misterios' and Mexican Missionary Plays in the Early Sixteenth Century," *Hispanic Review,* 19 (1951), 59-61.

Igo, John. *Los Pastores: An Annotated Bibliography with an Introduction.* San Antonio: College Library Publication, 1967.

Johnson, Winifred. "Early Theater in the Spanish Borderlands," *Mid-America,* 13 (October, 1931), 121-31.

[Lea] Lucero-White, Aurora. *Coloquios de los Pastores.* Santa Fe: Santa Fe Press, 1940.

———. *Literary Folklore of the Hispanic Southwest.* San Antonio: Naylor, 1953.

Martin, Charles B. *The Survivals of Medieval Religious Drama in New Mexico.* Unpubl. doctoral diss. Columbia: Univ. of Missouri, 1959. *DA,* 20, 3298-99.

McCrossan, Sister Joseph Marie. *The Role of the Church and the Folk in the Development of the Early Drama in New Mexico.* Philadelphia: Univ. of Pennsylvania Press, 1948.

Niggli, Josephine. *Mexican Folk Plays.* Chapel Hill: Univ. of North Carolina Press, 1938.

Painter, Muriel Thayer. *The Yaqui Easter Ceremony at Pascua.* Tucson: Chamber of Commerce, 1950.

Pearce, T. M. *"Los Moros y Los Cristianos:* Early American Play," *New Mexico Folklore Record,* 2 (1947-48), 58-65.

———. "Tracing a New Mexico Folk Play," *New Mexico Folklore Record,* IX (1954-55), 20-22.

———. "The New Mexican 'Shepherds' Play'," *Western Folklore,* 15 (1956), 77-88.

Place, Edwin B. "A Group of Mystery Plays Found in a Spanish-Speaking

Region of Southern Colorado," *University of Colorado Studies,* 18 (1930), 1-8.

Rael, Juan B. "More Light on the Origin of *Los Pastores,*" *New Mexico Folklore Record,* 6 (1951-52), 1-6.

————. *The Sources and Diffusion of the Mexican Shepherds' Plays.* Guadalajara, Mexico: Librería La Joyita, 1965.

Robe, Stanley L. *Coloquio de Pastores from Jalisco, Mexico.* Berkeley: Univ. of California Press, 1954. Folklore Studies, No. 4, 1954.

————. "The Relationship of *Los Pastores* to Other Spanish-American Folk Drama," *Western Folklore,* 16 (1957), 281-87.

Tully, Marjorie F., and Juan B. Rael. *An Annotated Bibliography of Spanish Folklore in New Mexico and Southern Colorado.* Albuquerque: Univ. of New Mexico Press, 1950.

Charles B. Martin
North Texas State University

Professional

Acheson, Sam, John William Rogers, and Kathleen Witherspoon. *Three Southwest Plays.* Dallas: Southwest Review, 1942.

Albertson, Vaughn S. "The Green Mask Players," [Houston]: *Southwest Review,* 16 (1930), 164-77.

Almaraz, Felix Diaz, Jr. *Standing Room Only: A History of the San Antonio Little Theatre, 1912-1962.* Waco: Texian Press, 1964.

Davis, Jackson. *A History of Professional Theatre in Dallas, Texas, 1920-1930.* Unpubl. doctoral diss. Baton Rouge: Louisiana State Univ., 1962. *DA,* 23, 4782-83.

Erhard, Thomas A. *Lynn Riggs, Southwest Playwright.* Austin: Steck-Vaughn, 1970.

Fletcher, Edward G. *The Beginnings of Professional Theatre in Texas.* Univ. of Texas Bulletin No. 3621 (June, 1936).

Jones, Margo. *Theatre-in-the-round.* New York: Rinehart, 1951.

King, C. Richard. *A History of the Theatre in Texas, 1722-1900.* Unpubl. doctoral diss. Waco: Baylor Univ. 1962.

Lawrence, D. H. "The Hopi Indian Snake Dance," *Theatre Arts Monthly,* 8 (December 1924), 836-60.

Major, Mabel, and T. M. Pearce. *Southwest Heritage, A Literary History with Bibliography.* Third ed. revised and enlarged. Albuquerque: Univ. of New Mexico Press, 1972. First edition (1938) and second edition, revised and enlarged (1948), by Mabel Major, Rebecca W. Smith, and T. M. Pearce.

Rogers, John William. "Drama of the Southwest," *Saturday Review of Literature,* 25 (May 16, 1942), 34.

Rosenfield, John. "10 Gallon Theatre," *Theatre Arts Monthly,* 37 (June 1953), 22-24.

Charles B. Martin
North Texas State University

Fiction

Pre-1918

Adams, Andy. "Western Interpreters," *Southwest Review,* 10 (October 1924), 70-74.

Agatha [Sheehan], Sister M. *Texas Prose Writings.* Dallas: Banks, Upshaw, 1936.

Arizona: A State Guide. New York: Hastings House, 1940.

Baker, Ernest Albert, and James Pachman. *A Guide to the Best Fiction.* New York: Macmillan, 1932.

Barns, Florence Elberta. *Texas Writers of Today.* Foreword by Robert Adger Law. Dallas: Tardy, 1935.

Boatright, Mody C. "The Beginnings of Cowboy Fiction," *Southwest Review,* 51 (Winter 1966), 11-28.

————. "The Formula in Cowboy Fiction and Drama," *Western Folklore,* 28 (April 1969), 136-45.

Boyer, Mary G. *Arizona in Literature: A Collection of the Best Writings of Arizona Authors from Early Spanish Days to the Present Time.* Glendale:: Arthur H. Clark, 1935.

Branch, Edward Douglas. *The Cowboy and His Interpreters.* New York: Appleton, 1926.

Campbell, Walter S. *The Book Lover's Southwest: A Guide to Good Reading.* Norman: Univ. of Oklahoma Press, 1955.

Dobie, J. Frank. *Guide to Life and Literature of the Southwest.* Rev. ed. Dallas: Southern Methodist Univ. Press, 1952.

Durham, Philip. "Riders of the Plains: American Westerns," *Neuphilologische Mitteilungen,* 58 (1957), 22-38.

Dykes, J. C. "Dime Novel Texas; or, the Sub-Literature of the Lone Star State," *The Southwestern Historical Quarterly,* 49 (January 1946), 327-40.

Eagleton, Davis F. *Writers and Writings of Texas.* New York: Broadway, 1913.

Folsom, James K. *The American Western Novel.* New Haven: College and University Press, 1966.

French, Warren. "The Cowboy in the Dime Novel," *The University of Texas Studies in English,* 30 (1951), 219-34.

Gaston, Edwin W., Jr. *The Early Novel of the Southwest.* Albuquerque: Univ. of New Mexico Press, 1961.

Ghodes, Clarence. "The Earliest Description of 'Western' Fiction?" *American Literature,* 37 (March 1965), 70-71.

Harkness, David J. *The Southwest and West Coast in Literature.* Knoxville: Univ. of Tennessee Press, 1954.

Harvey, Charles M. "The Dime Novel in American Life," *Atlantic,* 100 (July 1907), 37-45.

Hutchinson, W. H. "The Western Story as Literature," *Western Humanities Review,* 3 (January 1949), 33-37.

Johannsen, Albert. *The House of Beadle and Adams and Its Dime and Nickel Novels: The Story of a Vanished Literature.* Foreword by John T. McIntyre. 2 vols. Norman: Univ. of Oklahoma Press, 1950. Vol. 3, 1961.

Lee, Robert Edson. *From West to East: Studies in the Literature of the American West.* Urbana: Univ. of Illinois Press, 1966.

Leisy, Ernest E. *The American Historical Novel.* Norman: Univ. of Oklahoma Press, 1950.

Leithead, J. Edward. "Legendary Heroes and the Dime Novel," *American Book Collector,* 18 (March 1968) 22-27.

Major, Mabel, and T. M. Pearce. *Southwest Heritage.* Third edition, revised and enlarged. Albuquerque: Univ. of New Mexico Press, 1972. First edition (1938) and second edition, revised and enlarged (1948), by Mabel Major, Rebecca W. Smith, and T. M. Pearce.

Major, Mabel, and Rebecca Smith. *The Southwest in Literature.* New York: Macmillan, 1929.

Marable, Mary, and Elaine Boylan. *A Handbook of Oklahoma Writers.* Norman: Univ. of Oklahoma Press, 1939.

Milton, John R. "The Western Novel: Sources and Forms," *Chicago Review,* 16 (Summer 1963), 74-100.

138   *Southwestern American Literature*

New Mexico: A Guide to the Colorful State. New York: Hastings House, 1940.

Oklahoma: A Guide to the Sooner State. Norman: Univ. of Oklahoma Press, 1941.

Payne, Leonidas Warren, Jr. *A Survey of Texas Literature.* New York: Rand McNally, 1928.

Pearce, Thomas M., and Telfair Hendon, eds. *America in the Southwest: A Regional Anthology.* Albuquerque: Univ. of New Mexico Press, 1933.

––––––, and A. P. Thomason, eds. *Southwesterners Write.* Albuquerque: Univ. of New Mexico Press, 1947.

Perry, George Sessions, ed. *Roundup Time: A Collection of Southwestern Writing.* New York: Whittlesey House, 1943.

Peterson, Levi S. "The Primitive and the Civilized in Western Fiction," *Western American Literature,* 1 (Fall 1966), 197-207.

Powell, Lawrence Clark. *Books West Southwest.* Los Angeles: Ward Ritchie, 1957.

––––––. *Heart of the Southwest.* Los Angeles: Dawson's Book Shop, 1955.

Rader, Jesse. *South of Forty.* Norman: Univ. of Oklahoma Press, 1947.

Raines, C. W. *A Bibliography of Texas.* Rev. ed. Austin: Gammel, 1896. Rpt., 1934.

Saunders, Lyle. *Guide to the Literature of the Southwest.* Albuquerque: Univ. of New Mexico Press, 1952.

––––––. *A Guide to Materials Bearing on Cultural Relations in New Mexico.* Albuquerque: Univ. of New Mexico Press, 1944.

Smith, Henry Nash. *Virgin Land: The American West as Symbol and Myth.* Cambridge: Harvard Univ. Press, 1950.

––––––. "The Western Hero in the Dime Novel," *Southwest Review,* (Summer 1948), 276-84.

Smith, Rebecca W. "The Southwest in Fiction," *Saturday Review of Literature,* 25 (May 16, 1942), 12-13, 37.

Streeter, Thomas W. *Bibliography of Texas, 1795-1845.* 5 vols. Cambridge: Harvard Univ. Press, 1955-60.

Texas: A Guide to the Lone Star State. New York: Hastings House, 1940. Rev. ed., 1969.

Tucker, Mary. *Books of the Southwest.* New York: J. J. Augustin, 1937.

Walker, Don D. "The Mountain Man as Literary Hero," *Western American Literature,* 1 (Spring 1966), 15-25.

Walker, Franklin. *A Literary History of Southern California.* Berkeley:

Univ. of California Press, 1950.

Webb, Walter Prescott, and others, eds. *The Handbook of Texas.* 2 vols. Austin: Texas State Historical Association, 1952.

Westbrook, Max. "The Themes of Western Fiction," *Southwest Review,* 43 Summer 1958), 232-38.

Edwin W. Gaston, Jr.

Stephen F. Austin State University

Post-1918

Agatha [Sheehan], Sister M. *Texas Prose Writings.* Dallas: Banks, Upshaw, 1936.

Campbell, Walter S. *The Book Lover's Southwest: A Guide to Good Reading.* Norman: Univ. of Oklahoma Press, 1955.

Dobie, J. Frank. *Guide to Life and Literature of the Southwest.* Rev. ed. Dallas: Southern Methodist Univ. Press, 1952.

Etulain, Richard W. "Recent Western Fiction," *Journal of the West,* 8 (October 1969), 656-58.

Folsom, James K. *The American Western Novel.* New Haven: College and University Press, 1966.

Gaston, Edwin W., Jr. *The Early Novel of the Southwest.* Albuquerque: Univ. of New Mexico Press, 1961.

Goodwyn, Larry. "The Frontier Myth and Southwestern Literature," *American Libraries,* 2 (February 1971), 161-67, and 2 (April 1971), 359-66.

Kurtz, Kenneth. *Literature of the American Southwest: A Selective Bibliography.* Los Angeles: Occidental College, 1956.

Major, Mabel, and T. M. Pearce. *Southwest Heritage: A Literary History with Bibliography.* Third ed., revised and enlarged. Albuquerque: Univ. of New Mexico Press, 1972. First edition (1938) and second edition, revised and enlarged (1948), by Mabel Major, Rebecca W. Smith, and T. M. Pearce.

Marable, Mary Hays, and Elaine Boylan. *A Handbook of Oklahoma Writers.* Norman: Univ. of Oklahoma Press, 1938.

Milton, John R. "The American West: A Challenge to the Literary Imagination," *Western American Literature,* 1 (Winter 1967), 267-84.

Peterson, Levi S. "The Primitive and the Civilized in Western Fiction," *Western American Literature,* 1 (Fall 1966), 197-207.

Pilkington, William T. "The Recent Southwestern Novel," *Southwestern American Literature,* 1 (January 1971), 12-15.

————. *My Blood's Country: Studies in Southwestern Literature.* Fort Worth: Texas Christian Univ. Press, 1973.

Powell, Lawrence Clark. "Heart of the Southwest: A Selective Reading List of Good Novels and Stories with Settings in Arizona and New Mexico," *Arizona Highways,* 33 (February 1957), 4-13.

Robinson, Cecil. *With the Ears of Strangers: The Mexican in American Literature.* Tucson: Univ. of Arizona Press, 1963.

Sonnichsen, C. L. "The New Style Western," *South Dakota Review,* 4 (Summer 1966), 22-28.

————. "The Sharecropper Novel in the Southwest," *Agricultural History,* 43 (April 1969), 249-58.

William T. Pilkington
Tarleton State University

Humor

Boatright, Mody M. *Folk Laughter on the American Frontier.* New York: Macmillan, 1949.

Campbell, Walter S. "Humor," *The Book Lover's Southwest: A Guide to Good Reading.* Norman: Univ. of Oklahoma Press, 1955. Pp. 198-202.

Cohen, Hennig, and William B. Dillingham. *Humor of the Old Southwest.* Boston: Houghton Mifflin, 1964.

DeVoto, Bernard. "Preface," *A Treasury of Western Folklore.* Ed. B. A. Botkin. New York: Crown, 1961.

Dobie, J. Frank. "Introduction," *Sam Slick in Texas.* By W. Stanley Hoole. San Antonio: Naylor, 1947.

————. "Backwoods Life and Humor," *Guide to Life and Literature of the Southwest.* Rev. ed. Dallas: Southern Methodist Univ. Press, 1952. pp. 45-49.

Hoig, Stan. *The Humor of the American Cowboy.* Lincoln: Univ. of Nebraska Press, 1958. Rpt., 1970.

Miles, Elton. *Southwest Humorists.* Austin: Steck-Vaughn, 1969.

Elton Miles
Sul Ross State University

Poetry

General

Anthologies

Armstrong, Virginia Irving, comp. *I Have Spoken: American History Through the Voices of the Indians.* Chicago: Swallow, 1971.

Astrov, Margot, ed. *American Indian Prose and Poetry: An Anthology.* New York: Capricorn Books, 1962. Originally published in 1946 as *The Winged Serpent.*

Baldwin, Jo Gwyn, ed. *Southwestern Mosaics.* El Paso: Boots and Saddle Press, 1969.

Bierhorst, John, ed. *In the Trail of the Wind: American Indian Poems and Ritual Orations.* New York: Farrar, Straus, and Giroux, 1971.

Brandon, William, ed. *The Magic World: American Indian Songs and Poems.* New York: Morrow, 1971.

Cronyn, George W., ed. *American Indian Poetry.* Introduction by Mary Austin. New York: Liveright, 1934, 1962. Originally published in 1918 by Boni and Liveright as *The Path of the Rainbow.*

McLuhan, T. C., ed. *Touch the Earth: A Self Portrait of Indian Existence.* New York: Outerbridge and Diesentfrey, 1971.

Major, Mabel, and T. M. Pearce, eds. *Signature of the Sun: Southwest Verse, 1900-1950.* Albuquerque: Univ. of New Mexico Press, 1950.

Rothenberg, Jerome, ed. *Shaking the Pumpkin: Traditional Poetry of the Indian North Americas.* New York: Doubleday, 1972.

Sanders, Thomas E., and Walter W. Peek, eds. *Literature of the American Indian.* Beverly Hills: Glencoe Press, 1973.

Shockley, Martin, ed. *Southwest Writers Anthology.* Austin: Steck-Vaughn, 1967.

Stevens, Pearl Moore, ed. *Southwestern Anthology of Verse.* San Antonio: Naylor, 1941.

Taylor, J. Golden, ed. *The Literature of the American West.* Boston: Houghton Mifflin, 1971.

Turner, Frederick W. III, ed. *The Portable North American Indian Reader.* New York: Viking, 1973.

Arizona

Anthologies

Boyer, Mary G., ed. *Arizona in Literature.* Glendale, California: Arthur H. Clark, 1935.

142   *Southwestern American Literature*

Quick, James E., ed. *Poetry of the Desert Southwest.* Phoenix: Baleen
    Press, 1972.
Stevens, A. Wilber, ed. *Poems Southwest.* Prescott, Arizona: Prescott Col-
    lege, 1968.
Winslow Literary Society, comp. *Shifting Sands.* Winslow, Arizona: The
    Society, 1948.

Magazines

Changes. Edited by Barent Gjelsness. Bisbee, Arizona.
Inscape. Edited by Joe M. Ferguson, Jr. Phoenix, Arizona.
Ironwood. Edited by Michael Cuddihy. Tucson, Arizona.
Midwest Chapparal. Edited by M. N. Dewey. Tucson, Arizona. 1949.
Sandcutters. Edited by Genevieve Sargent. Phoenix, Arizona. Quarterly
    publication of the Arizona State Poetry Society. 1966.
Sun Tracks. Poetry edited by Carol Kirk. Tucson, Arizona. Quarterly pub-
    lication devoted to American Indian.

Societies

Arizona State Poetry Society. Quarterly publication *Sandcutters* since 1966.
    Anthologies: *Ballet on the Wind* (1969) and *Sing, Naked Spirit* (1970).

New Mexico

Anthologies

Fitzpatrick, George, ed. *Poems of New Mexico.* Santa Fe, New Mexico:
    New Mexico Magazine, 1936.
Henderson, Alice Corbin, ed. *The Turquoise Trail: An Anthology of New
    Mexico Poetry.* Boston: Houghton Mifflin, 1928.

Magazines

Deer and Dachshund. Ranches of Taos, New Mexico. 1952. Irregular.
Encore. Edited by Alice Briley. Albuquerque. 1966. Quarterly.
Desert Review. Edited by Terry Abbott. Santa Fe. Irregular.
Gale. Arroyo Hondo, New Mexico. 1949. Monthly.
Heritage, Llano Estacada. Edited by J. L. Burke. Hobbs, New Mexico.
Ninth Circle. Edited by P. R. Morgan. Las Cruces, New Mexico. 1966.
Outcast. Edited by Jean and Veryl Rosenbaum. Santa Fe. Quarterly.
SCTH/Sonnet, Cinquain, Tanka, Haiku. Edited by Rhoda DeLong Jewell.
    El Rito, New Mexico. 1964. Quarterly.

Societies

New Mexico Poetry Society. Yearbook in 1971; bulletins since 1969.

Oklahoma

Anthologies

Botkin, Benjamin, ed. *The Southwest Scene: An Anthology of Regional Verse.* Oklahoma City: Economy, 1931.

Conner, Mrs. A. C., ed. *An Anthology of Poetry by Oklahoma Writers.* Guthrie, Oklahoma: Cooperative Publishing, 1935.

Paxton, Joseph Francis, ed. *The Oklahoma Anthology for 1929.* Norman: Univ. of Oklahoma Press, 1929.

Poetry Society of Oklahoma. *Oklahoma Silver Jubilee Anthology, 25th Year 1934-1959.* Oklahoma City: Northwest Publishing, 1959.

Rossman, George, and Bess Truitt, eds. *The Red Earth.* 3 vols. Oklahoma City: n. p., 1944-46.

Magazines

Cimarron Review. Published by Oklahoma State University. Stillwater. 1967.

Nimrod. Published by the University of Tulsa. Tulsa. 1957.

Red Earth Poetry Magazine. Edited by George Rossman. Oklahoma City. 1944. Bi-monthly.

Seven. Edited by James Neill Northe. Oklahoma City. 1957. Irregular.

Societies

Oklahoma Poetry Society. Yearbooks since 1944; bulletins since 1951. *State Anthology* (1936).

Texas

Anthologies

Allan, Frances D., comp. *Lone Star Ballads.* Galveston: J. D. Sawyer, 1874.

Beaty, John O., L. W. Payne, Rebecca W. Smith, and W. H. Vann, comps. *Texas Poets.* Dallas: Dealey and Lowe, 1936.

Border Poets. *Cantando.* Dallas: Kaleidograph, 1939.

Boyle, Lois, ed. *Texas Legacy: An Anthology of Texas Poetry.* San Antonio: Naylor, 1935.

Bushby, D. Maitland, ed. *The Golden Stallion: An Anthology of Poems Concerning the Southwest and Written by Representative Southwestern Poets.* Dallas: Southwest Press, 1930.

Dixon, Samuel Houston, comp. *Poets and Poetry of Texas: Biographical Sketches of the Poets of Texas, with Selections from Their Writings.* Austin: Sam H. Dixon, 1885.

Eagleton, Davis Foute. *Texas Literature Reader.* Dallas: Southern, 1916.

Edwards, Margaret Royalty. *Poets Laureate of Texas.* San Antonio: Naylor, 1956. Rev. ed., 1966.

Graham, Philip, ed. *Early Texas Verse.* Austin: Steck, 1936.

Greer, Hilton Ross, ed. *Voices of the Southwest.* New York: Macmillan, 1923.

————, and Florence Elberta Barns, eds. *New Voices of the Southwest.* Dallas: Tardy, 1934.

Harrison, Henry, ed. *Texas Poets.* New York: Henry Harrison, 1936.

Lorraine, Lilith, ed. *Avalon Anthology of Texas Poets.* Corpus Christi: Different Press, 1963.

Montgomery, Vaida Stewart, comp. *A Century with Texas Poets and Poetry.* Dallas: Kaleidograph, 1934.

Montgomery, Whitney, ed. *The Road to Texas.* Dallas: Kaleidograph, 1940.

Morris, Marjorie, ed. *Surf, Stars, and Stone: An Anthology of Texas Verse.* Dallas: Royal, 1961.

Oliphant, Dave, ed. *The New Breed: An Anthology of Texas Poets.* Denmark, South Carolina: Prickley Pear Press, 1973.

Parker, Elsie Smith, and Miriam G. Beaird, eds. *Southwestern Anthology.* Dallas: American Poetry Association, 1937.

Magazines

The Bard, A Comrade of the Young Poet. Edited by C. O. Gill. Dallas. January, 1922, to April, 1924. 19 issues.

The Buccaneer, A Journal of Poetry. Edited by William Russell Clark and (later) Dawson Powell. Dallas. September, 1924, to 1926. 13 issues.

Cycle. Houston. 1935. Quarterly.

*Cyclo*Flame.* Edited by Vernon Payne. San Angelo, Texas. 1963. Quarterly, 1963-69; annual after 1969.

Different: The Voice of the Cultural Renaissance. Edited by Lilith Lorraine. Dallas. 1945.

Flame. Edited by Lilith Lorraine. Alpine, Texas. 1960. Quarterly.

The Harlequinade. Edited by Franz A. Finsberg. Abilene, Texas. October, 1929-Spring, 1931. Quarterly. 13 issues.

Kaleidograph: A National Magazine of Poetry. Edited by Whitney and Vaida Stewart Montgomery. Dallas. May, 1929-June, 1959. Monthly from May, 1929, through June, 1954; quarterly from July, 1954, through June, 1959.

Penny Poems from Midwestern University (formerly *Penny Poems from Amarillo College*). Wichita Falls, Texas. 1964. Irregular.

Quetzal. Edited by Randall W. Ackley. Abilene, Texas; later Pembroke, North Carolina. Spring, 1970. Three times a year.

Quicksilver: A Quarterly Magazine of Poetry. Edited by Grace Ross and Mabel M. Kuykendall. Fort Worth. 1948.

RE: Arts and Letters. Edited by Edwin W. Gaston, Jr. and (later) by Stanley Alexander. Published by the School of Liberal Arts of Stephen F. Austin State University. 1968. Twice a year.

Southwester. Edited by Jane Bailey Fitzgerald. Dallas. 1937-38. Monthly.

The Torch Bearer: A Magazine for the Coming Writers of Texas. Edited by William H. Vann. Belton, Texas. 1928-31. Quarterly. 12 issues.

Societies

Texas Poetry Society. Yearbooks since 1922; monthly bulletins. Book publication awards: *White Fire* (1925) by Grace Noll Crowell; *The Singing Heart* (1926) by Margaret Bell Houston; *The Death of a Buccaneer* (1927) by Stanley E. Babb; *Stardust and Stone* (1928) by Glen Ward Dresbach; *Black Poppies* (1929) by Jan Isbelle Fortune; *Winds of the Morning* (1930) by Hazel Harper Harris; *Arrow Unspent* (1931) by Patrick D. Moreland; *I Keep a Rainbow* (1932) by Lexie Dean Robertson; *A Little Flame Blown* (1933) by William E. Bard.

Alice Briley
Albuquerque

James E. Quick
Arizona State University

Arthur M. Sampley
North Texas State University

Winston Weathers
University of Tulsa

Juveniles

Works About

Campbell, Walter S. "Juveniles," *The Book Lover's Southwest: A Guide to Good Reading.* Norman: Univ. of Oklahoma Press, 1955. Pp. 203-13.

Harrington, Mildred P., ed. *The Southwest in Children's Books.* Baton Rouge: Louisiana State Univ. Press, 1952.

Major, Mabel, and T. M. Pearce. *Southwest Heritage: A Literary History with Bibliography.* Third ed., revised and enlarged. Albuquerque: Univ. of New Mexico Press, 1972. First edition (1938) and second edition, revised and enlarged (1948), by Mabel Major, Rebecca W. Smith, and T. M. Pearce.

"Southwestern Literature and Culture in the English Classroom," *Arizona English Bulletin,* 13 (April 1971), 1-118.

Representative Examples

Abbott, John Stevens Cabot. *Christopher Carson, Known as Kit Carson.* New York: Dodd, Mead, 1901.

————. *David Crockett and Early Texan History.* New York: Dodd, Mead, 1906.

————. *Kit Carson, the Pioneer of the Far West.* New York: Dodd, Mead. 1929.

Abeita, Louise. *I Am a Pueblo Indian Girl.* New York: Morrow, 1929.

Adams, Andy. *Wells Brothers, the Young Cattle Kings.* Boston: Houghton Mifflin, 1911.

————. *Ranch on the Beaver.* Boston: Houghton Mifflin, 1927.

Adams, Samuel H. *The Santa Fe Trail.* Eau Claire: E. M. Hale, 1952.

Alexander, Frances. *Mother Goose on the Rio Grande.* Skokie, Illinois: Banks, Upshaw, 1944.

Allen, Allyn (pseud.). *Real Book about the Texas Rangers.* Garden City, New York: Doubleday, 1952.

Allen, Edward. *Heroes of Texas.* New York: Julian Messner, 1970.

Altsheler, Joseph Alexander. *Herald of the West.* New York: Appleton, 1898.

————. *Apache Gold.* New York: Appleton-Century, 1913.

————. *Romance of the San Jacinto Campaign.* Des Moines: Appleton-Century-Crofts, 1913. Rpt., 1952.

————. *The Texas Scouts: A Story of the Alamo and of Goliad.* Des Moines: Appleton-Century-Crofts, 1913. Rpt., 1952.

————. *Horseman of the Plains.* New York: Macmillan, 1926.

————. *The Texan Star.* New York: Appleton-Century-Crofts, 1952.

American Heritage, eds. *Cowboys and Cattle Country.* New York: Harper & Row, 1961.

————. *Texas and the War with Mexico.* San Carlos, California: Golden Press, 1961.

Anglund, Joan Walsh. *The Brave Cowboy.* New York: Harcourt, Brace and World, 1959.

———. *Cowboy and His Friends.* New York: Harcourt, Brace and World, 1961.

———. *Cowboy's Secret Life.* New York: Harcourt, Brace and World, 1963.

Applegate, Frank G. *Native Tales of New Mexico.* Philadelphia: Lippincott, 1932.

Armer, Laura (Adams). *Waterless Mountain.* New York: Longmans, Green, 1931.

———. *Dark Circle of Branches.* New York: Longmans, Green 1933.

Association for Childhood Education International. *Told under the Stars and Stripes.* New York: Macmillan, 1945.

Austin, Mary. *The Children Sing in the Far West.* Boston: Houghton Mifflin, 1928.

Bailey, Mrs. Bernadine (Freeman). *Picture Book of Colorado.* Toronto: George F. McLeod, 1950.

———. *Picture Book of Texas.* Chicago: Albert Whitman, 1950.

———. *Picture Book of Oklahoma.* Chicago: Albert Whitman, 1952.

Bailey, Jean. *Cherokee Bill, Oklahoma Pacer.* New York: Abingdon-Cokesbury, 1952.

Baker, Betty. *The Shaman's Last Stand.* New York: Harper & Row, 1963.

Baker, Charlotte. *Necessary Nellie.* New York: Coward-McCann, 1945.

———. *Nellie and the Mayor's Hat.* New York: Coward-McCann, 1947.

———. *Green Poodles.* New York: McKay, 1956.

Baker, Elizabeth Whitemore. *Stocky, Boy of West Texas.* New York: John C. Winston, 1945.

Baker, Karle Wilson. *Texas Flag Primer.* Cleveland: World, 1925.

———. *Two Little Texans.* Cleveland: World, 1932.

Baker, Olaf. *Dusty Star.* New York: Dodd, Mead, 1922.

———. *Panther Magic.* New York: Dodd, Mead, 1928.

———. *Thunder Boy.* New York: Dodd, Mead, 1929.

———. *Shasta of the Wolves.* New York: Dodd, Mead, 1930.

Ball, Zachary (pseud.). *North to Abilene.* New York: Holiday House, 1960.

Barker, Eugene Campbell. *The Father of Texas.* Dallas: Southwest Press, 1925. Rpt., Indianapolis: Bobbs-Merrill, 1935.

Barnes, Nancy. *The Wonderful Year.* New York: Simon & Schuster, 1946.

Barr, Jene. *Texas Pete, Little Cowboy.* Chicago: Albert Whitman, 1950.

Barron, E. *Child's History of Texas.* San Antonio: Naylor, 1936.

Baylor, Frances Courtenay. *Juan and Juanita.* Boston: Houghton Mifflin, 1926.

Beebe, Burdetta Faye. *Coyote, Come Home.* New York: McKay, 1963.
Behn, Harry. *The Painted Cave.* New York: Harcourt, Brace and World, 1957.
Beim, Lorraine, and Jerrold. *The Burro that Had a Name.* New York: Harcourt, Brace and World, 1939.
Bendbow, Hesper (pseud. for George W. Archer). *More than She Could Bear: A Story of the Gachupin War in Texas, A. D. 1812-1813.* Philadelphia: Claxton, Remsen and Haffelfinger, 1872.
Bennett, Emerson. *Viola; or, Adventures in the Far South West.* Philadelphia: T. B. Peterson, 1852.
Benton, Jesse James. *Cow by the Tail.* Boston: Houghton Mifflin, 1943.
Berryman, Opal Leigh. *Pioneer Preacher.* New York: Crown, 1948.
Bishop, C. K. *Stout Rider.* Austin: Steck-Vaughn, 1953.
———. *First Texas Ranger: Jack Hays.* New York: Messner, 1959.
———. *Lone Star Leader: Sam Houston.* New York: Messner, 1961.
Blair, Walter. *Davy Crockett, Frontier Hero.* New York: Coward-McCann, 1955.
Bleeker, Sonia. *Horsemen of the Western Plateau.* New York: Morrow, 1957.
———. *The Navajo: Herders, Weavers and Silversmiths.* New York: Putman, 1961.
Bloch, M. H. *Tony of the Ghost Town.* New York: Coward-McCann, 1956.
Boehmer, Robert. *Trail to Santa Fe.* Chicago: Encyclopaedia Britannica, 1963.
Bogan, Samuel D. *Let the Coyote Howl.* New York: Putnam, 1946.
Booker, Jim. *Trail to Oklahoma.* Nashville: Broadman Press, 1959.
Bosworth, Allan R. *Wherever the Grass Grows.* Garden City: Doubleday, 1941.
———. *Cabin in the Hills.* Garden City: Doubleday, 1947.
———. *Hang and Rattle.* Garden City: Doubleday, 1947.
———. *Sancho of the Long, Long Horns.* Garden City: Doubleday, 1947.
———. *Bury Me Not.* Garden City: Doubleday, 1948.
Bracken, Dorothy Kendall. *Doak Walker; Three Times All-American.* Austin: Steck-Vaughn, 1950.
Britt, Henry Albert. *The Boy's Own Book of Frontiersmen.* New York: Macmillan, 1924.
Bronson, Wilfrid Swancourt. *Coyotes.* New York: Harcourt, Brace and World, 1946.

――――. *Pinto's Journey.* New York: Messner, 1948.

Brooks, Noah. *Boy Emigrants.* New York: Scribner's, 1914.

Brown, John Henry. *Life and Times of Henry Smith.* Austin: Steck-Vaughn, 1935. Fascimile of 1887 ed.

Buff, Mary. *Dancing Cloud, the Navajo Boy.* New York: Viking, 1937.

Campbell, Camilla. *Star Mountain and other Legends.* New York: McGraw-Hill, 1946.

――――. *Bartletts of Box B Ranch.* New York: McGraw-Hill, 1949.

Cannon, Cornelia (James). *The Pueblo Boy: A Story of Coronado's Search for the Seven Cities of Cibola.* Boston: Houghton Mifflin, 1926.

――――. *Pueblo Girl, the Story of Coronado on the Rio Grande.* Boston: Houghton Mifflin, 1930.

――――. *Fight for the Pueblo; the Story of Onate's Expedition and the Founding of Santa Fe.* Boston: Houghton Mifflin, 1934.

Carpenter, Allan. *Enchantment of America: Arizona.* Chicago: Children's Press, 1964.

――――. *Enchantment of America: Oklahoma.* Chicago: Children's Press, 1965.

――――. *Enchantment of America: Texas.* Chicago: Children's Press, 1965.

Carroll, Curt (pseud.). *Golden Herd.* New York: Morrow, 1950.

――――. *San Jacinto.* Austin: Steck-Vaughn, 1957.

Castor, Henry. *The First Book of the War with Mexico.* New York: Franklin Watts, 1964.

Caudle, Robert Emmet. *West of the Sabine.* San Antonio: Naylor, 1940.

Chamberlain, James Franklin. *North America.* London: Macmillan, 1927.

Champney, (Mrs.) Elizabeth Williams. *Great-Grandmother, Girl in New Mexico, 1670-1680.* Boston: Estes and Lauriot, 1888.

Chastian, Madge Lee. *Loblolly Farm.* New York: Harcourt, Brace and World, 1950.

Cheavens, Frank. *Arrow Lie Still.* Dallas: Story Book Press, 1950.

Cheavens, Martha Louise. *Crosswinds.* Boston: Houghton Mifflin, 1948.

Christensen, Gardell Dano. *Buffalo Kill.* New York: Thomas Nelson, 1959.

――――. *Buffalo Horse.* New York: Thomas Nelson, 1961.

Church, Margaret (Pond). *Burro of Angelitos.* New York: Holt, 1936.

Clark, Ann Nolan. *Child's Story of New Mexico.* Albuquerque: Univ. of New Mexico Press, 1941.

――――. *In My Mother's House.* New York: Viking, 1941.

――――. *Little Navajo Bluebird.* New York: Viking, 1943.

————. *Blue Canyon Horse.* New York: Viking, 1954.

————. *The Desert People.* New York: Viking, 1962.

————. *Paco's Miracle.* New York: Farrar, Straus, 1962.

————. *Medicine Man's Daughter.* New York: Farrar, Straus, 1963.

————. *Tia Maria's Garden.* New York: Viking, 1963.

Clark, Idena McFadin. *Little Dude.* New York: Ariel Books, 1952.

Clark, Joseph Lynn and Dorothy A. Linder. *Story of Texas.* Boston: Heath, 1955.

Clemens, Jeremiah. *Mustang Gray: A Romance.* Philadelphia: Lippincott, 1858.

Coatsworth, Elizabeth J. *Old Whirlwind; a Story of Davy Crockett.* New York: Macmillan, 1953.

Coe, Fanny E. *Makers of the Nation.* London: Macmillan, 1930.

Collin, Hedvig. *Nils, Globetrotter.* New York: Viking, 1957.

Constant, Alberta Wilson. *Miss Charity Comes to Stay.* New York: Crowell, 1959.

Coolidge, Dane. *Silver and Gold.* New York: Dutton, 1919.

————. *Wunpost.* New York: Dutton, 1920.

————. *Fighting Fool.* Indianapolis: Bobbs-Merrill, 1922.

————. *Man Killers.* Indianapolis: Bobbs-Merrill, 1922.

————. *Lost Wagons.* New York: Dutton, 1923.

————. *Lorenzo the Magnificent.* New York: Dutton, 1925.

————. *Not-afraid.* New York: Dutton, 1926.

————. *Scalp-lock.* Indianapolis: Bobbs-Merrill, 1926.

————. *Under the Sun.* New York: Dutton, 1926.

————. *Desert Trail.* New York: Grosset & Dunlap, 1927.

————. *Rimrock Jones.* New York: Grosset & Dunlap, 1927

————. *Shadow Mountain.* New York: Grosset & Dunlap, 1927.

————. *Texas Cowboys.* New York: Dutton, 1937.

Cousins, Margaret. *We Were There at the Battle of the Alamo.* New York: Grosset & Dunlap, 1958.

Craig, Martha and M. S. Carter. *Texas Under Six Flags.* Dallas: Southwest Press, 1935.

Crownfield, Gertrude. *Lone Star Rising.* New York: Crowell, 1940.

Crump, Irving. *Boys' Book of Cowboys.* New York: Dodd, Mead, 1934.

Cumming, Marian. *All about Marjory.* New York: Harcourt, Brace and World, 1950.

Daugherty, James. *Daniel Boone.* New York: Viking, 1939.

Davis, Julia. *Ride with the Eagle.* New York: Harcourt, Brace and World, 1962.

Davis, Russell G., and Brent K. Ashabranner. *Choctaw Code.* New York: McGraw-Hill, 1961.

De Huff, Elizabeth Willis. *Taytray's Tales.* New York: Harcourt, Brace, 1922.

———. *Memories Taytray's.* New York: Harcourt, Brace, 1924.

———. *Five Little Katchinas.* Boston: Houghton Mifflin, 1930.

———. *Two Little Hops.* Chicago: Mentzer, Bush, 1936.

———. *Hoppity Bunny's Hop.* Caldwell: Caxton Printers, 1939.

———. *Say the Bells of Old Missions.* St. Louis: Herder Co., 1943.

———. *Little Boy Dance.* Chicago: Wilcox, Follet, 1946.

De Shields, James T. *Cynthia Ann Parker.* San Antonio: Naylor, 1934.

Dodge, Natt N., and Herbert S. Zim. *The American Southwest.* New York: Golden Press, 1955.

Dorian, Edith, and W. N. Wilson. *Hokahey, American Indians Then and Now.* New York: McGraw-Hill, 1957.

Dubios, William Rene. *Otto in Texas.* New York: Viking, 1959.

Duncan, Lois. *Season of the Two-Heart.* New York: Dodd, Mead, 1964.

Eberle, Irmengarde. *Very Good Neighbors.* Philadelphia: Lippincott, 1945.

———. *Mustang on the Prairie.* Garden City: Doubleday, 1968.

Ellison, Eugenia Adams. *Exiled Heart, the Ballad of Sam Houston.* San Antonio: Naylor, 1965.

Evans, Augusta Jane. *Inez: A Tale of the Alamo.* New York: G. W. Carleton and Co., 1855; rpt., 1871.

Evans, Edna (Hoffman). *Written with Fire: The Story of Cattle Brands.* New York: Holt, Rinehart & Winston, 1962.

Finger, Charles Joseph. *Tales from Silver Lands.* Garden City: Doubleday, Doran, 1924.

———. *Frontier Ballads.* Garden City: Doubleday, 1927.

Fisher, Aileen. *All on a Mountain Day.* New York: Thomas Nelson, 1956.

———. *Cherokee Strip.* New York: Dutton, 1956.

Fletcher, Sidney E. *The Big Book of Cowboys.* New York: Grosset & Dunlap, 1950.

———. *Big Book of Indians.* New York: Grosset & Dunlap, 1950.

———. *Big Book of the Wild West.* New York: Grosset & Dunlap, 1951.

———. *Cowboy and His Horse.* New York: Grosset & Dunlap, 1951.

Floethe, Louise. *Cowboy on the Ranch.* New York: Scribner's, 1959.

Fogler, Doris, and Nina Nicol. *Rusty Pete of the Lazy A. B.* New York: Macmillan, 1929.

Folsom, Franklin. *Mystery at Payrock Canyon.* New York: Harvey House, 1962.

Ford, Paul Leicester. *Great K & A Train Robbery.* New York: Dodd, Mead, 1897.

Franklin, George Cory. *Wild Animals of the Southwest.* Boston: Houghton Mifflin, 1950.

———. *Wild Horses of the Rio Grande.* Boston: Houghton Mifflin, 1951.

———. *Back of Beyond.* New York: Dutton, 1952.

Friermood, Elizabeth Hamilton. *Candle in the Sun.* Garden City: Doubleday, 1958.

Gambrell, Herbert Pickens. *Texas—Its Story.* Dallas: Southwest Press, 1935.

Garst, Doris. *Kit Carson: Trail Blazer and Scout.* New York: Messner, 1942.

———. *Custer, Fighter of the Plains.* New York: Messner, 1944.

———. *Cowboy Books.* Nashville, Tennessee: Abingdon-Cokesbury, 1946.

———. *Sitting Bull, Champion of His People.* New York: Messner, 1946.

———. *Buffalo Bill.* New York: Messner, 1948.

———. *Big Foot Wallace of the Texas Rangers.* New York: Messner, 1951.

———. *Cowboys and Cattle Trails.* New York: Harper & Row, 1960.

Gay, Zhenya, and Jan Gay. *Pancho and His Burro.* New York: Morrow, 1930.

Gilstrap, Robert. *Ten Texas Tales.* Austin: Steck-Vaughn, 1963.

Grinnell, George Bird. *Jack, the Young Ranchman.* New York: Frederick A. Stokes, 1899; rpt., 1925.

———. *Jack Among the Indians; or, A Boy's Summer on the Buffalo Plains.* Philadelphia: Frederick A. Stokes, 1900.

———. *Jack, the Young Cowboy.* New York: Frederick A. Stokes, 1913.

———. *When Buffalo Ran.* New Haven: Yale Univ. Press, 1920.

Hader, Berta (Hoernen), and Elmer Hader. *Midget and Bridget.* New York: Macmillan, 1934.

Hager, Alice (Rogers). *Loop and Little in the Cowboy's Story.* New York: Macmillan, 1937.

Hall, Sam (Major S. S.) (Buckskin Sam). *Kit Carson, Jr., The Crack Shot of the West.* New York: Beadle and Adams Division New York Library, 1878.

Harrington, Isis L. *Komok of the Cliffs.* New York: Scribner's, 1934.

———. *Nah-le-Kah-de (He Herds Sheep)*. New York: Dutton, 1937.

———. *Told in the Twilight*. New York: Dutton, 1938.

Haywood, Carolyn. *Eddie and the Fire Engine*. New York: Morrow, 1949.

———. *Betsy's Little Star*. New York: Morrow, 1950.

———. *Eddie and Gardenia*. New York: Morrow, 1951.

———. *Mixed-up Twins*. New York: Morrow, 1952.

Heiderstadt, Dorothy. *Frontier Leaders and Pioneers*. New York: McKay, 1962.

Henderson, Le Grand. *Augustus Goes South*. Indianapolis: Bobbs-Merrill, 1940.

———. *Why Cowboys Sing in Texas*. Nashville: Abingdon-Cokesbury, 1950.

Henry, Marguerite. *Brighty of the Grand Canyon*. Chicago: Rand McNally, 1953.

Henry, Will. *The Texas Rangers*. New York: Random, 1957.

Hoff, Carol. *Johnny Texas*. Chicago: Follett, 1950.

———. *Johnny Texas on the San Antonio Road*. Chicago: Follett, 1953.

———. *Wilderness Pioneer: Stephen F. Austin of Texas*. Chicago: Follett, 1955.

———. *Head to the West*. Chicago: Follett, 1957.

Hogner, Dorothy Childs. *Navajo Winter Night*. New York: Thomas Nelson, 1935.

———. *Education of a Burro*. New York: Thomas Nelson, 1936.

Holbrook, Stewart Hall. *Wild Bill Hickok Tames the West*. New York: Random, 1952.

———. *Davy Crockett*. New York: Random, 1955.

Holling, Holling Clancy. *The Book of Indians*. New York: Platt and Munk Co., 1935.

———. *Book of Cowboys*. New York: Platt and Munk Co., 1936.

———. *Tree in the Trail*. Boston: Houghton Mifflin, 1942.

Hooker, Forrestine (Cooper). *The Little House on the Desert*. Garden City: Doubleday, 1924.

———. *Cricket: a Little Girl of the Old West*. Garden City: Doubleday, 1925.

———. *Just George*. Garden City: Doubleday, 1926.

———. *Civilizing Cricket; a Story for Girls*. Garden City: Doubleday, 1927.

Howard, Elizabeth (pseud. of Elizabeth Howard Mizner). *A Star to Follow*. New York: Morrow, 1954.

Hubbard, Margaret Ann. *Seraphina Told*. New York: Macmillan, 1941.

154   *Southwestern American Literature*

Hull, James Howard. *Trail and Pack Horses.* Garden City: Doubleday, 1925.

Hyde, Wayne. *What Does a Cowboy Do?* New York: Dodd, Mead, 1963.

Ingraham, Prentiss. *Buffalo Bill and the Robber Ranch King; or, The White Tarrantula of Texas.* New York: Street and Smith, 1913.

Jackson, William Henry. *The Pony Express Goes Through: An American Saga Told by Its Heroes.* Philadelphia: Lippincott, 1935.

Jacobs, Caroline Elliott (Hoggs). *A Texas Blue Bonnet.* Boston: L. C. Page, 1910.

———. *Blue Bonnet's Ranch Party.* Boston: L. C. Page, 1912.

James, Ahlee. *Tewa Firelight Tales.* New York: Longmans, 1927.

James, Bessie (Rowland), and Marquis James. *Six Feet Six: the Heroic Story of Sam Houston.* Indianapolis: Bobbs-Merrill, 1935.

Jensen, Ann (Oden). *The Time of Rosie.* Austin: Steck-Vaughn, 1967.

Johansen, Margaret (Alison). *Hawk of Hawk Clan.* New York: Longmans, Green, 1941.

Johnson, Dorothy Marie. *Famous Lawmen of the Old West.* New York: Dodd, Mead, 1963.

Johnson, William W. *Sam Houston, the Tallest Texan.* New York: Random, 1953.

———. *The Birth of Texas.* Boston: Houghton Mifflin, 1960.

Johnston, Annie Fellow. *The Little Colonel in Arizona.* Boston: L. C. Page, 1905.

Johnston, Leah Carter. *San Antonio, St. Anthony's Town.* San Antonio: San Antonio Public Library Librarian's Council, 1947.

Jones, Weyman B. *Edge of Two Worlds.* New York: Dial Press, 1968.

Kelly, Eric Philbrook. *On the Staked Plains.* New York: Macmillan, 1940.

King, General Charles. *An Apache Princess.* New York: Hobart Co., 1903.

Kjelgaard, Jim. *Lion Hound.* New York: Holiday House, 1955.

———. *Desert Dog.* New York: Holiday House, 1956.

Krumgold, Joseph . . . *and now, Miguel.* New York: Crowell, 1953.

Ladd, Ileta Kerr. *Seeing Texas.* Dallas: Mathis, Van Nort, 1943

Latham, Barbara. *Pedro, Nina and Perrito.* New York: Harper, 1939.

Lauritzen, Jonreed. *The Ordeal of the Young Hunter.* Boston: Little, Brown, 1954.

Leighton, Margaret (Carver). *Comanche of the Seventh.* New York: Rinehart, 1957.

Lenski, Lois. *Boom Town Boy.* Philadelphia: Lippincott, 1948.

————. *Cowboy Small.* New York: Henry Z. Walek, 1949.

————. *Texas Tomboy.* Philadelphia: Lippincott, 1950.

Le Sueur, Meridel. *Chanticleer of Wilderness Road: a Story of Davy Crockett.* New York: Knopf, 1951.

Lowrey, Jenette Sebring. *Annunciata and the Shepherds.* New York: Harper, 1938.

————. *The Silver Dollar.* New York: Harper & Row, 1940.

————. *Rings on Her Fingers.* New York: Harper & Row, 1941.

————. *Tap-a-Tap!* New York: Harper & Row, 1942.

————. *Lavender Cat.* New York: Harper & Row, 1944.

————. *The Bird.* New York: Harper, 1947.

————. *Margaret.* New York: Harper, 1950.

————. *Love, Bid Me Welcome.* New York: Harper & Row, 1964.

McCaleb, Walter Flavius. *Bigfoot Wallace.* San Antonio: Naylor, 1956.

————. *Stephen F. Austin.* San Antonio: Naylor, 1957.

————. *William Barret Travis,* San Antonio: Naylor, 1957.

————. *Sam Houston.* San Antonio: Naylor, 1958.

————. *Mier Expedition.* San Antonio: Naylor, 1959.

————. *The Alamo.* San Antonio: Naylor, 1961.

————. *Spanish Missions of Texas.* San Antonio: Naylor, 1961.

McCracken, Harold. *Winning of the West.* Garden City: Doubleday, 1955.

McGiffin, Lee. *Ten Tall Texans.* New York: Lothrop, Lee & Shepard, 1956.

McKee, Louise Virginia, and Richard Aldrich Summers. *Dusty Desert Tales.* Caldwell: Caxton, 1941.

McMullin, Mawd Llewellyn. *Child's Story of Oklahoma.* Oklahoma City: Modern Publishers, 1941.

McNeer, May Yonge. *Story of the Great Plains.* New York: Harper, 1943.

Maher, Ramona. *Their Shining Hour.* New York: John Day, 1960.

Malkus, Alida Sims. *Raquel of the Ranch Country.* New York: Harcourt, Brace, 1927.

————. *Dragon Fly of Zuni.* New York: Harcourt, Brace, 1928.

————. *Stone Knife Boy.* New York: Harcourt, Brace, 1930.

Marriott, Alice Lee. *The Ten Grandmothers.* Norman: Univ. of Oklahoma Press, 1945.

————. *Winter-Telling Stories.* New York: William Sloane, 1947.

————. *Indians on Horseback.* New York: Thomas Y. Crowell, 1948.

Marshall, Helen Laughlin. *New Mexican Boy.* New York: Holiday House, 1940.

Mauzey, Merritt. *Texas Ranch Boy.* New York: Abelard-Schuman, 1955.

Meadowcraft, Enid (La Monte). *Texas Star.* New York: Thomas Y. Crowell Co., 1950.

————. *Story of Davy Crockett.* New York: Grossett & Dunlap, 1952.

Means, Florence (Crannell). *Adella Mary in Old Mexico.* Boston: Houghton Mifflin, 1930.

————. *Bowlful of Stars; a Story of the Pioneer West.* Boston: Houghton Mifflin, 1934.

————. *Tangled Waters: A Navajo Story.* Boston: Houghton Mifflin, 1936.

————. *Whispering Girl, a Hopi Story of Today.* Boston: Houghton Mifflin, 1941.

————. *Shadow Over Wide Ruin.* Boston: Houghton Mifflin, 1942.

————. *Silver Fleece.* Philadelphia: John C. Winston, 1950.

Montgomery, Rutherford George [pseud. Al Avery, Everitt Proctor]. *The Mystery of the Turquoise Frog.* New York: Messner, 1946.

Moon, Carl. *The Flaming Arrow.* Philadelphia: Frederick A. Stokes, 1927.

————. *Painted Moccasin.* Philadelphia: Frederick A. Stokes, 1931.

Moon, Grace (Purdie). *Chi-Wee; the Adventure of a Little Indian Girl.* Garden City: Doubleday, 1925.

————. *Chi-Wee and Loki of the Desert.* Garden City: Doubleday, 1926.

————. *Nadita (Little Nothing).* Garden City: Doubleday, 1927.

————. *Arrow of Tee-May.* New York: A. L. Burt, 1934.

————. *Missing Katchina.* Garden City: Doubleday, 1934.

Morgan, Len. *Abilene Trail.* Camden: Thomas Nelson, 1941.

Morris, Ann (Axtell). *Digging in the Southwest.* Garden City: Doubleday, 1933.

Mulcahy, Lucille. *Pita.* New York: Coward-McCann, 1954.

————. *Blue Marshmallow Mountains.* New York: Thomas Nelson, 1959.

Nason, Thelma Campbell. *Under the Wide Sky, Tales of New Mexico and the Spanish Southwest.* Chicago: Follett, 1965.

Newcomb, Corelle. *Silver Saddles.* New York: Longmans, Green, 1943.

————. *Cortez, the Conqueror.* New York: Random, 1947.

Nichols, Walter Hammond. *Cowboy Hugh; the Odyssey of a Boy.* New York: Macmillan, 1927.

Norton, Andre (pseud. Mary Alice Norton). *Stand to Horse.* New York: Harcourt, Brace and World, 1956.

————. *Ride Proud Rebel!* Cleveland: World, 1961.

————. *Rebel Spurs.* Cleveland: World, 1962.

Olgin, Joseph. *Sam Houston: Friend of the Indians.* Boston: Houghton Mifflin, 1958.

Otero, Nina. *Old Spain in Our Southwest.* New York: Harcourt, Brace, 1936.

Pattullo, George. *The Sheriff of Badger: A Tale of the Southwest Borderland.* New York: Appleton, 1912.

Peck, Leigh. *Pecos Bill and Lightning.* Boston: Houghton Mifflin, 1940.

————. *Don Coyote.* Boston: Houghton Mifflin, 1942.

————. *They Were Made of Rawhide.* Boston: Houghton Mifflin, 1954.

Pope, Henry David. *A Lady and a Lone Star Flag.* San Antonio: Naylor, 1936.

Quinn, Vernon (pseud. Capini Vequin). *War-paint and Powder-horn.* Philadelphia: Frederick A. Stokes, 1929.

————. *Picture Map Geography of the United States.* Philadelphia: Lippincott, 1953.

Rachlis, Eugene, and John C. Ewers. *Indians of the Plains.* New York: American Heritage, 1960.

Reek, Alma Kehoe. *All Aboard for Tin Cup.* New York: Scribner's, 1962.

Robinson, William Powell. *Where the Panther Screams.* Cleveland: World, 1961.

Rollins, Philip Ashton. *The Cowboy: His Characteristics, His Equipment, and His Part in the Development of the West.* New York: Scribner's, 1922.

————. *Jinglebob: A True Story of a Real Cowboy.* New York: Scribner's, 1927.

Rouke, Constance Mayfield. *Davy Crockett.* New York: Harcourt, Brace, 1934.

Rounds, Glen. *The Blind Colt.* New York: Holiday House, 1941; rpt., 1960.

————. *Ol' Paul, the Mighty Logger.* New York: Holiday House, 1949.

————. *Rodeo: Bulls, Broncs and Buckaroos.* New York: Holiday Hause, 1949.

————. *Whitey Takes a Trip.* New York: Holiday House, 1954.

————. *Whitey Ropes and Rides.* New York: Holiday House, 1956.

————. *Whitey the Wild Horse.* New York: Holiday House, 1958.

————. *Whitey and the Colt Killer.* New York: Holiday House, 1962.

————. *Whitey's New Saddle.* New York: Holiday House, 1963.

Rushmore, Helen. *Cowboy Joe of the Circle S.* New York: Harcourt, Brace, 1950.

————. *Shadow of Robber's Roost.* Cleveland: World, 1960.

Salomon, Julian H. *The Book of Indian Crafts and Indian Lore.* New York: Harper & Row, 1928.

Sabin, Edward Legrand. *Bar B Boys; or The Young Cow-punchers.* New York: Crowell, 1909.

————. *Boy Settler; or, Terry in the New West.* New York: Crowell, 1916.

————. *Buffalo Bill and the Overland Trail.* Philadelphia: Lippincott, 1916.

————. *With Sam Houston in Texas.* Philadelphia: Lippincott, 1916.

————. *Rio Bravo; a Romance of the Texas Frontier.* Philadelphia: Macrae Smith, 1925.

————. *Rose of Santa Fe.* Philadelphia: Macrae Smith, 1925.

————. *Old Jim Bridger on the Moccasin Trail.* New York: Crowell, 1938.

Sanchez, Nellie (Van de Grift). *Stories of the States: Tales of Early Exploration and Settlement.* New York: Crowell, 1941; rpt., 1951.

Sasek, Miroslav. *This Is Texas.* New York: Macmillan, 1967.

Sayers, Frances Clarke. *Bluebonnets for Lucinda.* New York: Viking, 1934.

————. *Tag-along Tooloo.* New York: Viking, 1941.

————. *Sally Tait.* New York: Viking, 1948.

Schultz, James Willard. *In the Great Apaches Forest.* New York: Houghton Mifflin, 1920.

————. *The Trail of the Spanish Horse.* Boston: Houghton Mifflin, 1922.

————. *A Son of the Navajos.* Boston: Houghton Mifflin, 1927.

Scott, Lena Becker. *Dawn Boy of the Pueblo.* Philadelphia: John C. Winston, 1935.

Seton, Ernest Thompson. *The Little Savages.* Gloucester: Peter Smith, 1963.

————. *Wild Animals I Have Known: "Lobo, King of Currumpaw."* New York: Schocken Books, 1966.

Sexton, Irwin, and Kathryn M. Sexton. *Samuel A. Maverick.* San Antonio: Naylor, 1964.

Seymour, Flora Warren (Smith). *Boys' Life of Kit Carson.* New York: Appleton-Century, 1929.

Shapiro, Irwin. *Yankee Thunder: the Legendary Life of Davy Crockett.* New York: Messner, 1944.

————. *John Henry and the Double Jointed Steam Drill.* New York: Julian Messner, 1945.

Sharp, Adda Mai (Cummings). *Gee Whillikins.* Austin: Steck-Vaughn, 1950.

Shirreffs, Gordon Donald. *Swiftwagon.* Philadelphia: Westminster Press, 1950.

————. *The Rebel Trumpet.* Philadelphia: Westminster Press, 1961.
Sickels, Eleanor Maria. *In Calico and Crinoline.* New York: Viking, 1935.
Skinner, Constance L. *Becky Landers, Frontier Warrior.* New York: Macmillan, 1926.
Sorensen, Clarence Woodrow. *Ways of Our Land.* New York: Silver, Burdett, 1954.
Sperry, Armstrong. *Wagons Westward.* Philadelphia: John C. Winston, 1936.
————. *Little Eagle, A Navajo Boy.* Philadelphia: John C. Winston, 1938.
Stevens, Mary Ellen and E. B. Sayles. *Little Cloud and the Great Plains Hunters 15,000 Years Ago.* Chicago: Reilly & Lee, 1962.
Stevenson, Augusta. *Sam Houston: Boy Chieftain.* Indianapolis: Bobbs-Merrill, 1962.
Stevenson, Burton Egbert. *American History in Verse for Boys and Girls.* Boston: Houghton Mifflin, 1932.
Stong, Philip Duffield. *Buckskin Breeches.* New York: Grosset & Dunlap, 1938.
————. *Cowhand Goes to Town.* New York: Dodd, Mead, 1939.
————. *Captain Kidd's Cow.* New York: Dodd, Mead, 1941.
Swan, Oliver G. *Covered Wagon Days.* New York: Grosset & Dunlap, 1928.
Tavo, Gus (pseud. for Martha Ivan and Gustave Ivan). *Trail to Love Canyon.* New York: Knopf, 1962.
————. *Ride the Pale Stallion.* New York: Knopf, 1968.
Taylor, Florence (Walton). *Navy Wings of Gold.* Chicago: Albert Whitman, 1944.
Tireman, Loyd Spencer. *Baby Jack and Jumping Jack Rabbit.* Albuquerque: Univ. of New Mexico Press, 1943.
————. *Hop-a-Long.* Albuquerque: Univ. of New Mexico Press, 1944.
————. *Dumbee.* Albuquerque: Univ. of New Mexico Press, 1945.
————. *Cocky.* Albuquerque: Univ. of New Mexico Press, 1946.
————. *Big Fat.* Albuquerque: Univ. of New Mexico Press, 1947.
Toepperwein, Emilie, and Fritz Toepperwein. *Little Valley Quail.* Boerne, Texas: Highland Press, 1945.
————. *I Want to Be a Cowboy.* Boerne, Texas: Highland Press, 1947.
————. *Uncle Kris and His Pets.* Boerne, Texas: Highland Press, 1948.
————. *Little Deputy.* Boerne, Texas: Highland Press, 1949.
Tousey, Sanford. *Cowboy Tommy.* Garden City: Doubleday, 1932.
————. *Cowboy Tommy's Roundup.* Garden City: Doubleday, Doran, 1934.

————. *Cowboy Jimmy.* New York: Charles E. Merrill, 1935.

Treuhardt, Beverly, and Marie Murdock. *Sam Bass.* Austin: Steck-Vaughn, 1958.

Trevathen, Robert E. *Longhorns for Fort Sill.* New York: Criterion Books, 1962.

Trotter, Grace (pseud. Nancy Paschal). *Clover Creek.* New York: Nelson, 1946.

————. *Magnolia Heights.* New York: Nelson, 1947.

Walton, Eda Lou. *Turquoise Boy and White Shell Girl.* New York: Crowell, 1933.

Waltrip, Lela, and Rufus Waltrip. *White Harvest.* New York: Longmans, Green, 1960.

————. *Purple Hills.* New York: Longmans, Green, 1961.

Warren, Betsy. *Indians Who Lived in Texas.* Austin: Steck-Vaughn, 1970.

Warren, Robert Penn. *Remember the Alamo!* New York: Random, 1958.

Warren, William Stephen. *Ride, Cowboy, Ride.* Eau Claire, Wisconsin: Cadmus Books, 1951.

Webb, Walter P. *The Story of the Texas Rangers.* New York: Grosset & Dunlap, 1957.

Whitney, Phyllis A. *Mystery of the Black Diamonds.* Eau Claire, Wisconsin: E. M. Hale, 1954.

Wier, Ester. *The Wind Chasers.* New York: McKay, 1967.

Wilkie, Katharine Elliott. *Zack Taylor: Young Rough and Ready.* Indianapolis: Bobbs-Merrill, 1962.

Wooten, Mattie Lloyd, ed. *Women Tell the Story of the Southwest.* San Antonio: Naylor, 1940.

Wormser, Richard Edward. *The Kidnapped Circus.* New York: Morrow, 1968.

Wright, Frances (Fitzpatrick). *Sam Houston, Fighter and Leader.* New York: Abingdon, 1953.

Vetal Flores
Angelo State University

Periodicals and Journalism

Newspapers
(begun before 1918)

Arizona

Bisbee, *Daily Review.* 1897+ Title varies: *Daily Lyre, Daily Orb, Cochise Review and Arizona Daily Orb.*

Clifton, *Copper Era.* 1899+

Douglas, *Daily Dispatch.* 1902+

Flagstaff, *Cocomino Sun.* 1882+ Title varies.

Florence *Blade Tribune.* 1892+

Miami, *Arizona Silver Belt.* 1878+ Published first at Globe.

Prescott *Courier.* 1882+

Phoenix, *Arizona Weekly Gazette.* 1902+

Phoenix *Gazette.* 1880+ Published 1880-1928 as *Arizona Gazette.*

Phoenix, *Arizona Republican.* 1890+

Prescott, *Journal Miner.* 1864-1934. Title varies: *Arizona Miner, Weekly Arizona Miner, Arizona Weekly Miner,* etc. Published 1864 in Fort Whipple, 1867 in Tucson.

Safford, *Graham County Guardian.* 1895+

Tombstone *Epitaph.* 1880+

Tombstone, *Arizona Kicker.* 1892-1913?

Tubac, *Weekly Arizonian.* 1859-1871. Moved from Tubac to Tucson to Prescott to Tucson. In 1867 published as *Southern Arizonian.*

Tempe *News.* 1887+

Tucson, *Arizona Citizen.* 1870+. Title varies: *Arizona Citizen and Weekly Tribune, Arizona Weekly Citizen, Daily Arizona Citizen, Tucson Daily Citizen.*

Tucson, *Daily Star.* 1879+

Tucson, *Arizona Weekly Star.* 1877-1907.

Saint Johns, *Apache County Independent News.* 1885+ Published first as *St. Johns Herald.* In 1905 as *St. Johns, Herald and Apache News.*

Willcox, *Arizona Range News.* 1884+

Williams *News.* 1890+

Winslow *Mail.* 1880+

Yuma, *Daily Sun and Arizona Sentinel.* 1869+ Title varies.

Yuma *Examiner.* 1872+ Title varies: *Arizona Sentinel* 1872-1911, *Arizona Sentinel and Yuma Weekly Examiner* 1911-1915. Combined with *Yuma Weekly and Weekly Examiner* 1920.

162   *Southwestern American Literature*

New Mexico

Alamogordo *News.* 1898+
Albuquerque *El Independiente.* 1890+ In Spanish. Published 1894-1932 in Las Vegas.
Albuquerque *Journal.* 1890+
Aztec, *Independent Review.* 1888+
Carlsbad, *Current-Argus.* 1886+ Combination of *Carlsbad Argus* (1886-1927) and *Current* (1892-1927).
Carrizozo, *Lincoln County News.* 1900+ Was *Carrizozo News* (1900-1925).
Deming *Graphic.* 1902+
Deming *Headlight.* 1881+
Farmington Times. 1890+ Title varies: *San Juan Times* (1890-1891). United with *Hustler* (1901-1905).
Gallup *Independent.* 1889+
Las Cruces *Sun News.* 1882+ Title varies.
Las Vegas *Daily Optic.* 1879+
Lovington *Leader.* 1909+
Portales *News-Tribune.* 1901+ Title varies.
Raton *Range.* 1881+ Title varies.
Raton *Reporter.* 1890-1930?
Roswell *Record.* 1888+
Santa Fe, *New Mexican* 1848+ Title varies.
Silver City *Daily Press and Independent.* 1895+
Silver City *Enterprise.* 1882+
Socorro, *Defensor-Chieftain.* 1866+
Springer *Tribune.* 1912+ From 1912-1929 was Springer *Times.*
Taos *News.* 1910+ From 1910-1917 was Taos *Valley News.* In English and Spanish.
Taos *Valley Herald.* 1884-1890. From 1844 to 1889 was *Herald.* In English and Spanish.
Tucumcari *News.* 1901+ Tucumcari *Times* (1903-1919) merged with *News* to form *News-Times,* later *News.*

Oklahoma

Bartlesville, *Examiner-Enterprise.* 1898+
Cherokee Baptist Mission, Indian Territory, *The Cherokee Messenger.* 1844-1846. Briefly revived 1858-1859. A missionary organ and Oklahoma's earliest periodical.

Ardmore, *Daily Ardmoreite.* 1893+
Enid *Eagle.* 1893+
Guthrie *Leader.* 1889+
Guymon *Herald.* 1890+ Began as Hardesty *Times,* renamed Hardesty *Herald.*
Lawton *Constitution.* 1901+
Marietta *Monitor.* 1895+
Muskogee *Phoenix.* 1888+
Muskogee *Times-Democrat.* 1894+
Oklahoma City *Times.* 1889+ Title varies.
Oklahoma City, *Daily Oklahoman.* 1894+
Ponca City *News.* 1893+
Shawnee, *News-Star.* 1904+
Tahlequah *Arrow.* 1888-1920. Title varies.
Tahlequah, *Cherokee Advocate.* 1844-1906.
Tahlequah, *Star Citizen* 1882+
Tulsa *Tribune.* 1904+ Published first as Tulsa *Democrat.*
Tulsa *World.* 1906+
Vinita, *Indian Chieftain.* 1882-1912.
Watonga *Republican.* 1892+
Weatherford *News.* 1899+

Texas

Austin *American.* 1914+
Beaumont *Enterprise.* 1880+
Clarksville, *Northern Standard.* 1842-1888.
El Paso, *Herald-Post.* 1880+
Dallas *Express.* 1893+ (Negro)
Dallas *Morning News.* 1885+
Dallas *Times Herald.* 1876+ Began as *Times.* In 1888 combined with *Daily Herald* (1873-1887) to form Dallas *Daily Times Herald.*
Fort Worth, *Star Telegram.* 1895+ Title varies.
Galveston *Daily News.* 1842+
Houston *Chronicle.* 1901+
Houston *Post.* 1880+
Huntsville *Item.* 1850+
Jefferson *Jimplecute.* 1846+
San Antonio *Express.* 1865+ Title varies.

San Antonio, *Freie Presse für Texas*. 1865+ In German.
San Antonio, *La Prensa*. 1913+ In Spanish.
San Antonio *Light*. 1881+ Title varies.
San Felipe, *Texas Gazette*. 1829-1833? Title varies: *Mexican Citizen, Constitutional Advocate and Texas Public Adviser, Texas Gazette and Brazoria Commercial Advertiser*.
San Felipe, *Telegraph and Texas Register*. 1835-1877. Title varies: *Democratic Telegraph and Texas Register, Weekly Houston Telegraph*. Published also in Harrisburg and Columbia.
Victoria *Advocate*. 1864+ Began as *Texian Advocate*.

Magazines

Arizona
Arizona and the West. Tucson. 1959+
Arizona Educator. Kingman. 1895-1897.
Arizona Highways: The Friendly Journal of Life and Travel in the Old West. Phoenix 1921-22 (Vols. 1 and 2); renewed publication in 1925 and has continued to the present.
Arizona Journal of Education. Phoenix. 1910-1912.
Arizona Legislative Review. Phoenix. 1900+
Arizona Magazine. *Phoenix*. 1906+ Began as *Southwest Today*.
Arizona Magazine. Yuma. 1893.
Arizona Medical Journal. Phoenix. 1912-1916.
Arizona Mining Review. Prescott. 1906-1908?
Arizona State Magazine and Pathfinder. Phoenix. 1910-1925. Title varies.
Arizona Teacher. Phoenix. 1912+
Arizona Teacher Parent. Tucson. 1914+
Arizona Quarterly Illustrated. Tucson. 1880-1881.
Southwestern Art Scene. Tucson. 1967+

New Mexico
El Palacio. Santa Fe. 1813+ Published by Museum of New Mexico. Anthropology, History, Art.
Revista Ilustrada. Santa Fe. 1906-1931. In Spanish.
The Condor. Las Cruces. 1898+ Published by Cooper Ornithological Society.
New Mexico. Santa Fe 1923+ Began as *New Mexico Highway Journal* in 1923 and ran as such until Vol. 9, No. 6, in June 1937.
New Mexico Educational Association Journal. Santa Fe. 1886?-1933?

New Mexico Magazine. Santa Fe. 1923+
New Mexico Medical Journal. 1905+ Las Vegas. Became *Southwestern Medicine* in 1917+
Southwestern Mines. Albuquerque. 1909-1911.
New Mexico Journal of Education. Santa Fe. 1903-1920?

Oklahoma

Cherokee Rose Buds. Tahlequah, Indian Territory. 1854. A magazine published at the Cherokee Female Seminary and "Devoted to the Good, the Beautiful, and the True." In English and Cherokee. One number (No. 2, Vol. 1) extant.
Journal of the Oklahoma State Medical Association. Oklahoma City. 1910+
Oklahoma Farmer. Guthrie. 1890-1924. Title varies: Merged with *Oklahoma Farm Journal* to become *Oklahoma Farmer-Stockman,* later was *Farmer Stockman.*
Oklahoma Magazine. Oklahoma City. 1905-1912?
Oklahoma Magazine: A Journal of Oklahoma and the Indian Territories. Oklahoma City, 1893-1895.
Oklahoma School Herald. Norman. 1892-1922?
Oklahoma Teacher. Oklahoma City. 1918+
Our Monthly. Tullahassee, Indian Territory. 1870-1875. A four-page quarto publication, issued irregularly, but usually once a month. Almost wholly in Muskoki. Valuable linguistic contribution.
Red River Valley Historical Review. Canyon. 1972.
Southwest Journal of Medicine and Surgery. Oklahoma City. 1893-1922. Title and place of publication vary.
Sturm's Oklahoma Magazine. Tulsa. 1905-1911. Was *Sturm's Statehood Magazine.* 1905-1906.
Twin Territories: The Indian Magazine. Muskogee. 1899-1904?

Texas

The American Home Journal: A Monthly Magazine for the Home. Dallas. 1904?-1915.
Brann's Iconoclast. Austin and Waco. 1891-1898. Published as *Iconoclast* in Austin 1891. Suspended from October, 1891 to January, 1895. Published in Waco as *Brann's Iconoclast* (1895-1898). Sold and moved to Chicago in 1898, published there as *Windle's Liberal Magazine* (1926-1929) and *The Liberal* (1929-1934).

The American Sketch Book: An Historical and Home Monthly. Austin. 1878-1883. Began in La Crosse, Wisconsin in 1874. Published there until 1876.

The Bohemian. Fort Worth. 1899-1907.

Dixieland: The Illustrated Home Magazine of the South. Dallas. 1904-1906?

"D" Magazine. Dallas. 1974+

The Guardian. Waco. 1891?-1895?

The Gulf Messenger: Illustrated Monthly Magazine of the Gulf States. San Antonio, Houston, Dallas. 1891-1898. Successor to *The Ladies Messenger* established in 1888. Later known as *The Gulf—Messenger and Current Topics.*

Holland's: The Magazine of the South. Dallas. 1905-1953.

Hunter's Magazine of Frontier History, Border Tragedy, Pioneer Achievement. Carlsbad, Ozona, Melvin, San Antonio. 1910-1912. Suspended until 1916, then published for year as *Hunter's Frontier Magazine.* The same editor and publisher, J. Marvin Hunter, Sr., began editing and publishing *Frontier Times* in 1923, like its two predecessors in subject matter. Last published in 1954 by Hunter family. *Frontier Times* appeared again in 1957 and is current.

The Passing Show. San Antonio. 1906-1912. Title varies: Mackay's *Weekly, Southern Sentinel, Bohemian Scribbler.*

The Period. Dallas and Houston. 1893-1906. Title varies: *The Period— Lee's Magazine, Lee's Texas Magazine, Lee's Magazine.*

The Round Table. Dallas. 1890-1893.

The Prairie Flower: A Literary Monthly Devoted to the Pure, the True, the Beautiful. Corsicana. 1882-1885?

The School Forum. Dallas. 1894-1895.

Southwest Review. Austin, Dallas. 1915+ Began as *The Texas Review.* Name changed in 1924.

Southwest Historical Quarterly. Austin. 1897+ Began as *The Quarterly of the Texas State Historical Association.* Name changed in 1921.

Southwestern Art. Austin. 1966+

The Stylus: A Monthly Magazine Devoted to Literature, Science, and Art. Austin. 1876.

Texas Journal of Education. Huntsville. 1854. Earliest Texas educational magazine.

The Texas Magazine: The Texas Monthly Magazine. 1896-1898.

Texas Monthly. Austin. 1972+

The Texas Outlook. Austin. 1916+ First published as *Texas State Teachers Association Bulletin* in Fort Worth. Name changed in 1919.

Texas Quarterly. Austin. 1958+

Texas School Journal. Houston, Dallas, Austin. 1883-1929. Title varies: Began as *Texas Journal of Education* (1880-1882). In 1914 merged with *Texas School Magazine* (1898) and became *Texas School Journal and Magazine of Methods.* In 1920 became again *Texas School Journal.* In 1929 became *Texas School Board Journal.*

The Texian Monthly Magazine. Galveston. 1858. Earliest Texas literary magazine.

Bibliographical Guide

A Check List of New Mexico Newspapers. [University of New Mexico Library]. Albuquerque: Univ. of New Mexico Press, 1935.

Alliot, Hector. *Bibliography of Arizona.* [Books, pamphlets and periodicals collected by J. A. Munk and donated to Southwest Museum]. Los Angeles: The Southwest Museum, 1914.

Bray, Leonard, ed. *Ayer Directory Newspapers, Magazines and Trade Publications.* Philadelphia: Ayer Press, 1970.

Dickey, Imogene Bentley. *Early Literary Magazines of Texas.* Austin: Steck-Vaughn, 1970.

Foreman, Carolyn Thomas. *Oklahoma Imprints 1835-1907.* Norman: Univ. of Oklahoma Press, 1936.

Gregory, Winifred, ed. *American Newspapers 1821-1936, A Union List of Files Available in the United States and Canada.* New York: H. W. Wilson, 1937.

Hargrett, Lester. *Oklahoma Imprints 1835-1890.* New York: R. R. Bowker, 1951.

Lutrell, Estelle. *Newspapers and Periodicals of Arizona 1859-1911.* Tucson: The Univ. of Arizona Press, 1950.

Mott, Frank Luther. *A History of American Magazines.* Cambridge: Harvard Univ. Press, 1957.

Porter, A. Stratton. *The Territorial Press of New Mexico 1834-1912.* Albu. querque: Univ. of New Mexico Press, 1969.

Ray, Grace Ernestine. *Early Oklahoma Newspapers.* Norman: Univ. of Oklahoma Press, 1928.

Shelton, Wilma Loy. *Check List of New Mexico Publications, 1850-1953.* Albuquerque: Univ. of New Mexico Press, 1954.

Titus, Edna Brown, ed. *Union List of Serials in Libraries of the United States and Canada,* 3rd ed. New York: H. W. Wilson, 1965.

Winkler, Ernest W., ed. *Check List of Texas Imprints 1846-1860.* Austin: Texas State Historical Association, 1949.

————, and Llerena Friend. *Check List of Texas Imprints 1861-1876.* Austin: Texas State Historical Assoc., 1963.

Woodress, James, comp. *Dissertations in American Literature 1891-1955 with Supplement 1956-1961.* Durham: Duke Univ. Press, 1962.

Imogene B. Dickey
North Texas State University

PART III

The
Authors

Edward Abbey (1927-   )
novels, short stories, nonfiction

Jonathan Troy. New York: Dodd, Mead, 1954.
The Brave Cowboy: An Old Tale in a New Time. New York: Dodd, Mead, 1956.
Fire on the Mountain. New York: Dial Press, 1962.
Desert Solitaire: A Season in the Wilderness. New York: McGraw-Hill, 1968.
Black Sun. New York: Simon and Schuster, 1971.
Slickrock: The Canyon Country of Southeast Utah. San Francisco: Sierra Club, 1971.
Cactus Country. New York: Time-Life Books, 1973.

Edward Abbey has published approximately twenty short stories, articles, and essays in such journals as *Life, Harper's, Field and Stream, The American West, New Mexico Quarterly,* and *Accent.*

Works about Edward Abbey
Peterson, Levi S. "The Primitive and the Civilized in Western Fiction," *Western American Literature,* 1 (Fall 1966), 197-207.
Pilkington, William T. "Edward Abbey: Southwestern Anarchist," *Western Review,* 3 (Winter 1966), 58-62.
————. "Edward Abbey: Western Philosopher, or How to Be a 'Happy Hopi Hippie,'" *Western American Literature,* 9 (May 1974), 17-31.
Wylder, Delbert E. "Edward Abbey and the 'Power Elite,'" *Western Review,* 6 (Winter 1969), 18-22.

William T. Pilkington
Tarleton State College

Andy Adams (1859-1935)
novels, nonfiction

The Log of a Cowboy: A Narrative of the Old Trail Days. Boston, New York: Houghton, Mifflin, 1903.
A Texas Matchmaker. Boston, New York: Houghton, Mifflin, 1904.
The Outlet. Boston, New York: Houghton, Mifflin, 1905.

Cattle Brands: A Collection of Western Camp-Fire Stories. Boston, New York: Houghton, Mifflin, 1906.

Reed Anthony, Cowman: An Autobiography. Boston, New York: Houghton, Mifflin, 1907

Wells Brothers: The Young Cattle Kings. Boston, New York: Houghton, Mifflin, 1911.

The Ranch on the Beaver: A Sequel to Wells Brothers: The Young Cattle Kings. Boston, New York: Houghton, Mifflin, 1927.

Why the Chisolm Trail Forks and Other Tales of the Cattle Country. Ed. Wilson Hudson. Austin: Univ. of Texas Press, 1956.

Works about Andy Adams

Dobie, J. Frank. "Andy Adams, Cowboy Chronicler," *Southwest Review,* 11 (January 1926), 92-101.

———. "Frank Dobie Recounts What He Knew of Andy Adams, Texas Cowboy Writer," *Austin-American Statesman,* October 6, 1935, p. 16.

Hudson, Wilson M. *Andy Adams: His Life and Writings.* Dallas: Southern Methodist Univ. Press, 1964.

———. *Andy Adams: Storyteller and Novelist of the Great Plains.* Austin: Steck-Vaughn, 1967.

Rhodes, Eugene Manlove. "The Cowboy in Fiction," *Story World and Photodramatist,* August, 1923, pp. 17-21.

Wray, Henry Russell. "Literary Outfit Puts Its Brand on Veteran Cowman," *Colorado Springs Gazette and Telegraph,* New Year's Number, January 1, 1905, p. 21.

Chalonnes Lucas
Denton, Texas

Faye Carr Adams (-   )
poetry

Sweet Is the Homing Hour. Dallas: Kaleidograph, 1948.

More Than a Loaf. San Antonio: Naylor, 1968.

As Seasons Pass (with Pauline Crittenden; illus. by Faye Carr Adams). Dallas: Shipp, 1971.

Other poems have appeared in the yearbook publications of the Poetry Society of Texas, *Christian Science Monitor, Nevada Magazine, New Mexico Magazine,* and *The Progressive Farmer.*

Charles Gongre
Lamar University

Ramon F. Adams (1889-   )
bibliography, history, biography, nonfiction

Cowboy Lingo. Boston: Houghton Mifflin, 1936.

Charles M. Russell, the Cowboy Artist. (With Homer Britzman). Pasadena, California: Trail's End Publishing Co., 1948.

Come An' Get It: The Story of the Old Cowboy Cook. Norman: Univ. of Oklahoma Press, 1952.

Six-Guns and Saddle Leather: A Bibliography of Books and Pamphlets on Western Outlaws and Gunmen. Norman: Univ. of Oklahoma Press, 1954; rev. and enlarged, 1969.

Western Words: A Dictionary of the American West. Norman: Univ. of Oklahoma Press, 1954; rev., 1968.

The Best of the American Cowboy. ed. by Ramon Adams. Norman: Univ. of Oklahoma Press, 1957.

The Rampaging Herd: A Bibliography of Books and Pamphlets on Men and Events in the Cattle Industry. Norman: Univ. of Oklahoma Press, 1959.

A Fitting Death For Billy the Kid. Norman: Univ. of Oklahoma Press, 1960.

The Old-Time Cowhand. New York: Macmillan, 1961.

Burrs Under The Saddle: A Second Look at Books and Histories of the West. Norman: Univ. of Oklahoma Press, 1964.

From the Pecos to the Powder: A Cowboy's Autobiography. As told to Ramon F. Adams by Bob Kennon. Norman: Univ. of Oklahoma Press, 1965.

The Legendary West. Dallas: Library of the DeGolyer Foundation, 1965.

The Cowman and His Philosophy. Austin: Encino, 1967.

The Cowboy and His Humor. Austin: Encino, 1968.

The Cowman and His Code of Ethics. Austin: Encino, 1969.

Wayne Gard: Historian of the West. Austin: Steck-Vaughn, 1970.

The Cowman Says It Salty. Tucson: Univ. of Arizona Press, 1971.

The Horse Wrangler and His Remuda. Austin: Encino, 1971.

Judith Alter
Texas Christian University

Frances Alexander (1888-   )
poetry, juveniles, folklore

Seven White Birds (poems). Dallas: Kaleidograph, 1938.
Mother Goose on the Rio Grande (Mexican nursery folklore with rhymed English translations). Dallas: Banks Upshaw, 1944.
Time at the Window (poems). Dallas: Kaleidograph, 1948.
Conversation with a Lamb (poems). Austin: Steck, 1955.
Handbook on Chinese Art Symbols (with Mary C. Alexander). Austin: Von Boeckman-Jones, 1958.
Pebbles from a Broken Jar (Chinese folktales). New York: Bobbs Merrill, 1963.
Mary Charlotte Alexander (An Mo Ling): Missionary to China, 1920-1956. Austin: Von Boeckman-Jones, 1968.
Choc, the Chacalaca (prose). Austin: Von Boeckman-Jones, 1969.
The Diamond Tree (children's poems). Austin: Von Boeckman-Jones, 1970.
Orphans on the Guadalupe. Wichita Falls, Texas: Nortex, 1971.

Arthur M. Sampley
North Texas State University

John Houghton Allen (1909-   )
poetry, novels, short stories, nonfiction

Song to Randado. Dallas: Kaleidograph, 1935.
Song to America. Dallas: Kaleidograph, 1936.
The Minor Testament of John Houghton Allen. Dallas: Kaleidograph, 1941.
Four Tales. Dallas: Kaleidograph, 1943.
A Latin-American Miscellany. Dallas: Kaleidograph, 1943.
Poetry. n.p., 1944.
San Juan. San Antonio: n.p., 1945.
Translations. Dallas: privately printed, 1945.
Southwest. Philadelphia: Lippincott, 1952.

In addition to the books listed above, Allen published sixteen articles and stories between 1953 and 1970 in such journals as *Holiday, New Mexico Quarterly,* and *Southwest Review.*

Henry L. Alsmeyer, Jr.
Texas A&M University

William Allen (1940-   )
novels, nonfiction

Starkweather. Boston: Houghton Mifflin, 1975.
To Tojo from Billy-Bob Jones (novella) in *Antioch Review.* Forthcoming.

In addition, William Allen published nonfiction in *Saturday Review, Reader's Digest,* and *Westways Magazine.* He is editor of *The Ohio Journal.*

James W. Lee
North Texas State University

Rudolfo Anayo (1937-   )
novel

Bless Me Ultima. Berkeley, California: Quinto Sol Publications, 1972.

James W. Lee
North Texas State University

Curt Anders (1927-   )
novels, biography

The Price of Courage. New York: Sagamore Press, 1957.
Fighting Generals. New York: Putnam, 1965.
Fighting Airmen. New York: Putnam, 1966.
Warrior: The Story of George S. Patton. New York: Putnam, 1967.
Fighting Confederates. New York: Putnam, 1968.
Now I See (with Charley Boswell). New York: Meredith Press, 1969.

Gretchen H. Colehour
Knox City, Texas

Dillon Anderson (1906-1974)
novels, short stories

I and Claudie. Boston: Little, Brown, 1951.

Claudie's Kinfolks. Boston: Little, Brown, 1954.
The Billingsley Papers. New York: Simon and Schuster, 1961.

In addition to the books listed above, Anderson published over twenty short stories in *Atlantic* and *Collier's* between 1949 and 1961.

Orlan Sawey
Texas A&I University

Edward Anderson (1905-   )
novels

Hungry Men. Garden City, New York: Doubleday, 1935.
Thieves Like Us. New York and Concord, N. H.: The American Mercury, 1937. Also New York: Frederick A. Stokes, 1937. Rpt. paper New York: Avon, 1974.

Works about Edward Anderson
Gaston, Edwin W., Jr. *The Early Novels of the Southwest.* Albuquerque: Univ. of New Mexico Press, 1961. P. 208.

Lee Rosamond
Stephen F. Austin State University

George W. Archer (1824-1907)
[pseud. Hesper Bendbow]
novels, short stories, history, medical essays

More Than She Could Bear: Story of the Gachupin War in Texas, 1812-13. Philadelphia: Clayton, Remsen and Haffelfinger, 1872.
The Dismemberment of Maryland: An Historical and Critical Essay. Baltimore: J. Murphy and Company, 1890.
An Authentic History of Cokesbury College, with Sketches of Its Founders and Teachers. Bel Air, Maryland: N. N. Nock, 1894.

Leslie H. Palmer
North Texas State University

Elliott Arnold (1912-   )
novels, short stories, plays, nonfiction, juvenile

Two Loves. New York: Greenburg, 1934.

Personal Combat. New York: Greystone Press, 1936.

Finlandia: The Life of Sibelius. New York: Holt, 1938.

Only the Young. New York: Holt, 1939.

Nose for News: The Way of Life of a Reporter. Evanston, Illinois: Row, Peterson and Co., 1941.

The Commandos. New York: Duell, Sloan and Pearce, 1942; rpt. as *First Comes Courage.* New York: Triangle Books, 1943.

Mediterranean Sweep: Air Stories from El Alamein to Rome [with Richard Thruelson]. New York: Duell, Sloan and Pearce, 1944.

Big Distance [with Donald Hough]. New York: Duell, Sloan and Pearce, 1945.

Tomorrow Will Sing. New York: Duell, Sloan and Pearce, 1945.

Blood Brother. New York: Duell, Sloan and Pearce, 1947.

Everybody Slept Here. New York: Duell, Sloan and Pearce, 1948.

Deep in My Heart (biography of Sigmund Romberg). New York: Duell, Sloan and Pearce, 1949.

Walk with the Devil. New York: Knopf, 1950.

Time of the Gringo. New York: Knopf, 1953.

Broken Arrow. New York: Duell, Sloan and Pearce, 1954.

White Falcon. New York: Knopf, 1955.

Rescue. New York: Duell, Sloan and Pearce, 1956.

Flight from Ashiva. New York: Knopf, 1959.

Brave Jimmy Stone. New York: Knopf, 1962.

A Night of Watching. New York: Scribner, 1967.

A Kind of Secret Weapon. New York: Scribner, 1969.

Code of Conduct. New York: Scribner, 1970.

Forests of the Night. New York: Scribner, 1971.

The Spirit of Cochise (juvenile). New York: Scribner, 1972.

Proving Ground; a Novel. New York: Scribner, 1973.

In addition to the works listed above, Arnold published stories and articles in such national magazines as *Saturday Evening Post, Nation, Popular Science, Collier's,* and *Redbook.*

Works about Elliott Arnold
Commire, Anne. *Something about the Author.* Vol. 5. Detroit: Gale, 1973.

"One Brief, Shining Moment" (excerpts from interview). Ed. Haskel Frankel. *Saturday Review*, 2 Sept. 1967, p. 22.

Ward, Martha E., and D. A. Marquardt. *Authors of Books for Young People*. Metuchen, New Jersey: Scarecrow, 1967.

Leslie H. Palmer
North Texas State University

Alfred W. Arrington (1810-1867)
[pseud. Charles Summerfield]
novels, poetry, nonfiction

The Desperadoes of the South-West (biography and history). New York: W. H. Graham, 1847. Published in slightly altered form as *Illustrated Lives and Adventures of the Desperadoes of the New World* in 1849 by T. B. Peterson of Philadelphia; and as *The Lives and Adventures of Desperadoes of the South-West* also in 1849 by W. H. Graham of New York.

Duelists and Duelling in the South-West (second and concluding part of *Desperadoes*). New York: W. H. Graham, 1847; and Philadelphia: Zeiber, 1847.

O. S. House Versus Western Transportation Company (legal arguments). Chicago: Tribune Steam Print, 1858.

Poems (poetry and memoirs). Chicago: E. B. Meyers, 1869.

The Rangers and Regulators of the Tanaha; or, Life Among the Lawless, A Tale of the Republic of Texas (novel). New York: R. M. DeWitt, 1856. Also published under same title in 1871 by Carlton of New York and Low of London. Published under the title of *A Faithful Lover* in 1884 by Carlton of New York.

Works about Alfred W. Arrington

Gaston, Edwin W., Jr. *The Early Novel of the Southwest*. Albuquerque: Univ. of New Mexico Press, 1961. *Passim*.

Lee Rosamond
Stephen F. Austin State University

Philip Atlee
[see James Atlee Phillips]

Mary Hunter Austin (1868-1934)
[pseud. Gordon Carstairs]
novels, short stories, poetry, nonfiction

The Land of Little Rain. Boston and New York: Houghton Mifflin, 1903; rpt. Garden City: Doubleday, 1962.

Isidro. Boston and New York: Houghton Mifflin, 1905.

The Flock. Boston and New York: Houghton Mifflin, 1906.

Santa Lucia, A Common Story. London and New York: Harper's, 1908.

Lost Borders. London and New York: Harper's, 1909.

The Basket Woman. Boston and New York: Houghton Mifflin, 1910.

Outland [Gordon Carstairs]. London: John Murray, 1910. Rpt. under her own name. New York: Boni and Liveright, 1919.

The Arrow Maker. New York: Duffield, 1911; rev. Boston and New York: Houghton Mifflin, 1915.

California, Land of the Sun. London: A. and C. Black, 1914; New York: Macmillan, 1914. Rev. ed. titled *Lands of the Sun.* Boston and New York: Houghton Mifflin, 1927.

The Man Jesus. New York and London: Harper's, 1915; rpt. as *A Small Town Man,* 1925. Serialized in *North American Review* (1915).

The Ford. Boston and New York: Houghton Mifflin, 1917.

The Trail Book. Boston and New York: Houghton Mifflin, 1918.

The American Rhythm. New York: Harcourt, Brace, 1923. Rpt. Boston and New York: Houghton Mifflin, 1930.

The Land of Journeys' Ending. New York and London: Century, 1924.

The Children Sing in the Far West. Boston and New York: Houghton Mifflin, 1928.

Starry Adventure. Boston and New York: Houghton Mifflin, 1931.

Earth Horizon. An Autobiography. Boston and New York: Houghton Mifflin, 1932.

Indian Pottery of the Rio Grande. Pasadena, Calif.: Esto Pub. Co., 1934.

One Smoke Stories. Boston and New York: Houghton Mifflin, 1934.

Mother of Felipe and Other Early Stories. Ed. Franklin Walker. Los Angeles: Book Club of California, 1950.

One Hundred Miles on Horseback. Los Angeles: Dawson's Book Shop, 1963.

In addition to the books listed, Mary Austin published a number of essays in such journals as *Saturday Review, South Atlantic Quarterly, English Journal,* and *Theatre Arts Magazine.*

Works about Mary Austin

Barker, R. L. "Mary Austin: Novelist and Ethnologist," *Sunset,* 43 (September 1919), 49-50.

Brooks, Van Wyck. *The Confident Years: 1885-1915.* New York: Dutton, 1932.

Calverton, V. F. "From Sectionalism to Nationalism," *The Liberation of American Literature.* New York: Scribner, 1932.

Doyle, Helen McKnight. "Books and Mary Austin," *Wilson Library Bulletin,* 14 (June 1940), 715-19.

————. *Mary Austin: Woman of Genius.* New York: Gotham House, 1939.

Dubois, Arthur E. "Mary Hunter Austin, 1868-1934," *Southwest Review,* 20 (April 1935), 321-64.

Field, Louise Maunsell. "Mary Austin, American," *Bookman,* 75 (December 1932), 819-21.

Keiser, Albert. *The Indian in American Literature.* New York: Oxford Univ. Press, 1933.

Lyday, Jo W. *Mary Austin: The Southwest Works.* Austin: Steck-Vaughn, 1968.

Pearce, Thomas Matthews. *Mary Hunter Austin.* New York: Twayne, 1965.

Jo W. Lyday
San Jacinto College

Ruth Averitte (1901-1972)
poetry, nonfiction

Salute to Dawn (poems). Dallas: Tardy Pub. Co., 1936.
Let's Review a Book (criticism). Dallas: Tardy Pub. Co., 1938.
Cowboy Over Kiska (poems). Dallas: Avalon Press, 1945.
Carols in Flower (poems). Dallas: Avalon Press, 1946.

Ruth Averitte has published numerous poems, comments, and articles in such periodicals as *Southwest Review, Texas Review, Writer's Digest, Living Poetry, Fiddlehead, The Canadian Poetry Journal, Breve,* and in several yearbooks of the Poetry Society of Texas.

Barbara Albrecht McDaniel
North Texas State University

Dora Aydelotte (1878-   )
novels, short stories

Long Furrows. New York: Appleton-Century, 1935
Green Gravel (juvenile). New York: Appleton-Century, 1937.
Trumpets Calling. New York: Appleton-Century, 1938.
Full Harvest. New York: Appleton-Century, 1939.
Run of the Stars. New York: Appleton-Century, 1940.
Across the Prairie. New York: Appleton-Century, 1941.
Measure of a Man. New York: Appleton-Century, 1942.

In addition, Dora Aydelotte published a number of short stories in *Forum* between 1932 and 1935.

Patricia E. Russell
Stephen F. Austin State University

Stanley E. Babb (1899-   )
poetry

Death of a Buccaneer and Other Poems. Dallas: Southwest Press, 1927.

In addition to the volume of poetry listed above, Stanley E. Babb has several uncollected poems in such journals as *Midland, Liberator, Bard, Buccaneer, Baylorian,* and *Southwest Review.*

Patricia E. Russell
Stephen F. Austin State University

Charlotte Baker (1910-   )
novels, juveniles, nonfiction

The Birds of Tanglewood. Dallas: Southwest Press, 1930.
A Sombrero for Miss Brown. New York: Dutton, 1941.
Hope Hacienda. New York: Crowell, 1942.
House of the Roses. New York: Dutton, 1942.
Necessary Nellie. New York: Coward-McCann, 1945.

Nellie and the Mayor's Hat. New York: Coward-McCann, 1947.
The House on the River. New York: Coward-McCann, 1948.
Kinnery Camp: A Story of the Oregon Woods. New York: McKay, 1951.
Sunrise Island; a Story of the Northwest Coast Indians Before the Coming of the White Man. New York: McKay, 1952.
Magic for Mary M. New York: McKay, 1953.
The Return of the Thunderbird; Story of a Voyage from Canton, China, to Norfolk, Virginia, in the Ship Thunderbird, Commanded by Samuel Heflin, Begun in 1801 and Terminated One Year Later. New York: McKay, 1954.
The Venture of the Thunderbird; Story of a Voyage from Norfolk, Virginia, to the Northwest Coast of America in the Ship Thunderbird, Commanded by John Audley. Begun in 1800 and Terminated One Year Later. New York: McKay, 1954.
The Green Poodles. New York: McKay, 1956.
Thomas, the Ship's Cat. New York: McKay, 1958.
An ABC of Dog Care for Young Owners. New York: McKay, 1959.
Little Brother. New York: McKay, 1959.
The Best of Friends. New York: McKay, 1966.
The Kittens and the Cardinals. New York: McKay, 1969.

Patricia E. Russell
Stephen F. Austin State University

Karle Wilson Baker (1878-1960)
novels, short stories, poetry, juveniles, nonfiction

Blue Smoke: A Book of Verses. New Haven: Yale Univ. Press, 1919.
The Garden of the Plynck. New Haven: Yale Univ. Press, 1920.
Burning Bush. New Haven: Yale Univ. Press, 1922.
Old Coins. New Haven: Yale Univ. Press, 1923.
Texas Flag Primer. Yonkers-on-Hudson, New York: World Book, 1925.
The Birds of Tanglewood. Dallas: Southwest Press, 1930.
Dreamers on Horseback (collected verse). Dallas: Southwest Press, 1931.
Two Little Texans. Yonkers-on-Hudson, New York: World Book, 1932.
Family Style. New York: Coward-McCann, 1937.
Star of the Wilderness. New York: Coward-McCann, 1942.

In addition to the books listed above, Baker published ten articles and stories between 1907 and 1937 in *Century, Everybody's, Forum, Putnam's, Southwest Review,* and *Texas Review.*

W. M. Richardson
University of Texas at Arlington

Eve Ball
nonfiction

Ruidoso: The Last Frontier. San Antonio: Naylor, 1963.

Bob Crosby, World Champion Cowboy (with Thelma Crosby). Clarendon, Texas: Clarendon Press, 1966.

Ma'am Jones of the Pecos. Tucson: Univ. of Arizona Press, 1969.

In the Days of Victorio: Recollections of a Warm Springs Apache. Tucson: Univ. of Arizona Press, 1970.

My Girlhood Among Outlaws by Lily Klasner (edited by Eve Ball). Tucson: Univ. of Arizona Press, 1972.

Diane M. Dodson
North Texas State University

Adolph F. Bandelier (1840-1914)
novels, short stories, anthropology, history

A Report on the Ruins of the Pueblo of Pecos. Boston: A. Williams and Co., 1881.

Historical Introduction to Studies Among the Sedentary Indians of New Mexico. Boston: A. Williams & Co., 1881.

Report of an Archaeological Tour in Mexico in 1881. Cambridge: Univ. Press, John Wilson & Son, 1884. Also published as *An Archaeological Reconnoissance* [sic] *into Mexico in the Year 1881.* Boston: Cupples, 1884.

An Outline of the Documentary History of the Zuñi Tribe. Cambridge: Peabody Museum, 1890.

Final Report of Investigations Among the Indians of the Southwestern United States, Carried on Mainly in the Years from 1880-1885. Cambridge: Univ. Press, John Wilson & Son, 1890-1892. Bandelier's *Index to Final Report* . . . published in Albuquerque: New Mexico Historical Records Survey, 1942.

The Delight Makers (novel). New York: Dodd, Mead, 1890; rpt. 1916, 1954.

Hemenway Southwestern Expedition: Contributions to the History of the Southwestern Portion of the United States. Cambridge: Univ. Press, John Wilson & Son, 1890.

The Gilded Man (novel). New York: D. Appleton & Co., 1893.

The Journey of Alvar Nuñez Cabeza de Vaca and His Companions from Florida to the Pacific, 1528-1536. (Translated by Fanny Bandelier; ed. with introduction by A. Bandelier.) New York: A. S. Barnes, 1905.

Documentary History of the Rio Grande Pueblos of New Mexico. "Bibliographic Introduction" issued as No. 13, Papers of the School of American Archaeology, Archaeological Institute of America [Santa Fe?], New Mexico, 1910. Published without the "Bibliographic Introduction" in *New Mexico Historical Review,* 4 (1929), 303-35; 5 (1930), 38-66, 154-85, 240-62, 333-85.

Islands of Titicaca and Koati. New York: Hispanic Society of America, 1910.

Historical Documents Relating to New Mexico, Nueva Vizcaya, and Approaches Thereto, to 1773, Collected by Adolph F. A. Bandelier and Fanny R. Bandelier. Ed. Charles Wilson Hackett. 3 vols. Washington: Carnegie Institution, 1923, 1926, 1937.

The Journals of Adolphe Francis Alphonse Bandelier during the Years 1886-1889. . . . New York: Press of the Pioneers, 1934.

Indians of the Rio Grande Valley (with Edgar L. Hewett). Albuquerque: Univ. of New Mexico Press, 1937.

The Unpublished Letters of Adolphe F. Bandelier concerning the Writing and Publication of "The Delight Makers." Ed. with introduction by Paul Radin. El Paso: C. Hertzog, 1942. Also New York: Charles P. Everitt, 1942.

The Southwestern Journals of Adolph F. Bandelier, 1880-1882. Ed. and annotated by Charles H. Lange and Carroll L. Riley. Albuquerque: Univ. of New Mexico Press, 1966. *The Southwestern Journals* . . . *1883-1884* was published in 1970. Two more volumes are planned, the third to cover 1885 to 1888 and the fourth, 1889 to 1892.

In addition, Adolph Bandelier published a number of essays on anthropology in learned journals.

Works about Adolph F. Bandelier

Bandelier Collection of Copies of Documents Relating to the History of New Mexico and Arizona (350 titles). In the Peabody Museum, Harvard University.

Bandelier, Adolph F. *Diaries, 1880-1890.* 10 vols. (ms.) in Museum of New Mexico, Santa Fe.

Bandelier, Fanny Ritter. "Recollections Regarding the Early Years of Adolph F. Bandelier," Ms. in Archives, Museum of New Mexico, Santa Fe. Other material about Bandelier also in Archives.

Fontana, Bernard L. "Dedication to Adolph F. A. Bandelier," *Arizona and the West,* 2 (Spring 1960), 1-5.

Hammond, George P. and Edgar F. Goad, eds. *A Scientist on the Trail: Travel Letters of A. F. Bandelier, 1880-1881.* Berkeley, California: Quivira Society, 1949.

Hobbs, Hulda R. "Bandelier in the Southwest," *El Palacio,* 47 (1940), 121-36.

Hodge, Frederick Webb. "Bandelier Obituary," *American Anthropologist,* 16 (1914), 349-58.

————. "Biographical Sketch and Bibliography of Adolphe Francis Alphonse Bandelier," *New Mexico Historical Review,* 7 (1932), 353-70.

Lummis, Charles F. "Death of Bandelier, An Irreparable Loss," *El Palacio,* 1 (April-May 1914), 1, 3-4.

Schaefer, Jack Warner. *Adolphe Francis Alphonse Bandelier.* Santa Fe: Press of the Territorian, 1966.

Waterman, T. T. "Bandelier's Contribution to the Study of Ancient Mexican Social Organization," *University of California Publications in American Archaeology and Ethnology,* 12 (1917), 249-82.

White, Leslie A., ed. *Pioneers in American Anthropology: the Bandelier-Morgan Letters,* 1873-1883. 2 vols. Albuquerque: Univ. of New Mexico Press, 1940.

————, and Ignacio Bernal. *Correspondencia de Adolfo F. Bandelier [with Don Joaquín García Icazbalceta].* Mexico: Instituto Nacional de Antropologia e Historia, 1960.

Robert E. Fleming
University of New Mexico

William Earl Bard (1892-   )
poetry

A Little Flame Blown. Dallas: Southwest Press, 1934.
Feather in the Sun. Dallas: Kaleidograph Press, 1949.
This Land, This People. San Antonio: Naylor, 1966.
Burning Embers. Quanah, Texas: Nortex, 1970.
As a Wild Bird Returning. Quanah, Texas: Nortex, 1973.

In addition, Bard published poems in such journals as *Midland, Forge,* Yearbooks of the Poetry Society of Texas, *Kaleidograph, Harp, Troubadour,* and *West.* His work has also appeared in a number of anthologies.

Patricia E. Russell
Stephen F. Austin State University

Elliott Speer Barker (1886-   )
poetry, nonfiction

When the Dogs Bark "Treed." Albuquerque: Univ. of New Mexico Press, 1946.
Beatty's Cabin: Adventures in the Pecos High Country. Albuquerque: Univ. of New Mexico Press, 1953.
A Medley of Wilderness and Other Poems. Santa Fe: n.p., 1962.
Western Life and Adventures, 1889-1970. New York: Calvin Horn, 1971.

In addition, Barker published poems in periodicals such as *American Forests,* and he has written a number of sportsman's stories in *Outdoor Life, Field and Stream,* and *American Forests.*

Patricia E. Russell
Stephen F. Austin State University

Eugene Campbell Barker (1874-1956)
history

The Finances of the Texas Revolution. Boston: Ginn, 1904.
A School History of Texas (with Charles Shirley Potts and Charles W. Ramsdell). Chicago: Row, Peterson, 1912.

California as the Cause of the Mexican War. Austin, 1917.

The Austin Papers. Washington: Government Printing Office, 1924.

The Life of Stephen F. Austin. Nashville and Dallas: Cokesbury, 1927.

The Growth of a Nation (with Walter P. Webb and Willie E. Dodd). New York: Row, Peterson, 1928, 1934, 1937.

Mexico and Texas, 1821-1835. Dallas: Turner, 1928.

Readings in Texas History for High Schools and Colleges. Dallas: The Southwest Press, 1929.

The Story of Our Nation. The United States of America (with William E. Dodd and Walter P. Webb). New York: Row, Peterson, 1929.

Old Europe and Our Nation (with Frederic Duncalf and Francis Leonard Bacon). New York: Row, Peterson, 1932.

Our Nation Begins (with William E. Dodd and Walter P. Webb). New York: Row, Peterson, 1932.

Our Nation Grows (with William E. Dodd and Walter P. Webb). New York: Row, Peterson, 1933.

Our Nation: Development (with William E. Dodd and Henry Steele Commager). New York: Row, Peterson, 1934.

The Father of Texas, New York: Bobbs Merrill, 1935.

The Story of Earliest Times (with Mabel Rockwood Grimm and Matilda Hughes). New York: Row, Peterson, 1936.

The Building of Our Nation (with Henry Steele Commager and Walter P. Webb). New York: Row, Peterson, 1937.

The Story of Colonial Times (with Mabel Rockwood Grimm and Matilda Hughes). New York: Row, Peterson, 1937.

The Story of Old Europe and New America (with Mabel Rockwood Grimm and Matilda Hughes). New York: Row, Peterson, 1937.

The Writings of Sam Houston (with Amelia W. Williams). Austin: Univ. of Texas Press, 1938.

Our Nation (with Henry Steele Commager). New York: Row, Peterson, 1941.

Speeches, Responses, and Essays. Austin: Eugene C. Barker History Center, 1954.

In addition, Barker published numerous scholarly essays in such periodicals as *Mississippi Valley Historical Review, Southwestern Historical Quarterly,* and *Texas Review.*

John T. Smith
North Texas State University

Ruth Laughlin Barker (1889-   )
nonfiction

Caballeros. New York: Appleton, 1931; 1937; rpt. Caldwell, Idaho: Caxton, 1945.
The Wind Leaves No Shadow. New York: Whittlesey House, 1948; rpt. Caldwell, Idaho: Caxton, 1951.

In addition, Barker published seven articles between 1916 and 1929 in *Pan American Magazine, House and Garden, Sunset, House Beautiful,* and *North American Review.*

Fred Rodewald
Stephen F. Austin State University

S. Omar Barker (1894-   )
novels, short stories, poetry

Winds of the Mountains. Beulah, N.M.: n.p., 1924.
Buckaroo Ballads. Santa Fe: Santa Fe New Mexican Publishing, 1928.
Born to Battle. Albuquerque: Univ. of New Mexico Press, 1951.
Songs of the Saddlemen. Denver: Swallow, 1954.
Sunlight Through the Trees. Las Vegas, N.M.: Highlands Univ. Press, 1954.
Legends and Tales of the Old West. Ed. S. Omar Barker. Garden City, New York: Doubleday, 1962.
Little World Apart. Garden City, New York: Doubleday, 1966.
Rawhide Rhymes. n.p., 1968. [not seen]
The Cattleman's Steak Book (with Carol Truax). n.p., 1967.

Barker has published stories, articles, and poetry in about one hundred magazines, including *Saturday Evening Post, Adventure, Argosy, Field and Stream, New York Times, Zane Grey's Western, Look, American Legion Magazine,* and *Ranch Romances.*

Alice Bullock
Santa Fe, New Mexico

Leola Christie Barnes (1889-   )
poetry, juveniles

Crimson Dawning. Dallas: Cockrell Publishing House, 1931.
Purple Petals. Devonshire: Channing Press, 1934. Rpt. San Antonio: Naylor, 1960.
Silver Century. San Antonio: Naylor, 1936; rpt., 1973.
West to Glory. New York: Exposition Press, 1961.
Her Majesty Nevertheless. San Antonio: Naylor, 1968.

Fred Rodewald
Stephen F. Austin State University

Will C. Barnes (1858-1936)
[pseud. William Croft]
short stories, poetry, nonfiction

Western Grazing Grounds and Forest Ranges. Chicago: The Breeders' Gazette, 1913.
Tales from the X-Bar Horse Camp. Chicago: The Breeders' Gazette, 1920.
Cattle (with William MacLeod Raine). Garden City, New York: Doubleday Doran, 1930.
Arizona Place Names. Tucson: Univ. of Arizona, 1935.
Apaches and Longhorns. Ed. Frank Lockwood. Los Angeles: Ward Ritchie Press, 1941.

In addition, Barnes published thirty articles and stories between 1898 and 1934 in such publications as *Harper's Weekly, Atlantic, Saturday Evening Post, Technical World, Nature, Science, Scientific American, Sunset,* and others. Barnes also contributed to several U.S. Department of Agriculture bulletins and booklets.

Works about Will C. Barnes
T. M. Knappen. "West at Washington," *Sunset,* 59 (July 1927), 51.

Fred Rodewald
Stephen F. Austin State University

William D. Barney (1916-   )
poetry

Kneel from the Stone. Dallas: Kaleidograph Press, 1952.
Permitted Proof. Dallas: Kaleidograph Press, 1955.

In addition, Barney published poems in *Epos, Ladies Home Journal, New Orleans Poetry Journal, University Review, Virginia Quarterly Review,* and *Voices.* His poetry has appeared in several anthologies, including *Best Poems of 1958, A Part of Space: Ten Texas Writers* (ed. Betsy F. Colquitt), *Southwest Writers Anthology* (ed. Martin S. Shockley), and *Fire and Sleet and Candlelight* (ed. A. Derleth).

Fred Rodewald
Stephen F. Austin State University

Amelia Edith Huddleston Barr (1831-1919)
novels, short stories, poetry, nonfiction

Romances and Realities. New York: J. B. Ford, 1876.
Cluny MacPherson: A Tale of Brotherly Love. New York: American Tract Society; New York: Dodd, Mead, 1883.
Scottish Sketches. New York: American Tract Society, 1883; rpt. New York: Dodd Mead, 1898. Translated into German as *"Die Grenzhirtin"* by Emmy von Feilitzsch. Konstanz: C. Hirsch, 1909.
Hallam Succession: A Tale of Methodist Life in Two Countries. New York: Phillips and Hunt, 1885; Cincinnati: Granston and Stowe, 1885; New York: Dodd, Mead, 1884; Toronto: W. Briggs, 1887.
Jan Vedder's Wife. New York: Dodd, Mead, 1885; rpt. New York: Christian Herald, 1916.
Lost Silver of Briffault. New York: Phillips and Hunt; Cincinnati: Cranston & Stowe, 1885; rpt. New York: Dodd, Mead, 1898.
Between Two Loves: A Tale of the West Riding. New York: Harper, 1886; rpt. New York: Dodd, Mead, 1889; London: Frederick Warne, 1894.
Bow of Orange Ribbon: A Romance of New York. New York: Dodd, Mead, 1886; New York: P. F. Collier, 1886.
Daughter of Fife. New York: Dodd, Mead, 1886.
Last of the Macallisters. New York: Harper, 1886; rpt. New York: Dodd, Mead, 1889.

Squire of Sandal Side, A Pastoral Romance. New York: Dodd, Mead, 1886.

Border Shepherdess: A Romance of Eskdale. New York: Dodd, Mead, 1887; London: J. Clarke, n.d.

Christopher, and Other Stories. New York: Phillips and Hunt; Cincinnati: Cranston & Stowe, 1888; rpt. New York: Dodd, Mead, 1898.

In Spite of Himself: A Tale of West Riding. London: J. Clarke, 1888.

Master of His Fate. New York: Dodd, Mead, 1888.

Remember the Alamo. New York: Dodd, Mead, 1888.

Feet of Clay. New York: Dodd, Mead, 1889.

Friend Olivia. New York: Dodd, Mead, 1889.

Household of McNeil. New York: Dodd, Mead, 1890.

Beads of Tasmer. New York: R. Bonner's Sons, 1891; London: J. Clarke, 1893.

Love for an Hour Is Love Forever. New York: Dodd, Mead, 1891.

Mrs. Barr's Short Stories. New York: R. Bonner's Sons, 1891.

Rose of a Hundred Leaves. New York: Dodd, Mead, 1891.

She Loved a Sailor. New York: Dodd, Mead, 1891.

Sister to Esau. New York: Dodd, Mead; New York: Hunt & Eaton, 1891.

Michael and Theodora: A Russian Story. Boston: Bradley and Woodruff, 1892.

Preacher's Daughter. Boston: Bradley and Woodruff; New York: Ward and Drummond, 1892.

Girls of a Feather. New York: R. Bonner's Sons, 1893.

Lone House. New York: Dodd, Mead, 1893.

Mate of the "Easter Bell" and Other Stories. New York: R. Bonner's Sons, 1893.

Singer From The Sea. New York: Dodd, Mead, 1893.

Bernicia. New York: Dodd, Mead, 1895.

Flower of Gala Water. New York: R. Bonner's Sons, 1895.

Knight of the Nets. New York: Dodd, Mead, 1896.

Winter Evening Tales. New York: Christian Herald, 1896.

King's Highway. New York: Dodd, Mead, 1897.

Prisoners of Conscience. New York: Century, 1897.

Stories of Life and Love. New York: Christian Herald, 1897.

Maids, Wives and Bachelors. New York: Dodd, Mead, 1898.

Trinity Bells: A Tale of Old New York. New York: J. F. Taylor, 1899; New York: Christian Herald, 1899; rpts. New York: Dodd, Mead, 1908; New York: Grosset & Dunlap, 1915.

Was It Right to Forgive? Chicago and New York: H. S. Stone, 1899.

Woven of Love and Glory. London: F. Warne, 1899.

I, Thou, and the Other One: A Love Story. New York: Dodd, Mead, 1900.

Maid of Maiden Lane: A Sequel to Bow of Orange. New York: Dodd, Mead, 1900.

Lion's Whelp: A Story of Cromwell's Time. New York: Dodd, Mead, 1901.

Souls of Passage. New York: Dodd, Mead, 1901.

Song of a Single Note. New York: Dodd, Mead; New York: Christian Herald Bible House; New York: Grosset & Dunlap, 1902.

Black Shilling: A Tale of Boston Town. New York: Dodd, Mead, 1903.

Thyra Varrick: A Love Story. New York: J. F. Taylor, 1903; London: T. F. Unwin, 1904; rpt. New York: Grosset & Dunlap, n.d.

Belle of Bowling Green. New York: Dodd, Mead, 1904.

Cecilia's Lovers. New York: Dodd, Mead, 1905.

Man Between: An International Romance. New York and London: The Authors and Newspapers' Association, 1906.

Heart of Jessie Laurie. New York: Dodd, Mead, 1907.

Strawberry Handkerchief: A Romance of the Stamp Act. New York: Dodd, Mead; New York: A. L. Burt, 1908.

Hands of Compulsion. New York: Dodd, Mead, 1909.

House on Cherry Street. New York: Dodd, Mead, 1909.

Reconstructed Marriage. New York: Dodd, Mead; New York: A. L. Burt, 1910.

Maid of Old New York: A Romance of Peter Stuyvesant's Time. New York: Christian Herald, 1911.

Sheila Vedder. New York: Dodd, Mead; New York: Grosset & Dunlap, 1911.

All the Days of My Life: An Autobiography. New York and London: D. Appleton, 1913.

Three Score and Ten. New York and London: D. Appleton, 1913.

Playing with Fire. New York and London: D. Appleton, 1914.

Measure of a Man. New York and London: D. Appleton, 1915.

Winning of Lucia: A Love Story. New York and London: D. Appleton, 1915.

Profit and Loss. New York and London: D. Appleton, 1916.

Christine, a Fife Fisher Girl. New York and London: D. Appleton, 1917.

Joan: A Romance of an English Mining Village. New York: D. Appleton, 1917.

Orkney Maid. New York and London: D. Appleton, 1918.
Paper Cup: A Story of Love and Labor. New York and London: D. Appleton, 1918.
Songs in the Common Chord. New York and London: D. Appleton, 1919.

Works about Amelia Barr

Adams, Paul. "Amelia Barr in Texas, 1856-1868," *Southwest Historical Quarterly,* 49 (January 1946), 361-73.
Blake, H. E. "Mrs. Barr and Her Story," *Bookman,* 37 (August 1913), 617-21.
Hawthorne, H. "Amelia E. Barr: Some Reminiscences," *Bookman,* 51 (May 1920), 283-86.
Sweetser, K. D. "Amelia Barr and the Novice," *Bookman,* 58 (October 1923), 172-78.

Fred Rodewald
Stephen F. Austin State University

Monte Barrett (1897-1949)
novels

The Pelham Murder Case. Chicago: White House, 1930.
Murder Offstage. Indianapolis: Bobbs-Merrill, 1931.
Knotted Silk. London: Stanley Paul; New York: A. L. Burt, 1932.
The Wedding March Murder. Indianapolis: Bobbs-Merrill, 1933.
Murder at Belle Camille. Indianapolis: Bobbs-Merrill, 1943.
Sun in Their Eyes. Indianapolis: Bobbs-Merrill, 1944.
The Tempered Blade. Indianapolis: Bobbs-Merrill, 1946.
Smoke up the Valley. Indianapolis: Bobbs-Merrill, 1949. Serialized as *Rustler's Range* in *Saturday Evening Post* (Feb.-Mar. 1949).
Scream in the Night. London: Merit Books, 1954.

In addition, Barrett serialized novels and parts of novels in newspapers. The following titles are listed in Florence Barnes's *Texas Writers Today,* but they apparently were never published as separate books: *The Waster* (1922), *The Third Ruby* (1927), *Who* (1928), *The Lone Rebel* (1929), and *Runaway* (1931).

Fred Rodewald
Stephen F. Austin State University

Donald Barthelme (1931-   )
novels, short stories

Come Back, Dr. Caligari. New York: Little, Brown, 1964.
Snow White. New York: Atheneum, 1967.
Unspeakable Practices, Unnatural Acts. New York: Farrar, Straus & Giroux, 1968.
City Life. New York: Farrar, Straus & Giroux, 1970.
The Slightly Irregular Fire Engine of the Hithering, Thithering Djinn. New York: Farrar, Straus & Giroux, 1971.
Sadness. New York: Farrar, Straus & Giroux, 1972.
Guilty Pleasures. New York: Farrar, Straus & Giroux, 1974.

In addition, Barthelme published more than twenty short stories in such journals as *Esquire, Harper's,* and *The New Yorker.*

Works about Donald Barthelme
Gilman, Richard. *The Confusion of Realms.* New York: Random House, 1963. Pp. 42-52.
Longleigh, Peter J., Jr. "Donald Barthelme's *Snow White,*" *Critique: Studies in Modern Fiction,* 11 (1969), 30-34.
Mudrick, Marvin. "Sarraute, Duras, Burroughs, Barthelme, and a Postscript," *Hudson Review,* 20 (Autumn 1967), 473-86.
Trachtenberg, Stanley. "Modes of Imperception," *Kenyon Review,* 29 (Sept. 1967), 561-68.

William B. Warde, Jr.
North Texas State University

Lelia McAnally Batte (1887-1960)
[Mrs. Robert Lee Batte]
fiction, poetry, history

Master of the Sycamores (Fiction). Houston: The Anson Jones Press, 1947.
The Perfumed Garden (Poetry). Dexter, Mo.: Candor Press, 1952.
Leaves from the Sycamore (Poetry). Dallas: The Story Book Press, 1954.
History of Milam County, Texas. San Antonio: Naylor, 1956.

Alfred S. Shivers
Stephen F. Austin State University

Roy Bedichek (1878-1959)
nonfiction

Adventures with a Texas Naturalist. Garden City, New York: Doubleday, 1947; rpt. 1961 by Doubleday and by Univ. of Texas Press.
Karankaway Country. Garden City, New York: Doubleday, 1950.
Educational Competition. Austin: Univ. of Texas Press, 1956.
The Sense of Smell. Garden City, New York: Doubleday, 1960.

In addition, Bedichek published some thirty essays and reviews in such periodicals as *Southwest Review, Reader's Digest,* and *Audubon Magazine.*

Works about Roy Bedichek
Dugger, Ronnie, ed. *Three Men in Texas: Bedichek, Webb and Dobie.* Austin: Univ. of Texas Press, 1967.
James, Eleanor. *Roy Bedichek.* Austin: Steck-Vaughn, 1970.
Owens, William A. *Three Friends: Bedichek, Dobie, Webb.* Garden City, New York: Doubleday, 1969.

Eleanor James
Texas Woman's University

John Barry Benefield (1877-1971)
novels, short stories

The Chicken-wagon Family. New York: Century, 1925.
Short Turns (stories). New York: Century, 1926.
Bugles in the Night (stories). New York: Century, 1927.
A Little Clown Lost. New York: Century, 1928.
Valiant Is the Word for Carrie. New York: Reynal and Hitchcock, 1935.
April Was When It Began. New York: Reynal and Hitchcock, 1939.
Eddie and the Archangel Mike. New York: Reynal and Hitchcock, 1943.

Uncollected stories have appeared in *Century, Collier's, Good Housekeeping, Ladies Home Journal, Pictorial Review, Scribner's Magazine,* and *Woman's Home Companion.*

Works about Barry Benefield
"Folklore in the Fiction of Barry Benefield," *Mississippi Quarterly,* 21 (1968), 63-70.

Larry B. Corse
North Texas State University

Robert Ames Bennet (1870-1954)
[pseud. Lee Robinet]
novels, novelettes

Into the Primitive. Chicago: A. C. Mc Clurg, and New York: A. L. Burt, 1908.

A Volunteer with Pike: The True Narrative of One Dr. John Robinson and of His Love for the Fair Señorita Vallois. Chicago: A. C. Mc Clurg, 1909.

The Shogun's Daughter. Chicago: A. C. Mc Clurg, 1910.

Out of the Primitive. Chicago: A. C. Mc Clurg, 1911.

Which One? Chicago: A. C. Mc Clurg, 1912.

The In-Bad Man. n. p., 1913.

Out of the Depths: A Romance of the Reclamation. Chicago: A. C. Mc Clurg, 1913; rpt. as *Deep Canyon,* 1928.

The Forest Maiden. [Lee Robinet]. Chicago: Browne and Howell, 1914.

The Quarterbreed. Chicago: Browne and Howell, 1914.

The Blond Beast. Chicago: Reilly & Britton, 1918.

Bloom of Cactus. Garden City, New York: Doubleday Page, 1920.

Waters of Strife. New York: A. L. Burt and New York: W. J. Watt, 1921; rpt. as *Waters of Conflict.* London: Collins, 1926.

Tyrrel of the Cow Country. Chicago: A. C. Mc Clurg and London: Cassell, 1923.

Branded. Chicago: A. C. Mc Clurg and New York: A. L. Burt, 1924.

The Two-gun Man. Chicago: A. C. Mc Clurg and New York: A. L. Burt, 1924; rpt. as *Two-Gun Sid,* 1925.

The Cattle Baron. Chicago: A. C. Mc Clurg, 1925; rpt. as *The Two-Gun Girl.* London: Collins, 1928.

The Rough Rider. Chicago: A. C. Mc Clurg, 1925.

The Boss of the Diamond. Chicago: A. C. Mc Clurg and New York: A. L. Burt, 1926; rpt. as *The Diamond A Girl,* 1930.

Go-getter Gary. Chicago: A. C. Mc Clurg, 1926.
Ken the Courageous. Chicago: A. C. Mc Clurg and New York: A. L. Burt, 1927; rpt. as *Ken of the Cow Country.* London: Collins, 1933.
On the Rustler Trail. Chicago: A. C. Mc Clurg and New York: A. L. Burt, 1927; rpt. as *The Cow Country Killers,* 1928.
The Desert Girl. London: Collins, 1928.
The Tenderfoot. Chicago: A. C. Mc Clurg, 1928.
Vengeance Valley. London: Collins, 1929.
The Roped Wolf. London: Collins, 1930.
The Sheepman's Gold. London: Collins, 1930.
Sunny of Timberline. London: Collins, 1930.
The Border Wolf. New York: G. H. Watt, 1931.
Caught in the Wild. London: Collins, 1931.
The Deadwood Trail. London: Collins, 1931.
Bad Med'cine. London: Collins, 1932.
Feud of Cattle Kings. London: Collins, 1932.
The Gold Wolf. New York: G. H. Watt, 1932.
Wild West Story Club. London: n. p., 1932.
Avalanche Gulch. London: Collins, 1933.
The Hunted Wolf. New York: I. Washburn, 1933.
The Law of the Trail. London: Collins, 1933.
A Son of Texas. London: Collins, 1933.
Guns on the Rio Grande. New York: I. Washburn, 1934.
Raiding Rustlers. London: Collins, 1934.
Texas Man. New York: I. Washburn and New York: A. L. Burt, 1934.
Trial by Fire. London: Collins, 1934.
Death Rides the Range. New York: I. Washburn, 1935.
Gold in the Desert. London: Collins, 1935.
White Buffalo. New York: I. Washburn and New York: Blue Ribbon Books, 1935.
Horsethief Hole. New York: I. Washburn, 1936.
Man Against Mustang. New York: I. Washburn, 1936.
Bad Apache. London: Collins, 1937.
Crossed Trails. New York: I. Washburn, 1937.
Hot Lead. New York: I. Washburn, 1937.
Trail of the Split Hoof. London: Collins, 1937.
Cowboy Caballero. London: Collins, 1938.
The Gun Fighter. New York: I. Washburn, 1938.

The Brand Blotters. New York: I. Washburn, 1939.
Range Boss. London: Collins, 1939.

Alfred S. Shivers
Stephen F. Austin State University

Emerson Bennett (1822-1905)
novels, short stories, poetry

Wild Scenes on the Frontiers: Or Heroes of the West. Philadelphia: Hamelin, 1839. Reissued as *Forest and Prairie* (1860).
The Brigand: A Poem . . . in Two Cantos. New York: Xylographic Press, 1842.
The Unknown Countess: Or Crime and its Results. Cincinnati: U. P. James, n.d. First published in a newspaper contest in 1843; rpt. in *The Pioneer's Daughter* (1851).
The Bandits of the Osage: A Western Romance. Cincinnati: Robinson and Jones, 1847.
Kate Clarendon: Or Necromancy in the Wilderness: A Tale of the Little Miami. St. Louis and Cincinnati: Stratton and Barnard, 1848.
Mike Fink: A Legend of the Ohio. Cincinnati: Robinson and Jones, 1848. Revised 1852.
The Renegade. A Historical Romance of Border Life. Cincinnati: Robinson and Jones, 1848. Revised in 1854 as *Ella Barnwell.*
The Trapper's Bride: Or Spirit of Adventure. Cincinnati: Stratton and Barnard, 1848. Possibly by Bennett, but usually ascribed to Sir Charles Augustus Murray, although the novel is said to be written in Bennett's style and not in Murray's.
Leni Leoti: Or Adventures in the Far West. Cincinnati and St. Louis: Stratton and Barnard, 1849. Revised 1851. (Sequel to *The Prairie Flower.*)
The Prairie Flower: Or Adventures in the Far West. Philadelphia: T. B. Peterson, 1849. Revised 1850, 1881. Sequel to *Leni Leoti.* Authorship attributed also to Sidney Walter Moss.
The Forest Rose: A Tale of the Frontier. Cincinnati: J. A. and U. P. James, 1850. Revised 1852.
The League of the Miami. A New and Stereotyped Edition, Enlarged, Re-

vised, and Corrected by the Author. Louisville, Ky.: C. Hagan, and Nashville, Tenn.: F. Hagan, 1850. (Jacob Blanck reports that the first form appeared in 1845.)

Miranda: A Tale of the French Revolution. New York: Stringer and Townsend, 1850.

Oliver Goldfinch: Or The Hypocrite. Cincinnati: Stratton and Barnard, 1850. Reissued as *The Forged Will.*

The Traitor: Or The Fate of Ambition. 2 vols. Cincinnati and St. Louis: Stratton and Barnard, 1850.

The Female Spy: Or Treason in the Camp: A Story of the Revolution. Cincinnati: Lorenzo Stratton, 1851.

The Pioneer's Daughter: A Tale of Indian Captivity. Philadelphia: T. B. Peterson, 1851. Includes *The Unknown Countess.*

The Mysterious League. Philadelphia: n.p., 1851.

Rosalie Du Pont: Or Treason in the Camp. A Sequel to *The Female Spy.* Cincinnati: Lorenzo Stratton, 1851.

The Prairie Scout: Or Agatone the Renegade: A Romance of Border Life. New York: Dewitt and Davenport, 1852.

Viola: Or Adventures in the Far South-West. A Companion to *The Prairie Flower.* Philadelphia: T. B. Peterson, 1852.

Walde-Warren: A Tale of Circumstantial Evidence. A Companion to *The Prairie Flower.* Philadelphia: T. B. Peterson, 1852.

Clara Moreland: Or Adventures in the Far South-West. Philadelphia: T. B. Peterson, and New York: F. M. Lupton, 1853.

Ella Barnwell: A Historical Romance of Border Life. Cincinnati: J. A. and U. P. James, 1853. Revised edition of *The Renegade.*

The Fair Rebel: A Tale of Colonial Times. Cincinnati: H. M. Rubison, 1853.

The Forged Will: Or Crime and Retribution. Philadelphia: T. B. Peterson, 1853. A re-issue of *Oliver Goldfinch.*

The Bride of the Wilderness. Philadelphia: T. B. Peterson, and New York: F. M. Lupton, 1854.

Alfred Morland: Or the Legacy. Cincinnati: H. M. Rubison, 1855.

Ellen Norbury: Or The Adventures of an Orphan. Philadelphia: T. B. Peterson, 1855.

The Heiress of Bellefont. Philadelphia: T. B. Peterson, 1855.

The Artist's Bride: Or the Pawnbroker's Heir. New York: Garrett, Dick and Fitzgerald, 1857. Re-issued in 1874 as *Villeta Linden.*

The Border Rover. Philadelphia: T. B. Peterson, and New York: F. M. Lupton, 1857.

Intriguing for a Princess: An Adventure with Mexican Banditti. Philadelphia: J. W. Bradley, 1859.

Forest and Prairie: Or Life on the Frontier. Philadelphia: John E. Potter, 1860. New name for *Wild Scenes on the Frontiers.*

The Phantom of the Forest: A Tale of the Dark and Bloody Ground. Author's Revised Edition. Philadelphia: John E. Potter, 1868.

The Bandit Queen: A Tale of Italy. New York: Street & Smith, 1869. Serialized in *Weekly* beginning Sept. 16, 1869.

The Orphan's Trials: Or Alone in a Great City. Philadelphia: T. B. Peterson, 1874.

The Outlaw's Daughter: Or Adventures in the South. Philadelphia: Claxton, Remsen and Haffelfinger, 1874.

Villeta Linden: Or The Artist's Bride. Philadelphia: Claxton, Remsen and Haffelfinger, 1874. A reprint of *The Artist's Bride* (1857).

Mink Curtiss: Or Life in the Backwoods. New York: James Miller, 1877. Authorship doubtful.

The Lincoln Memorial: Albur-Immortelles. Edited by Osborn H. Oldroyd. New York: G. W. Carleton, 1882.

Kid Curry's Last Stand: Or Nick Carter in Dangerous Surroundings. Edited by Chickering Carter. New York: Street and Smith, 1907.

Works about Emerson Bennett

"Bennett, Emerson," *American Authors and Books, 1640 to the Present Day.* Ed. W. J. Burke and Will D. Howe. New York: Crown Publishers, 1962. P. 58.

Gaston, Edwin W., Jr. *The Early Novel of the Southwest.* Albuquerque: Univ. of New Mexico Press, 1961. pp. 38, 225, 267, passim.

Mills, Randall V. "Emerson Bennett's Two Oregon Novels," *Oregon Historical Quarterly,* 41 (December 1940), 367-81.

Trites, W. B. "Emerson Bennett, Author," *Century,* 120 (April 1930), 211-18.

Venable, William Henry. *Beginnings of Literary Culture in the Ohio Valley.* Cincinnati: R. Clarke, 1891. Pp. 291-93.

Alfred S. Shivers
Stephen F. Austin State University

John Allyn McAlpin Berryman (1914-1972)
fiction, poetry, nonfiction

"Twenty Poems," *Five Young American Poets.* Norfolk, Conn.: New Directions, 1940. pp. 41-80.

Poems. Norfolk, Conn.: New Directions, 1942.

The Dispossessed (poems). New York: Sloane, 1948.

Stephen Crane (critical biography). New York: Sloane, 1950; rpt. with a second preface, Cleveland: World Publishing, Meridian, 1962.

Homage to Mistress Bradstreet (poem). New York: Farrar, Straus and Giroux, 1956.

His Thought Made Pockets & the Plane Buckt (poems). Pawlet, Vermont: C. Fredericks, 1958.

77 Dream Songs. New York: Farrar, Straus and Giroux, 1964.

Berryman's Sonnets. New York: Farrar, Straus and Giroux, 1967.

Short Poems. New York: Farrar, Straus and Giroux, 1967. (Contains *The Dispossessed, His Thought Made Pockets & the Plane Buckt,* and "Formal Elegy").

His Toy, His Dream, His Rest: 308 Dream Songs. New York: Farrar, Straus and Giroux, 1968.

Homage to Mistress Bradstreet and Other Poems. New York: Farrar, Straus and Giroux, 1968. (Includes *Homage* and selections from *The Dispossessed* and *His Thought Made Pockets & the Plane Buckt.*)

The Dream Songs. New York: Farrar, Straus and Giroux, 1969. (A combined edition of *77 Dream Songs* and *His Toy, His Dream, His Rest.*)

Love & Fame (poems). New York: Farrar, Straus and Giroux, 1970.

Delusions, etc. (poems). New York: Farrar, Straus and Giroux, 1972.

Recovery (novel). New York: Farrar, Straus and Giroux, 1973.

In addition, Berryman published short stories, poems, essays, and criticism in various anthologies and in such journals as the *New Yorker, Hudson Review, Partisan Review, Kenyon Review, American Scholar,* and *New Republic.*

Works about John Berryman
(Among the most revealing articles about Berryman are his own essays, such as "One Answer to a Question," *Shenandoah,* 17 [Autumn 1965], 67-76.)

"Badge of Courage," *Times Literary Supplement,* June 8, 1951, p. 356.

Blum, Morgan. "Berryman as Biographer, "Stephen Crane as Poet," *Poetry,* 78 (August 1951), 298-307.

Ciardi, John. "The Researched Mistress," *Saturday Review,* 40 (March 23, 1957), 36-37.

"Congested Funeral: Berryman's New Dream Songs," *Times Literary Supplement,* June 26, 1969, p .680.

Cott, Jonathan. "Theodore Roethke and John Berryman: Two Dream Poets," *On Contemporary Literature,* ed. Richard Kostelanetz. New York: Avon, 1964. pp. 520-31.

Eckman, Frederick. "Moody's Ode: The Collapse of the Heroic," *University of Texas Studies in English,* 86 (1957), 80-92.

Evans, Arthur and Catherine. "Pieter Bruegel and John Berryman: Two Winter Landscapes," *Texas Studies in Language and Literature,* 5 (Autumn 1963), 309-18.

Fitts, Dudley. "Deep in the Unfriendly City," *New York Times Book Review,* June 20, 1948, p. 4.

Hamilton, Ian. "John Berryman," *London Magazine,* 4 (February 1965), 93-100.

Harvard Advocate, 103 (Spring 1969); special John Berryman issue. Contents include: "An Interview with John Berryman"; Adrienne Rich, "Living with Henry"; three new Dream Songs; Albert Gelpi, "Homage to Berryman's Homage"; Monroe Engel, "An Educational Incident"; William Meredith, "A Bright Surviving Actual Scene: Berryman's Sonnets"; Carol Johnson, "John Berryman: The Dream Songs"; as well as homage to the poet in pieces by Howard Nemerov, Mark Van Doren, Robert Lowell, Elizabeth Bishop, Conrad Aiken, and Robert Fitzgerald.

Holder, Alan. "Anne Bradstreet Resurrected," *Concerning Poetry,* 2 (Spring 1969), 11-18.

Howard, Jane. "Whisky and Ink, Whisky and Ink," *Life,* 63 (July 21, 1967), 67-76.

Jackson, Bruce. "Berryman's Chaplinesque," *The Minnesota Review,* 5 (Jan.-Apr. 1965), 90-94.

Kelly, Richard J. *John Berryman: A Checklist.* Metuchen, New Jersey: Scarecrow Press, 1972.

Kostelanetz, Richard. "Conversation with Berryman," *The Massachusetts Review,* 11 (Winter 1970), 340-47.

Linebarger, J. M. *John Berryman.* New York: Twayne, 1974.

Lowell, Robert. "The Poetry of John Berryman," *New York Review of*

Books, 2 (May 28, 1964), pp. 3-4.

Martz, William J. *John Berryman.* Minneapolis: Univ. of Minnesota Press, 1969.

McDaniel, Barbara Albrecht. "John Berryman: Songs to Terrify & Comfort," *The Sixties: Fiction, Poetry, Drama,* ed. Kenneth Frieling. Deland, Florida: Everett/Edwards, Forthcoming.

Meredith, William. "Henry Tasting All the Secret Bits of Life: Berryman's Dream Songs," *Wisconsin Studies in Contemporary Literature,* 6 (Winter-Spring 1965), 27-33.

Montague, John. "American Pegasus," *Studies,* 48 (Summer 1959), 183-91.

Nims, John Frederick. "The Dispossessed," "World's Fair," and "The Traveler," *Poetry: A Critical Supplement* (April 1948), pp. 1-6.

Oberg, Arthur. "The *Dream Songs* and the Horror of Unlove," *Univ. of Windsor Review,* 6 (1970), 1-11.

Pearson, Gabriel. "John Berryman—Poet as Medium," *The Review* (Oxford), No. 15 (April 1965), pp. 3-17.

Ricks, Christopher. "Recent American Poetry," *The Massachusetts Review,* 11 (Spring 1970), 313-37.

Rosenthal, M. L. *The New Poets: American and British Poetry Since World War II.* New York: Oxford Univ. Press, 1967. pp. 118-30.

Stepanchev, Stephen. "For an Excellent Lady: Berryman's Sonnets," *The New Leader,* 50 (May 22, 1967), 26-28.

Stitt, Peter A. "Berryman's Vein Profound," *The Minnesota Review,* 7 (1967), 356-59.

Thompson, John. "An Alphabet of Poets," *New York Review of Books,* 11 (August 1, 1968), 34-35, 36.

Toynbee, Philip. "Berryman's Songs," *Encounter,* 24 (March 1965), 76-78.

Vendler, Helen. "Savage, Rueful, Irrepressible Henry," *New York Times Book Review,* November 3, 1968, pp. 1, 58-9.

Wasserstrom, William. "Cagey John: Berryman as Medicine Man," *Centennial Review,* 12 (Summer 1968), 334-54.

Wilson, Edmund. "Stephen Crane—Hannah Whitall Smith," *New Yorker,* 26 (January 6, 1951), 77-85.

"Zoo-Maze: The World in Vaudeville," *Times Literary Supplement,* April 15, 1965, p. 292.

J. M. Linebarger
Barbara Albrecht McDaniel
North Texas State University

Opal Berryman (1897-   )
nonfiction

Pioneer Preacher. New York: Crowell, 1948.

Carroll Schoenewolf
Stephen F. Austin State University

Hoffman Birney (1891-1958)
[pseud. David Kent]
novels, children's stories

King of the Mesa. Philadelphia: The Penn Publ. Co., 1927.
The Masked Rider. Philadelphia: The Penn Publ. Co., 1928.
Steeldust, the Story of a Horse. Philadelphia: The Penn Publ. Co., 1928.
Vigilantes. Philadelphia: The Penn Publ. Co., 1929.
The Cañon of Lost Waters. Philadelphia: The Penn Publ. Co., 1930.
The Pinto Pony. Philadelphia: The Penn Publ. Co., 1930.
Roads to Roam. Philadelphia: The Penn Publ. Co., 1930.
Two Little Navajos. Philadelphia: The Penn Publ. Co., 1931.
Zealots of Zion. Philadelphia: The Penn Publ. Co., 1931.
Kudlu, the Eskimo Boy. Illustrated by Jean Macdonald. Philadelphia: The
   Penn Publ. Co., 1932.
Barrier Ranch. Philadelphia: The Penn Publ. Co., 1933.
Tu'Kwi of the Peaceful People. Philadelphia: The Penn Publ. Co., 1933.
Forgotten Cañon. Philadelphia: The Penn Publ. Co., 1934.
Grim Journey. New York: Minton, Balch, 1934.
Holy Murder (with Charles Kelly). New York: Minton, Balch, 1934.
Ay-chee, Son of the Desert. Philadelphia: The Penn Publ. Co., 1935.
Eagle in the Sun. New York: Putnam's, 1935.
A Stranger in Black Butte. Philadelphia: The Penn Pub. Co., 1936.
Dead Man's Trail. Philadelphia: The Penn Publ. Co., 1937.
Mountain Chief. Philadelphia: The Penn Publ. Co., 1938.
Ann Carmeny. New York: Putnam's, 1941.
Jason Burr's First Case. [David Kent]. New York: Random House, 1941.
Brothers of Doom. New York: Putnam's, 1942.

A Knife is Silent. [David Kent]. New York: Random House, 1947.
Dice of God. [David Kent]. New York: Holt, 1956.

Carroll Schoenewolf
Stephen F. Austin State University

Forrester Avery Blake (1912-   )
novels, history

Riding the Mustang Trail. New York: Scribner, 1935.
Denver, Rocky Mountain Capital, Nugget Histories No. 2. Denver: Rocky
Mountain Pamphlet House, 1945.
Rocky Mountain Tales (with Levette Jay Davidson). Norman: Univ. of
Oklahoma Press, 1947.
Johnny Christmas. New York: Morrow, 1948.
Wilderness Passage. New York: Random House, 1953.
The Franciscan. Garden City, New York: Doubleday, 1963.

Jarrell Richman
Stephen F. Austin State University

Lena Whittaker Blakeney (1882-   )
poetry

Ports of Call. New York: H. Vinal, 1926.

Jarrel Richman
Stephen F. Austin State University

Mody C. Boatright (1896-1970)
nonfiction, history, folklore

Alma Mater, The Immortal. Canyon, Texas: West Texas State Normal
College, 1920.
Tall Tales from Texas Cow Camps. Dallas: Southwest Press, 1934.
Accuracy in Thinking. New York: Farrar and Rinehart, 1938.

Gib Morgan, Minstrel of the Oil Fields. Austin: Texas Folklore Society, 1945.

Folk Laughter on the American Frontier. New York: Macmillan, 1949.

The Family Saga and Other Phases of American Folklore (with Robert B. Downs and John T. Flanagan). Urbana: Univ. of Illinois Press, 1958.

Folklore of the Oil Industry. Dallas: Southern Methodist Univ. Press, 1963.

Tales from the Derrick Floor (with William A. Owens). Garden City, New York: Doubleday, 1970.

Mody Boatright, Folklorist (collected essays). Ed. Ernest Speck. Austin: Univ. of Texas Press, 1973.

In addition, Boatright published over twenty articles between 1927 and 1970 in such publications as *American Quarterly, Journal of American Folklore, PMLA, South Atlantic Quarterly, Southwest Review, Studies in English* (Univ. of Texas), *Texas Quarterly,* and *Western Folklore.* He also published two plays in *Poet Lore* (1929 and 1930) and was a contributor to four volumes of the Texas Folklore Society Publication (vols. 33, 34, 37, and 38) and to the *Encyclopedia Americana.*

Works about Mody C. Boatright

Cline, Clarence L., Harry H. Ransom, and Mody Boatright. *Mody Boatright, Secretary and Editor, 1943-1964.* Austin: Texas Folklore Society, 1965.

Speck, Ernest B. *Mody C. Boatright.* Austin: Steck-Vaughn, 1971.

Ernest Speck
Sul Ross State University

Elroy Bode (1931-   )
sketches

Texas Sketchbook: A Sheaf of Prose Poems. El Paso: Texas Western Press, 1967.

Elroy Bode's Sketchbook II: Portraits in Nostalgia. El Paso: Texas Western Press, 1972.

Alone in the World Looking. El Paso: Texas Western Press, 1973.

Steve Lee
Denton, Texas

Herbert Eugene Bolton (1870-1953)
history

With the Makers of Texas: A Source Reader in Texas History. Austin: Gammel-Statesman Publ. Co., 1904.

Father Kino's Lost History, Its Discovery and Its Value. New York: privately printed, 1911.

Guide to Materials for the History of the United States in the Principal Archives of Mexico. Washington: Carnegie Institution of Washington, 1913.

Athanase de Mezieres and the Louisiana-Texas Frontier, 1768-1780. Cleveland: Arthur H. Clark Co., 1914.

Texas in the Middle Eighteenth Century: Studies in Spanish Colonial History and Administration. Berkeley: Univ. of California Press, 1915.

Spanish Exploration in the Southwest, 1542-1706. New York: Scribner, 1916; rpt. 1925.

The Colonization of North America, 1492-1783 (with Thomas Maitland Marchall). New York: Macmillan, 1920.

The Spanish Borderlands: A Chronicle of Old Florida and the Southwest. New Haven: Yale Univ. Press, 1921.

California's Story (with Ephrain D. Adams). Boston: Allyn and Bacon, 1922.

The Debatable Land. A Sketch of the Anglo-Spanish Contest for the Georgia Country (with Mary Ross). Berkeley: Univ. of California Press, 1925.

Palou and His Writings. Berkeley: Univ. of California Press, 1926.

History of the Americas. Boston: Ginn, 1928.

Anza's California Expeditions. Berkeley: Univ. of California Press, 1930.

Outpost of Empire: The Story of the Founding of San Francisco. New York: Knopf, 1931.

The Padre on Horseback: A Sketch of Eusebio Francisco Kino, S. J., Apostle to the Pimas. San Francisco: The Sonora Press, 1932.

Cross, Sword and Gold Pan: A Group of Notable Full-color Paintings in the Exploration and Settlement of the West, by Carl Oscar Borg and Willard Sheets: With Interpretive Essays by Herbert E. Bolton and John R. McCarthy. Los Angeles: The Primavera Press, 1936.

Rim of Christendom: A Biography of Eusebio Francisco Kino, Pacific Coast Pioneer. New York: Macmillan, 1936.

Wider Horizons of American History. New York: Appleton-Century, 1939.

American Neighbors (with Delia Goetz and Ernesto Galarza). Washington: The American National Red Cross, 1940.
Historical Memoir of Pimeria Alta: A Contemporary Account of the Beginnings of California, Sonora, and Arizona, 1683-1911. Berkeley: Univ. of California Press, 1948.
Coronado: Knight of Pueblo and Plains. New York: Whittlesey House, 1949.

In addition, Bolton published numerous scholarly essays in such periodicals as the *American Historical Review, Historical Outlook, Mississippi Valley Historical Review,* and the *Southwestern Historical Quarterly.*

John T. Smith
North Texas State University

Margie Belle Huffmaster Boswell (1875-1962?)
poetry, essays

The Mockingbird and Other Poems. Los Angeles: J. C. Farley, 1927.
The Upward Way. Dallas: Tardy, 1937.
Wings Against the Dawn. Dallas: Avalon Press, 1945.
The Light Still Burns. Dallas: Story Book Press, 1952.
Starward. Arlington, Texas: Dudley Hodgkins Co., 1956.
Sunrise in the Valley. Arlington, Texas: Dudley Hodgkins Co., 1959.

Jarrell Richman
Stephen F. Austin State University

B. M. Bower (1871-1940)
[Mrs. Bertha Muzzy Bower Sinclair Cowan]
novels, short stories

Chip, of the Flying U. New York: Dillingham, 1906; rpt. New York: Grosset, 1913.
Her Prairie Knight and Rowdy of the "Cross L." New York: Dillingham, 1907.

Lure of the Dim Trails. New York: Grosset, 1907.
Lonesome Trail. New York: Dillingham, 1909.
Long Shadow. New York: Grosset, 1909.
Happy Family. New York: Dillingham, 1910.
Good Indian. Boston: Little, 1912.
Lonesome Land. Boston: Little, 1912.
The Gringos; A Story of the Old California Days in 1849. Boston: Little, 1913.
Ranch at the Wolverine. Boston: Little, 1914.
Flying U's Last Stand. Boston: Little, 1915.
Flying U Ranch. New York: Grosset, 1915.
Jean of the Lazy A. Boston: Little, 1915.
Heritage of the Sioux. Boston: Little, 1916.
Phantom Head. Boston: Little, 1916.
Lookout Man. Boston: Little, 1917.
Starr of the Desert. Boston: Little, 1917.
Cabin Fever. Boston: Little, 1918.
Skyrider. Boston: Little, 1918.
Rim o' the World. Boston: Little, 1919.
Quirt. Boston: Little, 1920.
Casey Ryan. Boston: Little, 1921.
Cow-Country. Boston: Little, 1921.
Sawtooth Ranch. London: Methuen, 1921.
Trail of the White Mule. Boston: Little, 1922.
Parowan Bonanza. Boston: Little, 1923.
Voice at Johnnywater. Boston: Little, 1923.
Bellehelen Mine. Boston: Little, 1924.
Eagle's Wing, A Story of the Colorado. Boston: Little, 1924.
Desert Brew. Boston: Little, 1925.
Meadowlark Basin. Boston: Little, 1925.
Black Thunder. Boston: Little, 1926.
Van Patten. Boston: Little, 1926.
Adam Chasers. Boston: Little, 1927.
Outlaw Paradise. London: Hodder & Stoughton, 1927.
White Wolves. Boston: Little, 1927.
Points West. Boston: Little, 1928.
Rodeo. Boston: Little, 1929.
Swallowfork Bulls. Boston: Little, 1929.

Fool's Goal. Boston: Little, 1930.
Tiger Eye. Boston: Little, 1930.
Dark Horse: A Story of the Flying U. Boston: Little, 1931.
Long Loop. Boston: Little, 1931.
Laughing Water. Boston: Little, 1932.
Rocking Arrow. Boston: Little, 1932.
Open Land. Boston: Little, 1933.
Trails Meet. Boston: Little, 1933.
Whoop-Up Trail. Boston: Little, 1933.
Flying U Strikes. Boston: Little, 1934.
Haunted Hills. Boston: Little, 1934.
Dry Ridge Gang. Boston: Little, 1935.
Trouble Rides the Wind. Boston: Little, 1935.
Five Furies of Leaning Ladder. Boston: Little, 1936.
Shadow Mountain. Boston: Little, 1936.
North Wind Do Blow. Boston: Little, 1937.
Wind Blows West. Boston: Little 1938.
A Starry Night. Boston: Little, 1939.
Singing Hill. Boston: Little, 1939.
Man on Horseback. Boston: Little, 1940.
Spirit of the Range. Boston: Little, 1940.
Sweet Grass. Boston: Little, 1940.
Family Failing. Boston: Little, 1941.
Kings of the Prairie. New York: Collins, 1941.

In addition to the novels, Mrs. Cowan wrote six short stories in such magazines as *McClure's* and *American Magazine.*

Works about B. M. Bower

Davison, Stanley R. *"Chip of the Flying U:* The Author Was a Lady," *Montana: The Magazine of Western History,* 23 (Spring 1973), 2-15.

Engen, Orrin A. *Writer of the Plains.* Culver City, California: The Pontine Press, 1973.

Meyer, Roy B. "B. M. Bower: The Poor Man's Wister," *Journal of Popular Culture,* 7 (Winter 1973), 667-79.

Owen J. Reamer
University of Southwestern Louisiana

Richard Bradford (1932-   )
novels

Red Sky at Morning. New York: Lippincott, 1968.
So Far From Heaven. New York: Lippincott, 1973.

Helen Lang Leath
North Texas State University

William Brammer (1930-   )
novel

The Gay Place; Being Three Related Novels: The Flea Circus, Room Enough to Caper. Country Pleasures. Boston: Houghton Mifflin, 1961.

Charles Ramos
Midwestern University

Edward Douglas Branch (1905-   )
nonfiction

The Cowboy and his Interpreters. New York: Appleton, 1926.
The Hunting of the Buffalo. New York: Appleton, 1929.
Westward; The Romance of the American Frontier. New York: Appleton, 1930.
The Sentimental Years, 1836-1860. New York: Appleton-Century, 1934.
The Story of America in Pictures. Ed. Franklin J. Meine. Chicago: Spencer Press, 1954.

Harry M. Solomon
Auburn University

Anna Brand (-   )
novels, short stories

I Want You Myself. New York: Doubleday, 1938.
Thunder Before Seven. New York: Doubleday, 1941.

Uncollected stories have appeared in *Delineator, Good Housekeeping, Pictorial Review,* and *Scholastic.*

Harry M. Solomon
Auburn University

William Cowper Brann (1855-1898)
novel, play, nonfiction

Potiphar's Wife: Story of Joseph Revised. San Antonio: Guessaz & Ferlet, 1894.

Brann's Scrapbook. Waco: Knight Printing Company, 1895.

Brann's Speeches and Lectures. Waco: Knight Printing Company, 1896.

Brann the Iconoclast: A Collection of the Writings of W. C. Brann . . . with Biography by J. D. Shaw. 2 vols. Waco: Herz Brothers, 1898. Rpt. 1905 and 1911; contains a few articles not included in the so-called *Complete Works.*

The Complete Works of Brann the Iconoclast. 12 vols. New York: The Brann Publishers, 1919.

Brann's Defence Against Enemies of Catholicism. New York: The Brann Publishers, 1921.

That American Woman, in *Brann the Playwright,* by Edward G. Fletcher and Jack L. Hart. Austin: Univ. of Texas Press, 1941.

The Best of Brann. Ed. Roger N. Conger. Waco: Texian Press, 1967.

Works about William Cowper Brann

Anon. "The Brann Episode," *The Baylor Literary,* 6 No. 2 (1897), 72-74.

Armstrong, James J. *Brann X-Rayed.* San Antonio: Eureka Printing Co., 1896.

———. *Broadsides for Brann: A Romance of the Rubbernecks.* San Antonio: Eureka Printing Co., 1896.

Bedichek, Roy. "Introduction," in *Brann and the Iconoclast,* by Charles Carver. Austin: Univ. of Texas Press, 1957.

Carver, Charles. *Brann and the Iconoclast.* Austin: Univ. of Texas Press, 1957.

Davenport, Walter and J. C. Derieux. *Ladies, Gentlemen, and Editors.* Garden City, New York: Doubleday & Co., 1960.

Dawson, Joseph M. "Image-Breaker Brann, Six Decades After," *Southwest Review,* 43 (Spring 1958), 148-54.

212 *Southwestern American Literature*

Fletcher, Edward G. and Jack L. Hart. *Brann the Playwright.* Austin: Univ. of Texas Press, 1941.

Gage, Harold. "This Man Brann." Texas Collection, Baylor University, Waco.

Gunn, John W. *Brann: Smasher of Shams.* Girard, Kansas: Haldeman-Julius Co. [c. 1924].

Meyer, Adolph E. "Advocatus Diaboli," *American Mercury,* Sept. 1927, pp. 68-74.

Morrison, Joseph L. "Main Currents in Brann's *Iconoclast,*" *Journalism Quarterly,* 40 (Spring 1963), 219-27.

Mott, Frank Luther. *A History of American Magazines 1885-1905.* Cambridge: The Belknap Press, 1957.

Rivers, William L. "William Cowper Brann and His 'Iconoclast,'" *Journalism Quarterly,* 35 (Fall 1958), 433-38.

Rollins, Hyder E. "William Cowper Brann," *South Atlantic Quarterly,* 14 (1915), 53-67.

Windle, C. A. "Brann's Iconoclast," *Brann's Iconoclast,* March 1903, p. 2.

John L. Idol, Jr.
Clemson University

J. Mason Brewer (1896-1975)
poetry, history, folklore

Negrito: A Volume of Negro Dialect Poems. San Antonio: Naylor, 1933.

Negro Legislators of Texas. Dallas: Mathis, 1935. Rpt. Austin: Pemberton Press, 1970.

The Negro in Texas History. Dallas: Mathis, 1936.

The Life of Dr. John Wesley Anderson: A Story in Verse. Dallas: Privately Printed, 1938.

An Historical Outline of the Negro in Travis County, J. Mason Brewer, ed. Austin: Samuel Huston College, 1940.

Little Dan from Dixieland: A Story in Verse. Dallas: The Bookcraft, 1940.

Humorous Folktales of the South Carolina Negro. Orangeburg, S.C.: Claflin College Press, 1945.

More Truth Than Poetry. Austin: Privately Printed, 1947.

Silhouettes of Life: A Group of Short Stories. J. Mason Brewer, ed. Austin: Samuel Huston College, 1948.

The Word on the Brazos. Austin: Univ. of Texas Press, 1953.
Aunt Dicy Tales. Austin: Privately Printed, 1956.
Dog Ghosts and Other Texas Negro Folk Tales. Austin: The University of Texas Press, 1958.
Three Looks and Some Peeps. Salisbury, North Carolina: Privately Printed, 1963.
Worser Days and Better Times. Chicago: Quadrangle Books, 1965.
American Negro Folklore. Chicago: Quadrangle Books, 1968.

In addition, Brewer published poems, reviews, and articles in *The North American Magazine, Crisis Magazine, The Journal of American Folklore, Phylon, The New Mexico Quarterly, Southern Folklore Quarterly, Dallas Morning News, Ebony,* and *Interracial Review.*

Works about J. Mason Brewer
Byrd, James W. *J. Mason Brewer: Negro Folklorist.* Austin: Steck-Vaughn, 1967.
Erwin, Dorothie, "He Tells It Like It Was," *Southwest Scene, The Dallas Morning News Sunday Magazine,* 23 August 1970, 8-13.

James W. Byrd
East Texas State University

Robert Bright (1902-   )
novels, children's stories

The Travels of Ching. New York: W. R. Scott, 1943.
Georgie. Garden City, New York: Doubleday, 1944.
The Life and Death of Little Jo. Garden City, New York: Doubleday, 1944.
The Intruders. Garden City, New York: Doubleday, 1946.
The Olivers; the Story of an Artist and his Family. Garden City, N. Y.: Doubleday, 1947.
Me and the Bears. Garden City, New York: Doubleday, 1951.
Richard Brown and the Dragon; Retold from an Anecdote by Samuel Langhorne Clemens in A TRAMP ABROAD. Garden City, New York: Doubleday, 1952.
Hurrah for Freddie! (with Dorothy Brett). Garden City, New York: Doubleday, 1953.

Miss Pattie. Garden City, New York: Doubleday, 1954.
I Like Red. Garden City, New York: Doubleday, 1955.
Georgie to the Rescue. Garden City, New York: Doubleday, 1956.
The Spirit of the Chase. New York: Scribner, 1956.
The Friendly Bear. Garden City, New York: Doubleday, 1957.
Georgie's Halloween. Garden City, New York: Doubleday, 1958.
My Red Umbrella. New York: William Morrow, 1959. Trans. Marion Red-
    field as *Mi Paraguas Rojo.* New York: Morrow, 1968.
My Hopping Bunny. Garden City, New York: Doubleday, 1960.
Georgie and the Robbers. Garden City, New York: Doubleday, 1963.
Which is Willy? Garden City, New York: Doubleday, 1963.
Georgie and the Magician. Garden City, New York: Doubleday, 1966.
Gregory; the Noisiest and Strongest Boy in Grangers Grove. Garden City,
    New York: Doubleday, 1969.
Georgie and the Noisy Ghost. New York: Doubleday, 1971.
Georgie Goes West. New York: Doubleday, 1973.

Harry M. Solomon
Auburn University

Myron Brinig (1900-   )
novels

Madonna Without Child. Garden City, New York: Doubleday, Doran, 1929.
Singermann. New York: Farrar and Rinehart, 1929.
Anthony in the Nude. New York: Farrar and Rinehart, 1930.
Wide Open Town. New York: Farrar and Rinehart, 1931.
This Man is my Brother. New York: Farrar and Rinehart, 1932.
The Flutter of an Eyelid. New York: Farrar and Rinehart, 1933.
Out of Life. New York: Farrar and Rinehart, 1934.
The Sun Sets in the West. New York: Farrar and Rinehart, 1935.
The Sisters. New York: Farrar and Rinehart, 1937.
May Flavin. New York: Farrar and Rinehart, 1938.
Anne Minton's Life. New York: Farrar and Rinehart, 1939.
All of Their Lives. New York: Farrar and Rinehart, 1941.
The Family Way. New York: Farrar and Rinehart, 1942.
The Gambler Takes a Wife. New York: Farrar and Rinehart, 1943.

You and I. New York: Farrar and Rinehart, 1945.
Hour of Nightfall. New York: Rinehart, 1947.
No Marriage in Paradise. New York: Rinehart, 1948, 1949.
Footsteps on the Stair. New York: Rinehart, 1950.
The Sadness in Lexington Avenue. New York: Rinehart, 1951.
Street of the Three Friends. New York: Rinehart, 1953.
The Looking Glass Heart. New York: Sagamore Press, 1958.

> Harry M. Solomon
> Auburn University

Robert Lee Brothers (1908-   )
poetry

Democracy of Dust. Dallas: Kaleidograph, 1947.
The Hidden Harp. Dallas: Kaleidograph, 1952.
Threescore and Ten. San Antonio: Naylor, 1963.

> Harry M. Solomon
> Auburn University

J. P. S. Brown (1931-   )
novels

Jim Kane. New York: Dial, 1970.
The Outfit. New York: Dial, 1971.
The Forests of the Night. New York: Dial, 1974.

> James W. Lee
> North Texas State University

Jack Yeaman Bryan (1907-   )
novel

Come to the Bower. New York: Viking, 1963.

> Harry M. Solomon
> Auburn University

Alice Bullock (1904-   )
short stories, nonfiction

Living Legends of the Santa Fe Country. Denver: Green Mountain Press, 1970; rpt. Santa Fe: Sunstone, 1972.
Mountain Villages. Santa Fe: Sunstone Press, 1973.
Discover Santa Fe. Santa Fe: Rydal Press, 1973.
Face the Wind (Stories). Santa Fe: Sunstone, 1975.

In addition, Bullock published hundreds of book reviews and feature articles in newspapers and magazines.

Geraldine Barrons
North Texas State University

Lolah Burford (1931-   )
novels

Vice Avenged: A Moral Tale. New York: Macmillan, 1971.
The Vision of Stephen. New York: Macmillan, 1972.
Edward, Edward. New York: Macmillan, 1973.
Maclyon. New York: Macmillan, 1974.

Chalonnes Lucas
Denton, Texas

William Skelly Burford (1927-   )
poetry, short stories, non-fiction

Man Now. Dallas: Southern Methodist Univ. Press, 1954.
A World. Austin: Univ. of Texas Press, 1962.
A Beginning: Poems. New York: Norton, 1966.
In addition to the volumes of poetry listed above, William Burford has published poems in such journals as *Poetry, Partisan Review, Saturday Review, Virginia Quarterly Review,* and the *Texas Quarterly;* he has published stories in *Partisan Review* (1949) and *Southwest Review* (1952).

Works about William Burford
Baker, Donald W. "Five Poets," *Poetry,* 111 (December 1967), 195-202.

Cassity, Turner. "Five Poets," *Poetry,* 103 (December 1963), 192-8.
Plath, Sylvia. "Poets on Campus," *Mademoiselle,* 37 (August 1953), 291.

Richard B. Sale
North Texas State University

Lois Wood Burkhalter (-   )
biography

Gideon Lincecum, 1793-1874: A Biography. Austin: Univ. of Texas Press, 1965.
Marion Koogler McNay: A Biography, 1883-1950. San Antonio: Marion Koogler McNay Art Institute, 1968.

H. Harbour Winn
University of Houston

Elizabeth Burleson (-   )
novels

A Man of the Family. Chicago: Follett, 1965.
Middl'un. Chicago: Follett, 1968.

H. Harbour Winn
University of Houston

William Riley Burnett (1899-   )
[pseud. James Updyke]
novels, short stories

Little Caesar. New York: Dial, 1929.
Iron Man. New York: Dial, 1930.
Saint Johnson. New York: Dial, 1930.
The Silver Eagle. New York: Dial, 1931.
The Giant Swing. New York: Harper, 1932.

Dark Hazard. New York: Harper, 1933.
Goodbye to the Past: Scenes from the Life of William Meadows. New York: Harper, 1934.
The Goodhues of Sinking Creek. New York: Harper, 1934.
King Cole: A Novel. New York: Harper, 1936. (British title: *Six Days Grace*).
The Dark Command: A Kansas Illiad. New York: Knopf, 1938.
High Sierra. New York: Knopf, 1940.
The Quick Brown Fox. New York: Knopf, 1942.
Nobody Lives Forever. New York: Knopf, 1943.
Romelle. New York: Knopf, 1946.
The Asphalt Jungle. New York: Knopf, 1949.
Stretch Dawson. New York: Fawcett, 1950.
Little Men, Big World. New York: Knopf, 1951.
Vanity Row. New York: Knopf, 1952.
Adobe Walls: A Novel of the Last Apache Rising. New York: Knopf, 1953.
Captain Lightfoot. New York: Knopf, 1954.
It's Always Four O'Clock: A Novel. [James Updyke] New York: Random House, 1956.
Pale Moon. New York: Knopf, 1956.
Underdog. New York: Knopf, 1957.
Bitter Ground. New York: Knopf, 1958.
Mi Amigo: A Novel of the Southwest. New York: Knopf, 1959.
The Goldseekers. Garden City, N. Y.: Doubleday, 1962.
The Widow Barony London: Macdonald, 1962.
The Roar of the Crowd: Conversations with an Ex-big-leaguer. Foreword by Frank Frisch. New York: C. N. Potter, 1964.
The Winning of Mickey Free. New York: Bantam, 1965.
Cool Man. Greenwich: Fawcett, 1968.

In addition the novels listed, Burnett has a number of short stories in such magazines as *Collier's* and *Saturday Evening Post*. Five of his novels were serialized in *Collier's,* but not published elsewhere: *Protection* (1931), *Jail Breakers* (1934), *Dr. Socrates* (1935), *Odds Against the Girl* (1945), and *Racket Alley* (1950-51). He wrote three screenplays; the best known is *Action in the North Atlantic* (1942).

Sue Zanne Boone
University of Houston

Walter Noble Burnes (1872-1932)
novels, articles

A Year with a Whaler. New York: Outing Publishing Co., 1913. Rpt. New York: Macmillan Co., 1919.

The Saga of Billy the Kid. Garden City, New York: Doubleday, Page, 1926. Rpt. 1927, 1928. Rpt. Penguin Books, 1946.

Tombstone, an Iliad of the Southwest. Garden City, N. Y.: Doubleday, Page, 1927. Rpt. 1929. Also published as *Tombstone, an Epic of the Southwest.* London: G. Bles, 1928. Rpt. as *Tombstone, the Toughest Town in Arizona.*

Billy the Kid. London: G. Bles, 1930.

The One-Way Ride. Garden City, New York: Doubleday, Doran, 1931.

The Robin Hood of El Dorado. New York: Coward-McCann, 1932.

Muriel J. Tyssen
University of Houston

Anna Robeson Brown Burr (1873-1941)
novels, short stories, biography

Alain of Halfdene. Philadelphia: Lippincott, 1896.

The Black Lamb. Philadelphia: Lippincott, 1896.

Sir Mark; A Tale of the First Capital, Philadelphia. New York: Appleton, 1896.

A Cosmopolitan Comedy. New York: Appleton, 1899.

The House of Pan. Philadelphia: Lippincott, 1899.

The Immortal Garland. New York: Appleton, 1900.

The Millionaire's Son. Boston: Estes, 1903.

Truth and a Woman. Chicago: H. S. Stone, 1903.

The Wine-Press. New York: Appleton, 1905.

The Jessop Bequest. Boston: Houghton Mifflin, 1907.

The Autobiography. A Critical and Comparative Study. London: Constable, 1909; rpt. Boston & New York: Houghton, Mifflin, 1909.

Religious Confessions and Confessants. Boston: Houghton Mifflin, 1914.

The House on Charles Street. New York: Duffield, 1921.

220   *Southwestern American Literature*

The House on Smith Square. New York: Duffield, 1923.
The Wrong Move. New York: Macmillan, 1923.
The Great House in the Park. New York: Duffield, 1924.
St. Helios. New York: Duffield, 1925.
The City We Visit, Old Philadelphia. Philadelphia & London: Lippincott, 1926.
West of the Moon. New York: Duffield, 1926.
The Portrait of a Banker: James Stillman, 1850-1918. New York: Duffield, 1927.
Palludia. New York: Duffield, 1928.
Weir Mitchell: His Life and Letters. New York: Duffield, 1929, 1930.
The Same Person. New York: Duffield, 1931.
Wind in the East. New York: Duffield & Green, 1933.
Alice James, 1848-1892. Journal and letters edited by Anna R. Burr, with an introduction. London: Macmillan, 1934.
The Bottom of the Matter. New York, London: Appleton-Century, 1935.
The Golden Quicksand. New York: Appleton-Century, 1936.

Works about Anna Robeson Burr
Cather, Willa. " 'The House on Charles Street,' " *Literary Review,* 3 (1922), 173-74.

> Muriel J. Tyssen
> University of Houston

Don Maitland Bushby (1900-   )
poetry

Mesquite Smoke and Other Poems. Philadelphia: Dorrance, 1926.
Ocatilla Blossoms. Philadelphia: Dorrance, 1927
The Golden Stallion; an Anthology of Poems Concerning the Southwest. Dallas: South-West Press, 1930.
April Will Return. Dallas: Tardy, 1937.

> Edward McShane
> University of Houston

Witter Bynner (1881-1968)
[pseud. Emanuel Morgan]
poetry, plays, translations, nonfiction

An Ode to Harvard and Other Poems. Boston: Small, Maynard & Co., 1907.
Tiger (play). New York: Mitchell Kennerley, 1913.
The Little King (play). New York: Mitchell Kennerley, 1914.
New World. New York: Mitchell Kennerley, 1916.
Spectra ([Emanuel Morgan] with Anna Knish). New York: Mitchell Kennerley, 1916.
Grenstone Poems. New York: Frederick A. Stokes, 1917.
A Canticle of Praise. San Francisco: John Henry Nash, 1918.
Pins for Wings, [Emanuel Morgan]. New York: Sunwise Turn, 1920.
A Book of Plays (play). New York: Knopf, 1922.
An Import of China. Newark: Newark Museum and Public Library, 1924.
Caravan. New York: Knopf, 1925.
Cake (play). New York: Knopf, 1926.
Indian Earth. New York: Knopf, 1929.
The Persistence of Poetry. San Francisco: Book Club of California, 1929.
Roots. New York: Random House, 1929.
Anne. n.p.: Press of Johnck & Seeger, 1930.
Eden Tree. New York: Knopf, 1931.
Guest Book. New York: Knopf, 1935.
Selected Poems. New York: Knopf, 1936
Against The Cold. New York: Knopf, 1940.
Take Away the Darkness. New York: Knopf, 1947.
Journey With Genius: Recollections and Reflections Concerning the D. H. Lawrences. New York: John Day, 1951.
Book of Lyrics. New York: Knopf, 1955.
New Poems 1960. New York: Knopf, 1960.

In addition, Bynner published approximately nine hundred poems, over two hundred translations, and numerous miscellaneous non-fiction writings in such journals as *Poetry, Southwest Review, Saturday Review, Literary Review, Little Review, Freeman,* and *Nation.*

Works about Witter Bynner
Colony, Horatio. "Witter Bynner—Poet of Today," *Literary Review,* 3 (Spring 1960), 339-61.

Day, D. "The New and Old Poetry of Witter Bynner," *Shenandoah,* 12 (Winter 1961), 3-11.

Flanner, Hildegarde. "Witter Bynner's Poetry," *University of Kansas City Review,* 6 (June 1940), 269-74.

Haber, Tom B., ed. *Thirty Housman Letters to Witter Bynner.* New York: Knopf, 1957.

Lindsay, Robert O. *Witter Bynner: A Bibliography.* Albuquerque: Univ. of New Mexico Press, 1967.

Mearns, Hughes, ed. *Witter Bynner.* New York: Simon and Schuster, 1927.

The Works of Witter Bynner: Biographical Sketch and Critical Bibliography. New York: Knopf, 1940.

J. Wilkes Berry
Texas Tech University

Sigman Byrd (1909-   )
novels, short stories, nonfiction

Tall Grew the Pines. New York: Appleton-Century, 1936.
The Redlander. New York: Dutton, 1939.
Sig Byrd's Houston. New York: Viking, 1955.
The Valiant (with John Sutherland). New York: Jason Press, 1955.

In addition, Byrd published some twenty stories in *Saturday Evening Post, Collier's,* and *American Magazine.*

Sue Zanne Boone
University of Houston

Camilla Campbell (1905-   )
novels, short stories, juveniles

Galleons Sail Westward. Dallas: Mathis, Van Nort, and Co., 1939.
Star Mountain and Other Legends of Mexico. New York: McGraw-Hill, 1946. 2nd ed., 1968.
The Bartletts of Box B Ranch. New York: Whittlesey House, 1949.
Coronado and His Captains. Chicago: Follett, 1958.

William Eager Howard, a Short Biography. San Antonio: Carleton, 1961.
Viva La Patria. (Illus. Nils Santiago). New York: Hill and Wang, 1970.

Edward McShane
University of Houston

Isabel Jones Campbell (1895-   )
[Mrs. Walter S. Campbell]
novel, short stories, poetry

Jack Sprat. New York: Coward-McCann, 1929.

In addition, Campbell published stories, poems, and articles in *American Magazine, Poetry,* and *Saturday Evening Post.*

Mary Schiflett
University of Houston

Walter Stanley Campbell (1887-1957)
[pseud. Stanley Vestal]
novels, short stories, poetry, nonfiction

Fandango: Ballads of the Old West. Boston: Houghton Mifflin, 1927.
Kit Carson, the Happy Warrior of the Old West: A Biography. Boston: Houghton Mifflin, 1928.
Happy Hunting Grounds. Chicago: Lyons and Carnahan, 1928.
'Dobe Walls: A Story of Kit Carson's Southwest. Boston: Houghton Mifflin, 1929.
Sitting Bull: Champion of the Sioux: A Biography. Boston: Houghton Mifflin, 1932. Rpt. Norman: Univ. of Oklahoma Press, 1967.
Warpath: The True Story of the Fighting Sioux, Told in a Biography of Chief White Bull. Boston: Houghton Mifflin, 1934.
New Sources of Indian History 1850-1891, The Ghost Dance, The Prairie Sioux: A Miscellany. Norman: Univ. of Oklahoma Press, 1934.
The Wine Room Murder. Boston: Little, Brown, 1935.
Mountain Men. Boston: Houghton Mifflin, 1937.
Revolt on the Border. Boston: Houghton Mifflin, 1938.
Professional Writing. [Walter S. Campbell]. New York: The Macmillan Company, 1938.

The Old Santa Fe Trail. Boston: Houghton Mifflin, 1939. Rpt. New York: Bantam Books, 1955.

Writing Magazine Fiction. [Walter Stanley Campbell]. New York: Doubleday, Doran, 1940.

King of the Fur Traders: The Deeds and Deviltry of Pierre Esprit Radisson. Boston: Houghton Mifflin, 1940.

Short Grass Country. Ed. Erskine Caldwell. New York: Duell, Sloan & Pearce, 1941.

Bigfoot Wallace: A Biography. Boston: Houghton Mifflin, 1942.

Writing Non-Fiction. [Walter Stanley Campbell]. Boston: The Writer, Inc., 1944. Rev. 1949.

The Missouri. Rivers of America Series. New York and Toronto: Farrar & Rinehart, 1945.

Jim Bridger, Mountain Man. New York: William Morrow, 1946.

Wagons Southwest: Story of Old Trails to Santa Fe. New York: Pioneer Trails Association, 1946.

Warpath and Council Fire: The Plains Indians' Struggle for Survival in War and in Diplomacy, 1851-1859. New York: Random House, 1948.

Writing: Advices and Devices. [Walter Stanley Campbell]. New York: Doubleday, 1949.

Joe Meek, The Merry Mountain Man. Caldwell, Idaho: Caxton, 1952.

Queen of the Cowtowns: Dodge City. New York: Harper, 1952. Rpt. New York: Bantam Books, 1954.

The Book Lover's Southwest: A Guide to Good Reading. [Walter S. Campbell]. Norman: Univ. of Oklahoma Press, 1955.

Works about Walter Stanley Campbell

Tassin, Ray. *Stanley Vestal: Champion of the Old West.* Glendale, Calif.: Arthur H. Clark, 1973.

Mary Schiflett
University of Houston

Benjamin Capps (1922-   )
novels, nonfiction

Hanging at Comanche Wells. New York: Ballantine, 1962.

The Trail to Ogallala. New York: Duell, Sloan and Pearce, 1964.

Sam Chance. New York: Duell, Sloan and Pearce, 1965.
A Woman of the People. New York: Duell, Sloan and Pearce, 1966.
The Brothers of Uterica. New York: Meredith Press, 1967.
The White Man's Road. New York: Harper and Row, 1969.
The Indians. New York: Time-Life Books, 1972.
The True Memoirs of Charley Blankenship. New York: Lippincott, 1972.
The Warren Wagontrain Raid. New York: Dial, 1974.

Joyce Roach
Keller, Texas

Arthur Hawthorne Carhart (1892-   )
[pseud. Harold Thorne, Hart Thorne, V. A. VanSickle]
novels, short stories, juveniles, nonfiction

The Last Stand of the Pack (with Stanley P. Young). New York: J. H. Sears, 1929.
The Ordeal of Brad Ogden: A Romance of the Forest Rangers. New York: J. H. Sears, 1929.
Colorado. New York: Coward-McCann, 1932.
Bronc Twister. [Hart Thorne]. New York: Dodd, Mead, 1937.
Drum Up the Dawn. New York: Dodd, Mead, 1937.
Saddle Men of the C Bit Brand [Hart Thorne]. New York: Dodd, Mead, 1937.
The Wrong Body. [V. A. VanSickle]. New York: Knopf, 1937.
Son of the Forest. Philadelphia: Lippincott, 1952.
Pinto the Cowboy Pony. n. p., Nifty, 1953.

In addition to the above and books on conservation, travel, recreation, and landscape design, Arthur Carhart has contributed over four thousand short stories, novelettes, serials, articles, and essays to magazines such as *Better Homes and Gardens, Rotarian, Saturday Evening Post,* and *Sunset.*

Works about Arthur Hawthorne Carhart
Melville, McClellan. "Conservationist Conserves Learning," *American Forests,* 68 (April 1962), 15, 60-63.

Joyce Cornette Palmer
Texas Woman's University

Lorraine Carr (-   )
[Mrs. William E. Huddleston]
novel, short stories, autobiography

Mother of the Smiths. New York: The Macmillan Company, 1940.
To the Philippines with Love (autobiography). Los Angeles: Sherbourne
Press, 1965.

Joyce Cornette Palmer
Texas Woman's University

Aline Badger Carter (-1972)
poetry

Halo of Love. Rogers, Arkansas: Avalon Press, 1946.
Doubt Not The Dream. San Antonio: Naylor, 1968.

John Igo
San Antonio College

Gary Cartwright (1934-   )
novels

The Hundred-Yard War. New York: Doubleday, 1968.

Cartwright is the author (with Edwin Shrake) of the screenplay *Kid Blue.*

Arlene Kyle
North Texas State University

Bill H. Casey (1930-1966)
novel, short stories, articles

A Shroud for a Journey. Boston: Houghton Mifflin, 1960.

In addition, Casey published seven short stories and articles in such journals as *Southwest Review* and *Contact.*

Works about Bill Casey
Turner, Steve. "Bill Casey: Jottings Before a Journey," *Southwestern American Literature,* 1 (May 1971), 80-86.

Richard B. Sale
North Texas State University

Fray Angelico Chavez (1910-   )
[b. Manuel Chavez]
poetry, history

Clothed with the Sun (poems). Santa Fe: Rydal Press, 1939.
New Mexico Triptich (stories). Paterson, N. J.: St. Anthony Press, 1940.
Eleven Lady Lyrics (poems). Paterson, N. J.: St. Anthony Press, 1945.
The Single Rose (poem). Santa Fe: Los Santos Bookshop, 1948.
Our Lady of the Conquest (history). Santa Fe: Historical Society of New Mexico, 1948.
La Conquistadora (literary history). Paterson, N. J.: St. Anthony Guild, 1954.
Origins of New Mexico Families (history). Santa Fe: Historical Society of New Mexico, 1954.
The Missions of New Mexico, 1776 (history). Albuquerque: Univ. of New Mexico Press, 1956.
Archives of the Archdiocese of Santa Fe (history). Washington: Academy of American Franciscan History, 1957.
From an Altar Screen (stories). New York: Farrar, Straus & Cudahy, 1957.
The Virgin of Port Lligat (poem). Fresno, California: Academy Guild Press, 1959.
The Lady From Toledo (literary history). Fresno, California: Academy Guild Press, 1960.
Coronado's Friars (history). Washington: Academy of American Franciscan History, 1968.
Selected Poems. Santa Fe: Press of the Territorian, 1969.
The Oroz Codex (history). Washington: Academy of American Franciscan History, 1971.
St. Francis of Assisi. Flagstaff: Northland, 1973.
My Penitente Land. Albuquerque: Univ. of New Mexico Press, 1974.

Fray Angelico Chavez has published many research articles in *New Mexico Historical Review* and *El Palacio* (Museum of New Mexico).

Alice Bullock
Santa Fe, New Mexico

William Lawrence (Larry) Chittenden (1862-1934)
poetry

Ranch Verses. New York: Putnam, 1893.
Bermuda Verses. New York: Putnam, 1909.

Mary Schiflett
University of Houston

Peggy Pond Church (1903-   )
[Margaret P. Church; Mrs. Fermor Church]
novels, poetry, biography, nonfiction

Foretaste. Santa Fe: Writers' Editions, 1933.
The Burro of Angelitos. Los Angeles: Suttonhouse, 1936.
Familiar Journey. Santa Fe: Writers' Editions, 1936.
The House at Otowi Bridge: The Story of Edith Warner and Los Alamos. Albuquerque: Univ. of New Mexico Press, 1960.

In addition, Church published approximately twenty-five poems in such journals as *Survey Graphic, Atlantic, Saturday Review, New Republic,* and *Virginia Quarterly* and two articles in *Common Ground.*

J. Wilkes Berry
Texas Tech University

Charles Badger Clark, Jr. (1883-   )
poetry

Sun and Saddle Leather. Boston: R. G. Badger, 1915; rev. ed. with Preface, 1920; rpt., Boston: Chapman and Grimes, 1936.

Grass Grown Trails. Boston: R. G. Badger, 1917.
Sky and Wood Smoke. Custer, S. D.: The Chronicle Shop, 1935.

Works about Charles Badger Clark, Jr.
Campbell, Walter S. *The Book Lover's Southwest: a Guide to Good Reading.* Norman: Univ. of Oklahoma Press, 1955.
Carlin, Paige. "Badger Clark, Poet Lariat of the West," *Together,* (August 1959), pp. 45-46.
Gillis, Everett A. "Literary Origins of Some Western Ballads," *Western Folklore,* 13 (April 1954), 101-106.
———. "Laureates of the Western Range," *The Sunny Slopes of Long Ago.* Dallas: Southern Methodist Univ. Press, 1966.

Everett A. Gillis
Texas Tech University

James Anthony Clark (1907-   )
nonfiction

Spindeltop. (With Michael T. Halbouty). New York: Random House, 1952.
Three Stars for the Colonel (biography). New York: Random House, 1954.
The Tactful Texan: A Biography of Governor Will Hobby. (With Weldon Hart). New York: Random House, 1958.
A Biography of Robert Alonzo Welch. (With Nathan Brock). Houston: Clark Book Co., 1963.
The Chronological History of the Petroleum and Natural Gas Industries. (With C. A. Warner and H. E. Walton). Houston: Clark Book Co., 1963.
Schlumberger Well Surveying Corporation: Founders of the Industry: Calendar for the Year 1967. n. p., 1966
Marrs McLean, a Biography. Houston: Clark Book Co., 1969.
Ahead of His Time. (Ed. with Michael T. Halbouty.) Houston: Gulf Publishing Co., 1971.
The Last Boom. (With Michael T. Halbouty.) New York: Random House, 1972

Lois Williams Parker
Lamar University

L. D. Clark (1922-   )
novel, criticism

The Dove Tree. Garden City, New York: Doubleday, 1961.
Dark Night of the Body (D. H. Lawrence's *The Plumed Serpent*). Austin:
Univ. of Texas Press, 1964.

In addition, Clark published a number of short stories in *Forum, Re Arts
and Letters,* and *Stories Southwest;* also essays on D. H. Lawrence.

Sr. Diane Sanders
Ursuline Academy
Kirkwood, Missouri

William R. Clark (-   )
poetry

Dogwood and Wild Laurel, A Narrative Poem of the Soil. Amarillo, Texas:
Russell Stationery, 1931.
A Stained Glass Window and Other Poems. Memphis, Texas: The Mem-
phis Publishing Co., 1934.

Sr. Diane Sanders
Ursuline Academy
Kirkwood, Missouri

Jeremiah Clemens (1814-1865)
novels, political writing

*Remarks of Messrs. Clemens, Butler, and Jefferson Davis, on the Vermont
Resolutions Relating to Slavery.* Washington: The Congressional Globe
Office, 1850.
*Bernard Lile: An Historical Romance, Embracing the Periods of the Texas
Revolution, and the Mexican War.* Philadelphia: Lippincott, 1856.
Mustang Gray: A Romance. Philadelphia: Lippincott, 1858.
The Rivals: A Tale of the Times of Aaron Burr and Alexander Hamilton.
Philadelphia: Lippincott, 1860.
*The History and Debates of the Convention of the People of Alabama,
Begun and Held in the City of Montgomery, on the Seventh Day of Janu-
ary, 1861.* Montgomery: White, Pfester, 1861; rpt. Atlanta: Wood, Han-
leiter, Rice, 1861.

Letter from Hon. Jere. Clemens. Philadelphia: The Union League of Philadelphia, 1864.

Tobias Wilson: A Tale of the Great Rebellion. Philadelphia: Lippincott, 1865.

An American Colonel: A Story of Thrilling Times During the Revolution and the Great Rivalry of Aaron Burr and Alexander Hamilton. Akron, Ohio: Wolfe Publ. Co., 1900. A reprinting of *The Rivals.*

In addition, Clemens has had other speeches preserved in the newspapers and periodicals of the time. Some of Clemens's unpublished papers are at Duke University and some in the collections of the Missouri Historical Society.

Works about Jeremiah Clemens
Brewer, Willis. *Alabama: Her History, Resources, War Record, and Public Men.* Montgomery: Barrett & Brown, 1872.
Garrett, William. *Reminiscences of Public Men in Alabama, For Thirty Years.* Atlanta: Plantation Pub. Co., 1872.

Ann Carpenter
Angelo State University

Walter Clemons (1929-   )
short stories

The Poison Tree and Other Stories. Boston: Houghton Mifflin, 1959.

In addition, Clemons published stories in *Transatlantic Review, Accent,* and *Ladies' Home Journal.*

Sr. Diane Sanders
Ursuline Academy
Kirkwood, Missouri

Walt Coburn (1889-1971)
novels

The Ringtailed Rannyhans. New York: The Century Co., 1927.
Mavericks. New York: The Century Co., 1929.
Barb Wire. New York: The Century Co., 1931.

Walt Coburn's Action Novels: Four Western Novels. New York: Fiction House, 1931.
Law Rides the Range. New York: Appleton-Century, 1935.
Sky-Pilot Cowboy. New York: Appleton-Century, 1937.
Pardners of the Dim Trails. Philadelphia: Lippincott, 1951.
Drift Fence. London: Hammond, 1953.
Burnt Ranch. London: Hammond, 1954.
Gun Grudge. London: Hammond, 1954.
Square Shooter. London: Hammond, 1955.
Wet Cattle. London: Hammond, 1955.
Beyond the Wide Missouri. New York: Arcadia House, 1956.
Cayuse. London: Hammond, 1956.
Fear Branded. London: Hammond, 1957.
Stirrup High (juvenile). New York: J. Messner, 1957.
Border Jumper. London: Hammond, 1958.
Buffalo Run. London: Hammond, 1958.
Free Rangers. London: Hammond, 1959.
Feud Valley and Sleeper-marked. London: Hammond, 1960.
Ramrod and Sons of Gun Fighters. London: Hammond, 1960.
Guns Blaze on Spiderweb Ranch. London: Hammond, 1961.
Pioneer Cattleman in Montana: The Story of the Circle C. Ranch. Norman: Univ. of Oklahoma Press, 1968.
Renegade. New York: Belmont Books, 1969.
Invitation to a Hanging. New York: Macfadden-Bartell, 1970.
Way of a Texan. New York: Avon, 1971.
Beyond the Wild Missouri. Derby, Connecticut: Belmont-Tower, 1974.
Western Word Wrangler (autobiography). Flagstaff: Northland, 1974.

Carol A. Lafferty
North Texas State University

Daisy Lemon Coldiron (1876-1946)
poetry

Songs of Oklahoma. Dallas: Kaleidograph, 1935.
There Was a Garden. Dallas: Kaleidograph, 1940.
Who Touches This. Dallas: Kaleidograph, 1940.
Ballads of the Plains. Dallas: Kaleidograph, 1950.

In addition, Coldiron's poems have appeared in *American Author, Arrow, Harlow's Weekly, Kaleidograph, The Oklahoma Poetry Society Anthology,* and *The University of Oklahoma Magazine.*

Carol A. Lafferty
North Texas State University

Will Levington Comfort (1878-1932)
novels, short stories, nonfiction

Trooper Tales: A Series of Sketches of the Real American Private Soldier. New York: Street and Smith, 1899; rpt. Freeport, New York: Books for Libraries Press, 1970.

The Lady of Fallen Star Island. New York and London: Street and Smith, 1902.

Routledge Rides Again. Philadelphia and London: Lippincott, 1910.

She Buildeth Her House. Philadelphia and London: Lippincott, 1911.

Fate Knocks at the Door: A Novel. Philadelphia and London: Lippincott, 1912.

Down Among Men. New York: Doran, 1913.

The Road of Living Men: A Novel. Philadelphia and London: Lippincott, 1913.

Sport of Kings. Philadelphia: Lippincott, 1913.

Fatherland, with "The Army of the Dead," by Barry Pain. New York: Doran, 1914.

Midstream: A Chronicle at Halfway (autobiography). New York: Doran, 1914.

Lot and Company. New York: Doran, 1915.

Red Fleece. New York: Doran, 1915.

Child and Country: A Book of the Younger Generation. New York: Doran, 1916.

The Hive (essays and stories). New York: Doran, 1918.

The Shielding Wing. Boston: Small, Maynard & Co., 1918.

The Last Ditch. New York: Doran, 1916.

The Yellow Lord. New York: Doran, 1919.

Nine Great Little Books: The Story of a Quest Through a Myriad Books and Days to Find the Book of the Heart Which is Humanity. Los Angeles: n.p., 1920.

Son of Power (with Zamin Ki Dost Willimina Leonora Armstrong). Garden
City, New York: Doubleday, Page, 1920.

This Man's World. Garden City, New York, and Toronto: Doubleday, Page,
1921.

Samadhi. Boston and New York: Houghton Mifflin, 1927.

Apache. New York: Dutton, 1931. Pub. in England as *Mangas Coloradas.*

Mangas Coloradas. London: Stein, 1931. Pub. in America as *Apache.*

The Pilot Comes Aboard. New York: Dutton, 1932. London: Jarrolds, 1933.

In addition, Comfort has at least seventy short stories that appear in such
journals as the *Saturday Evening Post, Lippincott's Magazine, Cosmopolitan, Frank Leslie's Monthly, Everybody's, Era,* and *Craftsman.* Some twenty
volumes of his manuscripts are in the library of the University of California.

Works about Will Comfort
Heffron, Ida Cassa. *Will Levington Comfort: Man of Vision.* Los Angeles:
I. Deach, Jr., 1936.

Ann Carpenter
Angelo State University

Ellsworth Prouty Conkle (1899-   )
plays

Crick Bottom Plays. New York: Samuel French, 1928.

In the Shadow of a Rock. New York: Samuel French, 1937.

Loolie and Other Plays. New York: Samuel French, 1937.

Two Hundred Were Chosen. New York: Samuel French, 1937.

Five Plays. New York: Samuel French, 1938. Including "Bill and the
Widowmaker," "The Delectable Judge," "49 Dogs in the Meathouse,"
"Johnny Appleseed," and "Paul and the Blue Ox."

Prologue to Glory. New York: Random House, 1938.

Poor Old Boys. New York: Samuel French, 1954.

A Bauble for Baby. New York: Samuel French, 1955.

No More Wars but the Moon. New York: Samuel French, 1955.

Son-of-a-Biscuit-Eater. New York: Samuel French, 1958.

Granny's Little Cheery Room. New York: Samuel French, 1960.

Kitten in the Elm Tree. New York: Samuel French, 1962.

Lots of Old People Are Really Good for Something. New York: Samuel French, 1964.

In addition to the plays published separately, Conkle has twenty-six plays in anthologies, and several essays on the drama and the essay in *Theatre Arts, English Journal,* and *Educational Theatre Journal.*

Ernest Speck
Sul Ross State University

Alberta Wilson Constant (1908-   )
short stories, juveniles, nonfiction

Oklahoma Run. New York: Crowell, 1955.
Miss Charity Comes To Stay. New York: Crowell, 1959; rpt. as *The Claim by the Cottonwood Tree* (London: Deutsch, 1964).
Willie and the Wildcat Well. New York: Crowell, 1962.
Those Miller Girls. New York: Crowell, 1965.
The Motoring Millers. New York: Crowell, 1969.
Paintbox on the Frontier: The Life and Times of George Caleb Bingham. New York: Crowell, 1974.

In addition, Constant published seven articles and short stories between 1943 and 1956 in *Good Housekeeping, Library Journal, Saturday Evening Post, Southwest Review,* and *Univ. of Kansas City Review.*

Sr. Paula Hartwig
Ursuline Academy
Laredo, Texas

Neil C. Cook (1896-   )
novel

Welcome Stranger. New York: Appleton, 1929.

Sr. Paula Hartwig
Ursuline Academy
Laredo, Texas

Dane Coolidge (1873-1940)
novels, nonfiction

Hidden Water. Chicago: A. C. Mc Clurg, 1910.
The Texican. Chicago: A. C. Mc Clurg, 1911.
Bat Wing Bowles. New York: Frederick A. Stokes, 1914.
The Desert Trail. New York: W. J. Watt, 1915.
Rimrock Jones. New York: W. J. Watt, 1917.
The Fighting Fool. New York: Dutton, 1918.
Shadow Mountain. New York: W. J. Watt, 1919.
Silver and Gold. New York: Dutton, 1919.
Wunpost. New York: Dutton, 1920.
The Man-Killers. New York: Dutton, 1921.
Lost Wagons. New York: Dutton, 1923.
The Scalp Lock. New York: Dutton, 1924.
Not Afraid. New York: Dutton, 1926.
Under the Sun. New York: Dutton, 1926.
Gun-Smoke. New York: Dutton, 1928.
War Paint. New York: Dutton, 1929.
Horse-Ketchum. New York: Dutton, 1930.
The Navajo Indians (with Mary R. Coolidge). Boston and New York: Houghton Mifflin, 1930.
Maverick Makers. New York: Dutton, 1931.
The Fighting Men of the West. New York: Dutton, 1932.
Sheriff Killer. New York: Dutton, 1932.
Jess Roundtree, Texas Ranger. New York: Dutton, 1933; rpt. as *Texas Ranger,* 1936.
Navajo Rugs (with Mary R. Coolidge). Pasadena, California: Esto Publ. Co., 1933.
The Fighting Danites. New York: Dutton, 1934.
Other Men's Cattle. London: Skeffington, 1934.
Silver Hat. New York: Dutton, 1934.
Long Rope. New York: Dutton, 1935.
Lorenzo the Magnificent. New York: Dutton, 1935.
Wolf's Candle. New York: Dutton, 1935.
Rawhide Johnny. New York: Dutton, 1936.
Snake Bit Jones. New York: Dutton, 1936.
Death Valley Prospectors. New York: Dutton, 1937.

Ranger Two-Rifles. New York: Dutton, 1937.
Texas Cowboys. New York: Dutton, 1937.
The Trail of Gold. New York: Dutton, 1937.
Arizona Cowboys. New York: Dutton, 1938.
Comanche Chaser. New York: Dutton, 1938; rpt. as *Redskin Trail.* London: Skeffington, 1940.
Hell's Hip Pocket. New York: Dutton, 1938.
Gringo Gold. New York: Dutton, 1939.
The Last of the Series (with Mary R. Coolidge). New York: Dutton, 1939.
Old California Cowboys. New York: Dutton, 1939.
Wally Laughs Easy. New York: Dutton, 1939.
Bloody Head. New York: Dutton, 1940.
Yaqui Drums. New York: Dutton, 1940.
Bear Paw. New York: Dutton, 1941.

In addition, Coolidge contributed short stories to magazines such as *Delineator, Overland Monthly, Outing,* and *Sunset.*

Works about Dane Coolidge
Cleaveland, Agnes Morley. "Three Musketeers of Southwestern Fiction," *American Magazine,* 87 (December 1929), 385.

> Sr. Paula Hartwig
> Ursuline Academy
> Laredo, Texas

Courtney Ryley Cooper (1886-1940)
novels, biography, nonfiction

Us Kids. Kansas City: Kellogg Baster, 1910.
End of Steel. New York: Prospect Press, 1918.
The Quick Lunch Cabaret: A Versical Omelette in One Scramble for Male Quartette. Chicago: T. S. Denison, 1918.
The Eagle's Eye (with W. J. Flynn). New York: Prospect Press, 1918.
Memories of Buffalo Bill (with Louisa Cody). New York: Appleton, 1919.
Dear Folks at Home, by Kemper F. Cowing. Ed. Courtney Ryley Cooper. Boston and New York: Houghton, 1919.

The Cross-Cut. Boston: Little, Brown, 1921.
The White Desert. Boston: Little, Brown, 1922.
The Last Frontier. Boston: Little, Brown, 1923.
Under the Big Top. Boston: Little, Brown, 1923.
Lions 'n Tigers 'n Everything. Boston: Little, Brown, 1924.
High Country: The Rockies Yesterday and To-Day. Boston: Little, Brown, 1926.
Oklahoma. Boston: Little, Brown, 1926.
Annie Oakley: Woman at Arms. New York: Duffield, 1927.
Sawdust and Solitude, by Lucia Zora. Ed. Courtney Ryley Cooper. Boston: Little, Brown, 1928.
Avalanche. London: Hurst, 1929.
Go North, Young Man! Boston: Little, Brown, 1929.
Caged. Boston: Little, Brown, 1930.
Trigger Finger. New York and London: Collins, 1930.
Circus Day. New York: Farrar & Rinehart, 1931.
Ghost Country. New York and London: Collins, 1933.
Boss Elephant. Boston: Little, Brown, 1934.
Old Mom. n.p., 1934 [not seen]
Mystery of the Four Abreast. New York and London: Collins, 1935.
Ten Thousand Public Enemies. Boston: Little, Brown, 1935.
Poor Man's Gold. Boston: Little, Brown, 1936.
The Golden Bubble. Boston: Little, Brown, 1937.
Here's to Crime. Boston: Little, Brown, 1937.
The Pioneers. Boston: Little, Brown, 1938.
Designs in Scarlet. Boston: Little, Brown, 1939.
Action in Diamonds. New York: Penn, 1942.
The Challenge of the Bush. Boston: Little, Brown, n.d.

In addition, Cooper published some 500 stories and articles in magazines such as *American Magazine, Collier's, Delineator, Ladies' Home Journal, Overland Monthly, Popular Mechanics, Readers' Digest, Saturday Evening Post,* and *World's Work.* As a journalist, Cooper wrote for the *Kansas City Star, New York World, Chicago Tribune.*

Sr. Paula Hartwig
Ursuline Academy
Laredo, Texas

Madison A. Cooper (1895-1956)
novels

Sironia, Texas. 2 vols. Boston: Houghton Mifflin, 1952.
The Haunted Hacienda. Boston: Houghton Mifflin, 1955.

Works about Madison Cooper
Travis, Marion. *Madison Cooper.* Waco, Texas: Word Books, 1971.

Larry B. Corse
North Texas State University

Edwin Corle (1906-1956)
novels, nonfiction

Mojave: A Book of Stories. New York: Liveright, 1934.
Fig Tree John. New York: Liveright, 1935; rpt. Los Angeles: Ward Ritchie Press, 1962.
Burro Alley. New York: Random House, 1938.
Solitaire. New York: Dutton, 1940.
Desert Country. New York: Duell, Sloan & Pearce, 1941.
Coarse Gold. New York: Dutton, 1942; rpt. Duell, Sloan & Pearce, 1952.
Listen, Bright Angel. New York: Duell, Sloan & Pearce, 1946; rpt. as *The Story of the Grand Canyon.* London: S. Low, Marston, 1948; rpt. New York: Duell, Sloan & Pearce, 1951.
Three Ways to Mecca. New York: Duell, Sloan & Pearce, 1947.
John Studebaker, An American Dream. New York: Dutton, 1948.
Igor Stravinsky. Ed Edwin Corle. New York: Duell, Sloan & Pearce, 1949.
In Winter Light. New York: Duell, Sloan & Pearce, 1949.
The Royal Highway (El Camino Real). Indianapolis: Bobbs-Merrill, 1949; rpt. New York: Duell, Sloan & Pearce, 1949.
People on the Earth. New York: Random House, 1937; rpt. Santa Barbara: W. Hebberd, 1950.
The Gila, River of the Southwest. New York: Rinehart, 1951.
Death Valley and the Creek Called Furnace. Los Angeles: Ward Ritchie Press, 1952.
Billy the Kid. New York: Duell, Sloan & Pearce, 1953.

In addition, Corle wrote a number of articles for *Holiday, Atlantic,* and *Yale Review.*

Works about Edwin Corle

Pilkington, William T. "Edwin Corle and the Southwestern Indian," *Western Review,* 4 (Winter 1967) 51-57; rpt. in Pilkington's *My Blood's Country.* Ft. Worth: Texas Christian Univ. Press, 1973.

James W. Lee
North Texas State University

Margaret Cousins (1905-   )
[pseud. Mary Parrish]
novels, short stories, biography, nonfiction

Uncle Edgar and the Reluctant Saint. New York: Farrar, Straus, 1948.
Ben Franklin of Old Philadelphia. New York: Random House, Landmark Books, 1952.
Christmas Gift. Garden City, New York: Doubleday, 1952.
Souvenir (with M. Truman). New York: McGraw-Hill, 1956.
We Were There at the Alamo. New York: Grossett and Dunlap, 1958.
Love and Marriage. Ed. Margaret Cousins. Garden City, New York: Doubleday, 1961.
Thomas Alva Edison. New York: Random House, Landmark Books, 1965.

In addition, Cousins published several poems and articles and approximately seventy-five uncollected short stories in such magazines as *Good Housekeeping, McCall's, House Beautiful, American Magazine,* and *Ladies Home Journal.*

Patricia Felts
Maurine LeBeau
North Texas State University

Alice Lent Covert (1913-   )
[pseud. Elaine Lowell]
novels, short stories

Return to Dust. New York: Kinsey, 1939.
Fighting Parson. New York: Kinsey, 1941.

The Months of Rain. New York: Kinsey, 1941.
End of Reckoning. New York: Kinsey, 1942.
The Eternal Mountain. Garden City: Doubleday, Doran, 1944.
All That's Mine. New York: Curl, 1946.
And Answer None. New York: Curl, 1946.
Believe Me True [Elaine Lowell]. New York: Arcadia House, 1947.
Just Between Women. New York: Curl, 1947.
The Glass House. New York: Bouregy and Curl, 1950.
Wayward Heart. New York: Avalon, 1950.
Heart's Desire. New York: Bouregy and Curl, 1951.
We'll Find Our Way. New York: Bouregy and Curl, 1951.
Dearly Beloved. New York: Bouregy and Curl, 1952.
The Dark Passage. New York: Bouregy and Curl, 1952.
The Distant Drum. New York: Bouregy and Curl, 1952.
This Tangled Web. New York: Bouregy and Curl, 1952.
This Time Forever. New York: Bouregy and Curl, 1952.
Shadow of Truth. New York: Bouregy and Curl, 1953.
Winds of Heaven. New York: Avalon, 1954.
Long Ago, Far Away. New York: Avalon, 1955.
My Heart an Altar, A Novel. New York: Avalon, 1955.
Wings of Morning. New York: Avalon, 1956.
The Alien Heart. New York: Avalon, 1957.

Covert published over thirty short stories and several articles in *Saturday Evening Post, Good Housekeeping,* and *Reader's Digest.*

Judy Ponthieu
Geoffrey Grimes
Texas Tech University

Leo Crane (1881-   )
nonfiction

Indians of the Enchanted Desert. Boston: Little, Brown, 1925.
Desert Drums: The Pueblo Indians of New Mexico, 1540-1928. Boston: Little, Brown, 1928.

Carrie Sue Woods
Texas Christian University

William Crawford (1929-   )
novels, nonfiction

Give Me Tomorrow. New York: Putnam, 1962.
The Bronc Rider. New York: Putnam, 1965.
The United States Border Patrol. New York: Putnam, 1965.

William T. Pilkington
Tarleton State College

Kyle Samuel Crichton (1898-1960)
[pseud. Robert Forsythe]
novels, short stories, biography, nonfiction

Law & Order, Ltd., The Rousing Life of Elfego Baca of New Mexico. Santa
Fe: New Mexican Publishing Corp., 1928.
Redder Than the Rose [Robert Forsythe]. New York: Covici-Friede, 1935.
Reading From Left To Right [Robert Forsythe]. New York: Covici-Friede,
1938.
The Proud People. New York: Scribner, 1944.
The Marx Brothers. Garden City, New York: Doubleday, 1950.
*The History of the Adventures of George Whigham and His Friend, Mr.
Clancy Hobson.* New York: Crown, 1951.
My Philadelphia Father (by Cornelia Drexel Biddle, as told to Kyle
Crichton). Garden City, New York: Doubleday, 1955.
My Partner-in-Law: The Life of George Morton Levy (with Martin Wilie
Littleton). New York: Farrar, Straus & Cudahy, 1957.
Subway to the Met: Risë Stevens' Story. Garden City, New York: Double-
day, 1959.
Total Recoil. Garden City, New York: Doubleday, 1960.

Crichton also published over four hundred short stories and articles in *Collier's* and *Scribner's* between 1927 and 1949 and several short stories and
articles in *Atlantic, Holiday,* and *Theatre Arts* between 1951 and 1959.

Judith Alter
Texas Christian University

Stanley Francis Louis Crocchiola (1908-   )
[pseud. Father Stanley]
novels, historical nonfiction

Raton Chronicle. Denver: World Press, 1948.
Fort Bascom, Comanche-Kiowa Barrier. Pampa, Texas: n.p., 1952.
The Grant that Maxwell Bought. Canadian, Texas: n.p., 1952.
Desperadoes of New Mexico. Denver: n.p., 1953.
Rodeo Town (Canadian, Texas). Denver: World Press, 1953.
Clay Allison. Denver: World Press, 1956.
Jim Courtright, Two Gun Marshall of Fort Worth. Denver: World Press, 1957.
Ciudad Santa Fe. Denver: World Press, 1958.
No Tears for Black Jack Ketchum. Denver: World Press, 1958.
Ike Stockton. Denver: World Press, 1959.
Dave Rudabaugh, Border Ruffian. Denver: World Press, 1961.
The Apaches of New Mexico. Pampa, Texas: Pampa Print Shop, 1962.
The Odyssey of Juan Archibeque. Pantex, Texas: n.p., 1962.
The Duke City: The Story of Albuquerque, New Mexico, 1706-1956. Pampa, Texas: n.p., 1963.
The Dawson Tragedies. Pep, Texas: n.p., 1964.
E. V. Sumner, Major-General, U.S. Army, 1797-1863. Borger, Texas: J. Hess, 1968.
Santanta and the Kiowas. Borger, Texas: J. Hess, 1968.

In addition, Father Stanley has approximately forty-five historical pamphlets dealing with towns and villages of New Mexico.

H. Jerome Thompson
Texas Tech University

Martha Ruth Cross (1887-   )
novels, short stories, nonfiction

The Golden Cocoon. New York: Harper, 1924.
The Unknown Goddess. New York: Harper, 1926.
Enchantment. New York: Green, 1930.
The Big Road. New York: Green, 1931.

Soldier of Good Fortune. Dallas: Banks Upshaw, 1936.
Back Door to Happiness. New York: J. H. Hopkins & Son, 1937.
Eden on a Country Hill. New York: H. C. Kinsey, 1938.
Wake Up and Garden. New York: Prentice-Hall, 1942.

In addition, Cross published some twenty essays and stories in *Better Homes and Gardens, Saturday Evening Post,* and *American Home.*

Jim Bryant
Texas Christian University

Grace Noll Crowell (1877-1969)
poetry, prose meditations

White Fire. Fort Worth: n.p., 1925; rpt. Dallas: P.L. Turner, 1928.
Silver in the Sun. Dallas: P. L. Turner, 1928.
Miss Humpety Comes to Tea and Other Poems. Dallas: Southwest Press, 1929; rev. and enlarged, New York: Harper, 1938.
Flame in the Wind. Dallas: Southwest Press, 1930.
Songs for Courage. Dallas: Southwest Press, 1930; rpt. New York and London: Harper, 1938.
Bright Destiny; A Book of Texas Verse. Dallas: P. L. Turner, 1936.
Light of the Years. New York and London: Harper, 1936.
This Golden Summit. New York and London: Harper, 1937.
Songs of Hope. New York and London: Harper, 1938.
Songs of Faith. New York and London: Harper, 1939.
The Radiant Quest. New York and London: Harper, 1940.
Splendor Ahead. New York and London: Harper, 1940.
Facing the Stars. New York and London: Harper, 1941.
The Lifted Lamp. New York and London: Harper, 1942.
Happiness for Sale. Minneapolis: Augsburg Pub. House, 1943.
Some Brighter Dawn. New York and London: Harper, 1943.
Between Eternities. New York and London: Harper, 1944.
The Shining Hour. Minneapolis: Augsburg Pub. House, 1944.
A Child Kneels to Pray. Minneapolis: Augsburg Pub. House, 1945.
The Glory of Giving. Minneapolis: Augsburg Pub. House, 1945.
The Wind-Swept Harp. New York and London: Harper, 1946.

The Crystal Fountain. New York: Harper, 1948.
Songs for Comfort. New York: Harper, 1948.
Apples of Gold. New York: Harper, 1950.
Meditations: Devotions for Women. Nashville: Abingdon-Cokesbury Press, 1951.
Bright Harvest. New York: Harper, 1952.
Little Boy Down the Lane. Minneapolis: Augsburg Pub. House, 1952.
The Little Serving Maid. Minneapolis: Augsburg Pub. House, 1953.
Moments of Devotion: Meditations and Verse. Nashville: Abingdon-Cokesbury Press, 1953.
Riches of the Kingdom. Nashville: Abingdon Press, 1954.
The Wood Carver. Minneapolis: Augsburg Pub. House, 1954.
Journey into Dawn. New York: Harper, 1955.
My Book of Prayer and Praise. Minneapolis: Augsburg Pub. House, 1955.
Come See a Man. New York: Abingdon Press, 1956.
Proofs of His Presence. New York: Abingdon Press, 1958.
Songs of Triumph. New York: Harper, 1959.
Facing Christmas, in *Guidepost's Joy to the World.* Carmel, Calif. and New York: Guideposts Associates, 1960.
Vital Possessions. New York: Abingdon Press, 1960.
God's Masterpieces. New York: Abingdon Press, 1963.
Poems of Inspiration and Courage: The Best Verse of Grace Noll Crowell. New York: Harper and Row, 1965.
Let the Sun Shine In. Old Tappan, New Jersey: Fleming H. Revell, 1970; also pub. Toronto: G. R. Welch, 1970.

Works about Grace Noll Crowell
Edwards, Margaret R. *Poets Laureate of Texas.* San Antonio: Naylor, 1966. Pp. 13-18.
Major, Mabel, Rebecca Smith Lee, and T. M. Pearce. *Southwest Heritage.* Albuquerque: Univ. of New Mexico Press, 1948. Rev. ed., 1972.
Plumb, Beatrice. *Grace Noll Crowell: The Poet and the Woman.* New York: Harper, 1938. Rpt. in *Lives that Inspire.* Minneapolis: Denison, 1962. Pp. 119-44.
Stidger, W. L. "Grace Noll Crowell," *Human Side of Greatness.* New York: Harper, 1940. Pp. 176-94.

Peggy Dechert Skaggs
Angelo State University

Albert Benjamin Cunningham (1888-   )
[pseud. Garth Hale, Estil Dale]
novels, nonfiction

The Manse at Barren Rocks. New York: Doran, 1918.
The Chronicle of an Old Town. New York and Cincinnati: The Abingdon Press, 1919.
The Singing Mountains. New York: George H. Doran, 1919.
Old Black Bass. New York and Cincinnati: The Abingdon Press, 1922.
Animal Tales of the Rockies. New York and Cincinnati: The Abingdon Press, 1925.
Murder at Deer Lick. New York: Dutton, 1939.
Murder at the Schoolhouse. New York: Dutton, 1940.
The Strange Death of Manny Square. New York: Dutton, 1941.
The Bancock Murder Case. New York: Dutton, 1942.
Death at "The Bottoms." New York: Dutton, 1942.
The Affair at the Boat Landing. New York: Dutton, 1943.
The Great Yant Mystery. New York: Dutton, 1943.
The Cane-patch Mystery. New York: Dutton, 1944.
Death Visits the Apple Hole. New York: Dutton, 1945.
Murder before Midnight. New York: Dutton, 1945.
Death Rides a Sorrel Horse. New York: Dutton, 1946.
One Man Must Die. New York: Dutton, 1946.
Strait is the Gate [Garth Hale]. New York: Dutton, 1946.
Death of a Bullionaire. New York: Dutton, 1947.
The Pounding Wheel [Garth Hale]. New York: Dutton, 1947.
Death Haunts the Dark Lane. New York: Dutton, 1948.
The Death of a Worldly Woman. New York: Dutton, 1948.
The Victory of Paul Kent [Garth Hale]. New York: Dutton, 1948.
After the Storm [Garth Hale]. New York: Dutton, 1949.
Léona Strait Is the Gate [Garth Hale]. Traduit de l'Américain par Gabrielle Goneel. Paris: R. Julliard, 1949.
Murder Without Weapons. New York: Dutton, 1949.
Hunter Is the Hunted. New York: Dutton, 1950.
The Killer Watches the Manhunt. New York: Dutton, 1950.
One Big Family [Garth Hale]. New York: Dutton, 1950.
Skeleton in the Closet. New York: Dutton, 1951.
Substance of a Dream [Garth Hale]. New York: Dutton, 1951.

Who Killed Pretty Becky Low? New York: Dutton, 1951.
The Last Survivor [Estil Dale]. New York: Dutton, 1952.
Legacy for Our Sons [Garth Hale]. New York: Dutton, 1952.
Strange Return. New York: Dutton, 1952.
The Everlasting Arms [Garth Hale]. New York: Dutton, 1953.

In addition, Cunningham published scholarly articles in *College English* and *School and Society.*

Harold W. Lawrence
Texas Christian University

Eugene Cunningham (1896-1957)
[pseud. Leigh Carder]
novels, short stories, nonfiction

Gypsying Through Central America. London: T. F. Unwin, 1922; New York: Dutton, 1922.
The Regulation Guy (short stories). Boston and New York: The Cornhill Publishing Co., 1922.
Trail to Apacaz. London: T. F. Unwin, 1924; New York: Dodd, Mead, 1924.
Whistling Lead. Boston and New York: Houghton Mifflin, 1936.
Famous in the West (short stories). El Paso, Texas: Hicks-Hayward, 1926.
Riders of the Night: A Novel of Cattle-land. Boston and New York: Houghton Mifflin, 1932; rpt. New York: Sun Dial Press, 1943.
Buckaroo, A Tale of the Texas Rangers. Boston and New York: Houghton Mifflin, 1933.
Hell-for-Leather Omnibus; containing two complete novels; Buckaroo; Diamond River Man. New York: Grosset & Dunlap, 1933-1934.
Diamond River Man. Boston and New York: Houghton Mifflin, 1934.
Texas Sheriff: A Novel of 'The Territory.' Boston and New York: Houghton Mifflin, 1934. Rpt. New York: Triangle Books, 1944.
Triggernometry: A Gallery of Gunfighters With Technical Notes on Leather Slapping as a Fine Art, Gathered from Many a Loose Holstered Expert Over the Years (Anthology). New York: The Press of the Pioneers, Inc., 1934. Rpt. Caldwell, Idaho: Caxton, 1941, 1947.
Border Guns [Leigh Carder]. New York: Covici, Friede, 1935.
Bravo Trail [Leigh Carder]. New York: Covici, Friede, 1935.
Outlaw Justice [Leigh Carder]. New York: Covici, Friede, 1935.

248   *Southwestern American Literature*

Quick Triggers. Boston and New York: Houghton Mifflin, 1935.
Redshirts of Destiny: A Novel of the Filibusters. New York: Empire Books, 1935.
Trail of the Macaw: Soldiers of Fortune in Banana Land. Boston and New York: Houghton Mifflin, 1935.
Pistol Passport: A Novel of the Texas Border. Boston and New York: Houghton Mifflin, 1936.
The Ranger Way. Boston and New York: Houghton Mifflin, 1937.
Texas Triggers. Boston and New York: Houghton Mifflin, 1938.
Gun Bulldogger. Boston and New York: Houghton Mifflin, 1939.
Red Range. Boston and New York: Houghton Mifflin, 1939.
Spiderweb Trail: A Texas Ranger Novel. Boston and New York: Houghton Mifflin, 1940.
Trail from the River. New York: Collins, 1940.
Riding Gun: A Buscadero Novel [Leigh Carder]. Boston and New York: Houghton Mifflin, 1951.

In addition, Cunningham published fiction and nonfiction western material in journals and edited Thomas Cruse's *Apache Days and After* (Caxton, 1941) and *Sophie Poe's Buckboard Days* (Caxton, 1936).

Harold W. Lawrence
Texas Christian University

William Cunningham (1901-   )
novels, short stories

Green Corn Rebellion. New York: Vanguard, 1935; rpt. London: John Long, 1937.
Pretty Boy. New York: The Vanguard Press, 1936. Also published under title *Tough Guy.* London: John Long, 1939.
The Real Book About Daniel Boone (juvenile book). Garden City, New York: Garden City Books, 1952.
Danny (with Sarah Cunningham). New York: Crown, 1953.

In addition, Cunningham published stories, poems, and essays in *Collier's* and *American Mercury.*

Harold W. Lawrence
Texas Christian University

Newton Mallory Curtis (c. 1800)
novels

The Bride of the Northern Wilds. New York: Burgess, Stringer & Co., 1843.
The Doom of the Tory's Guard. Troy, New York: L. Willard, 1843.
The Hunted Chief. New York: Williams Brothers, 1847.
The Patrol of the Mountain. New York: Williams Brothers, 1847.
The Ranger of Ravenstream. New York: Williams Brothers, 1847.
The Foundling of the Mohawk. New York: Williams Brothers, 1848.
The Marksmen of Monmouth. Troy, New York: L. Willard, 1848.

Jane Prokesch
Texas Christian University

Edward Everett Dale (1879-1972)
biography, history, nonfiction

Tales of the Tepee. Boston: Heath, 1919.
Letters of Lafayette. Oklahoma City: Harlow Publications, 1925.
The Prairie Schooner and Other Poems. Guthrie, Okla.: Co-operative Publishing Co., 1929.
Frontier Trails. Ed. E. E. Dale. Boston: Houghton Mifflin, 1920.
The Range Cattle Industry. Norman: Univ. of Oklahoma Press, 1930.
A Rider of the Cherokee Strip. Ed. E. E Dale. Boston: Houghton Mifflin, 1936.
Cherokee Cavaliers (with Gaston Litton). Norman: Univ. of Oklahoma Press, 1939.
Cow Country. Norman: Univ. of Oklahoma Press, 1942.
History of Oklahoma (with M. L. Wardell). New York: Prentice-Hall, 1948.
Indians of the Southwest: A Century of Federal Relations. Norman: Univ. of Oklahoma Press, 1949.
Oklahoma: The Story of a State. Evanston, Ill.: Row, Peterson, 1949.
Pioneer Judge: The Life of Robert Lee Williams (with J. D. Morrison). Cedar Rapids, Iowa: The Torch Press, 1958.
Frontier Ways: Sketches of Life in the Old West. Austin: Univ. of Texas Press, 1959. Rpt. USIA in several languages.
The Cross Timbers: Memories of a North Texas Boyhood. Austin: Univ. of Texas Press, 1966.
The Vanquished Prairie. Chicago: Windfall Press, 1972.

In addition, Dale published some twenty-five essays in learned journals, and left three manuscript volumes, including *The West Wind Blows: An Autobiography.*

M. E. Bradford
University of Dallas

James Wilmer Dallam (1818-1847)
novels, nonfiction

The Lone Star: A Tale of Texas; Founded Upon Incidents in the History of Texas. New York, Philadelphia: E. Ferrett & Co., 1845.
The Deaf Spy: A Tale Founded Upon Incidents in the History of Texas. Baltimore: W. Taylor, 1848.

In addition, Dallam published a digest of the laws of the Republic of Texas and several volumes of legal opinions by various state courts.

James W. Lee
North Texas State University

Captain Kit Dalton (-   )
nonfiction

Under the Black Flag. Memphis, Tennessee: Lockard Pub. Co., 1914.

Jim Bryant
Texas Christian University

Anne Pence Davis (-   )
novels

Mimi at Camp: The Adventures of a Tomboy. Chicago: Goldsmith, 1935.
Wishes Are Horses. Dallas: Mathis, Van Nort, 1938.
The Customer Is Always Right. New York: Macmillan, 1940.
The Top Hand of Lone Tree Ranch. New York: Crowell, 1960.

Uncollected essays have appeared in *The Writer.*

Martha Shipley
Sweetwater, Texas

Bruce Davis (1912-1974)
poetry

Hog Killin Time and Other Poems. Denton, Texas: Trilobite Press, 1973.

In addition, Davis wrote *Revised City Charter and Codification of the Ordinances of the City of Denton, Texas.* Denton, 1941.

Richard B. Sale
North Texas State University

Harold Lenoir Davis (1896-1960)
novels, short stories, poetry, nonfiction

Honey in the Horn. New York and London: Harper, 1935.
Proud Riders and Other Poems. New York: Harper, 1942.
Harp of a Thousand Strings. New York: Morrow, 1947.
Beulah Land. New York: Morrow, 1949.
Winds of Morning. New York: Morrow, 1952.
Team Bells Woke Me (stories). New York: Morrow, 1953.
The Distant Music. New York: Morrow, 1957.
Kettle of Fire. New York: Morrow, 1959.

In addition, Davis published poems in *Poetry* and sketches in *American Mercury.*

Works about Harold Lenoir Davis
Kohler, Dayton. "H.L. Davis: Writer in the West," *College English,* 14 (December 1952), 133-40.

Dahlia Terrell
Texas Tech University

James Francis (J. Frank) Davis (1870-1942)
[pseud. Nick Sherlock Collier]
novels, plays, nonfiction

Frenological Finance: Being a True History of the Life and Adventures of Mortimer Kensington Queen [Nick Sherlock Collier]. Boston: C. M. Clark, 1907.

Almanzar. New York: Holt, 1918.
The Chinese Label. Boston: Little, Brown, 1920
Almanzar Evarts, Hero. Macon, Georgia: J. W. Burke, 1925.
The Ladder (play). Unpublished; produced on Broadway in 1926.
Gold in the Hills; or, the Dead Sister's Secret. (Play). Boston: Baker, 1929.
A Series of Appreciations of Seven Immortal Texans for Whom Dining Cars and Lounge Cars Operated on the Texas Special are Named. Cover title: *Pioneers of the Great Southwest.* n. p.: written for the Missouri-Kansas-Texas Lines, 1933 (pamphlet).
Ladies Night (play). Boston: Baker, 1934.
The Road to San Jacinto. Indianapolis: Bobbs-Merrill, 1936.
Texas: Its History and Its Heroes. n.p.: written for the Missouri-Kansas-Texas Lines, 1936 (pamphlet).

In addition, Davis' one-act plays include "Appearances," "Freckles," "Midnight," and "A Modern Buccaneer." Uncollected essays, a novelette, stories, and plays have appeared in *American, Blue Book, Ladies Home Journal, Saturday Evening Post, Scribner's Magazine,* and *Sunset.*

Works about J. Frank Davis
Bellamy, Frances R. "We Have with Us—'The Ladder,' " *Outlook*, 9 (May 1928), 63.
Davis, J. Frank (as told to Louis J. Mogelever). "The Truth About 'The Ladder,' " *Theatre Magazine,* 48 (November 1928), 15-16.

Martha Shipley
Sweetwater, Texas

Mary (Mollie) Evelyn Moore Davis (1844-1909)
novels, short stories, poetry, plays

Minding the Gap and Other Poems. By Mollie E. Moore. Houston: Cushing & Cave, 1867.
Poems. By Mollie E. Moore. Houston: E. H. Cushing, 1869; rpt. 1872.
In War Times at La Rose Blanche. Boston: D. Lathrop, 1888.
The Mistress of Odd Corner. By M. E. M. Davis. The Yellow Apples. By Patience Stapleton. Boston: The Two Tales Pub. Co., 1892.

Under the Man-Fig. Boston and New York: Houghton Mifflin, 1895.
A Christmas Masque of Saint Roch, Pere Dagobert, and Throwing the Wanga. Chicago: A. C. McClurg, 1896.
An Elephant's Track and Other Stories. New York: Harper, 1897.
Under Six Flags; the Story of Texas. Boston and London: Ginn, 1897; rpt. Dallas: Cokesbury Book Store, 1953.
The Wire Cutters. Boston and New York: Houghton Mifflin, 1899.
The Queen's Garden. Boston and New York: Houghton Mifflin, 1900.
Jaconetta: Her Loves. Boston and New York: Houghton Mifflin, 1901.
Karen-Happuch and I. New Orleans: Picayune Job Office, 1901.
Tulane Songs. New Orleans: Tulane Univ. Press, 1901.
A Bunch of Roses, and Other Parlor Plays. Boston: Small, Maynard, 1903.
The Little Chevalier. Boston and New York: Houghton Mifflin, 1903.
Two Poems: Pere Dagobert; Throwing the Wanga. New Orleans: Picayune Job Office, c. 1906.
Christmas Boxes: Comedy for Four Males and Four Females. New York: Edgar S. Werner, c. 1907.
A Dress Rehearsal; Comedy for Four Males and Four Females. New York: E. S. Werner, c. 1907.
His Lordship; Romantic Comedy. New York: n.p., 1907.
The New System: Comedy for Four Males and Four Females. New York: Edgar S. Werner, c. 1907.
The Price of Silence. Boston and New York: Houghton Mifflin, 1907.
Queen Anne Cottages: Romantic Comedy for Five Males, Three Females and Supes. New York: Werner, c. 1907.
The Moons of Balbanca. Boston and New York: Houghton Mifflin, 1908.
Selected Poems of Mollie E. Moore Davis. New Orleans: Green Shutter Book Shop, 1927.
Letters of M. E. M. Davis to Kate Minor of Southdown Plantation. Tokyo: Hokuseido, 1955.
The Ships of Desire. Tokyo: Hokuseido, 1955.

Work about Mollie Moore Davis
Anderson, John Q. "Folklore in the Texas Fiction of Mollie E. Moore Davis (1844-1909)," *Journal of the American Studies Assn. of Texas,* 1 (1970), 20-27.
———. "Notes on Mollie E. Moore Davis," *Louisiana Studies,* 1 (1962), 20-27.

Friend, Llerena. "New Acquisitions [Mollie E. Moore Davis]," *The Library Chronicle of the University of Texas,* 6 (1957), 50-52.

In Memoriam: Mary Evelyn Moore Davis. New Orleans: Privately printed. n.p.: n.d. [1909?].

Moore, Fred H. "Notes on the Life of Mollie E. Moore Davis," *Chronicles of Smith County, Texas,* 9 (1970), 45-53.

Nott, Charles C. *Sketches in Prison Camps.* New York: A. D. F. Randolph, 1865.

John Q. Anderson
University of Houston

Cleo Dawson
novel

She Came to the Valley. New York: Morrow, 1943.

Henry L. Alsmeyer, Jr.
Texas A&M University

Donald Day (1899-   )
nonfiction

Backwoods to Border. Ed. with Mody C. Boatright. Texas Folk-Lore Society Publications, 18. Dallas: Southern Methodist Univ. Press, 1943.

From Hell to Breakfast. Ed. with Mody C. Boatright. Texas Folk-Lore Society Publications, 19. Dallas: Southern Methodist Univ. Press, 1944.

Big Country: Texas. New York: Duell, Sloan & Pearce, 1947.

The Autobiography of Will Rogers. Ed. Donald Day. Boston: Houghton Mifflin, 1949.

Will Rogers, Boy Roper. Boston: Houghton Mifflin, 1950.

Franklin D. Roosevelt's Own Story. Ed. Donald Day. Boston: Little, Brown, 1951.

How We Elect Our Presidents. Ed. Donald Day. Boston: Little, Brown, 1952.

Woodrow Wilson's Own Story. Ed. Donald Day. Boston: Little, Brown, 1952.

Uncle Sam's Uncle Josh, or, Josh Billings on Practically Everything. Ed. Donald Day. Boston: Little, Brown, 1953.
The Autobiography of Sam Houston. Ed. with Harry Herbert Ullom. Norman: Univ. of Oklahoma Press, 1954.
The Evolution of Love. New York: Dial Press, 1954.
Hunting and Exploring Adventures of Theodore Roosevelt. Ed. Donald Day New York: Dial Press, 1955.
Will Rogers: A Biography. New York: McKay, 1962.

In addition, Day published over a dozen articles in *Southwest Review* and in various folklore and history publications.

Jack D. Wages
Texas Tech University

Angie Elbertha Debo (1890-   )
history

The Historical Background of the American Policy of Isolation (with J. Fred Rippy.) Northampton, Massachusetts: Smith College Studies in History, 1924.
The Rise and Fall of the Choctaw Republic. Norman: Univ. of Oklahoma Press, 1934.
And Still the Waters Run. Princeton: Princeton Univ. Press, 1940.
The Road to Disappearance. Norman: Univ. of Oklahoma Press, 1941.
Oklahoma; a Guide to the Sooner State. Ed. Angie Debo and John M. Oskison. Norman: Univ. of Oklahoma Press, 1941. 2nd ed., 1947.
Tulsa: from Creek to Oil Capital. Norman: Univ. of Oklahoma Press, 1943.
Prairie City, the Story of an American Community. New York: Knopf, 1944.
Oklahoma, Foot-loose and Fancy-free. Norman: Univ. of Oklahoma Press, 1949.
The Five Civilized Tribes of Oklahoma; Report on the Social and Economic Conditions. Philadelphia: Indian Rights Association, 1951.
The Cowman's Southwest: Being the Reminiscences of Oliver Nelson, Freighter, Camp Cook, Cowboy, Frontiersman in Kansas, Indian Territory, Texas and Oklahoma, 1878-1893. Ed. Angie Debo. Glendale, California: Arthur H. Clark, 1953.

A History of the Choctaw, Chicasaw, and Natchez Indians. By Horatio B.
Cushman. Ed. Angie Debo. Stillwater, Oklahoma: Redlands Press, 1962.
A History of the Indians of the United States. Norman: Univ. of Oklahoma
Press, 1970.

In addition, Debo published many articles and book reviews in such periodi-
cals as *Southwest Review, New York Times Book Review, Chronicles of
Oklahoma, Pacific Historical Quarterly, American Academy of Political and
Social Sciences Annals, Journal of Southern History, The American Indian,
Mississippi Valley Historical Review.*

Works about Angie Debo
"Angie Debo," *Oklahoma Libraries,* 21 (Jan. 1971), 14-15.

> Gretchen C. Colehour
> Knox City, Texas

Frances Denning (-   )
poetry

Discovery and Other Poems. Dallas: Kaleidograph, 1946.
Verbs and Seasons: Poems. San Antonio: Naylor, 1962.

> Diane M. Dodson
> North Texas State University

James Thomas Deshields (1861-1948)
nonfiction

Frontier Sketches (series of newspaper articles). *Fort Worth Gazette,* 1883.
Cynthia Ann Parker: The Story of Her Capture. St. Louis: Charles B.
Woodward Printing Co., 1886.
Border Wars of Texas. Tioga, Texas: The Herald Co., 1912.
The Fergusons: "Jim and Ma." Dallas: Cockrell Publishing Co., 1932.
Tall Men with Long Rifles. San Antonio: Naylor, 1935.
They Sat in High Places: The Presidents and Governors of Texas. San
Antonio: Naylor, 1940.

> Dahlia Terrell
> Texas Tech University

Al Dewlen (1921-   )
novels, short stories, nonfiction

The Night of the Tiger. New York: McGraw-Hill, 1956.
The Bone Pickers. New York: McGraw-Hill, 1958.
Twilight of Honor. New York: McGraw-Hill, 1961.
Servants of Corruption. New York: Doubleday, 1971.

In addition, Dewlen published approximately fifteen short stories and articles in such periodicals as *Saturday Evening Post, Coronet,* and *The Writer.*

Works about Al Dewlen
Merren, John. "Character and Theme in the Amarillo Novels of Al Dewlen," *Western Review,* 6 (Summer 1969), 3-9.

Richard B. Sale
North Texas State University

J. Frank Dobie (1888-1964)
nonfiction

A Vaquero of the Brush Country. Boston: Little, Brown, 1929.
Coronado's Children. New York: Grosset and Dunlap, 1930.
On the Open Range. Dallas: Southwest Press, 1931.
Tongues of the Monte. Boston: Little, Brown, 1935.
Tales of the Mustang. Dallas: The Book Club of Texas, 1936.
The Flavor of Texas. Dallas: Dealey and Lowe, 1936.
Apache Gold and Yaqui Silver. Boston: Little, Brown, 1939.
John C. Duval: First Texas Man of Letters. Dallas: Southwest Review, 1939.
The Longhorns. Boston: Little, Brown, 1941.
Guide to Life and Literature of the Southwest. Dallas: Southern Methodist Univ. Press, 1942; revised and enlarged in 1952.
A Texan in England. Boston: Little, Brown, 1944.
The Voice of the Coyote. Boston: Little, Brown, 1949.
The Ben Lilly Legend. Boston: Little, Brown, 1950.
The Mustangs. Boston: Little, Brown, 1952.
Tales of Old-Time Texas. Boston: Little, Brown, 1955.

Up the Trail from Texas. New York: Random House, 1955.
I'll Tell You a Tale. Boston, Little, Brown, 1960.
Cow People. Boston: Little, Brown, 1964
Rattlesnakes. Bertha McKee Dobie, ed. Boston: Little, Brown, 1965.
Carl Sandburg and St. Peter at the Gate. Austin: Encino, 1966.
Some Part of Myself. Bertha McKee Dobie, ed. Boston: Little, Brown, 1967.
Out of the Old Rock. Boston: Little, Brown, 1972.

In addition to the listed major works, Dobie published thirty-six articles in the publications of the Texas Folklore Society between 1923 and 1966 and fifty-three articles in *Southwest Review* between 1926 and 1963. Dobie wrote columns for the *Dallas Morning News* and the *Austin American-Statesman* and marketed his stories regularly with such popular magazines as *The Country Gentleman, The Cattleman, Saturday Evening Post, Frontier Times, Nature Magazine, Hollands Magazine,* and *Holiday*. The bulk of his shorter publications eventually found its way, edited and improved, into his major works. See the bibliographies by McVicker and Cook for information concerning these minor publications.

Works about J. Frank Dobie
Abernethy, Francis Edward. *J. Frank Dobie*. Austin: Steck-Vaughn, 1967.
Bode, Winston. *A Portrait of Pancho*. Second edition. Austin: Steck-Vaughn, 1968.
Cook, Spruill. *J. Frank Dobie: Bibliography*. Waco, Texas: The Texian Press, 1968.
Dugger, Ronnie, ed. *Three Men in Texas: Bedichek, Webb, and Dobie*. Austin: Univ. of Texas Press, 1967.
"J. Frank Dobie," *Austin American-Statesman*, (special issue, Sunday, October 25, 1964).
"J. Frank Dobie of Texas," *The Texas Observer*, July 24, 1964.
McVicker, Mary Louise. *The Writings of J. Frank Dobie: A Bibliography*. Lawton, Okla.: Museum of the Great Plains, 1968.
Owens, William A. *Three Friends*. New York: Doubleday, 1969.
Powell, Lawrence Clark. "Mr. Southwest: J. Frank Dobie of Texas," *Arizona Highways,* 33 (June 1957), pp. 4-9.
Tinkle, Lon. *J. Frank Dobie: The Makings of an Ample Mind*. Austin: Encino, 1968.
Webb, Walter Prescott. *Concerning Mr. Dobie of the University of Texas.*

Austin: Brick Row Bookshop, 1964.
Yarborough, Ralph W. *Frank Dobie: Man and Friend*. Washington D. C.:
Potomac Corral, The Westerners, 1967.

Francis Edward Abernethy
Stephen F. Austin State University

Harry Sinclair Drago (1888-   )
[pseud. Bliss Lomax, Will Ermine, Kirk Deming, Steward Cross,
J. Wesley Putnam, Grant Sinclair]
novels, short stories, history

Whoso Findeth a Wife [J. Wesley Putnam]. New York: Macaulay, 1914.
The Hidden Things [J. Wesley Putnam]. New York: Macaulay, 1915.
Whispering Sage (with Joseph Noel). New York: The Century Co., 1922.
Following the Grass. New York: Macaulay, 1924.
Out of the Silent North. New York: Macaulay, 1925.
The Woman Thou Art [Grant Sinclair]. New York: Macaulay, 1925.
Wild Fruit [Grant Sinclair]. New York: G. H. Watt, 1926.
The Desert Hawk. New York: Macaulay, 1927.
Women to Love. New York: Amour Press, 1931.
Guardians of the Sage. New York: Macaulay, 1932; rpt. as *Top Hand With
a Gun*. New York: Fawcett Publications, 1955.
Desert Water. New York: Macaulay, 1933.
This Way to Hell [Steward Cross]. New York: Macaulay, 1933.
The Wild Bunch (short stories). New York: A. L. Burt, 1934.
Montana Road. New York: Morrow, 1935.
Plundered Range [Will Ermine]. New York: Morrow, 1936.
Closed Range [Bliss Lomax]. New York: Macaulay, 1937.
Law Bringers [Bliss Lomax]. New York: Macaulay, 1937.
Grass Means Fight [Kirk Deming]. New York: Macaulay, 1938.
Lawless Region [Will Ermine]. New York: Macaulay, 1938.
Mavericks of the Plains [Bliss Lomax]. New York: Greenberg, 1938.
Leather Burners [Bliss Lomax]. Garden City, New York: Doubleday, 1940.
Revised as *Ambush at Coffin Canyon* [Bliss Liomax]. New York: Ace
Books, 1954.
Secret of the Wastelands [Bliss Lomax]. New York: Doubleday, 1940.
Buckskin Empire. Garden City, New York: Doubleday, 1942.

Stagecoach Kingdom. Garden City: Doubleday, 1943. Serialized in *Western Story.*

River of Gold. New York: Dodd, 1945.

War on the Saddle Rock [Will Ermine]. New York: Morrow, 1945.

Last of the Longhorns [Will Ermine]. Garden City: Doubleday, 1948.

Shadow Mountain [Bliss Lomax]. New York: Dodd, 1948.

Apache Crossing [Will Ermine]. Garden City: Doubleday, 1950.

The Fight for Sweetwater [Bliss Lomax]. New York: Dodd, 1950.

Silver Star [Will Ermine]. Garden City: Doubleday, 1951.

Riders of the Buffalo Grass [Bliss Lomax]. New York: Dodd, 1952.

Longhorn Empire [Will Ermine]. Garden City: Doubleday, 1953.

Frenchman's River [Will Ermine]. New York: Permabooks, 1955.

Their Guns Were Fast (short stories). New York: Dodd, 1955.

Decision at Broken Butte. New York: Permabooks, 1957.

Wild Grass. New York: Permabooks, 1957.

Buckskin Affair. Garden City: Doubleday, 1958.

Appointment on the Yellowstone [Bliss Lomax]. New York: Dodd, 1959.

Fenced Off. Garden City: Doubleday, 1959.

Wild, Woolly, and Wicked; The History of the Kansas Cow Towns and the Texas Cattle Trade. New York: C. N. Potter, 1960.

Red River Valley; The Mainstream of Frontier History from the Louisiana Bayous to the Texas Panhandle. New York: C. N. Potter, 1962.

Outlaws on Horseback; The History of the Organized Bands of Bank and Train Robbers Who Terrorized the Prairie Towns of Missouri, Kansas, Indian Territory, and Oklahoma for Half a Century. New York: Dodd, 1964.

Great American Cattle Trails; The Story of the Old Cow Paths of the East, and the Longhorn Highways of the Plains. New York: Dodd, 1965.

Lost Bonanzas; Tales of the Legendary Lost Mines of the American West. New York: Dodd, 1966.

Many Beavers; The Story of a Cree Indian Boy. New York: Dodd, 1967.

The Steamboaters; From the Early Side-Wheelers to the Big Packets. New York: Dodd, 1967.

Roads to Empire; The Dramatic Conquest of the American West. New York: Dodd, 1968.

Notorious Ladies of the Frontier. New York: Dodd, 1969.

Great Range Wars; Violence on the Grasslands. New York: Dodd, 1970.

Canal Days in America. New York: C. N. Potter, 1972.

Road Agents and Train Robbers. New York: Dodd, Mead, 1973.

Bill F. Fowler
Southwest Texas State University

Glenn Ward Dresbach (1889-1968)
poetry

The Road to Everywhere. Boston: Gorham Press, 1916.
In the Paths of the Wind. Boston: Four Seas, 1917.
Morning, Noon, and Night. Boston: Four Seas, 1920.
In Colors of the West. New York: Holt, Rinehart, Winston, 1922.
The Enchanted Mesa. New York: Holt, Rinehart, Winston, 1924.
Cliff Dwellings and Other Poems. New York: Vinal, 1926.
Star Dust and Stone. Dallas: P. L. Turner, 1928.
This Side of Avalon. New York: Vinal, 1928.
The Wind in the Cedars. New York: Holt, Rinehart, Winston, 1929.
Selected Poems. New York: Holt, Rinehart, Winston, 1930.
Collected Poems, 1914-1948, of Glenn Ward Dresbach. Caldwell, Idaho: Caxton, 1950.

In addition, Dresbach published approximately two hundred uncollected poems in such journals as *Atlantic, The Saturday Evening Post, Commonweal, New Republic, Poetry, McCalls,* and *London Poetry Magazine;* Dresbach's poems have also been published in many anthologies of poetry, such as *Moult's Best Poems,* and *Home Book of Modern Verse.*

Works about Glenn Ward Dresbach
Ford, Edsel. "Glenn Ward Dresbach: The New Mexico Years, 1915-1920," *New Mexico Quarterly,* 34 (1964), 78-96.

Robert C. Braden
Southwest Texas State University

Robert Luther Duffus (1888-   )
novels, nonfiction

Roads Going South. New York: Macmillan, 1921.
The Coast of Eden. New York: n.p., 1923
The American Renaissance. New York: Knopf, 1928.
Tomorrow Never Comes. New York: Houghton-Mifflin, 1929.
Books—Their Place in a Democracy. New York: Houghton-Mifflin, 1930.

Mastering the Metropolis. New York: Harper, 1930.

The Santa Fe Trail. New York: Longmans, Green, 1930. Rpt. Albuquerque: Univ. of New Mexico Press, 1972.

The Arts in American Life. New York: Houghton-Mifflin, 1933.

Our Starving Libraries. New York: Houghton-Mifflin, 1933.

Jornada. New York: Covici-Friede, 1935.

Democracy Enters College. New York: Scribner's, 1936.

The Sky But Not the Heart. New York: Macmillan, 1936.

Night Between the Rivers. New York: Macmillan, 1937.

Lillian Wald: Neighbor and Crusader. New York: Macmillan, 1938.

L. Emmett Holt: A Pioneer of a Children's Century. New York: Appleton-Century-Crofts, 1940.

That Was Alderbury. New York: Macmillan, 1941.

Victory on West Hill. New York: Macmillan, 1942.

The Innocents at Cedro. New York: Macmillan, 1944.

The Valley and Its People. New York: Knopf, 1944.

Non-Scheduled Flight. New York: Macmillan, 1950.

Williamstown Branch: Impersonal Memoirs of a Vermont Boyhood. New York: Norton, 1958.

Waterbury Record (II). New York: Norton, 1959.

The Tower of Jewels. New York: Norton, 1960.

Nostalgia, U.S.A., Or If You Don't Like the 1960's, Why Don't You Go Back Where You Came From. New York: Norton, 1963.

Adventure in Retirement. New York: Norton, 1964.

Queen Calafia's Island. New York: Norton, 1965.

Jimmy's Place. New York: Norton, 1966.

The Cat's Pajamas. New York: Norton, 1967.

Tomorrow's News: A Primer for Profits. New York: Norton, 1967.

West of the Dateline. New York: Norton, 1968.

Jason Goose. New York: Norton, 1969.

Polar Route to Time Gone By. New York: Norton, 1969.

Jason Potter's Space Walk. New York: Norton, 1970.

In addition, Duffus published approximately two hundred articles between 1918 and 1960 in such publications as *American Mercury, American Scholar, Dial, Harper's, Scribner's Magazine, World's Work,* and others.

Robert C. Braden
Southwest Texas State University

Bob Duncan (1927-   )
[pseud. James Hall Roberts]
novels, nonfiction

Dicky Bird Was Singing; Men, Women, and Black Gold. New York: Rinehart, 1952.

Castles in the Air (with Irene Castle, as told to Bob and Wanda Duncan). New York: Doubleday, 1958.

Buffalo Country. New York: E. P. Dutton, 1959.

If It Moves, Salute It. New York: Doubleday, 1960.

Reluctant General; The Life and Times of Albert Pike. New York: E. P. Dutton, 1961.

The Voice of Strangers. Toronto: Doubleday, 1961.

The February Plan [James Hall Roberts]. New York: William Morrow, 1967.

The Day the Sun Fell. New York: William Morrow, 1970.

In addition, Duncan published approximately a hundred short stories and magazine articles. Collaborating with his wife Wanda, he has also written approximately a hundred documentary films and several television scripts.

Works about Bob Duncan

Serebnick, J. "New Creative Writers," *Library Journal,* 84 (1 October 1959), 3018.

Walter A. Winsett
Southwest Texas State University

Mary Maude Dunn (1894-1967)
[pseud. Lilith Lorraine]
poetry, nonfiction

Songs for Tomorrow. Corpus Christi, Texas: United Daughters of the Confederacy, n.d. (Identified by the author as "my first book.")

The Brain of the Planet. New York: Stellar Publishing, 1929.

Banners of Victory. Atlanta: Banner Press, 1937.

Knight in White Armor. Ed. Lilith Lorraine. San Antonio: Avalon Poetry Shrine, 1941.

Beyond Bewilderment. Atlanta: Banner Press, 1942.

Lilith Tells All. San Antonio: Avalon Press, 1942.

Wings Over Chaos. Ed. Lilith Lorraine. San Antonio: Avalon Press, 1942.

They. N.p.: Avalon Press, 1943.

The Day Before Judgment. Atlanta: Banner Press, 1944.

Let Dreamers Wake. Dallas: Avalon Press, 1945.

Voices from Avalon. Ed. Lilith Lorraine. Dallas: Avalon Press, 1945.

Character Against Chaos. Rogers, Arkansas: Avalon Press, 1947.

Let the Patter Break. Rogers, Arkansas: Avalon Press, 1947.

The Lost Word. Rogers, Arkansas: Avalon Press, 1949.

Wine of Wonder. Dallas: Book Craft, 1952.

These Shall Endure. Ed. Lilith Lorraine. Alpine, Texas: Different Press, 1955.

Not for Oblivion. Alpine, Texas: Different Press, 1956.

Indispensable: The Poets' Deskmate. Comp. Lilith Lorraine. Alpine, Texas: Different Press, 1957.

With No Secret Meaning. Comp. Lilith Lorraine. Alpine, Texas: Different Press, 1957.

Today the Stars. Comp. Lilith Lorraine. Alpine, Texas: Different Press, 1960.

Avalon Golden Book. Comp. Lilith Lorraine. Alpine, Texas: Different Press, 1961.

The Minds Create. Comp. Lilith Lorraine. Alpine, Texas: Different Press, 1961.

Sing Loud for Loveliness. Comp. Lilith Lorraine. Brooklyn, New York: Parthenon, 1962.

Avalon Anthology of Texas Poets. Comp. Lilith Lorraine. Corpus Christi, Texas: Different Press, 1963.

Light from Other Stars. New York: Poets of America, 1963.

Publishing Poets Directory, 1963. Comp. Lilith Lorraine. Corpus Christi, Texas: Different Press, 1963.

Warriors of Eternity. Comp. Lilith Lorraine. Corpus Christi, Texas: Different Press, 1963.

Flame Annual 1964. Ed. Lilith Lorraine. Corpus Christi, Texas: Different Press, 1964.

Flame Annual 1965. Ed. Lilith Lorraine. Corpus Christi, Texas: Different Press, 1965.

In addition, Lorraine published approximately one thousand uncollected poems in periodicals such as *American Bard, Flame, Epos, New York Times,* and *Quicksilver.*

Works about Lilith Lorraine
Wright, Cleveland Lamar. *The Story of Avalon*. Alpine, Texas: Different
Press, c. 1962.

John Igo
San Antonio College

John Crittenden Duval (1816-1897)
novels, nonfiction

The Treasure Cave; Or, The Buccaneer's Secret. New York: G. Munro,
1870. Vol. 2, No. 6, of the Alden Chase Collection of Dime Novels.

The War-Trail of the Seminoles; Or, A Tale of the Florida Everglades.
New York: G. Munro, 1870. Vol. 10, No. 3, of the C. M. Hulett Collection of Dime Novels.

The Adventures of Big-Foot Wallace, The Texas Ranger and Hunter. Philadelphia and Macon, Georgia: Claxson, Remsen and Haffelfinger and
J. W. Burke, 1871 [joint publication]. Rpt. Austin: Steck-Vaughn, 1947
[facsimile of the 1871 ed.].

Early Times in Texas; Or the Adventures of Jack Dobell. Austin: H. P. N.
Gammel & Co., 1892; rpt. 1967 (Introduction by John Q. Anderson).

The Adventures of Big-Foot Wallace. Ed. Mabel Major and Rebecca W.
Smith. Dallas: Tardy Publishing Co., 1936; rpt. Lincoln: Univ. of Nebraska Press, 1966.

Early Times in Texas; Or, The Adventures of Jack Dobell. Ed. Mabel
Major and Rebecca W. Smith. Dallas: Tardy, 1936.

Works about John C. Duval

Anderson, John Q. *John C. Duval: First Texas Man of Letters.* Austin:
Steck-Vaughn, 1967.

Corner, William. "John Crittenden Duval: The Last Survivor of the Goliad
Massacre," *Quarterly of the Texas State Historical Association,* 1 (1897-
1898), 47-67.

Dobie, J. Frank. *John C. Duval, First Texas Man of Letters; His Life and
Some of His Unpublished Writings.* Dallas: Southern Methodist Univ.
Press, 1939; 2nd ed., 1965.

Vestal, Stanley. *Bigfoot Wallace.* Boston: Houghton Mifflin, 1942.

John Q. Anderson
University of Houston

William Eastlake (1917-   )
novels, short stories

Go in Beauty. New York: Harper, 1956.
The Bronc People. New York: Harcourt, Brace, 1958.
Portrait of an Artist with 26 Horses. New York: Simon and Schuster, 1963.
Castle Keep. New York: Simon and Schuster, 1965.
The Bamboo Bed. New York: Simon and Schuster, 1969.
Child's Garden of Verses for the Revolution. New York: Grove, 1971.

In addition, Eastlake has about fifty short stories in such journals as *Atlantic, Kenyon Review, Harper's,* and *Evergreen Review.*

Works about William Eastlake
Angell, Richard C. "Complete Bibliography," *New Mexico Quarterly,* 34 (Spring 1965), 208-09.
————. "Eastlake at Home and Abroad," *New Mexico Quarterly,* 34 (Spring 1965), 204-07.
Haslam, Gerald. *William Eastlake.* Austin: Steck-Vaughn, 1970.
Wylder, Delbert. "The Novels of William Eastlake," *New Mexico Quarterly,* 39 (Spring 1965), 188-203.

Gerald Haslam
Sonoma State College

Lucile Selk Edgerton (c. 1919-   )
novels, short stories

In Walked Anny. n.p.: McLeod, 1940.
Pillars of Gold. New York: Knopf, 1941.

In addition, Edgerton has several uncollected short stories in such journals as *Liberty* and *This Week* and many feature articles in Chicago and Milwaukee newspapers.

Works about Lucile S. Edgerton
"New Writers: Lucile Selk Edgerton," *The Publishers' Weekly,* 140 (26 July 1941), 246-47.

Walter A. Winsett
Southwest Texas State University

Ralph Ellison (1914-   )
novel, short stories, nonfiction

Invisible Man. New York: Random House, 1952.
Shadow and Act (essays). New York: Random House, 1964.

In addition, Ellison published fiction, essays, and criticism in such journals as *Atlantic, New Republic,* and *Quarterly Review of Literature,* and in various anthologies.

Works about Ralph Ellison

Baumbach, Jonathan. "Nightmare of a Native Son," *Critique,* 6 (Spring 1963), 48-65; rpt. in *The Landscape of Nightmare.* New York: New York Univ. Press, 1965.

Bennett, John Z. "The Race and the Runner: Ellison's *Invisible Man,*" *Xavier Univ. Studies,* 5 (March 1966), 12-26.

Bloch, Alice. "Sight Imagery in *Invisible Man,*" *English Journal,* 55 (November 1966), 1019-21.

Bluestein, Gene. "The Blues as a Literary Theme," *Massachusetts Review,* 8 (Summer 1967), 593-617.

Bone, Robert A. *The Negro Novel in America.* New Haven: Yale Univ. Press, 1958.

————. "Ralph Ellison and the Uses of Imagination," in *Anger and Beyond.* Ed. Herbert Hill. New York: Harper and Row, 1966. Pp. 86-111.

Chester, Alfred and Vilma Howard. "The Art of Fiction; Ralph Ellison," *Paris Review,* No. 8 (Spring 1955), pp. 54-71.

Covo, Jacqueline. *The Blinking Eye: Ralph Waldo Ellison and His American, French, German, and Italian Critics.* Metuchen, New Jersey: Scarecrow Press, 1974.

Fraiberg, Selma. "Two Modern Incest Heroes," *Partisan Review,* 28 (1961), 646-61.

Geller, Allen. "An Interview with Ralph Ellison," *Tamarack Review,* No. 32 (Summer 1964), pp. 3-24.

Glicksberg, Charles I. "The Symbolism of Vision," *Southwest Review,* 39 (Summer 1954), 259-65.

Hassan, Ihab. "The Qualified Encounter," in *Radical Innocence.* Princeton, N.J.: Princeton Univ. Press, 1961. Pp. 168-79.

Horowitz, Ellin. "The Rebirth of the Artist," in *On Contemporary Literature.* Ed. Richard Kostelanetz. New York: Avon Books, 1964. Pp. 330-46.

Horowitz, Floyd Ross. "The Enigma of Ellison's Intellectual Man," *College Language Association Journal,* 7 (December 1963), 126-32.

————. "Ralph Ellison's Modern Version of Brer Bear and Brer Rabbit in Invisible Man," *Midcontinent American Studies Journal,* 4 (Fall 1963), 21-7.

Howe, Irving. "Black Boys and Native Sons," *Dissent* (Autumn 1963), pp. 353-68. [Ellison replied to this article through "The World and the Jug" in *Shadow and Act.* Howe answered Ellison in *The New Leader,* February 3, 1964.] "Black Boys and Native Sons" also appears in *A World More Attractive* by Irving Howe, New York: Horizon Press, 1963.

Hyman, Stanley Edgar. "The Negro Writer in America: An Exchange," *Partisan Review,* 25 (Spring 1958), 197-211. Ellison's reply, "Change the Joke and Slip the Yoke," appeared in the same issue of *Partisan Review* and in *Shadow and Act.*

————. "Ralph Ellison in Our Time," in *Standards: A Chronicle of Books for Our Time.* New York: Horizon Press, 1966. Pp. 249-53.

Isaacs, Harold R. "Five Writers and Their African Ancestors," *Phylon,* 21 (Fall 1960), 317-22.

Jackson, Esther Merle. "The American Negro and the Image of the Absurd,"*Phylon,* 23 (Winter 1962), 359-71.

Klein, Marcus. "Ralph Ellison's *Invisible Man,*" in *After Alienation.* Cleveland: World Publishing Co., 1964. Pp. 71-146. Rpt. in *Images of the Negro in American Literature.* Ed. Seymour L. Gross and John Edward Hardy. Chicago: Univ. of Chicago Press, 1966. Pp. 249-64.

Kostelanetz, Richard. "The Politics of Ellison's Booker: *Invisible Man* as Symbolic History," *Chicago Review,* 19 (1967), 5-26.

Lee, L. L. "The Proper Self: Ralph Ellison's *Invisible Man,*" *Descant,* 10 (Spring 1966), 33-48.

Littlejohn, David. *Black on White.* New York: Grossman, 1966.

Mengeling, Marvin E. "Whitman and Ellison: Older Symbols in a Modern Mainstream," *Walt Whitman Review,* 12 (September 1966), 67-70.

Nash, R. W. "Stereotypes and Social Types in Ellison's *Invisible Man,*" *Sociological Quarterly* 6 (Autumn 1965), 349-60.

O'Daniel, Therman B. "The Image of Man as Portrayed by Ralph Ellison," *College Language Association Journal,* 10 (June 1967), 277-84.

Olderman, Raymond M. "Ralph Ellison's Blues and *Invisible Man,*" *Wisconsin Studies in Contemporary Literature,* 7 (Summer 1966), 142-59.

Rodnon, Stewart. "Ralph Ellison's *Invisible Man:* Six Tentative Approaches," *College Language Association Journal,* 12 (September 1968), 244-56.

Rovit, Earl H. "Ralph Ellison and the American Comic Tradition," *Wisconsin Studies in Contemporary Literature,* 1 (Fall 1960), 34-42. Rpt. in *Recent American Fiction: Some Critical Views.* Ed. Joseph J. Waldmeir. Boston: Houghton Mifflin, 1963.

Schafer, William J. "Irony from Underground—Satiric Elements in *Invisible Man,*" *Satire Newsletter,* 7 (Fall 1969), 22-28.

Singleton, M. K. "Leadership Mirages as Antagonists in *Invisible Man,*" *Arizona Quarterly,* 22 (Summer 1966), 157-71.

Thompson, James, Lennox Raphael, and Steve Cannon. " 'A Very Stern Discipline': An Interview with Ralph Ellison," *Harper's,* (March 1967), pp. 76-95.

Twentieth Century Interpretations of INVISIBLE MAN. Ed. John M. Reilly. Englewood Cliffs, N.J.: Prentice-Hall, 1970.

Warren, Robert Penn. "The Unity of Experience," *Commentary,* 39 (May 1965), 91-96.

Webster, Harvey Curtis. "Inside a Dark Shell," *Saturday Review of Literature,* 2 April 1952, pp. 22-23.

West, Anthony. "Ralph Ellison," in *Principles and Persuasions.* New York: Harcourt, Brace and Co., 1957. pp. 212-28.

Barbara Albrecht McDaniel
North Texas State University

Loula Grace Erdman (-   )
novels, short stories

A Wonderful Thing and Other Stories. New York: Dodd, Mead, 1940.
Separate Star. New York: Longmans, Green, 1944.
Fair Is the Morning. New York: Longmans, Green, 1945.
The Years of the Locust. New York: Dodd, Mead, 1947.
Life Was Simpler Then. New York: Dodd, Mead, 1948. Rpt. 1963.
Lonely Passage. New York: Dodd, Mead, 1948.
The Edge of Time. New York: Dodd, Mead, 1950.
The Wind Blows Free. New York: Dodd, Mead, 1952.
My Sky Is Blue. New York: Longmans, Green, 1953.

Three at the Wedding. New York: Dodd, Mead, 1953.
The Wide Horizon: A Story of the Texas Panhandle. New York: Dodd, Mead, 1956.
Short Summer. New York: Dodd, Mead, 1958.
The Far Journey. New York: Dodd, Mead, 1959.
The Good Land. New York: Dodd, Mead, 1959.
Many a Voyage. New York: Dodd, Mead, 1960.
The Man Who Told the Truth and Six Other Stories. New York: Dodd, Mead, 1962.
Room to Grow. New York: Dodd, Mead, 1962.
Another Spring. New York: Dodd, Mead, 1966.
A Time to Write. New York: Dodd, Mead, 1969.
A Bluebird Will Do. New York: Dodd, Mead, 1973.
Save Weeping For the Night. New York: Dodd, Mead, 1975.

In addition, Erdman has a number of uncollected stories, articles, and essays in such magazines as *Redbook, Christian Herald, American Girl, Country Home, and Progressive Farmer.*

Works about Loula Grace Erdman
Karolides, Nicholas J. *The Pioneer in the American Novel: 1900-1950.* Norman: Univ. of Oklahoma Press, 1967.
Sewell, Ernestine P. *Loula Grace Erdman.* Austin: Steck-Vaughn, 1970.
Vestal, Stanley. *The Book Lover's Southwest.* Norman: Univ. of Oklahoma Press, 1955.

Ernestine P. Sewell
University of Texas, Arlington

Winston M. Estes (1917-   )
novels, sketches

Winston in Wonderland. Harrisburg, Pa.: Eagle Books, 1956.
Another Part of the House. Philadelphia: Lippincott, 1970.
A Streetful of People. Philadelphia: Lippincott, 1972.
A Simple Act of Kindness. Philadelphia: Lippincott, 1973.

Phillip L. Fry
University of Texas at Austin

Joe Evans (1882-1966)
humor, folk wisdom, devotionals

A Corral Full of Stories. El Paso: Privately printed, 1939.
The Cow. El Paso: Privately printed, 1944.
The Cowboys' Hitchin' Post. El Paso: Privately printed, 1946.
Collecting Friends, My Hobby. El Paso: Privately printed, 1952.
After Dinner Stories. El Paso: Privately printed, 1952.
Pecos' Poems [with Pecos Higgins]. El Paso: Privately printed, 1956.
Bloys: Cowboy Camp Meeting. El Paso: Privately printed, 1959.
The Horse. El Paso: Privately printed, 1962.
Ol' Spot, the Lead Steer. El Paso: Privately printed, 1964.

Durrett Wagner
Chicago, Illinois

Max Evans (1925-   )
novels, short stories, nonfiction

Southwest Wind (stories). San Antonio: Naylor, 1958.
Long John Dunn of Taos. Los Angeles: Westernlore Press, 1959.
The Rounders. New York: Macmillan, 1960.
Hi-Lo Country. New York: Macmillan, 1961.
Three Short Novels: The Great Wedding, The One-eyed Sky, and My Pardner. Boston: Houghton Mifflin, 1963.
The Mountain of Gold. Dunwoody, Georgia: N. S. Berg, 1965.
Shadow of Thunder. Chicago: Swallow, 1969.
Sam Peckinpaugh, Master of Violence: Being the Account of the Making of a Movie and Other Sundry Things. Vermillion, S.D.: Dakota Press, 1972.
Bobby Jack Smith—You Dirty Coward. Freeport, N.Y.: Nash, 1974.

Works about Max Evans
Milton, John R. ed. "Interview: Max Evans." *South Dakota Review,* 5 (Summer 1967), 77-87.
———. *Three West: Conversations with Vardis Fisher, Max Evans, Michael Straight.* Vermillion, S.D.: Dakota Press, 1970.
Sonnichsen, C. L. "The New Style Western." *South Dakota Review* 4 (Summer 1966), 22-28.

James W. Lee
North Texas State University

Odie B. Faulk (1933-   )
nonfiction

Tom Green: A Fightin' Texan. Waco: Texian Press, 1963.

The Last Years of Spanish Texas, 1778-1821. The Hague: Mouton, 1964.

A Successful Failure, 1519-1910. Austin: Steck-Vaughn, 1965.

Lancers for the King (with Sidney Brickerhoff). Tucson: Arizona Historical Foundation, 1965.

Texas After Spindletop, 1901-1965 (with Seth McKay). Austin: Steck-Vaughn, 1965.

Arizona's State Historical Society: Its History and Leaders, and Its Services to the Public. Ed. Odie B. Faulk. Tucson: Arizona Pioneers' Historical Society, 1966.

Too Far North, Too Far South. Los Angeles: Westernlore Press, 1967.

Land of Many Frontiers: A History of the American Southwest. New York: Oxford Univ. Press, 1968.

Derby's Report on Opening the Colorado. Ed. Odie B. Faulk. Albuquerque: Univ. of New Mexico Press, 1969.

The Geronimo Campaign. New York: Oxford Univ. Press, 1969.

Arizona: A Short History. Norman: Univ. of Oklahoma Press, 1970.

North America Divided: The Mexican War, 1846-1848 (with Seymour V. Connor). New York: Oxford Univ. Press, 1971.

Tombstone: Myth and Reality. New York: Oxford Univ. Press, 1972.

Destiny Road: The Gila Trail and the Opening of the Southwest. New York: Oxford Univ. Press, 1973.

This Beats Working for a Living [By Professor X]. New Rochelle, N.Y.: Arlington House, 1973.

A Short History of the American West (with Joseph Stout). New York: Harper and Row, 1974.

In addition, Faulk has contributed many essays to learned journals.

James W. Lee
North Texas State University

Erna Fergusson (1888-1964)
nonfiction

Dancing Gods: Indian Ceremonials of New Mexico and Arizona. New York: Knopf, 1931.

Mexican Cookbook. Santa Fe: The Rydal Press, 1934; rev. ed., 1940; rpt. Albuquerque: Univ. of New Mexico Press, 1945.
Fiesta in Mexico. New York: Knopf, 1934.
Guatemala. New York: Knopf, 1937.
Venezuela. New York: Knopf, 1939.
Our Southwest. New York: Knopf, 1940.
Our Hawaii. New York: Knopf, 1942.
Chile. New York: Knopf, 1943.
Cuba. New York: Knopf, 1946.
Erna Fergusson's Albuquerque. Albuquerque: Merle Armitage Editions, 1947.
Murder and Mystery in New Mexico. Albuquerque: Merle Armitage Editions, 1948.
Hawaii (juvenile). Grand Rapids, Michigan: The Fideler Co., 1950.
Let's Read About Hawaiian Islands (juvenile). Grand Rapids, Michigan: The Fideler Co., 1950.
New Mexico: A Pageant of Three Peoples. New York: Knopf, 1951; 2nd ed., rev., 1964.
Mexico Revisited. New York: Knopf, 1955.

In addition, Fergusson wrote a great many travel essays and many book reviews in newspapers and magazines.

Works about Erna Fergusson

Cassidy, Louise Lowber. "A 'Delight Maker,'" *Sunset Magazine*, 54 (January 1925), 38-39.
Fergusson, Harvey. *Home in the West: An Inquiry into My Origins*. New York: Duell, Sloan and Pearce, 1945.
Keleher, William A. "Erna Fergusson," *The Historical Society of New Mexico Hall of Fame Essays* (Albuquerque, 1965), 27-54.
McMullen, Frances Drewry. "Ask Miss Fergusson," *Woman Citizen*, 11 (January 1927), 26-27, 41-42.
Powell, Lawrence Clark. "First Lady of Letters," *New Mexico Magazine*, 40 (March 1962), 22-23, 37-39.
Remley, David. *Erna Fergusson*. Austin: Steck-Vaughn, 1970.
Woodward, Dorothy. "Erna Fergusson," *New Mexico Quarterly*, 22 (Spring 1952), 75-89.

David A. Remley
University of New Mexico

Harvey Fergusson (1890-1971)
novels, nonfiction

The Blood of the Conquerors. New York: Knopf, 1921.
Capitol Hill: A Novel of Washington Life. New York: Knopf, 1923.
Women and Wives. New York: Knopf, 1924.
Hot Saturday. New York: Knopf. 1926.
Wolf Song. New York: Knopf, 1927.
In Those Days: An Impression of Change. New York: Knopf, 1929.
Footloose McGarnigal. New York: Knopf, 1930.
Rio Grande. New York: Knopf, 1933.
Modern Man: His Belief and Behavior. New York: Knopf, 1936.
Followers of the Sun: A Trilogy of the Santa Fe Trail; rpt. of *Wolf Song, In Those Days,* and *The Blood of the Conquerors.* New York: Knopf, 1936.
The Life of Riley. New York: Knopf, 1937.
Home in the West: An Inquiry into My Origins. New York: Duell, Sloan and Pearce, 1944.
People and Power: A Study of Political Behavior in America. New York: William Morrow, 1947.
Grant of Kingdom. New York: William Morrow, 1950.
The Conquest of Don Pedro. New York: William Morrow, 1954.

Works about Harvey Fergusson
Folsom, James K. *Harvey Fergusson.* Austin: Steck-Vaughn, 1969.
Milton, John. "Conversation with Harvey Fergusson," *South Dakota Review,* 9 (Spring 1971), 39-45.
Pilkington, William T. "The Southwestern Novels of Harvey Fergusson," *New Mexico Quarterly,* 35 (Winter 1965-66), 330-43; rpt. in Pilkington's *My Blood's Country.* Ft. Worth: Texas Christian Univ. Press, 1973.
Powell, Lawrence Clark. "Books Determine," *Wilson Library Bulletin,* 30 (September 1955), 62-65.
Robinson, Cecil. "Legend of Destiny: The American Southwest in the Novels of Harvey Fergusson," *American West,* 4 (November 1967), 16-18, 67-68.
————. *With the Ears of Strangers. The Mexican in American Literature.* Tucson: Univ. of Arizona Press, 1963.

James K. Folsom
University of Colorado

Timothy Flint (1780-1840)
novels, short stories, nonfiction

A Sermon Preached May 11, 1808, at the Ordination of the Rev. Ebenezer Hubbard. Newburyport: E. W. Allen, 1808.

An Oration, Delivered at Leominster, July 4, 1815 . . . Worcester, Mass.: William Manning, 1815.

A Sermon Delivered in Leominster, at the Commencement of the Year, Lord's Day, January 1st, 1815. Leicester, Mass.: Hori Brown, 1815.

The Columbian Harmonist. Cincinnati: Coleman and Phillips, 1816.

Francis Berrian; or, The Mexican Patriot. Boston: Cummings, Hilliard and Co., 1826.

Recollections of the Last Ten Years . . . Boston: Cummings, Hilliard and Co., 1826.

A Condensed Geography and History of the Western States. Cincinnati: E. H. Flint, 1828. Rpt. 1832 as *A History and Geography of the Mississippi Valley.*

The Life and Adventures of Arthur Clenning. Philadelphia: Tower & Hogan, 1828.

The Lost Child. Boston: Carter & Hendee, and Putnam & Hunt, 1830.

The Shoshonee Valley: A Romance. Cincinnati: E. H. Flint, 1830.

The Personal Narrative of James O. Pattie, of Kentucky. Cincinnati: J. H. Wood, 1831.

The Art of Being Happy: From the French of Droz, "Sur L'Art D'Etre Heureux." (Trans. Timothy Flint). Boston: Carter and Hendee, 1832.

The United States and the Other Divisions of the American Continent. Cincinnati: E. H. Flint and L. R. Lincoln, 1832. An extended edition of *A Condensed Geography.*

Biographical Memoir of Daniel Boone, the First Settler of Kentucky. Cincinnati: N. & G. Guilford, 1833. Later editions occasionally entitled *The First White Man of the West.*

Don't Give Up the Ship; or, the Good Son. London: Harvey and Darton, 1833. Abridged from *George Mason, the Young Backwoodsman.* Boston: Hilliard, Gray, Little, and Wilkins, 1829.

Indian Wars of the West. Cincinnati: E. H. Flint, 1833.

Lectures Upon Natural History, Geology, Chemistry. . . . Boston: Lilly, Wait, Colman, and Holden. Cincinnati: E. H. Flint, 1833.

The Bachelor Reclaimed or Celibacy Vanquished, from the French. (Trans. Timothy Flint). Philadelphia: Key & Biddle, 1834.

Journal of the Rev. Timothy Flint. Alexandria, La., 1835.
The Hunters of Kentucky. New York: William H. Graham, 1847.
Little Henry, the Stolen Child. Boston: S. G. Simpkins, 1847.
The Life and Adventures of Daniel Boone. Cincinnati: U. P. James, 1868.
A new edition of *Biographical Memoir* with an account of Captain Estill's defeat.
The Western Monthly Review (May 1827-June 1830). Ed. Timothy Flint. 3 vols. Cincinnati, 1827-1930.

In addition, Flint has approximately forty articles and short stories in such periodicals as *The Western Monthly Review, The Knickerbocker,* and *The Athenaeum.* His poems appear in *The Western Monthly Review, Recollections,* and *The Knickerbocker.*

Works about Timothy Flint
Carelton, Phillips D. "The Indian Captivity," *American Literature,* 25 (May 1943), 169-80.
Cowie, Alexander. "Contemporaries and Immediate Followers of Cooper, I: Timothy Flint (1780-1840) and Early Western Fiction," in *The Rise of the American Novel.* New York: American Book Company, 1948. pp. 212-27.
Folsom, James K. *Timothy Flint.* New York: Twayne, 1965.
Hamilton, John A. "Timothy Flint's 'Lost Novel,' " *American Literature,* 22 (March 1950), 54-56.
Kirkpatrick, John E. *Timothy Flint: Pioneer, Missionary, Author, Editor, 1780-1840.* Cleveland: Arthur H. Clark, 1911.
Lombard, C. A. "Timothy Flint: Early American Disciple of French Romanticism," *Revue de Littérature Comparée,* 36 (April-June 1962), 276-82.
Morris, Robert L. "Three Arkansas Travelers," *Arkansas Historical Quarterly,* 4 (Autumn 1945), 215-30.
Seelye, John D. "Timothy Flint's 'Wicked River' and *The Confidence-Man,*" *PMLA,* 78 (March 1963), 75-79.
Smith, Henry Nash. *Virgin Land; The American West as Symbol and Myth.* Cambridge, Mass.: Harvard Univ. Press, 1950.
Stimson, Frederick S. " 'Francis Berrian': Hispanic Influence on American Romanticism," *Hispanica,* 42 (December 1959), 511-16.
Trollope, Frances M. *Domestic Manners of the Americans.* 2 vols. New York: Dodd, Mead, and Co., 1927.

Tuckerman, Henry T. *America and Her Commentators*. New York: Scribner, 1864. Pp. 401-04.

Turner, Arlin. "James Kirke Paulding and Timothy Flint," *Mississippi Valley Historical Review*, 34 (June 1947), 105-11.

Venable, William H. "Timothy Flint," *Beginnings of Literary Culture in the Ohio Valley*. Cincinnati: R. Clarke and Co., 1891. Pp. 323-60. Rpt. New York: Peter Smith, 1949.

Waler, Lennie M. "Picturesque New Mexico Revealed in Novel as Early as 1826," *New Mexico Historical Review*, 13 (July 1938), 325-28.

David B. Kesterson
North Texas State University

Robert Flynn (1932-   )
novels, short stories, play

Journey to Jefferson (unpublished play). Produced at Theater of Nations, Paris, 1964. Special Jury Award. Dallas Theater Center, Dallas, Texas, 1962, 1967, 1969.

North To Yesterday. New York: Knopf, 1967.

In The House of the Lord. New York: Knopf, 1969.

Lampassas, Oder Der Lange Weg. Translated by Helga Wingert-Uhde. Frankfurt-Am-Main: Fischer Verlag, 1969.

The Sounds of Rescue, The Signs of Hope. New York: Knopf, 1970.

In addition, Flynn has several uncollected stories in *Saturday Evening Post, Yale Review*, and *Descant*.

John D. Brantley
Trinity University

Horton Foote (1916-   )
novels, plays

Only the Heart. New York: Dramatists Play Service, 1944.

The Chase. New York: Dramatists Play Service, 1952. Published as a novel, New York: Rinehart, 1956; rpt. New York: New American Library, 1966.

The Trip to Bountiful. New York: Dramatists Play Service, 1954.
A Young Lady of Property: Six Short Plays. New York: Dramatists Play Service, 1955.
The Traveling Lady. New York: Dramatists Play Service, 1955.
Harrison, Texas: Eight Television Plays. New York: Harcourt Brace, 1956.
The Midnight Caller; A Play in One Act. New York: Dramatists Play Service, 1959.
Roots in Parched Ground. New York: Dramatists Play Service, 1962.
Three Plays. New York: Harcourt, Brace & World, 1962.
Tomorrow; A Play Adapted from a Story by William Faulkner. New York: Dramatists Play Service, 1963.
The Screenplay of To Kill a Mockingbird. New York: Harcourt, Brace & World, 1964.
Baby The Rain Must Fall. New York: Popular Library, 1965.

In addition, a number of Foote's unpublished plays have been presented on stage.

James W. Lee
North Texas State University

Mary Hallock Foote (1847-1938)
novels, short stories, sketches

The Led-Horse Claim. Boston: James R. Osgood, 1883.
John Bodewin's Testimony. Boston: Tichnor, 1886.
The Last Assembly Ball. Boston: Houghton Mifflin, 1889.
The Chosen Valley. Boston: Houghton Mifflin, 1892.
Coeur d'Alene. Boston: Houghton Mifflin, 1894.
The Cup of Trembling, and Other Stories. Boston: Houghton Mifflin, 1895.
The Little Fig-Tree Stories. Boston: Houghton Mifflin, 1899.
The Prodigal. Boston: Houghton Mifflin, 1900.
The Desert and the Sown. Boston: Houghton Mifflin, 1902.
A Touch of Sun, and Other Stories. Boston: Houghton Mifflin, 1903.
The Royal Americans. Boston: Houghton Mifflin, 1910.
A Picked Company. Boston: Houghton Mifflin, 1912.
The Valley Road. Boston: Houghton Mifflin, 1915.
Edith Bonham. Boston: Houghton Mifflin, 1917.
The Ground-Swell. Boston: Houghton Mifflin, 1919.

A Victorian Gentlewoman in the Far West: The Reminiscences of Mary Hallock Foote. Ed. Paul W. Rodman. San Marino, California: The Huntington Library, 1972.

In addition, Foote had a great many stories and sketches published in *Atlantic, Scribner's,* and the *Century Magazine.*

Works about Mary Hallock Foote

Armstrong, Regina. "Representative American Illustrators," *Critic,* 37 (August 1900), 131-41.

Benn, Mary Lou. "Mary Hallock Foote: Early Leadville Writer," *Colorado Magazine,* 33 (April 1956), 93-108.

Davidson, Levette Jay. "Letters from Authors," *The Colorado Magazine,* 19 (July 1942), 122-25.

Etulain, Richard W. "Mary Hallock Foote (1847-1938)," *American Literary Realism 1870-1910,* 5 (Spring 1972), 145-50.

Foote, Arthur B. "Memoir of Arthur De Wint Foote," *Transactions of the American Society of Civil Engineers,* 99 (1934), 1449-52.

"Foote, Mary Hallock," *The National Cyclopedia of American Biography,* Vol. VI. New York: James T. White and Company, 1929, pp. 472-73.

Gilder, Helena DeKay. "Mary Hallock Foote," *Bookbuyer,* 11 (August 18, 1894), 338-42.

Gilder, Rosamond, ed. *Letters of Richard Watson Gilder.* Boston: Houghton Mifflin, 1916, pp. 64-65, 214-19, 304-6.

Maguire, James. *Mary Hallock Foote.* Boise: Boise State College Press, 1972.

Taft, Robert. *Artists and Illustrators of the Old West: 1850-1900.* New York: Charles Scribner's Sons, 1953, pp. 172-75, 345-47.

Richard Etulain
Idaho State University

Grant Foreman (1869-1935)
history

Pioneer Days in the Early Southwest. Cleveland: Arthur H. Clark Company, 1926.

Indians and Pioneers, the Story of the American Southwest Before 1830.

280 *Southwestern American Literature*

New Haven: Yale Univ. Press; London: H. Milford, Oxford Univ. Press, 1930. Rev. ed. Norman: Univ. of Oklahoma Press, 1936.
Indian Removal, The Emigration of the Five Civilized Tribes of Indians. Norman: Univ. of Oklahoma Press, 1932.
Advancing the Frontier, 1830-1860. Norman: Univ. of Oklahoma Press, 1933.
The Five Civilized Tribes. Norman: Univ. of Oklahoma Press, 1934.
Down the Texas Road, Historic Places along Highway 69 Through Oklahoma. Norman: Univ. of Oklahoma Press, 1936.
Fort Gibson, A Brief History. Norman: Univ. of Oklahoma Press, 1936.
The Adventures of James Collier, First Collector of the Port of San Francisco. Chicago: The Black Cat Press, 1937.
Sequoyah. Norman: Univ. of Oklahoma Press, 1938.
Marcy and the Gold Seekers, The Journal of Captain R. B. Marcy with an Account of the Gold Rush over the Southern Route. Norman: Univ. of Oklahoma Press, 1939.
A History of Oklahoma. Norman: Univ. of Oklahoma Press, 1942.
Muskogee, The Biography of an Oklahoma Town. Norman: Univ. of Oklahoma Press, 1943. (Also St. Louis: privately printed for Grant Foreman by Blackwell Wielandy Company, 1947.)
The Last Trek of the Indians. Chicago: Univ. of Chicago Press, 1946.
Lore and Lure of Eastern Oklahoma. Published by Muskogee Chamber of Commerce, 1947.

In addition, Foreman edited four other historical works and contributed some twenty-five essays to learned journals.

Works about Grant Foreman
Clark, Stanley. "Grant Foreman," *Chronicles of Oklahoma,* 31 (1953), 226-242.
Dale, Edward Everett. *Grant Foreman, A Brief Biography, with Bibliography.* Norman: Univ. of Oklahoma Press, 1933.
Key, William S. "Dr. Grant Foreman, A Eulogy," *Chronicles of Oklahoma,* 31 (1953), 243-46.
Wiesendanger, Martin W. *Grant and Carolyn Foreman: A Bibliography.* Tulsa: Univ. of Tulsa Press, 1948.

Martha L. Brunson
Southwest Texas State University

Joseph O'Kane Foster (1898-   )
novels, short stories, plays, nonfiction

The Great Montezuma. Ranchos de Taos, New Mexico: Ranchos Press, 1940.
In the Night Did I Sing. New York: Scribner, 1942.
A Cow Is Too Much Trouble in Los Angeles. New York: Duell, Sloan & Pearce, 1952.
Street of the Barefoot Lovers. New York: Duell, Sloan & Pearce, 1953.
Time to Embrace. New York: Popular Library, 1955.
Danielle. New York: Beacon Books, 1959.
Stephana. New York: Duell, Sloan & Pearce, 1959.
D. H. Lawrence in Taos. Albuquerque: Univ. of New Mexico Press, 1971.

In addition, Foster published seven stories between 1939 and 1947 in *Arizona Quarterly, Atlantic Monthly, New Mexico Quarterly, Story Magazine,* and *Southwest Review.*

Martha L. Brunson
Southwest Texas State University

Oscar J. Friend (1897-   )
[pseud. Ford Smith, Owen Fox Jerome]
novels

The Round-up. Chicago: A. C. McClurg, 1924.
The Bullet Eater. Chicago: A. C. McClurg, 1925.
Click of Triangle T. Chicago: A. C. McClurg, 1925.
The Wolf of Wildcat Mountain. Chicago: A. C. McClurg, 1926.
Gun Harvest. Chicago: A. C. McClurg, 1927.
The Hand of Horror [Owen Fox Jerome]. New York: E. J. Clode, 1927.
Bloody Ground. Chicago: A. C. McClurg, 1928.
The Red Kite Clue [Owen Fox Jerome]. New York: E. J. Clode, 1928.
Domes of Silence. London: Stanley Paul, 1929.
The Golf Club Murder [Owen Fox Jerome]. New York: E. J. Clode, 1929.
The Mississippi Hawk. Chicago: A. C. McClurg, 1929.
Half-moon Ranch. New York: G. H. Watt, 1931.
The Murder at Avalon Arms [Owen Fox Jerome]. New York: E. J. Clode, 1931.
The Range Maverick. New York: G. Howard Watt, 1931.

The Long Noose. New York: Gateway Books, 1942.
Murder as Usual [Owen Fox Jerome]. New York: Gateway Books, 1942.
The Corpse Awaits [Owen Fox Jerome]. New York: Bouregy and Thomas, 1946.
The Range Doctor. London: Ward, Lock, 1948.
The Kid from Mars. New York: Frederick Fell, 1949.
Barricade. Kingston, New York: Quinn Publishing, 1950.
Trouble at the Lazy-S. London: Hammond, Hammond, 1951.
Buzzard Meat Range. London: Hammond, Hammond, 1953.
Deputies of Death. London: Hammond, Hammond, 1954.
Lobo Brand. New York: Avalon, 1954.
Guntrap Trail: A Dark Knight Story [Ford Smith]. London: William Foulsham, 1955.
Montana Ermine. New York: Avalon, 1955.
Oklahoma Gun-song: A Dark Knight Story [Ford Smith]. London: William Foulsham, 1955.
Gun-Runner. London: Hammond, Hammond, 1956.
Five Assassins [Owen Fox Jerome]. New York: Bouregy and Thomas, 1958.
Leave Everything to Me [Owen Fox Jerome]. New York: Bouregy and Thomas, 1959.
Buzzard's Roost [Ford Smith]. New York: Avalon, 1961.
Action at Powder River [Ford Smith]. New York: Bouregy and Thomas, 1963.
The Star Men. New York: Avalon, 1963.

Friend was also joint editor with Leo Margulies of three anthologies: *From Off This World; Gems of Science Fiction* (New York: Merlin Press, 1949), *The Giant Anthology of Science Fiction* (New York: Merlin Press, 1954), and *My Best Science Fiction Story, As Selected by 25 Outstanding Writers* (New York: Merlin Press, 1950).

George M. Pisk
Southwest Texas State University

Patricia Gallagher (-   )
novels

The Sons and the Daughters. New York: J. Messner, 1961.

Answer to Heaven. London: Muller, 1962.
The Fires of Brimstone. New York: Avon, 1966.
Shannon. New York: Avon, 1967.
Shadows. New York: Avon, 1971.
Summer of Sighs. New York: Avon, 1971.

Nancy Grayson
Southwest Texas State University

Herbert Pickens Gambrell (1898-   )
history

A Social and Political History of Texas (with Lewis W. Newton). Dallas: Southwest Press, 1932. Rev. ed. Dallas: Turner Company, 1935.
Mirabeau Buonaparte Lamar, Troubadour and Crusader. Dallas: Southwest Press, 1934.
Texian Who's Who (with others). Dallas: The Texian Company, 1937.
The Philosophical Society of Texas: Proceedings of the Centennial Meetings, 1937. Dallas: Regional Press, 1938.
Memoirs of Mary Israel Ellet, 1780-1870. Ed. Gambrell. Doylestown, Pennsylvania: Bucks County Historical Society, 1940.
Anson Jones: The Last President of Texas. Garden City, New York: Doubleday, 1948. 2nd ed. Austin: Univ. of Texas Press, 1964.
Texas, Yesterday and Today, with the Constitution of the State of Texas (with Lewis W. Newton). Dallas: Turner Co., 1949.
A Pictorial History of Texas (with Virginia L. Gambrell). New York: Dutton, 1960.
Texas Today and Tomorrow (with others). Dallas: Southern Methodist Univ. Press, 1961.

In addition, Gambrell published some thirty essays on history in numerous learned journals.

Works about Herbert Gambrell
Moore, Mary. "Meet Mr. History," *Junior Historian, Texas,* 13 (May, 1953), 16-18.

Nancy Grayson
Southwest Texas State University

Wayne Gard (1899-   )
history, biography, folklore, journalism

Book Reviewing. New York: Knopf, 1927.

Sam Bass. Boston: Houghton Mifflin, 1936; rpt. Lincoln: Univ. of Nebraska Press, 1969.

Frontier Justice. Norman: Univ. of Oklahoma Press, 1954.

The Chisolm Trail. Norman: Univ. of Oklahoma Press, 1954.

Cattle Brands of Texas. Dallas: First National Bank, 1956.

Fabulous Quarter Horse: Steel Dust. New York: Duell, Sloan and Pearce, 1958.

The Great Buffalo Hunt. New York: Knopf, 1959; rpt. Lincoln: Univ. of Nebraska Press, 1968.

Rawhide Texas. Norman: Univ. of Oklahoma Press, 1965.

The First 100 Years of Texas Oil and Gas. Dallas: Mid-Continent Oil and Gas Association, 1966.

Up the Trail in '79 by John B. Fletcher. Ed. Wayne Gard. Norman: Univ. of Oklahoma Press, 1968.

Reminiscences of Range Life. Austin: Steck-Vaughn, 1970.

In addition, Gard has published over a hundred articles about the West in such periodicals as *American Heritage, American West, Southwest Review, True West,* and *Cattleman.* For thirty-one years, Gard was a member of the staff of the Dallas *Morning News* where he wrote editorials, signed articles, and books reviews.

Works about Wayne Gard
Adams, Ramon F. *Wayne Gard: Historian of the West.* Austin: Steck-Vaughn, 1970.

Helen Lang Leath
North Texas State University

George Garland [see Garland Roark]

Claud Wilton Garner (1891-   )
novels, nonfiction

Wetback. New York: Coward-McCann, 1947.

Cornbread Aristocrat. New York: Creative Art Press, 1950.
The Young Texans. New York: Farrar, Straus, & Giroux, 1960.
Word of Honor. New York: Farrar, Straus, & Giroux, 1964.
Sam Houston: Texas Giant. San Antonio: Naylor, 1969.

Armando San Miguel
Sue Noles
Wallace Jones
Angelo State University

George Palmer Garrett (1929-   )
novels, short stories, poetry, nonfiction

King of the Mountain. New York: Scribner, 1957.
The Reverand Ghost. New York: Scribner, 1957.
The Sleeping Gypsy and Other Poems. Austin: Univ. of Texas Press, 1958.
The Finished Man. New York: Scribner, 1960.
Abraham's Knife and Other Poems. Chapel Hill, N.C.: Univ. of North Carolina Press, 1961.
In the Briar Patch. Austin: Univ. of Texas Press, 1961.
Sir Slob and the Princess. New York: Samuel French, 1962.
Cold Ground Was My Bed Last Night. Columbia: Univ. of Missouri Press, 1964.
Do, Lord, Remember Me. Garden City, New York: Doubleday, 1965.
The Girl in the Black Raincoat. New York: Duell, 1966.
For a Bitter Season. Columbia: Univ. of Missouri Press, 1967.
Which Ones are the Enemy? Boston: Little, Brown, 1969.
A Wreath for Garibaldi and Other Stories. New York: Hart Davis, 1969.
Death of The Fox. Garden City, N.Y.: Doubleday, 1971.

In addition, Garrett published articles in *American Law Review, Criminal Law,* and *Kenyon Review.*

Gloria Bigham
Gary Randall Hill
Donna Rockwell
Angelo State University

Peter Gent (1942-   )
novel

North Dallas Forty. New York: Morrow, 1973.

Phillip L. Fry
University of Texas at Austin

Jewel Gibson (1904-   )
novels

Joshua Beene and God. New York: Random House, 1946; rpt. London: Eyre & Spottiswood, 1948.
Black Gold. New York: Random House, 1950.

In addition, Gibson is a contributor to the *Houston Chronicle Magazine,* and co-author, with Hal Lewis and Cliff Sage, of a play—*Creep Past the Mountain Lion.*

Chalonnes Lucas
Denton, Texas

Everett A. Gillis (1914-   )
poetry, nonfiction

Hello the House! Dallas: Kaleidograph, 1944.
Who Can Retreat? Los Angeles: Wagon and Star Publishers, 1944.
Sunrise in Texas. San Antonio: Fotolith Corp., 1949.
Angles of the Wind. Dallas: Kaleidograph, 1954.
Oliver La Farge. Austin: Steck-Vaughn, 1967.

Gillis has been widely published in periodicals such as *Prairie Schooner, The Southwester, The New York Times, PMLA,* and *Texas Studies in Lanuage and Literature.*

Works about Everett A. Gillis
Green, Lola Beth, and Terrell, Dahlia. "Everett A. Gillis," in *Bold Land, A Bibliography.* Lubbock: Texas Tech Library Bulletin No. 8, (1970). Pp. 20-25.

Marilyn Neiman
Denton, Texas

Frances Gillmor (1903-   )
novels, nonfiction

Thumbcap Weir. New York: Minton, 1929.
Windsinger. New York: Minton, 1930.
Traders to the Navajos (with Louisa Wade Wetherill). Boston: Houghton, 1934.
Fruit Out of the Rock. New York: Duell, Sloan, 1940.
Dance Dramas of Mexican Villages. Tucson: Univ. of Arizona Press, 1943.
Spanish Texts of Three Dance Dramas from Mexican Villages. Tucson: Univ. of Arizona Press, 1943.
Flute of the Smoking Mirror [A portrait of Nezahualcoyotl, Poet-King of the Aztecs]. Albuquerque: Univ. of New Mexico Press, 1949.
The King Danced in the Market Place [Biography of Mctezuma Ilhuicamina]. Tucson: Univ. of Arizona Press, 1964.

In addition, Gillmor has essays and reviews in such journals as *Mademoiselle, Tomorrow, Western Folklore,* and *Western Humanities Review.*

Judy Richardson
Arlington Public Library

Fred Gipson (1908-1973)
novels, short stories, nonfiction

Fabulous Empire: Colonel Zack Miller's Story. Boston: Houghton Mifflin, 1946.
Hound-Dog Man. New York: Harper, 1949.
The Home Place. New York: Harper, 1950.
Big Bend: A Homesteader's Story (with J. O. Langford). Austin: Univ. of Texas Press, 1952.
Cowhand: The Story of a Working Cowboy. New York: Harper, 1953.
Recollection Creek. New York: Harper, 1955.
The Trail-Driving Rooster. New York: Harper, 1955.
Old Yeller. New York: Harper, 1956.
The Cow Killers. Austin: Univ. of Texas Press, 1956.
Savage Sam. New York: Harper & Row, 1962.

In addition, Gipson published numerous short stories, tales, and sketches

288   *Southwestern American Literature*

in such periodicals as *Southwest Review, Frontier Times, True West,* and *Reader's Digest.*

Works about Fred Gipson

Gipson, Tommie. "Helpless in Hollywood: or, How Much Is that Hound Dog," *Southwest Review,* 45 (Summer 1960), 259-65.

Henderson, Sam H. *Fred Gipson.* Austin: Steck-Vaughn, 1967.

Tinsley, Russell. "Maverick Author," *The Alcalde,* (February 1961), 18-19.

Walbridge, Earle F. "Fred Gipson," *Wilson Library Bulletin,* 32 (October 1957), 96.

Sam H. Henderson
North Texas State University

Oliver Gloux (1818-1883)
[pseud. Gustave Aimard]
novels

The Border Rifles: A Tale of the Texan War. Philadelphia: T. B. Peterson and Brothers, 1840. Rpt. New York: Beadle and Adams (Beadle's Dime Library), 1881. Published in France as *Les Rodeurs de Frontière.* Paris: Amyot, 1868.

The Freebooters; A Story of the Texan War. Philadelphia: T. B. Peterson, 1840 [?]. Published in France as *Les Francs Tireurs.* Paris: Amyot, 1861.

The Gold Finders. A Romance of California. New York: E. D. Long, 1840. Later retitled *The Gold Seekers: A Tale of California.* London: Ward and Lock, 1861. Published in France as *La Fievre d'Or.* Paris: Amyot, 1860.

The Indian Scout; or, Life on the Frontier; A Story of the Aztec City. Philadelphia: T. B. Peterson, 1850 [?]. Published in France as *L'Eclaireur.* Paris: Amyot, 1859.

The Frontiersman. New York: F. M. Lupton, 1854.

The Guide of the Desert; or, Life in the Pampas. London: J. A. Berger, [186?]. First published as *Le Guaranis.* Paris: Amyot, 1854.

The Chief of the Aucas; or, The Foster Brothers. London: Routledge, Warne & Routledge, 1859. Later retitled *The Pearl of the Andes. A Tale of Love and Adventure.* London: Ward and Lock, 1863. First published as *Le Grand Chef des Aucas.* Paris: Amyot, 1858.

The Trail Hunter; A Tale of the Far West. London: Ward and Lock, 1861. Later retitled *The Trail Hunter; or, Red Cedar, the Prairie Outlaw.* New

York: Beadle and Adams (American Tales), 1868. First published as *Le Chercher de Pistes*. Paris: Amyot, 1858.

The Trapper's Daughter. A Story of the Rocky Mountains. London: Ward and Lock, 1861. Later retitled *The Trapper's Daughter; or, The Outlaw's Fate. A Story of the Rocky Mountains.* New York: Beadle and Adams (American Tales), 1869. Also published under the title *Lynch Law; or, The Hunter's Revenge.* Publisher and date unknown. First published as *Le Loi de Lynch.* Paris: Amyot, 1859.

The Buccaneer Chief. London: J. A. Berger, 1865 [?]. First published as *Le Grand Filibuste.* Paris: Amyot, 1860.

The Indian Chief; The Story of a Revolution. London: Ward and Lock, 1861. Later retitled *The Indian Chief; A Tale of the Desert.* London: J. & R. Maxwell, 1879 [?]. First published as *Curumilla.* Paris: Amyot, 1860.

The Tiger Slayer; A Tale of the Indian Desert. London: Ward and Lock, 1860. Later retitled *The Tiger Slayer; or, Eagle Head to the Rescue.* New York: Beadle and Adams (American Tales), 1869. Published in France as *Le Grande Filibuste.* Paris: Amyot, 1860.

Loyal Heart, the Pale Face Hunter; or, The Trappers of Arkansas. New York: Beadle and Adams (American Tales), 1868. First published as *Le Coeur-Loyal.* Paris: Amyot, 1861.

The Pirates of the Prairies; Adventures in the American Desert. London: Ward and Lock, 1861. Later retitled *The Bandits at Bay; or, The Pirates of the Prairies.* New York: Beadle and Adams (American Tales), 1868. Later retitled *The Pirates of the Prairies; Adventures in the American Desert; or, Fighting for Texas.* Chicago: Max Stein, [19??]. Published in France as *Pirates des Praires.* Paris: Amyot, 1868.

Prairie Flower. Adventures on the Indian Border. London: Ward and Lock, 1861. Later retitled *The Prairie Flower; or, The Baffled Chief.* New York: Beadle and Adams (Frank Starr's American Novels), 1875. Published in France as *Balle-Franche.* Paris: Amyot, 1861.

The White Scalper; A Story of the Texan War. London: Ward and Lock, 1861. Rpt. New York: Beadle and Adams. (Dime Library), 1881. Published in France as *Les Scalpeurs Blancs.* Paris: E. Dentu, 1873.

The Last of the Incas. London: Ward and Lock, 1862. Later retitled *The Last of the Aucas.* London: G. Vickers, 1877. Published in France as *L'Araucan.* Paris: Cadot, 1864.

The Queen of the Savannah; A Story of the Mexican War. London: Ward,

Lock, and Tyler, 1862. Published in France as *L'Eau-Qui-Court*. Paris: 1867.

The Red Track; A Story of Social Life in Mexico. London: Ward and Lock, 1862. Published in France as *Valentin Guillois*. Paris: Amyot, 1862.

Stronghand; or, The Noble Revenge. A Tale of the Disinherited. London: J. & R. Maxwell, 1863. First published as *La Main-Ferme*. Paris: 1862.

The Adventurers. A Story of a Love Chase. London: Ward and Lock, 1863. Published in France as *Les Aventuriers*. Paris: Amyot, 1864.

The Bee Hunters; A Tale of Adventure. London: J. & R. Maxwell, 1864. Published in France as *Les Chasseurs d'Abeilles*. Paris: Amyot, 1864.

The Flying Horseman. London: C. H. Clarke, 1868. First published as *Zeno Cabral*. Paris: Amyot, 1864.

The Insurgent Chief. London: C. H. Clarke, 1868. First published as *Le Montonero*. Paris: 1864.

The Rebel Chief; A Tale of Guerilla Life. London: Ward and Lock, 1865. First published as *Les Nuits Mexicaines*. Paris: De Soye, 1864.

The Smuggler Chief. A Novel. London: Ward and Lock, 1864. Later retitled *The Smuggler Hero. A Story*. London: George Vickers, 1877. Published in France as *Les Fils de la Tortue*. Paris: 1864.

Stoneheart. A Romance. London: Ward, Lock, and Tyler, 1865. First published as *Le Coeur De Pierre*. Paris: Amyot, 1864.

The Missouri Outlaws. London: J. & R. Maxwell, 1879. First published as *Les Outlaws du Missouri*. Paris: Amyot, 1868.

The Prairie Pirates; or, The Hunter's Revenge. New York: Beadle and Adams (Frank Starr's American Novels), 1869. (This book is a rewritten version of three novels listed elsewhere in this bibliography: *The Pirates of the Prairies, The Trail Hunter,* and *The Trapper's Daughter*.)

The Treasure of Pearls; A Romance of Adventure in California. London: J. & R. Maxwell, 1884.

The Red River Half Breed; A Tale of the Wild Northwest. London: J. & R. Maxwell, 1885 [?].

As far as can be told, the only translator of Aimard is Sir F. C. L. Wraxall. Bibliographic information concerning the translations of Aimard's novels is difficult to authenticate. Also, the entries above give only the dates of the earliest appearance of the novels in English and French. Almost all of them, however, went through several editions and eventually were printed in the United States.

Works about Gustave Aimard
Gaston, Edwin. *The Early Novel of the Southwest.* Albuquerque: The University of New Mexico Press, 1961. Pp. 263-64. (The short discussion of Aimard found here is apparently the only work that has been done on him in English.)

Charles Gongre
Lamar University

Frank Goodwyn (1911-   )
novels, nonfiction

The Devil in Texas. Dallas: Dealy and Lowe, 1936.
The Magic of Limping John. New York: Rinehart, 1944.
Life on the King Ranch. New York: Thomas Y. Crowell, 1951.
Lone Star Land. New York: Knopf, 1955.
The Black Bull. New York: Doubleday, 1958.

In addition, Goodwyn published numerous articles on folklore in such publications as *Journal of American Folklore, Southern Folklore Quarterly,* and *Western Folklore.*

Orlan Sawey
Texas A&I University

William Goyen (1915-   )
novels, short stories

The House of Breath. New York: Random House, 1950.
Ghost and Flesh. New York: Random House, 1952.
In a Farther Country. New York: Random House, 1955.
The Faces of Blood Kindred. New York: Random House, 1960.
The Fair Sister. New York: Doubleday, 1963.
A Book of Jesus. New York: Doubleday, 1973.
Come, The Restorer. New York: Doubleday, 1974.
Selected Writings of William Goyen. New York and Berkeley: Random House and The Bookworks, 1974.

In addition, Goyen published short fiction, articles, reviews, and poems in a variety of periodicals and has written and had produced dramatic works for both the stage and television.

Works about William Goyen

Bachelard, Gaston. *The Poetics of Space.* Trans. Maria Jolas. New York: Orion Press, 1964.

Breit, Harvey. "Talk with William Goyen." *New York Times Book Review,* September 10, 1950, p. 12.

Coindreau, Maurice Edgar. "Preface to *The House of Breath*" in *The Times of William Faulkner: A French View of Modern American Fiction.* Ed. and trans. George M. Reeves. Columbia: University of South Carolina Press, 1971.

Curtius, Ernst Robert. "William Goyen" in *Essays on European Literature.* Trans. Michael Kowel. Princeton: Princeton University Press, 1973.

Gossett, Louise Y. "The Voices of Distance: William Goyen," in *Violence in Recent Southern Fiction.* Durham: Duke University Press, 1965.

Hoffman, Frederick J. *The Art of Southern Fiction.* Carbondale: Southern Illinois University Press, 1967.

Isherwood, Christopher. "Young American Writers." *Observer,* May 13, 1951, p. 7.

Korges, James. "William Goyen" in *Contemporary Novelists.* Ed. James Vinson. New York: St. Martin's Press, 1972.

Nin, Anais. *The Novel of the Future.* New York: Macmillan, 1966.

Peden, William. *The American Short Story.* Boston: Houghton Mifflin, 1964.

Phillips, Robert. "Samuels and Samson: Theme and Legend in 'The White Rooster.' " *Studies in Short Fiction,* 6 (1969), 331-333.

————. "Secret and Symbol: Entrances to Goyen's House of Breath." *Southwest Review,* 59 (1974), 248-253.

————. "The Romance of Prophecy: Goyen's *In a Farther Country.*" *Southwest Review,* 56 (1971), 213-221.

Stern, Daniel. "On William Goyen's *The House of Breath*" in *Rediscoveries: Informal Essays in Which Well-Known Novelists Rediscover Neglected Works of Fiction by One of Their Favorite Authors.* Ed. David Madden. New York: Crown, 1971.

Clyde L. Grimm, Jr.
Southwest Texas State University

John Alexander Graves (1920-   )
nonfiction, short stories

Goodbye to a River. New York: Knopf, 1960.
Hard Scrabble. New York: Knopf, 1974.

In addition, Graves has stories and essays in such journals as *Holiday, New Yorker, Atlantic,* and *American Heritage.*

Marilyn Neiman
Denton, Texas

Ben K. Green (1912-1974)
nonfiction

Horse Conformation: Horse Trades of Yesteryear. Wolfe City, Texas: Privately published, 1962.
Horse Tradin'. New York: Knopf, 1967.
Shield Mares. Austin, Texas: Encino Press, 1967.
Wild Cow Tales. New York: Knopf, 1969.
Back to Back. Austin, Texas: Encino Press, 1970.
The Last Trail Drive Through Down-Town Dallas. Flagstaff: Northland, 1971.
The Village Horse Doctor, West of the Pecos. New York: Knopf, 1971.
A Thousand Miles of Mustanging. Flagstaff: Northland, 1972.
Some More Horse Tradin'. New York: Knopf, 1972.
Ben Green Tales (4 vols). Flagstaff: Northland, 1974.
The Color of Horses. Flagstaff: Northland, 1974.

James W. Byrd
East Texas State University

A. C. Greene (1923-   )
nonfiction

A Personal Country. New York: Knopf, 1969.
The Last Captive. Austin: Encino, 1972.
The Santa Claus Bank Robbery. New York: Knopf, 1972.
The Christmas Tree. Austin: Encino, 1973.
Dallas: The Deciding Years—A Historical Portrait. Austin: Encino, 1974.

In addition, Greene published essays in *Southwest Review, Atlantic,* and *Arlington Quarterly.*

Sylvia McGowan
Tarleton State University

Hilton Ross Greer (1869-1949)
poetry, anthologies

Sun Gleams and Gossamers. Boston: R. G. Badger, 1903.

The Spiders, and Other Poems. Nashville: Publishing House Methodist Episcopal Church, South, 1906.

A Prairie Prayer, and Other Poems. Boston: Sherman, French, 1912.

Voices of the Southwest. New York: Macmillan, 1923.

Best Short Stories of the Southwest. Dallas: Southwest Press, 1928.

Best Short Stories of the Southwest, Second Series. Dallas: Southwest Press, 1931.

New Voices of the Southwest (with Florence Elberta Barns). Dallas: Tardy, 1934.

Ten and Twenty Aprils: Selected Verse of Hilton Ross Greer. Dallas: Tardy, 1935.

An Introduction to Texas Literature. Dallas: Helms Printing Co., 1941.

Works about Hilton Ross Greer

Montgomery, Vaida Stewart. *A Century with Texas Poets and Poetry.* Dallas: Kaleidograph Press, 1934.

Smith, Goldie Capers. *The Creative Arts in Texas: A Handbook of Biography.* Nashville: Cokesbury, 1926.

Arthur M. Sampley
North Texas State University

Zane Grey (1872-1939)
novels, short stories

Betty Zane. New York: C. Francis Press, 1903.

The Spirit of the Border: A Romance of the Early Settlers in the Ohio Valley. New York: A. L. Burt, 1906.

The Last of the Plainsmen. New York: The Outing Publishing Co.: Grosset & Dunlap, 1909.

The Last Trail: A Story of Early Days in the Ohio Valley. New York: A. L. Burt, 1909.

The Short-Stop. Chicago: A. C. McClurg, 1909.

The Heritage of the Desert: A Novel. New York: Harper, 1910.

The Young Forester. New York: Harper, 1910.

The Young Lion-Hunter. New York: Harper, 1911.

The Young Pitcher. New York: Harper, 1911.

Ken Ward in the Jungle: Thrilling Adventures in Tropical Wilds. New York: Harper, 1912.

Riders of the Purple Sage: A Novel. New York: Harper, 1912.

Desert Gold: A Romance of the Border. New York: Harper, 1913.

The Light of Western Stars: A Romance. New York: Grosset & Dunlap; Harper, 1914.

The Lone Star Ranger: A Romance of the Border. New York: Harper, 1915.

The Rainbow Trail. New York: Grosset & Dunlap; Harper, 1915.

The Border Legion. New York: Harper, 1916.

Wildfire. New York: Grosset & Dunlap; Harper, 1917.

The Desert of Wheat: A Novel. New York: Grosset & Dunlap, 1918.

The U. P. Trail: A Novel. New York: Harper; Grosset & Dunlap, 1918.

Tales of Fishes. New York: Harper, 1919.

The Man of the Forest: A Novel. New York: Harper, 1920.

The Red-Headed Outfield and Other Baseball Stories. New York: Grosset & Dunlap, 1920.

The Mysterious Rider: A Novel. New York: Harper, 1921.

The Day of the Beast. New York: Harper, 1922.

Tales of Lonely Trails. New York: Harper, 1922.

To the Last Man. New York: Harper; McKinlay, Stone & Mackenzie, 1922.

Tappan's Burro and Other Stories. New York: Harper, 1923.

Wanderer of the Wasteland. New York: Harper, 1923.

The Call of the Canyon. New York: Harper, 1924.

Roping Lions in the Grand Canyon. New York: Harper, 1924.

Tales of Southern Rivers. New York: Harper, 1924.

The Deer Stalker. New York: Harper, 1925.

Tales of Fishing Virgin Seas. New York: Harper, 1925.

Tales of the Angler's Eldorado. New York: Harper, 1925.

The Thundering Herd. New York: Harper, 1925.

The Vanishing American. New York: Harper, 1925.
Captives of the Desert. New York: Harper, 1926.
Under the Tonto Rim. New York: Harper, 1926.
Forlorn River: A Romance. New York: Harper, 1927.
Tales of Swordfish and Tuna. New York: Harper, 1927.
Don: The Story of a Lion Dog. New York: Harper, 1928.
"Nevada": A Romance. New York: Harper, 1928.
Tales of the Fresh Water Fishing. New York: Harper, 1928.
Wild Horse Mesa. New York: Harper, 1928.
Fighting Caravans. New York: Harper, 1929.
The Shepherd of Guadaloupe. New York: Harper, 1930.
The Wolf Tracker. New York: Harper, 1930.
Sunset Pass. New York: Harper, 1931.
Tales of Tahitian Waters. New York: Harper, 1931.
Zane Grey's Book of Camps and Trails. New York: Harper, 1931.
Arizona Ames. New York: Harper, 1932.
The Drift Fence. New York: Harper, 1932.
Robber's Roost. New York: Harper, 1932.
The Hash Knife Outfit. New York: Harper, 1933.
Code of the West. New York: Harper, 1934.
Thunder Mountain. New York: Harper, 1935.
The Lost Wagon Train. New York: Harper, 1936.
The Trail Driver. New York: Harper, 1936.
An American Angler in Australia. New York: Harper, 1937.
West of the Pecos. New York: Harper, 1937.
Majesty's Rancho. New York: Harper, 1938.
Raiders of Spanish Peaks. New York: Harper, 1938.
Knights of the Range. New York: Harper, 1939.
The Roaring U. P. Trail. London: Hodder and Stoughton, 1939.
Western Union. New York: Harper, 1939.
30,000 on the Hoof. New York: Harper, 1940.
Twin Sombreros. New York: Harper, 1940.
Stairs of Sand. New York: Harper, 1943.
The Zane Grey Omnibus. Ed. Ruth G. Gentles. New York: Harper, 1943.
Wilderness Trek: A Novel of Australia. New York: Harper, 1944.
King of the Royal Mounted and the Ghost Guns of Roaring River. Racine, Wis.: Whitman, 1946.
Shadow on the Trail. New York: Harper, 1946.

Valley of Wild Horses. New York: Harper, 1947.
Rogue River Feud. New York: Harper, 1948.
The Maverick Queen. New York: Harper, 1950.
The Dude Ranger. New York: Harper, 1951.
Zane Grey's Adventures in Fishing. Ed. Ed Zern. New York: Harper, 1952.
Wyoming. New York: Harper, 1953.
Lost Pueblo. New York: Harper, 1954.
Black Mesa. New York: Harper, 1955.
Stranger from the Tonto. New York: Harper, 1956.
The Fugitive Trail. New York: Harper, 1957.

Works about Zane Grey
Boal, S. "Zane Grey: Writer of the Purple Sage," *Coronet,* 36 (June 1954), 112-17.
Boyle, R. H. "Man Who Lived Two Lives in One," *Sports Illustrated,* 29 April, 1968, pp. 68-70.
Karr, Jean. *Zane Grey, Man of the West.* New York: Greenberg, 1949.
Mott, F. L. *Golden Multitudes: The Story of Best Sellers in the United States.* New York: Macmillan, 1947.
Powell, L. C. "Books Determine," *Wilson Library Bulletin,* 30 (Sept. 1955), 62-65.
Schubert, P. "Roundup in Bloody Basin," *Saturday Evening Post,* 15 Feb. 1958, pp. 36-37+.
Scott, Kenneth W. "*The Heritage of the Desert:* Zane Grey Discovers the West," *Markham Review,* 2 (Feb. 1970), 10-12.

Mallory Chamberlin, Jr.
North Texas State University

John Howard Griffin (1920-   )
novels, nonfiction

The Devil Rides Outside. Fort Worth, Texas: Smiths, 1952.
Nuni. Boston: Houghton Mifflin in association with Smiths, Inc., Dallas, 1956.
Land of the High Sky. Midland, Texas: The First National Bank of Midland, 1959.
Black Like Me. Boston: Houghton Mifflin, 1961.

The John Howard Griffin Reader. Ed. Bradford Daniel. Boston: Houghton
Mifflin, 1968.

The Church and the Black Man. Dayton, Ohio: Pflaum Press, 1969.

A Hidden Wholeness: the Visual World of Thomas Merton. (Photos by
Thomas Merton and John Howard Griffin. Text by John Howard Griffin.)
Boston: Houghton Mifflin, 1968.

A Hidden Wilderness: The Visual World of Thomas Merton. Boston:
Houghton Mifflin, 1970.

Jacques Maritain: Homage in Words and Pictures (with Yves R. Simon).
Albany, N.Y.: Magi Books, 1973.

Photographic Portraits. Albany, N.Y.: Magi Books, 1973.

Twelve Photographic Portraits. Greensboro, N.C.: Unicorn Press, 1973.

In addition, Griffin has a monograph on school desegregation and some
thirty essays, short stories, and chapters in books.

Works about John Howard Griffin

Campbell, Jeff H. *John Howard Griffin.* Austin: Steck-Vaughn, 1970.

Geismar, Maxwell. "John Howard Griffin: The Devil in Texas," *American
Moderns.* New York: Hill and Wang, 1958. Pp. 251-65.

McDonnell, Thomas P. "John Howard Griffin: An Interview," *Ramparts,*
1 (January 1963), 6-16.

Rank, H. "Rhetorical Effectiveness of *Black Like Me,*" *English Journal,* 57
(September 1968), 813-17.

Jeff H. Campbell
Midwestern University

Patricia Browning Griffith (1935-   )
novel, short stories

The Future Is Not What It Used To Be. New York: Simon & Schuster,
1970.

In addition, Griffith published stories in *Harper's, Colorado Quarterly,* and
Texas Observer.

Albert J. Griffith
Our Lady of the Lake College
San Antonio, Texas

Grover C. (Bill) Gulick (1916-   )
novels, short stories

Abilene or Bust! New York: Cupples and Leon, 1946.

Desolation Trail. New York: Cupples and Leon, 1946.

Bend of the Snake. Boston: Houghton Mifflin, 1950.

A Drum Calls West. Boston: Houghton Mifflin, 1952.

A Thousand for the Cariboo. Boston: Houghton Mifflin, 1954.

White Men, Red Men, and Mountain Men. Boston: Houghton Mifflin, 1955.

The Land Beyond. Boston: Houghton Mifflin, 1958.

The Shaming of Broken Horn and Other Stories. Garden City, New York: Doubleday, 1961.

Hallelujah Trail. Garden City, New York: Doubleday, 1965.

They Came to a Valley. Garden City, New York: Doubleday, 1966.

Liveliest Town in the West. Garden City, New York: Doubleday, 1969.

The Moon-eyed Appaloosa. Garden City, New York: Doubleday, 1969.

The Country Club Caper. Garden City, New York: Doubleday, 1971.

Snake River Country. Caldwell, Idaho: Caxton, 1971.

In addition, Gulick published over a dozen stories in *Collier's* and *Saturday Evening Post* between 1949 and 1961.

James Hamilton
Randy Lichnovsky
Ricky Menchaca
Angelo State University

Archibald Clavering Gunter (1847-1907)
novels

Mr. Barnes of New York. New York: Leipzig B. Tanehnitz, 1888.

Mr. Potter of Texas. New York: Home Publishing, 1888.

That Frenchman! New York: Home Publishing, 1889.

Small Boys in Big Boots. New York: Home Publishing, 1890.

A Florida Enchantment. New York: Home Publishing, 1892.

The First of the English. New York: Home Publishing, 1894.

The King's Stockbroker. New York: Home Publishing, 1894.

A Princess of Paris. New York: Home Publishing, 1894.
The Ladies' Juggernaut. New York: Home Publishing, 1895.
The Love Adventures of Al-Mansur. New York: Home Publishing, 1895.
Don Balasco of Key West. New York: Home Publishing, 1896.
Her Senator. New York: Home Publishing, 1896.
The Power of Woman. New York: Home Publishing, 1897.
The Adventures of a Naval Officer. New York: Home Publishing, 1898.
Baron Montez of Panama and Paris. New York: Home Publishing, 1898.
Billy Hamilton. New York: Home Publishing, 1898.
Jack Curzon. New York: Home Publishing, 1898.
A Lost American. New York: Home Publishing, 1898.
Miss Nobody of Nowhere. New York: Home Publishing, 1898.
The Fighting Troubadour. New York: Home Publishing, 1899.
M. S. Bradford. New York: Home Publishing, 1899.
Adrienne de Portalis. New York: Home Publishing, 1900.
The Princess of Copper. New York: Home Publishing, 1900.
Tangled Flags. New York: Home Publishing, 1900.
The Deacon's Second Wind. New York: Home Publishing, 1901.
The City of Mystery. New York: Home Publishing, 1902.
The Spy Company. New York: Home Publishing, 1902.
The Surprises of an Empty Hotel. New York: Home Publishing, 1902.
The Conscience of a King. New York: Home Publishing, 1903.
Phil Conway. New York: Home Publishing, 1903.
The Man Behind the Door. New York: Home Publishing, 1904.
My Japanese Prince. New York: Home Publishing, 1904.
The Changing Pulse of Madame Touraine. New York: Home Publishing, 1905.
The Adventures of Dr. Burton. New York: Home Publishing, 1905.
A Prince in the Garret. New York: Home Publishing, 1905.
Mr. Barnes, American. New York: Home Publishing, 1907.
Prince Karl. New York: G. W. Dillingham, 1907.

Works about Archibald Clavering Gunter
Mott, Frank L. *Golden Multitudes.* New York: Macmillan, 1947.

Gary Burns
Janis Galloway
Keryth Stubblefield
Angelo State University

A. B. Guthrie, Jr. (1901-   )
novels, short stories, nonfiction

Murders at Moon Dance. New York: Dutton, 1943; rpt. as *Trouble at Moon Dance.* New York: Popular Library, 1951.

The Big Sky. New York: William Sloane, 1947.

The Way West. New York: William Sloane, 1949.

These Thousand Hills. Boston: Houghton Mifflin, 1956.

The Big It and Other Stories. Boston: Houghton Mifflin, 1960; rpt. as *Mountain Medicine.* New York: Pocket Books, 1961.

The Blue Hen's Chick. New York: McGraw-Hill, 1965.

Arfive. Boston: Houghton Mifflin, 1971.

Wild Pitch. Boston: Houghton Mifflin, 1973.

Guthrie has also published approximately forty stories, articles and poems between 1922 and 1969 in such magazines as *Atlantic Monthly, Boys' Life, Esquire, Frontier, Harper's, Holiday, Life, Saturday Evening Post, Saturday Review,* and *Writer.*

Works about A. B. Guthrie, Jr.

"A. B. Guthrie, Jr.," in *Kentucky Story.* Ed. Hollis S. Summers. Lexington: Univ. of Kentucky Press, 1954. Pp. 242-43.

Cournos, John, and H. S. Cournos. *Famous Modern American Novelists.* New York: Dodd, Mead, 1952. Pp. 145-50.

Cracroft, Richard H. *"The Big Sky:* A. B. Guthrie's Use of Historical Sources." *Western American Literature,* 6 (Fall 1971), 163-176.

Folsom, James K. *The American Western Novel.* New Haven: College and University Press, 1966. Pp. 64-76.

Ford, Thomas W. *A. B. Guthrie, Jr.* Austin: Steck-Vaughn, 1968.

Goodwyn, Frank. "The Frontier in American Fiction," *Inter-American Review of Bibliography,* 10 (October-December, 1960), 356-69.

Hairston, Joe B. "Community in the West." *South Dakota Review,* 11 (Spring, 1973), 17-27.

Hood, Charles E., Jr. "The Man and the Book: Guthrie's *The Big Sky." Montana Journalism Review,* 14 (1971), 6-15.

Kohler, Dayton. "A. B. Guthrie, Jr., and the West." *College English,* 12 (February 1951), 249-56; rpt. in *English Journal,* 40 (February 1951), 65-72.

Prescott, Orville. "The Art of Historical Fiction: Richter, Guthrie," in *In*

My Opinion: An Inquiry into the Contemporary Novel. Indianapolis: Bobbs-Merrill, 1952. pp. 133-45.

Stegner, Wallace. Foreword to *The Big Sky* by A. B. Guthrie. Boston: Houghton Mifflin, 1965.

Stineback, David C. "On History and Its Consequences: A. B. Guthrie's *These Thousand Hills.*" *Western American Literature,* 6 (Fall 1971), 177-89.

Todd, Edgeley W. "A Note on 'The Mountain Man as Literary Hero,'" *Western American Literature,* 1 (Fall 1966), 219-21.

Walker, Don D. "The Mountain Man as Literary Hero," *Western American Literature,* 1 (Spring 1966), 15-25.

Warfel, Harry R. "Alfred Bertram Guthrie, Jr.," in *American Novelists of Today.* New York: American Book Company, 1951. p. 189.

"West of the Mississippi: An Interview with Frederick Manfred," *Critique,* 2 (Winter 1959), 35-56.

Williams, John. "The 'Western': Definition of the Myth," *Nation,* 193 (November 18, 1961), 401-06.

Young, Vernon. "An American Dream and Its Parody," *Arizona Quarterly,* 6 (Summer 1950), 112-23.

Thomas W. Ford
University of Houston

Leon Hale (1921-   )
novel, nonfiction

Turn South at the Second Bridge. New York: Doubleday, 1965.
Bonney's Place. New York: Doubleday, 1972. Rpt. New York: Popular Library, 1973.

Lee Sullenger
Stephen F. Austin State University

J. Evetts Haley (1901-   )
biography, history, nonfiction

The XIT Ranch of Texas and the Early Days of the Llano Estacado. Chicago: The Lakeside Press, 1929; rev., Norman: Univ. of Oklahoma Press, 1953 and 1967.

Charles Goodnight: Cowman and Plainsman. Boston: Houghton Mifflin, 1936; rpt., Norman: Univ. of Oklahoma Press, 1949.
George W. Littlefield, Texan. Norman: Univ. of Oklahoma Press, 1943.
Charles Schreiner, General Merchandise: The Story of a Country Store. Austin: Texas State Historical Association, 1944.
Jeff Milton: A Good Man with a Gun. Norman: Univ. of Oklahoma Press, 1948.
The Heraldry of the Range: Some Southwestern Brands. Canyon, Texas: Panhandle-Plains Historical Society, 1949.
Fort Concho and the Texas Frontier. San Angelo: San Angelo *Standard-Times,* 1952.
Life on the Texas Range (with Erwin E. Smith). Austin: Univ. of Texas Press, 1952.
Story of Shamrock. Amarillo: The Shamrock Oil and Gas Corp., 1954.
Focus on the Frontier. Amarillo: The Shamrock Oil and Gas Corp., 1957.
Erle P. Halliburton: Genius with Cement. Duncan and El Paso: Carl Hertzog, 1959.
F. Reaugh, Man and Artist. El Paso: Carl Hertzog for the Shamrock Oil and Gas Corp., 1960.
Men of Fiber. El Paso: Carl Hertzog, 1963.
A Texas Looks at Lyndon, A Study in Illegitimate Power. Canyon, Texas: Palo Duro Press, 1964.
Earl Vandale on the Trail of Texas Books. Canyon, Texas: Palo Duro Press, 1965.
The Flamboyant Judge: James D. Hamlin (ed. with William C. Holden). Canyon: Palo Duro Press, 1972.
Robbing Banks Was My Business: The Story of J. Harvey Bailey, America's Most Successful Bank Robber. Canyon: Palo Duro Press, 1973.

In addition, Haley has a number of essays on Western subjects and on politics in such publications as *The Shamrock, Southwest Review,* and *The Cattleman;* and edited *Bill Oden: Early Days on the Texas-New Mexico Plains.* Canyon: Palo Duro Press, 1965.

Works about J. Evetts Haley
Bradford, M. E. "The Care and Keeping of Memory: J. Evetts Haley and Plutarchian Biography," *Southwestern American Literature,* forthcoming.
Frantz, Joe B. and Julian Ernest Choate, Jr. *The American Cowboy.* Norman: Univ. of Oklahoma Press, 1955.

Hill, Joseph A. *The Panhandle-Plains Historical Society and Its Museum.*
    Canyon, Texas: West Texas State Univ. Press, 1955.
Robinson, Chandler A. *J. Evetts Haley: Cowman-Historian.* El Paso: Carl
    Hertzog, 1967. (Full bibliography).

M. E. Bradford
University of Dallas

Dick Wick Hall (1877-1926)
humor

Stories from the Salome Sun (collected by Frances Dorothy Nutt). Flagstaff: Northland, 1968.

In addition to his collection of short stories, Hall contributed numerous
stories and sketches to the *Saturday Evening Post.*

Works about Dick Wick Hall
Boyer, Mary G. ed. "Dick Wick Hall," *Arizona in Literature.* Glendale,
    California: Arthur H. Clark, 1935. pp. 495-511.
Miles, Elton. *Southwest Humorists.* Austin: Steck-Vaughn, 1969.

Elton Miles
Sul Ross State University

Sharlot Mabridth Hall (1870-1943)
poetry, nonfiction

Cactus and Pine; Songs of the Southwest (poems). Boston: Sherman, 1910.
    2nd ed. revised and enlarged, Phoenix, Arizona: Arizona Republican,
    1924.
The Story of the Smoki People. Privately printed, 1923.
Poems of a Ranch Woman. Phoenix: Historical Society of Arizona, 1953.

In addition, Hall has essays, poems, and stories in such publications as *Out
West, Atlantic,* and *Ladies Home Journal.*

Works about Sharlot Hall
"Sharlot Hall," *Writer* (July, 1901), p. 106.

"Arizona Territorial Historian," *Van Norden Magazine,* 6 (January 1910), 455.

Weston, J. J. "Sharlot Hall: Arizona's Pioneer Lady of Literature," *Journal of the West,* 4 (October 1965), 539-52.

Judy Richardson
Arlington Public Library

Samuel Adams Hammett (1816-1865)
[pseud. Philip Paxton]
humor

A Stray Yankee in Texas. New York: Redfield, 1854.
Piney Woods Tavern; or, Sam Slick in Texas. New York: Redfield, 1858.

Works about Samuel A. Hammett

Hoole, W. Stanley. *Sam Slick in Texas,* "Introduction" by J. Frank Dobie. San Antonio: Naylor, 1945.

Miles, Elton. *Southwest Humorists.* Austin: Steck-Vaughn, 1969.

Elton Miles
Sul Ross State University

Lewis Ulysses Hanke (1905-   )
history

The Spanish Struggle for Justice in the Conquest of America. Boston: Little, Brown, 1949.

Bartolome de las Casas, Historiador. Mexico: Fonde de Cultura Economica, 1951; rpt. Gainesville: Univ. of Florida Press, 1952.

Bartilome de las Casas. Oxford: Univ. of Pennsylvania Press; Gainsville, Fla.: Univ. of Florida Press, 1952.

Imperial City of Potosi. New York: Heinman, 1956.

Aristotle and the American Indians: A Study in Race Prejudice in the Modern World. Chicago: Henry Regnery, 1959.

Biblioteca de Autores Españoles. Madrid: Juan Pérez de Tudela Bueso, 1959.

Modern Latin America: A Continent in Ferment. New York: Van Nostrand, 1960.
Handbook of Latin American Studies. Cambridge, Mass.: Harvard Univ. Press; Gainsville, Fla.: Univ. of Florida Press, 1963.
Do the Americans Have a Common History?: A Critique of the Bolton Theory. New York: Knopf, 1964.
Bartolome Arzans de Orsia y Vela's History of Potosi. Providence, R.I.: Brown Univ. Press, 1965.
First Social Experiments in America. Boston: Little, Brown, 1967.
History of the Latin American Civilization: Source and Interpretations. Boston: Little, Brown, 1967.
Mexico and the Caribbean. New York: Van Nostrand, 1967.
Contemporary Latin America. New York: Van Nostrand, 1968.
Defense of the Indians by las Casas. DeKalb: Northern Illinois Univ. Press, 1973.
All Mankind Is One. DeKalb: Northern Illinois Univ. Press, 1974.

Rose Cano
Rhonda Hammit
Angelo State University

Alberta Hannum (1906-   )
novels, plays

Spin A Silver Dollar. New York: Viking, 1931; rpt., Viking, 1961; rpt., New York: Ballantine, 1972.
Thursday April. New York: Harper, 1931.
Tommy's Temper: A One-Act Christmas Play. Franklin, Ohio: Eldridge Publishing Co., 1931.
The Hills Step Lightly. New York: William Morrow, 1934.
The Gods and One. New York: Duell, Sloan, and Pearce, 1941.
Roseanna McCoy. New York: Holt, 1947.
Paint the Wind. New York: Viking, 1958; rpt., New York: Ballantine, 1972.
Look Back With Love: A Recollection of the Blue Ridge. New York: Vanguard, 1967.

Nancy Young
Angelo State University

Hazel Harris (1902-   )
short stories, poetry, plays

When A Man Wanders: A One-Act Play for Women, in *Poet Lore.* Boston, 1929.
Wings of the Morning. Dallas: C. C. Cockrell Co., 1931.
Stars of the Morning. Dallas: C. C. Cockrell Co., 1957.

In addition, Harris published two short stories, one each in *Good House-keeping* (May 1935) and in *Nature Magazine* (November 1942).

Lee McNair
Angelo State University

Merton L. Harris (-   )
novel

The Golden Mirage. New York: Fleming H. Revell, 1925.

Paula Ellis
Joe Kollmyer
Angelo State University

Samuel Bertram Harrison (-   )
novels

Yonder Lies Jericho. New York: Appleton, 1933.
The White King. Garden City, New York: Doubleday, 1950. London: Redman, 1952.
Madrigal. Los Angeles: Nash, 1969. Rpt. New York: Avon, 1972.

Charlene Herrera
Angelo State University

Edith Aileen Heal (1903-   )
novels, short stories, juvenile nonfiction

Into Everywhere: A Play for the Mind's Eye. Boston: n. p., 1927.
Robin Hood. Chicago: Rand McNally, 1928.

The Topaz Seal: A Mystery Romance of the Jamestown Colony. River
    Forest, Illinois: Laidlaw Brothers, 1928.
How the World Began. Chicago: Rockwell, 1930.
Siegfried. Chicago: Rockwell, 1930.
Hound of Culain. Chicago: Rockwell, 1931.
World of Insects. Chicago: Rockwell, 1931.
Mr. Pink and the House on the Roof. New York: Julian Messner, 1941.
Send No Money. New York: Abrams, 1942.
Dogie Boy. Chicago: Albert Whitman, 1944.
The Very Sun. New York: Crown, 1944.
The Golden Bowl. New York: Lothrop, 1947.
Teen-Age Manual. New York: Simon & Schuster, 1948.
First Book of America. New York: Franklin Watts, 1952.
Tim Trains His Terrier. Chicago: Whitman, 1952.
The Shadow Boxers. New York: Scribner, 1956.
I Wanted to Write a Poem. New York: Beacon, 1958.
The Young Executive's Wife. New York: Dodd, 1958.
Fashion As A Career. New York: Julian Messner, 1961.
What Happened to Jenny. New York: Atheneum, 1962.
Visual Thinking in Advertising. New York: Holt, Rinehart & Winston, 1963.

Heal published short stories in *Vogue* (1961) and in *Literary Review* (1965).

Works about Edith Heal
Ghent, Dorothy Van. "Forms of Fiction and the Duties of Conscience," *Yale
    Review,* 46 (Autumn 1956), 158-60.

> Bobbie Endicott
> Angelo State University

Shelby Hearon (1931-   )
novels, nonfiction

Armadillo in the Grass. New York: Curtis, 1972.
The Second Dune. New York: Knopf, 1973.

In addition, Hearon published nonfiction in *Texas Monthly.*

> Monte D. Fite
> North Texas State University

Alice Corbin Henderson (1881-1949)
poetry, nonfiction, juveniles

Linnet Songs. Chicago: Wind-Tryst Press, 1898.
Adam's Dream and Two Other Miracle Plays for Children. New York: Scribner's, 1909.
Andersen's Best Fairy Tales. Chicago, New York: Rand McNally, 1911.
The Spinning Woman of the Sky. Chicago: Ralph Fletcher Seymour, 1912.
Red Earth. Chicago: Ralph Fletcher Seymour, 1920. Rpt. 1921.
The Turquoise Trail, An Anthology of New Mexico Poetry. Ed. Alice Corbin Henderson. Boston and New York: Houghton Mifflin, 1928.
The Sun Turns West. Santa Fe: Writers' Editions, 1933.
A Child's Bouquet (music by Mary Morley). Santa Fe: Writers' Editions, 1935.
Brothers of Light, the Penitentes of the Southwest. New York: Harcourt, Brace, 1937.
The New Poetry, An Anthology (ed. with Harriet Monroe). New York: Macmillan, 1917, 1923, 1932.

In addition, Henderson published hundreds of essays, poems, and reviews in most of the major literary journals in America.

Works about Alice Corbin Henderson
Bynner, Witter and Oliver La Farge, eds. "Alice Corbin: An Appreciation," *New Mexico Quarterly Review,* 19 (Spring 1949), 33-79. Contains ten essays by well-known literary figures.
Monroe, Harriet. *A Poet's Life.* New York: Macmillan, 1938.
Pearce, T. M. *Alice Corbin Henderson.* Austin: Steck-Vaughn, 1969.

T. M. Pearce
University of New Mexico

Archibald Henderson (1916-   )
poetry

Omphale's Wheel, and Other Poems. Francestown, New Hampshire: Golden Quill Press, 1966.
Mehy in His Carriage. (Poems by Archibald Henderson, Judson Crews, and others). Ed. Robert Loyd Williams. Austin, Texas: Summit Press, 1968.

The Puzzled Picture. Houston: Pierre St. Le Macs Press, 1971.

In addition, Henderson has several uncollected poems and critical articles in various journals.

J. F. Kobler
North Texas State University

O. Henry [see William Sidney Porter]

James Leo Herlihy (1927-   )
novels, plays

Blue Denim (a play with William A. Noble). New York: Random House, 1958.
The Sleep of Baby Filbertson, and Other Stories. New York: Dutton, 1959.
All Fall Down (novel). New York: Dutton, 1960.
Midnight Cowboy (novel). New York: Simon and Schuster, 1965.
A Story That Ends With a Scream, and Eight Others. New York: Simon and Schuster, 1967.
Stop, You're Killing Me; Three Short Plays. New York: Simon and Schuster, 1970.
The Season of the Witch (novel). New York: Simon and Schuster, 1971.

In addition, Herlihy has shorter fiction and plays in *Paris Review, Esquire,* and *Mademoiselle.*

Works about James Leo Herlihy
Serebnick, J. "New Creative Writers," *Library Journal,* 85 (June 1, 1960), 2201.

Judy Richardson
Arlington Public Library

Virginia D. Hersch (1896-   )
novels, short stories

Bird of God: The Romance of El Greco. New York: Harper & Brilliam, 1930.

Woman Under Glass: St. Teresa of Avila. New York: Harper & Brilliam, 1930.
Storm Beach. Boston: Houghton Mifflin, 1933.
Seven Cities of Gold. New York: Duell, Sloan & Pearce, 1946.
To Seize a Dream. New York: Crown, 1948.

Hersch published short stories in *Menorah* (April 1933) and in *Atlantic Monthly* (September 1932).

Works about Virginia D. Hersch
"Lee and Virginia Hersch," *Overland News,* November 1930, p. 342.
"Virginia Hersch," *Wilson Bulletin for Libraries,* 8 (December 1933), 202.

> Johnny Z. Garcia
> Cynthia Hays
> Karyn Stubblefield
> Angelo State University

Clyde Walton Hill (1883-1932)
poetry

Shining Trails. Dallas, Texas: Shining Trails Sales Co., 1926.

In addition, Hill has several uncollected poems in *Literary Digest* and in various anthologies.

> Carol Block
> Jan Cooney
> William F. Williams
> Angelo State University

Pendleton Hogan (1907-   )
novels, short stories

Bishop of Havanna. New York: Ives Washburn, 1933.
Dark Comes Early. New York: Ives Washburn, 1934.
Mortal Be Proud. New York: Ives Washburn, 1938.

In addition, Hogan published stories and essays in such journals as *Collier's, The New Yorker,* and *Virginia Quarterly Review.*

Works about Pendleton Hogan
Davis, Richard. *Tennessee Studies in Literature.* Knoxville: Univ. of Tennessee Press, 1965. Pp. 1-6, 165.

Rebecca Ross
J. B. White
Angelo State University

William Curry Holden (1896-   )
history

Alkali Trails. Dallas: Southwest Press, 1930.
Rollie Burns; or, An Account of the Ranching Industry on the South Plains. Dallas: Southwest Press, 1932.
The Spur Ranch: A Study of the Enclosed Ranch Phase of the Cattle Industry in Texas. Boston: The Christopher Publ. House, 1934.
Why Use Dobe? Lubbock: Texas Technological College, 1934.
Studies of the Yaqui Indians. Lubbock: Texas Technological College, 1936.
Hill of the Rooster. New York: Holt, 1956.
The Espuela Land and Cattle Company. Austin: Texas State Historical Association, 1970.

In addition, Holden published a number of essays on similar subjects in learned journals.

Glenn Christian
Steven Grafa
Greg Pittmon
Angelo State University

Claudia Jones Holland (1903-   )
novel

There's No Return. San Antonio: Naylor, 1937.

In addition, Holland has approximately fifty uncollected brief informal essays in *The Farmer Stockman* from 1935 through 1957. She also wrote a weekly column titled "Women Tell Me" for the *Temple Daily Telegram* from 1936 through 1941.

Kenneth W. Davis
Texas Tech University

Rupert Sargent Holland (1878-1952)
novels, short stories, history

Historic Boyhoods. New York: MaCrae Smith, 1909.
Historic Girlhoods. New York: MaCrae Smith, 1910.
Boy Scouts of Birch-bark Island. Philadelphia: Lippincott, 1911.
Historic Inventions. New York: MaCrae Smith, 1911.
Historic Poems and Ballads. New York: MaCrae Smith, 1912.
Historic Adventures. New York: MaCrae Smith, 1913.
Historic Heroes of Chivalry. New York: MaCrae Smith, 1914.
Boy Scouts of Snow-shoe Lodge. Philadelphia: Lippincott, 1915.
William Penn. New York: Macmillan, 1915.
Blackbeard's Island. Philadelphia: Lippincott, 1916.
Historic Events of Colonial Days. New York: MaCrae Smith, 1916.
Blue Heron's Feather. Philadelphia: Lippincott, 1917.
All 'round Our House. New York: MaCrae Smith, 1919.
Neptune's Son. New York: MaCrae Smith, 1919.
Man in the Moonlight. New York: MaCrae Smith, 1920.
Refugee Rock. New York: MaCrae Smith, 1920.
Panelled Room. New York: MaCrae Smith, 1921.
House of Delusion. New York: MaCrae Smith, 1922.
Knights of the Golden Spur. New York: Century, 1922.
Lafayette for Young Americans. New York: MaCrae Smith, 1922.
Peter Cotterell's Treasure. Philadelphia: Lippincott, 1922.
Crooked Lanes. New York: MaCrae Smith, 1923.
Mystery of the Opal. New York: MaCrae Smith, 1924.
Minot's Folly. New York: MaCrae Smith, 1925.
Pirates of the Delaware. Philadelphia: Lippincott, 1925.
Historic Ships. New York: MaCrae Smith, 1926.
Rider in the Green Mask. Philadelphia: Lippincott, 1926.
Historic Railroads. New York: MaCrae Smith, 1927.
Red Beard of Virginia. Philadelphia: Lippincott, 1927.
Historic Airships. New York: MaCrae Smith, 1928.
Splendid Buccaneer. New York: Lippincott, 1928.
Drake's Lad. New York: Century, 1929.
Pirate of the Gulf. New York: Lippincott, 1929.
Sons of Seven Cities. New York: MaCrae Smith, 1929.
Dauntless Company. New York: Century, 1930.

Mad Anthony. New York: Century, 1931.
Piper of Salem. New York: Penn, 1931.
Race for a Fortune. New York: Lippincott, 1931.
Yankee Ships in Pirate Waters. New York: MaCrae Smith, 1931.
Captain Tripp. New York: Century, 1932.
How to Murder Speaks. New York: Sears, 1932.
Rescue. New York: MaCrae Smith, 1932.
Big Bridge. New York: MaCrae Smith, 1934.
Chateau of the Swan. New York: Farrar, 1935.
Sea Scouts of Birch-Bark Island. New York: Lippincott, 1936.
Plays of American Colonies. New York: Harper, 1937.
Boy Who Lived on London Bridge. New York: MaCrae Smith, 1938.
Steadfast at Valley Forge. New York: MaCrae Smith, 1939.
Secret of Blennerhassett. New York: MaCrae Smith, 1941.
Wreaker's Reef. New York: MaCrae Smith, 1941.
Freedom's Flag. New York: MaCrae Smith, 1943.

In addition, Holland published stories and articles between 1907 and 1948 in *St. Nicholas, Scribner's Magazine, World's Work, Ladies Home Journal, Woman's Home Companion, Lippincott's Magazine, Atlantic,* and *New York Times Magazine.*

Works about Rupert Sargent Holland
"Holland, Rupert Sargent," *Wilson Library Bulletin,* New York: H. W. Wilson and Company, 1952.

Gayle Hamilton
Steve Van Hoozer
Angelo State University

W. Eugene Hollon (1913-   )
non-fiction

The Lost Pathfinder: Zebulon Montgomery Pike. Norman: Univ. of Oklahoma Press, 1949.
Beyond the Cross Timbers: The Travels of Randolph B. Marcy. Norman: Univ. of Oklahoma Press, 1955.
William Bollaert's Texas. Norman: Univ. of Oklahoma Press, 1956.

A History of the Stovall Museum of Science and History. Norman: Univ. of Oklahoma Press, 1956.
The Southwest: Old and New (with Ruth L. Butler). New York: Knopf, 1961.
The Great American Desert: Then and Now. New York: Oxford Univ. Press, 1966.
Frontier Violence. New York: Oxford Univ. Press, 1974.

In addition, W. Eugene Hollon has published numerous essays and reviews in learned journals and in *American Heritage* and *The New York Times.*

Diane M. Dodson
North Texas State University

Mary Austin Holley (1784-1846)
nonfiction

Texas. Observations, Historical, Geographical and Descriptive, in a series of Letters, Written during a Visit to Austin's Colony, with a view to permanent settlement in that country, in the Autumn of 1831. With an Appendix, Containing specific answers to certain questions relative to Colonization in Texas, issued sometime since by the London Geographical Society. Also, some notice of the recent political events in that quarter. Baltimore: Armstrong and Plaskitt, 1833. Rpt. as *Texas.* Austin: Steck, 1935.
Mary Austin Holley; the Texas Diary, 1835-1838. Austin: Univ. of Texas Press, 1965.

Works about Mary Austin Holley
Clapp, Rev. Theodore. "Obituary of Mary Austin Holley," *New Orleans Courier,* 3 August, 1846, n.p.
Hatcher, Mattie Austin. *Letters of an Early American traveller, Mary Austin Holley; her life and her works, 1784-1846.* Dallas: Southwest Press, 1933.
Lee, Rebecca Smith. *Mary Austin Holley, a Biography.* Austin: Univ. of Texas Press, 1962.

Haley Heidelberg
Gay Roycroft
Angelo State University

Byrd Hooper (1905-   )
novel

Beef for Beauregard. New York: Putnam, 1959.

John Goble
Angelo State University

William L. Hopson (c.1914-   )
[pseud. John Sims]
novels, nonfiction

Gun-Thrower. New York: Phoenix Press, 1940.
Cowpoke Justice. New York: Phoenix Press, 1941.
The Laughing Vaquero. New York: Phoenix Press, 1943.
Sunset Ranch. New York: Phoenix Press, 1943.
Silver Gulch. New York: Phoenix Press, 1944.
Hell's Horseman. New York: Phoenix Press, 1946.
Rambling Top Hand. New York: Phoenix Press, 1946.
The Gringo Bandit. New York: Phoenix Press, 1947.
Notched Guns. New York: Phoenix Press, 1947.
Straight from Boothill. New York: Phoenix Press, 1947.
Arizona Roundup. New York: Phoenix Press, 1948.
Man from Sonora. New York: Phoenix Press, 1948.
NP Puncher. New York: Phoenix Press, 1948.
Tombstone Stage. New York: Phoenix Press, 1948.
The Border Raider. New York: Phoenix Press, 1949.
Horse Thief Masquerade. New York: Phoenix Press, 1949.
The New Cowhand. New York: Phoenix Press, 1949.
Outlaw of Hidden Valley. New York: Phoenix Press, 1949.
Yucca City Outlaw. New York: Phoenix Press, 1949.
Desert Campfire. New York: Phoenix Press, 1951.
The Last Apaches. New York: Phoenix Press, 1951.
Wild West Show. New York: Phoenix Press, 1951.
Gunfighter's Pay. New York: Phoenix Press, 1952. Rpt. New York: Avalon, 1973.
Hangtree Range. New York: Phoenix Press, 1952.
High Saddle. New York: Phoenix Press, 1952.

Cow Thief Empire. New York: Phoenix Press, 1953.
Cry Viva. New York: Phoenix Press, 1953.
Apache Kill. New York: Phoenix Press, 1954.
Mexico After Dark (with Lois O'Connor). New York: Macfadden-Bartell, 1964.
A Gunman Rode North. New York: Phoenix Press, 1954.
Trouble Rides Tall. New York: Fawcett, 1955.
The Guns of MacCameron. New York: Phoenix Press, 1959.
Six Shooter from Socorro. New York: Phoenix Press, 1959.

Arvil A. Barnes, Jr.
Chuck McRae
Angelo State University

Paul Horgan (1903-   )
novels, nonfiction

Men of Arms. New York: McKay, 1931.
The Fault of Angels. New York: Harper, 1933.
No Quarter Given. New York: Harper, 1935.
Main Line West. New York: Harper, 1936.
From the Royal City of the Holy Faith of St. Francis of Assisi. Santa Fe: Rydal, 1936.
Return of the Weed (short stories). New York: Harper, 1936. (Published in England as *Lingering Walls;* London: Constable, 1936).
A Lamp on the Plains. New York: Harper, 1937.
The Habit of Empire. Santa Fe: Rydal, 1938.
Far from Cibola (short stories). New York: Harper, 1938.
Figures in a Landscape (short stories). New York: Harper, 1940.
Yours, A. Lincoln (drama). 1942.
A Tree on the Plains (An American opera with music by Ernst Bacon). New York: A. L. Williams, 1942.
The Common Heart. New York: Harper, 1942.
Look at America: The Southwest. Boston: Houghton Mifflin, 1947.
The Devil in the Desert. Toronto: Longmans, Green, 1952.
One Red Rose for Christmas. Toronto: Longmans, Green, 1952.
Great River: The Rio Grande in North American History. 2 vol. New York: Rinehart, 1954.

Humble Powers (Three novelettes). London: Macmillan, 1954; New York: Image Books, 1956.
The Saintmaker's Christmas Eve. New York: Farrar, Straus, 1955.
The Centuries of Santa Fe. New York: Dutton, 1956.
Give Me Possession. New York: Farrar, Straus, 1957.
Rome Eternal. New York: Farrar, Straus, 1959.
A Distant Trumpet. New York: Farrar, Straus, 1960.
Citizen of New Salem. New York: Macmillan, 1961. (Published in England as *Abraham Lincoln, Citizen of New Salem,* Macmillan, 1961.)
Martyrdom in Washington: A Play in Three Acts. New York: A. L. Williams, 1961.
Mountain Standard Time (Three volumes in one: *Main Line West, Far from Cibola, The Common Heart*). New York: Farrar, Straus, 1962.
Toby and the Nighttime. New York: Farrar, Straus, 1963.
Conquistadors in North American History. New York: Farrar, Straus, 1963. (Published in England as *Conquistadors in North America,* Macmillan, 1963.)
Things as They Are. New York: Farrar, Straus, 1964.
Songs After Lincoln. New York: Farrar, Straus, 1965.
Peter Hurd: A Portrait Sketch from Life. Austin: Univ. of Texas Press, 1965.
Memories of the Future. New York: Farrar, Straus, 1966.
The Peach Stone (stories). New York: Farrar, Straus, 1967.
Everything to Live For. New York: Farrar, Straus, 1968.
Whitewater. New York: Farrar, Straus, 1970.
Encounters With Stravinsky: A Personal Record. New York: Farrar, Straus, 1972.

In addition, Horgan has scores of stories and poems in such journals as *Poetry, Harper's, Atlantic,* and *Yale Review.*

Works about Paul Horgan
Carter, Alfred. "On the Fiction of Paul Horgan," *New Mexico Quarterly,* 7 (August 1937), 207-16.
Day, James. *Paul Horgan.* Austin: Steck-Vaughn, 1967.
Pilkington, William T. "Paul Horgan," *My Blood's Country.* Fort Worth: Texas Christian Univ. Press, 1973.

Judy Richardson
Arlington Public Library

Boyce House (1896-1961)
poetry, humor, journalism

Were You in Ranger? Dallas: Tardy Publ. Co., 1935.

Oil Boom; the Story of Spindletop, Burkburnett, Mexia, Smackover, Desdemona, and Ranger. Caldwell, Idaho: Caxton, 1941.

How I Took Hollywood by Storm. Dallas: Banks Upshaw, 1942.

I Give You Texas! 500 Jokes of the Lone Star State. San Antonio: Naylor, 1943; rpt. 1962.

Tall Talk from Texas. San Antonio: Naylor, 1944.

Texas, Proud and Loud. San Antonio: Naylor, 1945.

Cowtown Columnist. San Antonio: Naylor, 1946.

Cub Reporter, Being Mainly About Mr. Mooney and the Commercial Appeal. Dallas: Hightower Press, 1947.

Laugh Parade of States, Star-Spangled Wit and Humor. San Antonio: Naylor, 1948.

City of Flaming Adventure; The Chronicle of San Antonio. San Antonio: Naylor, 1949. Rev. and enl. ed. as *San Antonio; City of Flaming Adventure.* San Antonio: Naylor, 1968.

Roundup of Texas Humor; Being Three Books: I Give You Texas! Tall Talk from Texas and *Texas, Proud and Loud.* San Antonio: Naylor, 1949.

Texas Laughs and the Amazing Truth About Texas. San Antonio: Naylor, 1950.

Texas Rhythm, and Other Poems. Dallas: Dealey, n.d. Rpt. San Antonio: Naylor, 1950.

Roaring Ranger; the World's Biggest Boom. San Antonio: Naylor, 1951.

Oil Field Fury. San Antonio: Naylor, 1954.

You Can Always Tell a Texan (But You Can't Tell Him Very Much). San Antonio: Naylor, 1955; rev. ed., 1958.

Texas Treasure Chest. San Antonio: Naylor, 1956.

As I was Saying (humor). San Antonio: Naylor, 1957.

Friendly Feudin'; Alaska vs. Texas. San Antonio: Naylor, 1959.

A journalist, House wrote news articles, humorous features, and, for many years, a regular column. His articles and poems appeared in *Poet Lore, Southwest Review,* and *Saturday Evening Post.*

Works about Boyce House
Morris, D. "Texas Booster," *Life,* 17 March 1947, pp. 4+.

Edra Charlotte Bogle
North Texas State University

Margaret Bell Houston (c.1878-1966)
novels, poetry

Prairie Flowers (poems). Boston: Badger, 1907.
The Little Straw Wife. New York: H. K. Fly, 1914.
The Witch Man. Boston: Small, Maynard, 1922.
The Singing Heart and Other Poems. Nashville: Cokesbury, 1926.
Lanterns in the Dusk (poems). New York: Dodd, Mead, 1930.
Moon of Delight. New York: Dodd, Mead, 1931.
Hurdy-Gurdy. New York: Appleton, 1932.
Magic Valley. New York: Appleton, 1934.
Gypsy Weather. New York: Appleton, 1935.
Window in Heaven. New York: Appleton, 1937.
Pilgrim in Manhattan. New York: Appleton, 1940.
Dark of the Moon. New York: Arcadia House, 1943.
Bride's Island. New York: Crown, 1951.
Yonder. New York: Crown, 1955.
Cottonwoods Grow Tall. New York: Crown, 1958.
Collected Poems. San Antonio: Naylor, 1967.

Edra Charlotte Bogle
North Texas State University

Robert Ervin Howard (1906-1936)
novels, short stories, poetry

The Garden of Fear. Los Angeles: Crawford, 1945.
Skull Face and Others. Sauk City, Wisconsin: Arkham House, 1946.
Conan the Conqueror. New York: Gnome Press, 1950.
The Coming of Conan. New York: Gnome Press, 1953.
Conan the Barbarian. New York: Gnome Press, 1954.
Always Comes Evening; the Collected Poems of Robert E. Howard. Sauk City, Wisconsin: Arkham House, 1957.
King Conan. New York: Gnome Press, 1958.
The Dark Man and Others. Sauk City, Wisconsin: Arkham House, 1963.
The Gent from Bear Creek. West Kingston, Rhode Island: Donald M. Grant, 1965.
The Pride of Bear Creek. West Kingston, Rhode Island: Donald M. Grant, 1968.

Red Shadows. West Kingston, Rhode Island: Donald M. Grant, 1963.
Singers in the Shadows. West Kingston, Rhode Island: Donald M. Grant, 1970.

Most of Howard's works are available in paperback, primarily from Lancer Books. Many other uncollected stories appeared in magazines such as *Weird Tales, Oriental Stories, Action Stories,* and *Fight Stories.*

Works about Robert Ervin Howard
The Howard Collector. Ed. Glenn Lord. No. 1 (1964). Contains articles, bibliographies, and previously unpublished fragments of Howard's work.
de Camp, L. Sprague. "Skald in the Post Oaks," *Fantastic,* 20 (June 1971), 99-108.

H. W. Hall
Texas A&M University

Dorothy Belle Flanagan Hughes (1904-   )
novels, short stories, poetry, nonfiction

Dark Certainty (poems). [Dorothy Belle Flanagan]. New Haven: Yale Univ. Press, 1931.
Pueblo on the Mesa, The First Fifty Years at the University of New Mexico. Albuquerque: Univ. of New Mexico Press, 1939.
The Cross-Eyed Bear. New York: Duell, Sloan and Pearce, 1940.
This So Blue Marble. New York: Duell, Sloan and Pearce, 1940.
The Bamboo Blonde. New York: Duell, Sloan and Pearce, 1941.
The Fallen Sparrow. New York: Duell, Sloan and Pearce, 1942.
An Omnibus of Terror (Contains *The So Blue Marble, The Cross-Eyed Bear,* and *The Bamboo Blonde*). New York: Duell, Sloan and Pearce, 1942.
The Blackbirder. New York: Duell, Sloan and Pearce, 1943.
The Delicate Ape. New York: Duell, Sloan and Pearce, 1944.
Johnnie. New York: Duell, Sloan and Pearce, 1944.
Dread Journey. New York: Duell, Sloan and Pearce, 1945.
Ride the Pink Horse. New York: Duell, Sloan and Pearce, 1946. Rpt. New York: Dell, 1958.
In a Lonely Place. New York: Duell, Sloan and Pearce, 1947.
The Big Barbecue. New York: Random House, 1949.

The Candy Kid. New York: Duell, Sloan and Pearce, 1950. Serialized in *Collier's* (1950).
The Davidson Report, A Novel of Suspense. New York: Duell, Sloan and Pearce, 1952.
The Expendable Man. New York: Random House, 1963; rpt. London: Andre Deutsch, 1964.

In addition, Hughes published several short stories and a poem in *American Magazine, Saturday Evening Post,* and *Woman's Home Companion* and two articles on mystery writing to *Writer.*

Edra Charlotte Bogle
North Texas State University

William Humphrey (1924-   )
novels, short stories

The Last Husband and Other Stories. New York: William Morrow, 1953.
Home From the Hill. New York: Knopf, 1958.
The Ordways. New York: Knopf, 1965.
A Time and a Place (stories). New York: Knopf, 1968.
The Spawning Run. New York: Knopf, 1971.
Proud Flesh. New York: Knopf, 1973. Rpt. Popular Library, 1974.

Works about William Humphrey
Lee, James W. *William Humphrey.* Austin: Steck-Vaughn, 1967.

James W. Lee
North Texas State University

John Igo (1927-   )
poetry, translations, articles

God of Gardens. Cleveland: American Weave Press, 1962.
A Chamber Faust. Coral Gables: Wake-Brook House, 1964.
Igo on Poetry. San Antonio: Philippi, 1965.
Los Pastores: A Triple Tradition. San Antonio: San Antonio College Library, 1967.
The Tempted Monk: A Dance Poem. Torrance, California: Hors Commerce Press,1967.

No Harbor, Else. San Antonio: Et Cetera, 1972.
Golgotha. San Antonio: Et Cetera, 1973.
Day of Elegies. San Antonio: Et Cetera, 1974.

Zula Williams Vizard
San Antonio College

Marquis James (1891-1955)
novels, short stories, nonfiction

A History of the American Legion. New York: William Green, 1923.
The Raven: A Biography of Sam Houston. New York: Halcyon House, 1929.
Andrew Jackson: The Border Captain. New York: Bobbs-Merrill, 1933.
Andrew Jackson: Portrait of a President. New York: Grosset and Dunlap, 1937.
Mr. Garner of Texas. New York: Bobbs-Merrill, 1939.
Alfred I. DuPont, the Family Rebel. New York: Bobbs-Merrill, 1941.
Biography of a Business. New York: Bobbs-Merrill, 1942.
They Had Their Hour. New York: World, 1942.
The Cherokee Strip. New York: Viking, 1945.
The Metropolitan Life. New York: Viking, 1947.
The Texaco Story. New York: Harper, 1953.
Biography of a Bank (with Bessie Rowland James). New York: Harper, 1954.

In addition, James published a number of short stories in *New Yorker, North American Review,* and *Saturday Evening Post.*

Marilyn Neiman
Denton, Texas

William Roderick (Will) James (1892-1942)
novels, short stories

Smoky, the Cowhorse. New York: Scribner, 1926.
Cow Country. New York: Scribner, 1927.
Lone Cowboy (autobiography). New York: Scribner, 1930.

Big Enough. New York: World, 1931.
Cowboys North and South. New York: Scribner, 1931.
Drifting Cowboy. New York: Scribner, 1931.
Sun Up. New York: Scribner, 1931.
Uncle Bill. New York: Scribner, 1932.
All in the Day's Riding. New York: Scribner, 1933.
Home Ranch. New York: Scribner, 1935.
Scorpion: A Good Bad Horse. New York: Scribner, 1936.
Cowboy in the Making. New York: Scribner, 1937.
Flint Spears. New York: World, 1938.
Will James Cowboy Book. Ed. Alice Dalgliesh. New York: Scribner, 1938.
Horses I've Known. New York: World, 1940.
My First Horse. New York: Scribner, 1940.
American Cowboy. New York: Scribner, 1942.
Dark Horse. New York: Grosset and Dunlap, 1946.
Sand. New York: Grosset and Dunlap, 1946.
Three Mustangers. New York: World, 1946.
Book of Cowboy Stories. New York: Scribner, 1951.

In addition, James has approximately twenty-five uncollected short stories in such publications as *The Saturday Evening Post, Sunset,* and *Scribner's Magazine.*

Works about Will James
Amaral, Anthony. "A Dedication to the Memory of Will James, 1892-1942," *Arizona and the West,* 10 (Autumn 1968), 206-10.
————. *Will James: The Gilt Edged Cowboy.* Los Angeles: Westernlore, 1967.
Montague, D. "Bucked and Battered to Fame," *American Magazine,* 111 (May 1931), 78.

Marilyn Neiman
Denton, Texas

Bradley Carter Jefferson (1894-   )
novel

Fair Havens. New York: Macmillan, 1948.

Diane Dodson
North Texas State University

Dan Jenkins (1929-   )
novels, nonfiction

Sports Illustrated's the Best 18 Golf Holes in America. New York: Dela-
  corte, 1966.
The Dogged Victim of Inexorable Fate. New York: Little-Brown, 1970.
Saturday's America. Boston: Little, Brown, 1970.
  1973.
Dead Solid Perfect. New York: Atheneum, 1974.

In addition, Jenkins, a senior editor of *Sports Illustrated,* has numerous
articles in that magazine.

Monte D. Fite
North Texas State University

Richard Johnson (-   )
[pseud. Sikes Johnson]
novel

The Hope of Refuge. Boston: Little, Brown, 1956.

John Lee
Denton Texas

Siddie Joe Johnson (1905-   )
poetry, nonfiction, juveniles

Agarita Berry. Dallas: The Southwest Press, 1933.
Debby. New York: Longmans, Green, 1940.
New Town in Texas. New York: Longmans, Green, 1942.
Texas: The Land of the Tejas. New York: Random House, 1943.
Gallant the Hour. Dallas: Kaleidograph, 1945.
Cathy. New York: Longmans, Green, 1945.
Susan's Year. New York: Longmans, Green. 1948.
Joe and Andy Want a Boat. Austin: Steck, 1951.
Rabbit Fires. Boerne, Texas: Highland Press, 1951.
Month of Christmases. New York: Longmans, Green, 1952.
Cat Hotel. New York: Longmans, Green, 1955.
About the Engineer of a Train. Chicago: Melmont Publishers, 1959.
Feather in My Hand. New York: Atheneum, 1967.

In addition, Johnson also wrote essays on children's literature and the following books of juvenile literature: *About the Engineer of a Train* (1959); *Cat Hotel* (1955); *Cathy* (1945); *Debby* (1940); *Joe and Andy Want a Boat* (1951); *Month of Christmases* (1952); *New Town in Texas* (1942); *Rabbit Fires* (1951); *Susan's Year* (1948); and *Texas: The Land of the Tejas* (1943).

Laura B. Kennelly
North Texas State University

Margaret Olive Jordan (-   )
poetry, nonfiction

God's Smiles and a Look into His Face. New York: F. T. Neely, 1901.
Ways of the World. New York: F. T. Neely, 1902.
Scattered Rose Leaves (poems). San Antonio: T. Kunzman, 1903.
Wine for the Soul, in Prose and Verse. Los Angeles: J. F. Rowny, 1919.

Diane Dodson
North Texas State University

Donald Joseph (1898-   )
novels, nonfiction

October's Child. New York: Frederick A. Stokes, 1929; London: Mathews, 1932.
Long Bondage. New York: Stokes, 1930; London: Mathews, 1932.
Four Blind Mice. New York: Stokes, 1932.
Straw in the South Wind. New York: Macmillan, 1946.
Ten Million Acres: The Life of William Benjamin Munson (with Mary Tonkin Smith). Denison, Texas: privately printed; New York: William E. Rudge's Sons, 1946.
Lud Daingerfield: Life of a Young Man. San Antonio: Naylor, 1956.

Works about Donald Joseph
Warfel, Harry R. *American Novelists of Today.* New York: American Book Co., 1951. P. 233.

A. C. Dodson
Dallas, Texas

Sherry Kafka (1937-   )
novels

Hannah Jackson. New York: Morrow, 1966.
Big Enough. New York: Putnam, 1970.
I Need a Friend. New York: Putnam, 1971.

Albert J. Griffith
Our Lady of the Lake College
San Antonio, Texas

Kenneth Carlyle Kaufman (1887-   )
poetry

Level Land: A Book of Western Verse. Dallas: Kaleidograph Press, 1935.

In addition, Kaufman is an editor and translator.

Works about Kenneth Kaufman
Marable, Mary Hays and Elaine Boylan. *A Handbook of Oklahoma Writers.*
Norman: Univ. of Oklahoma Press, 1939. pp. 65-66.

Steven Lee
Denton, Texas

Karon Kehoe (-   )
novel

City in the Sun. New York: Dodd, Mead, 1946.

William Aloysius Keleher (1886-1972)
history, biography

Maxwell Land Grant: A New Mexico Item. Santa Fe: Rydal Press, 1942.
The Fabulous Frontier: Twelve New Mexico Items. Santa Fe: Rydal Press, 1945.
Turmoil in New Mexico, 1846-1868. Santa Fe: Rydal Press, 1951.

Violence in Lincoln County, 1869-1881: A New Mexico Item. Albuquerque: Univ. of New Mexico Press, 1957.
Memoirs: A New Mexico Item, 1892-1969. Santa Fe: Rydal Press, 1970.

Eleanor Dodson
Dallas, Texas

Walter E. Kidd (1911-   )
[pseud. Conrad Pendleton]
poetry, nonfiction

Slow Fire of Time [Conrad Pendleton]. Denver: Swallow, 1956.
Time Turns West [Conrad Pendleton]. Cleveland: American Weave Press, 1961.
Adventures of Frelf. Racine: Western, 1963.
West: Manhattan to Oregon [Conrad Pendleton]. Denver: Swallow, 1966.
American Winners of the Nobel Literary Prize (coeditor with Warren G. French). Norman: Univ. of Oklahoma Press, 1968.
British Winners of the Nobel Literary Prize. Norman: Univ. of Oklahoma Press, 1973.
Oregon Odyssey of Wheels. Ft. Smith, Arkansas: South & West Press, 1973.

In addition, Kidd published numerous poems in *Catholic World, New Republic, Poetry, Prairie Schooner, University of Kansas City Review, Voices,* and other periodicals.

James W. Lee
North Texas State University

Larry L. King (1929-   )
novel, short stories, nonfiction

The One-Eyed Man. New York: New American Library, 1966.
And Other Dirty Stories. New York: World, 1968.
Confessions of a White Racist. New York: Viking, 1971.
The Old Man and Lesser Mortals. New York: Viking, 1974.

In addition, King published approximately thirty articles and reviews in publications such as *Esquire, Harper's, Holiday, Nation, New Republic, Saturday Evening Post,* and others. He is also contributing editor to the *Texas Observer,* where much of his journalistic writing has appeared.

Works about Larry L. King
Pilkington, William T. "The Dirt Farmer and the Cowboy: Notes on Two Texas Essayists," *RE: Arts and Letters,* 3 (Fall 1969), 42-54. Rpt. in *My Blood's Country.* Ft. Worth: Texas Christian Univ. Press, 1973.

Don R. Swadley
University of Texas at Arlington

Henry Herbert Knibbs (1874-1945)
novels, short stories, poetry

Lost Farm Camp. Boston: Houghton Mifflin, 1912.

Stephen March's Way. Boston: Houghton Mifflin, 1913.

Overland Red: A Romance of the Moonstone Cañon Trail. Boston: Houghton Mifflin, 1914.

Songs of the Outlands; Ballads of the Hoboes and Other Verse. Boston: Houghton Mifflin, 1914.

Sundown Slim. Boston: Houghton Mifflin, 1915.

Riders of the Stars: A Book of Western Verse. Boston: Houghton Mifflin, 1916.

Tang of Life. Boston: Houghton Mifflin, 1918.

Ridin' Kid from Powder River. Boston: Houghton Mifflin, 1919.

Songs of the Trail. Boston: Houghton Mifflin, 1920.

Partners of Chance. Boston: Houghton Mifflin, 1921.

Saddle Songs and Other Verse. Boston: Houghton Mifflin, 1922.

Wild Horses. Boston: Houghton Mifflin, 1924.

Temescal. Boston: Houghton Mifflin, 1925.

Sungazers. Boston: Houghton Mifflin, 1926.

Sunny Mateel. Boston: Houghton Mifflin, 1927.

Songs of the Lost Frontier. Boston: Houghton Mifflin, 1930.

Gentlemen, Hush! (with Turbesé Lummis). Boston: Houghton Mifflin, 1933.

Tonto Kid. Boston: Houghton Mifflin, 1936.

In addition, Knibbs published a score of poems and short stories in such periodicals as *American Magazine, Literary Digest,* and *Saturday Evening Post.*

Owen J. Reamer
University of Southwestern
Louisiana

J. Armoy Knox (1858-1901)
humor

Sketches from "Texas Siftings" (with Alexander Edwin Sweet). New York: Texas Siftings Publishing Company, 1882.
On a Mexican Mustang through Texas from the Gulf to the Rio Grande (with Alexander Edwin Sweet). Hartford: S. S. Scranton, 1883.
Three Dozen Good Stories from Texas Siftings (with Alexander Edwin Sweet). New York: J. S. Ogilvie and Company, 1887.

Works about J. Armoy Knox
Miles, Elton. *Southwest Humorists.* Austin: Steck-Vaughn, 1969. pp. 15-23.

Ernest Speck
Sul Ross State University

Laura Krey (1890-   )
[pseud. Mary Everett]
novels, short stories

And Tell of Time. Boston: Houghton Mifflin, 1938.
On the Long Tide. Boston: Houghton Mifflin, 1940.

In addition, Krey published ten or twelve short stories—some under the pseudonym of Mary Everett—in such periodicals as *Sewanee Review, Southwest Review,* and *Good Housekeeping.*

Jeff H. Campbell
Midwestern University

Fania Kruger (1893-   )
poetry, nonfiction

Cossack Laughter (poems). Dallas: Kaleidograph Press, 1937.
The Tenth Jew (poems). Dallas: Kaleidograph Press, 1949.
Selected Poems. Austin: American Universal Artforms, 1973.

Kruger also published numerous poems in *Contemporary Poetry, Prairie Schooner, Southwest Review, Texas Quarterly, Voices,* and other periodicals.

Works about Fania Kruger
Barnes, Florence Elberta. *Texas Writers of Today*. Dallas: Taylor, 1935.
p. 270.
Major, Mabel, et al. *Southwest Heritage: A Literary History with Bibliography*. Albuquerque: Univ. of New Mexico Press, 1948. Rev. ed., 1972.

James W. Lee
North Texas State University

Joseph Wood Krutch (1893-1970)
nonfiction

Comedy and Conscience After the Restoration. New York: Columbia Univ. Press, 1924; 2nd ed., 1961.
Edgar Allan Poe: A Study in Genius. New York: Knopf, 1926.
The Modern Temper: A Study and a Confession. New York: Harcourt, Brace, 1929.
Five Masters: A Study in the Mutation of the Novel. New York: J. Cape & H. Smith, 1930.
Experience and Art: Some Aspects of the Esthetics of Literature. New York: H. Smith and R. Haas, 1932.
Was Europe a Success? New York: Farrar & Rinehart, 1934.
The American Drama Since 1918: An Informal History. New York: Random House, 1939; rev. New York: Braziller, 1957.
Samuel Johnson: A Biography. New York: Holt, 1944.
Henry David Thoreau. New York: William Sloane, 1948.
The Twelve Seasons: A Perpetual Calendar for the Country. New York: William Sloane, 1949; 2nd ed. 1961.
The Desert Year. New York: William Sloane, 1952.
The Best of Two Worlds. New York: William Sloane, 1953.
"Modernism" in Modern Drama: A Definition and an Estimate. Ithaca, New York: Cornell Univ. Press, 1953.
The Measure of Man: On Freedom, Human Values, Survival, and the Modern Temper. Indianapolis: Bobbs-Merrill, 1954.
The Voice of the Desert; A Naturalist's Interpretation. New York: William Sloane, 1955.

The Great Chain of Life. Boston: Houghton-Mifflin, 1957.
Grand Canyon: Today and All Its Yesterdays. New York: William Sloane, 1958.
Human Nature and the Human Condition. New York: Random House, 1959.
The Forgotten Peninsula: A Naturalist in Baja California. New York: William Sloane, 1961.
The World of Animals: A Treasury of Lore, Legend, and Literature by Great Writers and Naturalists from the Fifth Century B.C. to the Present. New York: Simon & Schuster, 1961.
Modern Literature and the Image of Man. San Francisco: Industrial Indemnity Co., 1962.
More Lives than One. New York: William Sloane, 1962.
If You Don't Mind My Saying So . . .: Essays on Man and Nature. New York: William Sloane, 1964.
Herbal. New York: Putnam, 1965.
And Even If You Do: Essays on Man, Manners & Machines. New York: William Morrow, 1967.
Baja California and the Geography of Hope. San Francisco: Sierra Club, 1967.

In addition, Krutch contributed over seventy essays to anthologies and to such publications as *Nation, Natural History, Saturday Review,* and *Theatre Arts.*

Works about Joseph Wood Krutch
Brown, John Mason. *Still Seeing More Things.* New York: McGraw-Hill, 1950.
Davis, R. B. and J. L. Livesay, eds. *Studies in Honor of John C. Hodges and Alwin Thaler.* Knoxville: Univ. of Tennessee Press, 1961.
Glicksberg, Charles I. "Joseph Wood Krutch: Critic of Despair," *Sewanee Review,* 44 (Jan.-March 1936), 77-93.
Green, Joseph G. "Joseph Wood Krutch: The Critic of Tragedy Looks at Comedy," *Quarterly Journal of Speech,* 54 (Feb. 1968), 37-46.
Harris, Mark. *The Case for Tragedy: Being a Challenge to Those Who Deny the Possibility of a Tragic Spirit in the Modern World.* New York: Putnam's, 1932.
Thompson, Alan Reynolds. "Farewell to Achilles," *Bookman,* 70 (Jan. 1930), 465-71.

Waggoner, Hyatt Howe, "The Modern Temper," *South Atlantic Quarterly,* 27 (July 1938), 282-90.

Mallory Chamberlin, Jr.
North Texas State University

Mabel McKinney Weir Keykendall (-   )
poetry

Divert the Interim (with Grace Ross). Dallas: Kaleidograph, 1949.
Poetry Out Where the West Begins (comp. with Grace Ross). Dallas: Kaleidograph, 1949.

In addition, Kuykendall published many individual poems in magazines of verse and regional anthologies. She and Grace Ross served for several years as co-editors of *Quicksilver,* a quarterly devoted to the publication of poetry.

James W. Lee
North Texas State University

Horatio Oliver Ladd (1839-1932)
history, religion

A Memorial of John S. C. Abbott, D.D. Boston: A. Williams, 1878.
Fighting in Mexico. New York: Dodd, Mead, 1883.
History of the War with Mexico. New York: Dodd, Mead, 1883.
Ramona Days, March 1887-October 1888. 2 vols. Santa Fe: Indian Department of the Univ. of New Mexico, 1887-1888.
The Story of New Mexico. Boston: D. Lothrop, 1891.
Chunda, A Story of the Navajos. New York: Eaton and Mains; Cincinnati: Jennings and Graham, 1906.
The Trend of a Scientific Thought Away from Religious Beliefs. Boston: R. G. Badger, 1909.
The Origin and History of Grace Church, Jamaica, New York. New York: Shakespeare Press, 1914.
A Genealogical Record of Samuel Greenleaf Ladd and Caroline de Olivier Vinal Ladd, His Wife. Boston: Alpine Press, 1927.

Ladd also published a sermon in *Outlook* (26 May 1894). His unpublished writings are housed in the University of New Mexico Library.

Works about Horatio Oliver Ladd

Bohme, Frederick George. "Horatio Oliver Ladd: A New England Conscience for New Mexico," *Bibliography of Church History,* 26 (June 1957), 143-55.

Lois A. Marchino
University of New Mexico

Oliver La Farge (1901-1963)
novels, short stories, nonfiction

Laughing Boy. Boston: Houghton Mifflin, 1929; Rpt. 1963.

Sparks Fly Upward. Boston: Houghton Mifflin, 1931.

Tribes and Temples (with Frans Blom). 2 vols. New Orleans: Tulane Univ. Press, 1931.

The Year Bearer's People (with Doughlas Byers). New Orleans: Tulane Univ. Press, 1931.

Long Pennant. Boston: Houghton Mifflin, 1933.

All the Young Men. Boston: Houghton Mifflin, 1935.

The Enemy Gods. Boston: Houghton Mifflin, 1937.

As Long as the Grass Shall Grow. New York: Alliance Book Corp., 1940.

The Changing Indian. Ed. Oliver La Farge. Norman: Univ. of Oklahoma Press, 1942.

The Copper Pot. Boston: Houghton Mifflin, 1942.

War Below Zero (with Corey Ford and Bernt Balchen). Boston: Houghton Mifflin, 1944.

Raw Material. Boston: Houghton Mifflin, 1945.

Santa Eulalia. Chicago: Univ. of Chicago Publications in Anthropology, 1947.

The Eagle in the Egg. Boston: Houghton Mifflin, 1949.

Cochise of Arizona. The American Heritage Series. New York: Aladdin Books, 1953.

The Mother Ditch. Boston: Houghton Mifflin, 1954.

Behind the Mountains. Boston: Houghton Mifflin, 1956.

A Pictorial History of the American Indian. New York: Crown, 1956.

A Pause in the Desert. Boston: Houghton Mifflin, 1957.

Santa Fe: The Autobiography of a Southwestern Town (with Arthur N. Morgan). Norman: Univ. of Oklahoma Press, 1959.

The Door in the Wall. Boston: Houghton Mifflin, 1965.
The Man with the Calabash Pipe. Ed. Winfield Townley Scott. Boston: Houghton Mifflin, 1966.

Works about Oliver La Farge

Allen, Charles. "The Fiction of Oliver La Farge," *Arizona Quarterly,* 1 (Winter 1945), 74-81.
Bunker, Robert. "Oliver La Farge: In Search of Self," *New Mexico Quarterly Review,* 20 (Summer 1951), 221-24.
Gillis, Everett A. *Oliver La Farge.* Austin: Steck-Vaughn, 1967.
Pearce, T. M. *Oliver La Farge.* New York: Twayne, 1972.

Everett A. Gillis
Texas Tech University

Mirabeau Buonaparte Lamar (1798-1859)
poetry, nonfiction

Life and Poems of Mirabeau B. Lamar. Ed. Philip Graham. Chapel Hill: Univ. of North Carolina Press, 1938.
Papers of Mirabeau B. Lamar. Ed. Charles A. Gulick, Jr. and Katherine Elliot. 6 vols. Austin: A. C. Baldwin, 1928; rpt. 7 vols. Austin: Pemberton Press, 1968.
Verse Memorials. New York: Privately printed, 1857.

Works about Lamar

Barker, Eugene C. "Mirabeau Buonaparte Lamar," *University of Texas Record,* 5 (August 1903), 146-60.
Christian, Asa K. *Mirabeau Buonaparte Lamar.* Austin: Von Boeckmann-Jones, 1922.
Dictionary of American Biography. 10 (1933), 553-54.
Dixon, Sam H. *The Poets and Poetry of Texas.* Austin: Sam H. Dixon Company, 1885.
Eagleton, Davis F. *Writers of Texas.* New York: Broadway Publishing Company, 1913.
Gambrell, Herbert P. *Mirabeau Buonaparte Lamar, Troubadour and Crusader.* Dallas: Southwest Press, 1934.
Graham, Philip. "Mirabeau Lamar's First Trip to Texas," *Southwest Review,* 21 (1936), 369-80.

Terrell, Alex W. "Mirabeau B. Lamar," *Library of Southern Literature,*
7:2987-3002.

Lois Williams Parker
Lamar University

Dama Langley [see Dama Margaret Smith]

Edwin Moultrie Lanham (1904-   )
novels, short stories

Sailors Don't Care. New York: J. Cape and H. Smith, 1930.
The Wind Blew West. New York and Toronto: Longmans, Green, 1935.
Banner at Daybreak. New York and Toronto: Longmans, Green, 1937.
Another Ophelia. New York and Toronto: Longmans, Green, 1938.
The Stricklands. Boston: Little, Brown, 1939.
Thunder in the Earth. New York: Harcourt Brace, 1941.
Slug it Slay. New York: Harcourt Brace, 1946.
Politics is Murder. New York: Harcourt Brace, 1947.
One Murder Too Many. New York: Harcourt Brace, 1952.
Death of a Corinthian. New York: Harcourt Brace, 1953.
The Iron Maiden. New York: Harcourt Brace, 1954.
Death in the Wind. New York: Harcourt Brace, 1955.
Murder on My Street. London: Victor Gollanez; Toronto: Longmans, 1958.
Double Jeopardy. New York: Harcourt Brace, 1959.
Six Black Camels. New York: Harcourt Brace, 1961.
No Hiding Place. New York: Harcourt, Brace and World, 1962.
Passage to Danger. New York: Harcourt, Brace and World, 1962.
Monkey on a Chain. New York: Harcourt Brace, 1963.
Speak Not Evil. New York: Farrar, Straus and Giroux, 1965.
The Paste-Pot Man. New York: Farrar, Straus and Giroux, 1967.
The Clock at Eight Sixteen. Garden City, New York: Doubleday, 1970.
Translations of Lanham's novels have been published in Germany, France,
South America, and elsewhere. Lanham has published over fifty short stories
and serialized novels in such magazines as *Collier's, McCalls, Redbook, Sat-
urday Evening Post,* and *Woman's Home Companion.*

Lois A. Marchino
University of New Mexico

Mary Lasswell (1905-   )
novels, humor, nonfiction

Suds in Your Eye. Boston: Houghton-Mifflin, 1942.
High Time. Boston: Houghton-Mifflin, 1944.
Mrs. Rasmussen's Book of One-Arm Cookery. Boston: Houghton-Mifflin, 1946.
Bread for the Living (novel). Boston: Houghton-Mifflin, 1948.
One on the House. Boston: Houghton-Mifflin, 1949.
Tooner Schooner. Boston: Houghton-Mifflin, 1951.
Wait for the Wagon. Boston: Houghton-Mifflin, 1951.
I'll Take Texas (travel). Boston: Houghton-Mifflin, 1958.
Rags and Hope: The Recollections of Val C. Giles, Four Years with Hood's Brigade, Fourth Texas Infantry, 1861-1865. Compiled and edited by Mary Lasswell. New York: Coward-McCann, 1961.
Let's Go for Broke. Boston: Houghton-Mifflin, 1962.
Tio Pepe. Boston: Houghton-Mifflin, 1963.

Works about Mary Lasswell
Miles, Elton. *Southwest Humorists*. Austin: Steck-Vaughn, 1969. pp. 39-41.

Elton Miles
Sul Ross State University

John H. Latham (1917-   )
novels

Lonesome Longhorn. Philadelphia: Westminster, 1951.
Brasada Badmen. New York: Ace Books, 1957.
Johnny Six-Gun. New York: Ace Books, 1957.
Meskin Hound. New York: Putnam, 1958.
The Long Fuse. New York: Ace Books, 1959.

Kenneth Johnson
University of New Mexico

Jonreed Lauritzen (1902-   )
novels, short stories

Arrows into the Sun. New York: A. A. Knopf, 1943.
Song Before Sunrise. Garden City: Doubleday, 1948.

The Rose and the Flame. Garden City: Doubleday, 1951.
The Ordeal of the Young Hunter. Boston: Little, Brown, 1954.
Suzanne. Garden City: Hanover, 1955.
The Young Mustangers. Boston: Little, Brown, 1957.
Treasure of the High Country. Boston: Little, Brown, 1959.
The Glitter-Eyed Wouser. Boston: Little, Brown, 1960.
The Legend of Billy Bluesage. Boston: Little, Brown, 1961.
The Everlasting Fire. Garden City: Doubleday, 1962.
Captain Sutter's Gold. Garden City: Doubleday, 1964.
The Cross and the Sword. Garden City: Doubleday, 1965.
Colonel Anza's Impossible Journey. New York: Putnam, 1966.
Blood, Banners and Wild Boars: Tales of Early Spain. Boston: Little, Brown, 1967.
Battle of San Pascual. New York: Putnam, 1968.

Kenneth Johnson
University of New Mexico

Tom Lea (1907-   )
novels, short stories, nonfiction

A Grizzly from the Coral Sea. El Paso: Carl Hertzog, 1944.
Peleliu Landing. El Paso: Carl Hertzog, 1945.
Calendar of Twelve Travelers Through the Pass of the North. El Paso: Carl Hertzog, 1946.
Bullfight Manual for Spectators. El Paso: Carl Hertzog, 1947.
The Brave Bulls. Boston: Little, Brown, 1949.
The Wonderful Country. Boston: Little, Brown, 1952.
The King Ranch. Boston: Little, Brown, 1957.
The Primal Yoke. Boston: Little, Brown, 1960.
The Hands of Cantu. Boston: Little, Brown, 1964.
Western Beef Cattle: A Series of Eleven Paintings. Austin: Encino Press, 1967.
A Picture Gallery. Paintings and Drawings with Text by the Artist. Boston: Little, Brown, 1968.
Tom Lea: A Selection of Paintings and Drawings from the Nineteen-sixties. San Antonio: Encino Press, 1969.
In the Crucible of the Sun. Kingsville, Texas: King Ranch, 1974.

In addition, Lea published seven articles between 1943 and 1957 in *Atlantic Monthly* and *Life*.

Works about Tom Lea

Ashby, Nannette M. "Hertzog Books," *Western Review*, 1 (Fall 1964), 28-36.

Braddy, Haldeen. "Artist Illustrators of the Southwest: H. D. Bugbee, Tom Lea and Jose Cisneros," *Western Review*, 1 (Fall 1964), 37-41.

West, John O. *Tom Lea: Artist in Two Mediums*. Austin: Steck-Vaughn, 1967.

John O. West
University of Texas at El Paso

Rebecca Smith Lee (1894-   )
short stories, poetry, biography, nonfiction

The Southwest in Literature (Ed. with Mabel Major). New York: Macmillan, 1929.

Texas Poems (with J. O. Beaty and L. W. Payne). Dallas: Dealey and Lowe, 1936.

Duval's The Adventures of Bigfoot Wallace (Ed. with Mabel Major). Dallas: Tardy, 1936.

Duval's Early Times in Texas (Ed. with Mabel Major). Dallas: Tardy, 1936.

My Foot's in the Stirrup (Ed. with Mabel Major). Dallas: Dealey and Lowe, 1937.

Glad Days (Ed. with Mamie H. Whittaker). Oklahoma City: The Economy Co., 1937.

Southwest Heritage: A Literary History with Bibliography (with Mabel Major and T. M. Pearce). Albuquerque: Univ. of New Mexico Press, 1938; Rev. 1948, 1972.

Mary Austin Holley: A Biography. Austin: Univ. of Texas Press, 1962.

In addition, Lee contributed numerous biographical and historical articles to such journals as *Filson Club Historical Quarterly, Modern Philology,* and *Publications of the Texas Folk-Lore Society;* several of her poems and short stories are in *Southwest Review*.

Bessie M. Pearce
San Antonio College

James Lehrer (1934-   )
novel

Viva Max! New York: Meredith Press, 1966.

Sylvia McGowan
Tarleton State College

Alan Le May (1899-   )
novels, short stories

Painted Ponies. New York: George H. Doran, 1927.
Old Father of Waters. Garden City, N. Y.: Doubleday, Doran, 1928.
Pelican Coast. Garden City, N. Y.: Doubleday, Doran, 1929.
Bug Eye. New York: Farrar & Rinehart, 1931.
Gunsight Trail. New York: Farrar & Rinehart, 1931.
Winter Range. New York: Farrar & Rinehart, 1932.
Cattle Kingdom. New York: Farrar & Rinehart, 1933.
Thunder in the Dust. New York: Farrar & Rinehart, 1934.
The Smoky Years. New York: Farrar & Rinehart, 1935.
Deepwater Island. New York: Farrar & Rinehart, 1936.
Empire for a Lady. New York: Farrar & Rinehart, 1937.
Useless Cowboy. New York: Farrar & Rinehart, 1943.
The Searchers. New York: Harper & Brothers, 1954.
The Unforgiven. New York: Harper & Brothers, 1957.
By Dim and Flaring Lamps. New York: Harper & Brothers, 1962.

In addition, Le May published some twenty short stories in *Collier's* magazine.

Robert Deamer
University of New Mexico

Warren Leslie (1927-   )
novels, nonfiction

The Best Thing that Ever Happened. New York: McGraw-Hill, 1952.
Love or Whatever It Is. New York: McGraw-Hill, 1960.

Dallas, Public and Private (nonfiction). New York: Grossman, 1964.
Under the Skin. New York: Geis, 1971.

Billie Phillips
San Antonio College

Alfred Henry Lewis (1858-1914)
novels, humor

Wolfville. New York: Frederick A. Stokes, 1897; rpt. 1923.
Sandburrs. New York: Frederick A. Stokes, 1900.
Wolfville Days. New York: Frederick A. Stokes, 1902.
Wolfville Nights. New York: Frederick A. Stokes, 1902; rpt. New York: Grossett & Dunlap, 1905.
The Sunset Trail (novel). New York: A. S. Barnes, 1905; A. L. Burt, 1906.
The Throwback: A Romance of the Southwest (novel). New York: A. L. Burt, 1906; New York: The Outing Publishing Co., 1906.
Wolfville Folks. New York: The Macauley Co., 1908; New York: Appleton, 1908.
Faro Nell and Her Friends: Wolfville Stories. New York: G. W. Dillingham Co., 1913.

Works about Alfred Henry Lewis
Filler, Louis. "Introduction" (and commentary), in *Old Wolfville: Chapters from the Fiction of Alfred Henry Lewis*. Yellow Springs, Ohio: The Antioch Press, 1968.
Humphries, Rolfe. "Introduction," in *Wolfville Yarns of Alfred Henry Lewis*. Ed. Rolfe and John Humphries. Kent State Univ. Press, 1968.

Elton Miles
Sul Ross State University

Judd Mortimer Lewis (1867-1945)
poetry

Sing the South. Houston: J. V. Dealy, 1905.
Lilts o' Love. Houston: J. V. Dealy, 1906.
Toddle-Town Trails. Houston: J. V. Dealy, 1914.

In addition, Lewis has approximately twenty-five uncollected poems in such magazines as *Ladies Home Journal, Good Housekeeping,* and *Collier's.*

Robert Deamer
University of New Mexico

Therese Lindsey (1870-1957)
poetry

Blue Norther, Texas Poems. New York: H. Vinal, 1925.
The Cardinal Flower. Dallas: Kaleidograph, 1934.
A Tale of the Galveston Storm. Dallas: Kaleidograph, 1936.

Work about Therese Lindsey
Montgomery, Vaida Stewart. *A Century with Texas Poets and Poetry.* Dallas: Kaleidograph Press, 1934.

Arthur M. Sampley
North Texas State University

John Avery Lomax (1872-1948)
nonfiction

Cowboy Songs and Other Frontier Ballads. New York: Macmillan, 1910. Revised (with Alan Lomax), 1938.
The Book of Texas (with Harry Yandell Benedict). Garden City, N. Y.: Doubleday, Page, 1916.
Songs of the Cattle Trail and Cow Camp. New York: Duell, Sloan and Pearce, 1919; rpt. 1947.
American Ballads and Folk Songs. New York: Macmillan, 1934; rpt. 1942.
Negro Folk Songs as Sung by Leadbelly (with Alan Lomax). New York: Macmillan, 1936.
Our Singing Country. New York: Macmillan, 1941.
Adventures of a Ballad Hunter. New York: Macmillan, 1947.
Folk Song: U. S. A. New York: Duell, Sloan and Pearce, 1947; rpt. as *Best Loved American Folk Songs.* New York: Grosset and Dunlap, 1954.
Leadbelly: A Collection of World Famous Songs (ed. with Alan Lomax). New York: Folkways, 1959.
Will Hogg, Texan. Austin: Univ. of Texas Press, 1956.

In addition, Lomax published articles in such journals as *Atlantic, Saturday Review of Literature, Nation,* and *Publications of the Texas Folklore Society.*

Maurine LeBeau
Patricia Felts
North Texas State University

Haniel Long (1888-1956)
poetry, nonfiction

The Soldier's Progress. Pittsburgh: Carnegie Institute of Technology, 1918.

Poems. New York: Moffat, Yard & Co., 1920.

Notes for a New Mythology. Chicago: The Bookfellows, 1926; rpt. with *Pittsburgh Memoranda.* New York and London: Johnson Reprint Corp., 1971.

Atlantides. Santa Fe: Writers' Editions, 1933.

Pittsburgh Memoranda. Santa Fe: Writers' Editions, 1935; rpt. with *Notes for a New Mythology.* New York and London: Johnson Reprint Corp., 1971.

Interlinear to Cabeza de Vaca: His Relation of the Journey from Florida to the Pacific, 1528-1536. Santa Fe: Writers' Editions, 1936; rpt. West Newbury, Mass.: Frontier Press, 1969.

Walt Whitman and the Springs of Courage. Santa Fe: Writers' Editions, 1938.

Malinche (Doña Marina). Santa Fe: Writers' Editions, 1939.

Piñon Country. New York: Duell, Sloan & Pearce, 1941.

Children, Students, and a Few Adults. Santa Fe: The Santa Fe Press, 1942.

French Soldier Home from Being a War Prisoner. Santa Fe: Santa Fe Press, 1942.

The Power Within Us: Cabeza de Vaca's Relation of His Journey from Florida to the Pacific. New York: Duell, Sloan & Pearce, 1944.

The Grist Mill. Santa Fe: Rydal Press, 1945.

A Letter to St. Augustine after Re-reading His Confessions. New York: Duell, Sloan & Pearce, 1950.

Spring Returns. New York: Pantheon Books, 1958.

Die Kraft in Uns. Translated by Hildegard von Barloewen. Hamburg: Grillen-Presse, 1963.

If He Can Make Her So. Pittsburgh: Frontier Press, 1968.

Long had approximately twenty uncollected poems in such journals as *Southwest Review, New Mexico Quarterly, Nation,* and *Poetry;* and some fifteen essays in such journals as *Southwest Review, Space, Forum,* and *New Mexico Quarterly.*

Works about Haniel Long

Burlingame, Robert. "More Than We Had Thought: Cabeza de Vaca, Haniel Long, and Our Day." *Southwest Review,* 53 (Autumn 1968), 360-74.

McCord, Howard. "The Existence of Augustine: A Counterplaint with Haniel Long," *whe're/1,* (Spring 1966), 39-43.

Major, Mabel; Smith, Rebecca W. and T. M. Pearce. *Southwest Heritage: A Literary History with Bibliography.* Albuquerque: Univ. of New Mexico Press, 1938. Pp. 128-9, 149.

Powell, Lawrence Clark. "A Friendship with Haniel Long," *Wilson Library Bulletin* (September 1957).

—————. "Through the Burning Glass," Reprinted in *A Passion for Books,* World Publishing Co., 1958. Pp. 238-49.

—————. "Southwest Classics Reread: Haniel Long and Interlinear to Cabeza de Vaca," *Westways,* 63 (April 1971), 26-9, 78-9.

Raines, Lester. *Writers and Writings of New Mexico.* Las Vegas, N. M.: New Mexico Normal University, 1935, p. 88.

—————. *More New Mexico Writers and Writings.* Las Vegas, N. M.: New Mexico Normal University, 1935, p. 49.

Sergeant, Elizabeth Shepley, "The Santa Fe Group," *Saturday Review of Literature,* 11 (December 8, 1934), p. 352.

Sylvester, Harry. "Cabeza de Vaca and Haniel Long," *The Commonweal,* 37 (February 12, 1943), 414-17.

Margaret Hartley
Southern Methodist University

Charles F. Lummis (1859-1928)
novels, poetry, nonfiction

Birch Bark Poems. Chillicothe, Ohio: by the author, 1883.

A New Mexico David and Other Stories and Sketches of the Southwest. New York: Scribner, 1891.

A Tramp Across the Continent. New York: Scribner, 1892.

Some Strange Corners of Our Country: The Wonderland of the Southwest.
New York: Century, 1892. Rev. and expanded as *Mesa, Canyon and
Pueblo: Our Wonderland of the Southwest.* New York: Century, 1925.
The Land of Poco Tiempo. New York: Scribner, 1893. Rpt. Albuquerque:
Univ. of New Mexico Press, 1966.
Spanish Pioneers. Chicago: A. C. McClurg, 1893. Rev. under the title *The
Spanish Pioneers and the California Missions.* Chicago: A. C. McClurg,
1929; rpt. Denver: Rio Grande Press, 1963.
The Man Who Married the Moon and Other Pueblo Indian Folk-Stories.
New York: Century, 1894. Published in 1910 as *Pueblo Indian Folk-
Stories.*
The Gold Fish of Gran Cimú (novel). Boston: Lamson, Wolffe, 1895.
The Enchanted Burro and Other Stories. Chicago: Way & Williams, 1897;
New York: Doubleday & McClure, 1897.
The King of the Broncos and Other Stories of New Mexico. New York:
Scribner, 1897.
The Awakening of a Nation: Mexico of Today. New York and London:
Harper, 1898.
My Friend Will. Chicago: A. C. McClurg, 1911.
The Memorial of Fray Alonso de Benavides, 1630. (Ed. with F. W. Hodge
and translated by Mrs. Edward E. Ayer). Chicago: R. R. Donnelly &
Sons, 1916; rpt. Albuquerque: Horn and Wallace, 1965.
Spanish Songs of Old California. Los Angeles: by the author, 1923.
A Bronco Pegasus (poetry). Boston and New York: Houghton Mifflin, 1928.
Flowers of Our Lost Romance (essays). Boston: Houghton Mifflin, 1929.
General Crook and the Apache Wars (Ed. by Turbese Lummis Fiske and
foreword by Dudley Gordon). Flagstaff, Arizona: Northland Press, 1966.
Bullying the Moqui (Articles from *Out West* edited and with introduction
by Robert Easton and MacKenzie Brown). Prescott, Arizona: Prescott
College Press, 1968.

In the late 1880s and early 1890s Lummis was a frequent contributor to
such magazines as *Harper's, Century,* and *Scribner's.*

Works about Charles F. Lummis
Bingham, Edwin R. *Charles F. Lummis: Editor of the Southwest.* San Ma-
rino: Huntington Library, 1955.
Earle, Henry Edmond. "An Old-Time Collector: Reminiscences of Charles
F. Lummis," *California Folklore Quarterly,* 1 (1942), 179-83.

Espinosa, J. Manuel. "Some Charles F. Lummis Letters, 1897-1903," *New Mexico Quarterly Review,* 11 (1941), 147-56.

Field, Ben. "Charles Fletcher Lummis," *Overland Monthly,* N.S. 89 (1929), 197-203, 223.

Gordon, Dudley C. "Charles Fletcher Lummis, Cultural Pioneer of the Southwest," *Arizona and the West,* 1 (1959), 305-16.

————. "Southwest Crusader," *New Mexico Magazine,* 19 (Oct. 1941), 10-11, 31-32.

Hewett, Edgar L. "Lummis the Inimitable," *Papers of the School of American Research,* Archaeological Institute of America, Santa Fe, New Mexico (1944). Pp. 1-13.

James, George Wharton. "Charles F. Lummis: A Unique Literary Personage of Modern America," *National Magazine,* 27 (Oct. 1912), 129-43.

Newmark, Marco R. "Charles Fletcher Lummis," *Historical Society of Southern California Quarterly,* 32, no. 1 (March 1950), 45-60.

Salzman, Maurice. "Charles Fletcher Lummis: The Very Last of the Mohicans," *Progressive Arizona and the Great Southwest,* 8 (Jan. 1929), 14-18.

Simmons, Marc. *Two Southwesterners: Charles Lummis and Amado Chaves* (letters). Cerrillos, N. M.: San Marcos Press, 1968.

Watkins, Frances E. "Charles F. Lummis and the Sequoya League," *Historical Society of Southern California Quarterly,* 26, no. 2 and 3 (June-Sept. 1944), 99-114.

Robert E. Fleming
University of New Mexico

Mabel Major (1894-1974)
nonfiction

The Southwest in Literature (ed. with Rebecca W. Smith). New York: Macmillan, 1929.

Duval's Big-Foot Wallace (Ed. with Rebecca W. Smith). Dallas: Tardy, 1936. Reissued in paperback. Lincoln: Univ. of Nebraska Press, 1966.

Duval's Early Times in Texas (ed. with Rebecca W. Smith). Dallas: Tardy, 1936.

My Foot's in the Stirrup (with William Bartlett and Rebecca W. Smith). Dallas: Dealey and Lowe, 1937.

Southwest Heritage, A Literary History (with Rebecca W. Smith and T. M.

Pearce). Albuquerque: Univ. of New Mexico Press, 1938; rev. and enlarged, 1948; rev. and enlarged with T. M. Pearce, 1972.

Signature of the Sun: Southwest Verse 1900-1950 (ed. with T. M. Pearce). Albuquerque: Univ. of New Mexico Press, 1950.

In addition, Major published some twelve essays and reviews in such journals as *Southwest Review, New Mexico Quarterly,* and Publications of the Texas Folklore Society.

Joyce Roach
Keller, Texas

Alida Sims Malkus (1895-   )
novels, nonfiction

Racquel of the Ranch Country. New York: Harcourt, Brace, 1927.
The Dragon Fly of Zuni. New York: Harcourt, Brace, 1928.
Caravans to Santa Fe. New York: Harper, 1928.
Timber Line. New York: Harcourt, Brace, 1929.
Pirates' Port. New York: Harper, 1929.
The Dark Star of Itza. New York: Harcourt, Brace, 1930.
The Spindle Imp. New York: Harcourt, Brace, 1931.
A Fifth for the King. New York: Harper, 1931.
Stone Knife Boy. New York: Harcourt, Brace, 1933.
Eastward Sweeps the Current. Philadelphia: Winston, 1937.
The Silver Llama. Philadelphia: Winston, 1939.
The Citadel of a Hundred Stairways. Philadelphia: Winston, 1941.
Along the Inca Highway. Boston: Heath, 1941.
Constancia Lona. Garden City, New York: Doubleday, 1947.
Chula of the Magic Islands. Akron, Ohio: Saalfield Publishing Co., 1948.
The Colt of Destiny. New York: Winston, 1950.
Little Giant of the North. New York: Winston, 1952.
The Story of Louis Pasteur. New York: Grosset & Dunlap, 1952.
The Story of Good Queen Bess. New York: Grosset & Dunlap, 1953.
We Were There at the Battle of Gettysburg. New York: Grosset & Dunlap, 1955.
The Sea and Its Rivers. Garden City, New York: Doubleday, 1956.
Sidi, Boy of the Desert. New York: Winston, 1956.
Young Inca Prince. New York: Knopf, 1957.

The Story of Winston Churchill. New York: Grosset & Dunlap, 1957.
Blue Water Boundary. New York: Hastings House, 1960.
Outpost of Peril. New York: John Day, 1961.
Exploring the Sky and Sea: Auguste and Jacques Piccard. Chicago: Kingston House, 1961.
Through the Wall. New York: Grosset & Dunlap, 1962.
There Really Was a Hiawatha. New York: Grosset & Dunlap, 1963.
Animals of the High Andes, New York: Abelard-Schuman, 1966.
The Strange Voyagers. Philadelphia: Chilton, 1966.
The Beloved Island. Philadelphia: Chilton, 1967.
The Story of Jacqueline Kennedy. New York: Grosset & Dunlap, 1967.
The Amazon. New York: McGraw-Hill, 1970.

In addition Malkus has essays and stories in *Horn Book, Travel, American Mercury,* and *St. Nicholas.*

Arlene E. Kyle
North Texas State University

Emma Louise Mally (1908-   )
novels, poetry

Dedications (poems). New York: Coward-McCann, 1937.
The Mocking Bird Is Singing (novel). New York: Holt, 1944.
A Treasury of Animal Stories. Selected and with a foreword by E. Louise Mally. New York: The Citadel Press, 1946.
The Tides of Dawn (novel). New York: William Sloan, 1949.
Abigail (novel). New York: Appleton-Century-Crofts, 1956.
Immortal Lieder. Translated by Emma Louise Mally. Berlin: Seven Seas Publishing, 1962.

Kay F. Reinartz
University of New Mexico

Alice Marriott (1910-   )
short stories, anthropology

The Ten Grandmothers. Norman: Univ. of Oklahoma Press, 1945.
Winter-Telling Stories. New York: William Sloane, 1947.
Indians on Horseback. New York: Crowell, 1948.

Maria: The Potter of San Ildefonso. Norman: Univ. of Oklahoma Press, 1948.
The Valley Below. Norman: Univ. of Oklahoma Press, 1949.
Indians of the Four Corners. New York: Crowell, 1952.
Greener Fields. New York: Crowell, 1953.
Hell on Horses and Women. Norman: Univ. of Oklahoma Press, 1953.
Sequoyah: Leader of the Cherokees. New York: Random House, 1956.
The Black Stone Knife. New York: Crowell, 1957.
These Are the People. Santa Fe: Laboratory of Anthropology, 1958.
The First Comers. New York: David McKay, 1960.
Oklahoma: The Story of Its Past and Present (with Edwin C. McReynolds and Estelle Faulconer). Norman: Univ. of Oklahoma Press, 1963.
Saynday's People. Lincoln: Univ. of Nebraska Press, 1963.
Indian Annie: Kiowa Captive. New York: David McKay, 1965.
Kiowa Years. New York: Macmillan Co., 1967.
American Indian Mythology (with Carol K. Rachlin). New York: Crowell, 1968.
American Epic: The Story of the American Indian (with Carol K. Rachlin). New York: Putnam's, 1969.
Peyote (with Carol K. Rachlin). New York: Crowell, 1971.
Oklahoma, The Forty-Sixth Star (with Carol K. Rachlin). Garden City: Doubleday, 1973.
Anthropological Study of the Osage Indians (with Carol K. Rachlin). New York: Clearwater Pub. Co., 1973.

In addition, Marriott published over thirty articles between 1942 and 1974 in such publications as *American Mercury, Harper's, Mademoiselle, New Yorker, Oklahoma Today,* and *Southwest Review.* All of the most recent longer works have been brought out in paperback editions.

Works about Alice Marriott
Kobler, Turner S. *Alice Mariott.* Austin: Steck-Vaughn, 1969.
————. "Alice Marriott: The Anthropologist as Artist," *Southwestern American Literature,* 1 (May 1971), 72-79.
Taylor, Helene Scherff, "Alice Marriott," *Wilson Library Bulletin,* 24 (February 1950), 396. Rpt. in *Current Biography Yearbook,* 1951.

Turner S. Kobler
Texas Woman's University

Ellis Martin [see Marah Ellis Ryan]

John Joseph Mathews (1895-   )
novels, nonfiction

Wah'Kon-Tah. Norman: Univ. of Oklahoma Press, 1932; rpt. 1968.
Sundown. New York: Longmans, Green, 1934.
. . . Talking to the Moon. Chicago: Univ. of Chicago Press, 1945.
Life and Death of an Oilman. Norman: Univ. of Oklahoma Press, 1951.
The Osages, Children of the Middle Waters. Norman: Univ. of Oklahoma Press, 1961.

Arlene E. Kyle
North Texas State University

Hamilton (Tex) Maule (1915-   )
juveniles, journalism

Jeremy Todd. New York: Random House, 1959.
Footsteps. New York: Random House, 1960.
Rookie, New York: David McKay, 1961.
The Quarterback. New York: David McKay, 1962.
The Shortstop. New York: David McKay, 1962.
Beatty of the Yankees. New York: David McKay, 1963.
The Championship Quarterback. New York: David McKay, 1963.
Last Out. New York: David McKay, 1964.
Linebacker. New York: David McKay, 1965.
Running Back. New York: David McKay, 1966.
Cornerback. New York: David McKay, 1967.
Players. New York: New American Library, 1967.
Receiver. New York: David McKay, 1968.
Running Scared: The Odyssey of a Heart Attack Victim's Jogging Back to Health. New York: Saturday Review Press, 1972.
Bart Starr: Professional Quarterback. New York: Watts, 1973.

Maule, a senior editor of *Sports Illustrated,* has published hundreds of uncollected articles on sports.

Sam G. Terry
Appalachian State University

Tom Mayer (1943-   )
short stories

Bubble Gum and Kipling. New York: Viking, 1964.
The Weary Falcon. Boston: Houghton Mifflin, 1971.
Climb for the Evening Star. Boston: Houghton-Mifflin, 1974.

In addition, Mayer has published several uncollected stories in such journals as *Saturday Evening Post, Atlantic, The New Yorker,* and *New Mexico Quarterly.*

Works about Tom Mayer
Davis, Kenneth W. "The Themes of Initiation in the Works of Larry Mc-Murtry and Tom Mayer," *The Arlington Quarterly,* 2 (Winter 1969-70), 29-43.

William T. Pilkington
Tarleton State College

Horace McCoy (1897-1955)
novels, screenplays, journalism

They Shoot Horses Don't They. New York: Simon and Schuster, 1935.
No Pockets in a Shroud. London: Barker, 1937.
I Should Have Stayed Home. New York: Knopf, 1938.
Kiss Tomorrow Goodbye. New York: Random House, 1948.
Scapel. New York: Appleton, 1952.

Diane Dodson
North Texas State University

Bonner McMillion (1921-   )
novels

The Lot of Her Neighbors. Philadelphia: Lippincott, 1953.
The Long Ride Home. Philadelphia: Lippincott, 1955.
So Long at the Fair. Garden City, New York: Doubleday, 1964.

Arlene E. Kyle
North Texas State University

Larry McMurtry (1936-   )
novels, short stories, nonfiction

Horseman, Pass By. New York: Harper and Row, 1961.
Leaving Cheyenne. New York: Harper and Row, 1963.
The Last Picture Show. New York: Dial, 1966.
In a Narrow Grave: Essays on Texas. Austin: Encino Press, 1968.
Moving On. New York: Simon and Schuster, 1970.
All My Friends Are Going to Be Strangers. New York: Simon and Schuster, 1972.

McMurtry has also published articles in *Gentlemen's Quarterly, Holiday,* and *Texas Quarterly.*

Works about Larry McMurtry
Davis, Kenneth W. "The Themes of Initiation in the Works of Larry McMurtry and Tom Mayer," *The Arlington Quarterly,* 2 (Winter 1969-70), 29-43.
Landess, Thomas H. *Larry McMurtry.* Austin: Steck-Vaughn, 1969.
Peavy, Charles D. "A Larry McMurtry Bibliography," *Western American Literature,* 3 (Fall 1968), 235-48.
Pilkington, William T. "The Dirt Farmer and the Cowboy: Notes on Two Texas Essayists," *RE: Arts and Letters,* 3 (Fall 1969), 42-54; rpt. in *My Blood's Country.* Ft. Worth: Texas Christian Univ. Press, 1973.

Thomas Landess
University of Dallas

Thomas Hill McNeal (1893-1959)
poetry, criticism

Motley's the Only Wear. Dallas: Kaleidograph, 1942.
Three Lyric Poets. (Alice Moser, Tom H. McNeal, Bryan Herbert Reece). Ed. with introduction by Alan Swallow. Prairie City, Illinois: The Press of J. A. Decker, 1942.

In addition, McNeal had poetry published in *Poetry, The Dallas Morning News, Texas Review, Kaleidograph, Literary Lantern,* and other publications; his criticism appeared in *Shakespeare Quarterly, Modern Language Quarterly,* and *Huntington Library Quarterly.*

Gretchen H. Colehour
Knox City, Texas

Florence Crannell Means (1891-   )
novels, nonfiction

Rafael and Consuelo (with Harriet Fullen). New York: Friendship Press, 1929.
Children of the Great Spirit (with Frances Riggs). New York: Friendship Press, 1932.
Ranch and Ring. Boston: Houghton Mifflin, 1932.
A Bowlful of Stars. Boston: Houghton Mifflin, 1934.
Rainbow Bridge. New York: Friendship Press, 1934.
Penny for Luck. Boston: Houghton Mifflin, 1935.
Tangled Waters. Boston: Houghton Mifflin, 1936.
The Singing Wood. Boston: Houghton Mifflin, 1937.
Shuttered Windows. Boston: Houghton Mifflin, 1938.
Adella Mary in Old Mexico. Boston: Houghton Mifflin, 1939.
Across the Fruited Plains. New York: Friendship Press, 1940.
At the End of Nowhere. Boston: Houghton Mifflin, 1940.
Children of the Promise. New York: Friendship Press, 1941.
Whispering Girl. Boston: Houghton Mifflin, 1941.
Shadow Over Wide Ruin. Boston: Houghton Mifflin, 1942.
Teresita of the Valley. Boston: Houghton Mifflin, 1943.
Peter of the Mesa. New York: Friendship Press, 1944.
The Moved-Outers. Boston: Houghton Mifflin, 1945.
Great Day in the Morning. Boston: Houghton Mifflin, 1946.
Assorted Sisters. Boston: Houghton Mifflin, 1947.
House Under the Hill. Boston: Houghton Mifflin, 1949.
The Silver Fleece (with Carl Means). New York: Winston, 1950.
Hetty of the Grande Deluxe. Boston: Houghton Mifflin, 1951.
Carver's George. Boston: Houghton Mifflin, 1952.
Alicia. Boston: Houghton Mifflin, 1953.
The Rains Will Come. Boston: Houghton Mifflin, 1954.
Sagebrush Surgeon. New York: Friendship Press, 1956.
Knock at the Door, Emmy. Boston: Houghton Mifflin, 1956.
Reach for a Star. Boston: Houghton Mifflin, 1958.
Borrowed Brother. Boston: Houghton Mifflin, 1958.
Emmy and the Blue Door. Boston: Houghton Mifflin, 1959.
Sunlight on the Hopi Mesas. New York: Judson, 1960.
But I Am Sara. Boston: Houghton Mifflin, 1961.

That Girl Andy. Boston: Houghton Mifflin, 1962.
Tolliver. Boston: Houghton Mifflin, 1963.
Us Maltbys. Boston: Houghton Mifflin, 1966.

In addition, Means has uncollected stories and essays in *Horn Book, Saint Nicholas,* and *Writer.*

Works about Florence Crannell Means

Andrews, S. "Florence Crannell Means" (bibliography), *Horn Book,* (22 January 1946), pp. 15-30.
Moore, A. C. "Three Owl's Notebook," *Horn Book,* (21 March 1945), pp. 108-09.
"Mosaic," *Horn Book,* (16 January 1940), pp. 34-40.
Pease, H. "Without Evasion: Some Reflections After Reading Mrs. Means' *The Moved-Outers," Horn Book,* (21 January 1945), pp. 8-17.
Rider, Elizabeth. *The Story Behind Modern Books.* New York: Dodd, Mead, 1949.

Kay F. Reinartz
University of New Mexico

Rudolph Mellard (1903-   )
novels, short stories

Sun and Sage: A Cowboy's Word Picture of the Southwest. San Antonio: Naylor, 1939.
Hills and Horizons: Pioneering the Big Bend Country of Texas. San Antonio: Naylor, 1940.
South by Southwest. Denver: Swallow, 1960.
Across the Crevass. Denver: Swallow, 1966.
The Chihuahua Trail–1868. Salado, Texas: The Anson Jones Press, 1973.
The Track of the Albatross. Salado, Texas: The Anson Jones Press, 1974.

In addition, Mellard published four short stories in *Naylor's Epic Century* during 1939 and one in collaboration with Evelyn Mellard in *Sul Ross State College Bulletin* (September 1964).

Vetal Flores
Angelo State University

Michael F. Mewshaw (1943-   )
novels, short stories

Man in Motion. New York: Random House, 1970.
Waking Slow. New York: Random House, 1972.
The Toll. New York: Random House, 1974.

Phillip L. Fry
University of Texas at Austin

George Milburn (1906-1966)
novels, short stories, nonfiction

The Hobo's Hornbook. New York: Ives Washburn, 1930.
Oklahoma Town. New York: Harcourt, Brace, 1931.
No More Trumpets and Other Stories. New York: Harcourt, Brace, 1933.
Catalogue. New York: Harcourt, Brace, 1936.
Flannigan's Folly. New York: Whittlesey House, McGraw-Hill, 1947.

In addition, fourteen stories by Milburn appeared in *American Mercury, Collier's, Esquire, Southern Review,* and *Vanity Fair* between 1929 and 1945; fourteen articles by Milburn appeared in *American Literature, American Mercury, American Speech, Harper's, Nation,* and *Yale Review* between 1930 and 1953. For more complete bibliographical listing, see below.

Works about George Milburn
Turner, Steven. *George Milburn.* Austin: Steck-Vaughn, 1970.

Steven Turner
University of Texas at Arlington

Helen Topping Miller (1884-1960)
novels, juveniles

Sharon. Philadelphia: Penn, 1931.
Blue Marigolds. Philadelphia: Penn, 1934.
Flaming Gahagans. Philadelphia: Penn, 1935.
Splendor of Eagles. Philadelphia: Penn, 1935.

Hawk in the Wind. New York: Appleton, 1938.
Whispering River. New York: Appleton, 1938.
Let Me Die Tuesday. New York: Grossett, 1939.
Next to My Heart. New York: Appleton, 1939.
Dark Lightning. New York: Appleton, 1940.
Love Comes Last. Philadelphia: Triangle Books, 1941.
Never Another Moon. New York: Grossett, 1943.
When a Girl's in Love. New York: Grossett, 1943.
Who Is This Girl? New York: Grossett, 1943.
Desperate Angel. New York: Grossett, 1944.
Last Lover. New York: Appleton, 1944.
Mulberry Bush. Philadelphia: Blakiston, 1944.
Sheridan Road. New York: Grossett, 1944.
Storm Over Eden. New York: Grossett, 1944.
Dark Sails: A Tale of Old St. Simon's. Indianapolis: Bobbs-Merrill, 1945.
Wicked Sister. New York: Appleton, 1945.
Hunter's Moon. New York: Appleton, 1946.
Shod with Flame. Indianapolis: Bobbs-Merrill, 1946.
Spotlight. New York: Appleton, 1946.
Candle in the Morning. New York: Appleton, 1947.
Sound of Chariots: The Novel of John Sevier and the State of Franklin.
    Indianapolis: Bobbs-Merrill, 1947.
Flame Vine. New York: Appleton, 1948.
Song After Midnight. Philadelphia: Triangle Books, 1948.
Trumpet in the City. Indianapolis: Bobbs-Merrill, 1948.
Born Strangers: A Chronicle of Two Families. Indianapolis: Bobbs-Merrill,
    1949.
Mirage. New York: Appleton, 1949.
Horns of Capricorn. New York: Appleton, 1950.
We Have Given Our Hearts Away. Indianapolis: Bobbs-Merrill, 1950.
Cameo. Indianapolis: Bobbs-Merrill, 1951.
Proud Young Thing. New York: Appleton, 1952.
Witch Water. Indianapolis: Bobbs-Merrill, 1952.
Hollow Silver. New York: Appleton, 1953.
No Tears for Christmas. Toronto: Longman's, 1954.
Rebellion Road, by Helen Topping Miller and J. D. Topping. Indianapolis:
    Bobbs-Merrill, 1954.
April to Remember. New York: Appleton, 1955.

Her Christmas at the Hermitage: A Tale About Rachel and Andrew Jackson. Toronto: Longman's, 1955.
Slow Dies the Thunder. Indianapolis: Bobbs-Merrill, 1955.
Christmas for Tad: A Story of Mary and Abraham Lincoln. Toronto: Longman's, 1956.
Sing One Song. New York: Appleton, 1956.
Nightshade. Indianapolis: Bobbs-Merrill, 1961.

Robert G. Cowser
University of Tennessee at Martin

Lewis Bennett Miller (1861-1933)
novels, short stories

A Crooked Trail. Pittsburgh, Pennsylvania: Axtell Rush Publishing Co., 1908. Originally serialized in *National Stockman and Farmer.*
The White River Raft. Boston: D. Estes & Co., 1910.
Saddles and Lariats. Boston: D. Estes & Co., 1912.
Fort Blocker Boys. Cincinnati: The Standard Publishing Co., 1917.

Miller published numerous serials and contributed short stories of adventure to *Youth's Companion, Century, Harper's, St. Nicholas, National Stockman and Farmer.*

George C. Greenlee
North Texas State University

Vassar Miller (1924-   )
poetry

Adam's Footprint. New Orleans: New Orleans Poetry Journal, 1956.
Wage War on Silence. Middletown, Connecticut: Wesleyan Univ. Press, 1960.
My Bones Being Wiser. Middletown, Connecticut: Wesleyan Univ. Press, 1963.
Onions and Roses. Middletown, Connecticut: Wesleyan Univ. Press, 1968.
If I Could Sleep Deeply Enough. New York: Liveright, 1974.

J. F. Kobler
North Texas State University

Francis Mitchell (c.1907-   )
novels

Dry Lake Ranch, New York: Arcadia House, 1957.
Brand of the Renegade. New York: Arcadia House, 1958.
Ranch of the Rio. New York: Arcadia House, 1958.
Panhandle Brand. New York: Arcadia House, 1964.

Bobbye Wood
North Texas State University

N. Scott Momaday (1934-   )
novels, poetry, short stories

Frederick Goddard Tuckerman, 1821-1873; Complete Poems. Ed. N. Scott
Momaday. New York: Oxford Univ. Press, 1965.
The Journey of Tai-me. Santa Barbara: Univ. of California, 1967.
House Made of Dawn. New York: Harper and Row, 1968.
The Way to Rainy Mountain. Albuquerque: Univ. of New Mexico Press,
1969.
Colorado: Summer/Fall/Winter/Spring. Chicago: Rand McNally, 1973.

In addition, Momaday has a score of poems and stories in such journals as
New Mexico Quarterly, Southern Review, and *Life.*

Works about N. Scott Momaday
Haslam, Gerald. "American Indians: Poets of the Cosmos," *Western Amer-
ican Literature,* 5 (Spring 1970), 15-29.
————. *Forgotten Pages of American Literature.* New York: Houghton
Mifflin, 1970. Pp. 7, 23-25.
Hylton, Marion Willard. "On a Trail of Pollen: Momaday's *House Made
of Dawn.*" *Critique,* 14 (No. 2), 60-69.
Oleson, Carole. "The Remembered Earth: Momaday's *House Made of
Dawn.*" *South Dakota Review,* 11 (Spring 1973), 59-78.
Porter, Mark. "Mysticism of the Land and the Western Novel." *South
Dakota Review,* 11 (Spring 1973), 79-91.
Smith, Marie. "Rainy Mountain, Legends, and Students," *Arizona English
Bulletin,* (April 1971), 41-44.
Trimble, Martha Scott. *N. Scott Momaday.* Western Writers Series. Boise:
Boise State College, 1973.

Winters, Yvor. *Forms of Discovery*. Denver: Swallow, 1967. Pp. 279-84.

Richard Etulain
Idaho State University

Vaida Stewart Montgomery (1888-1959)
poetry, handbooks, anthologies

Kaleidograph, A National Magazine of Poetry (edited with Whitney Montgomery). Dallas, May 1929-June 1959.
Locoed and Other Poems. Dallas: Kaleidoscope, 1930.
The Practical Rhymer (handbook on verse-writing). Dallas: Kaleidoscope, 1931.
Signs and Markers, Road Information for Hitch-Hikers Along the Literary Highway. Dallas: Kaleidoscope, 1931; rev. ed., 1933.
Bright Excalibur: A Collection of Poems Selected from Kaleidograph. A National Magazine of Poetry (edited with Whitney Montgomery). Dallas: Kaleidograph, 1933.
First Aid for Fictionists. Dallas: Kaleidograph, 1933.
Verse Forms—Old and New. Dallas: Kaleidograph, 1933.
Verse Technique—Simplified. Dallas: Kaleidograph, 1933.
A Century with Texas Poets and Poetry (biographies, bibliographies, selections). Dallas: Kaleidograph, 1934.
Secrets of Selling Verse. Dallas: Kaleidograph, 1934.
Merry-Go-Round (anthology edited with Whitney Montgomery). Dallas: Kaleidograph, 1935.
Sparks Afar (anthology edited with Whitney Montgomery). Dallas: Kaleidograph, 1936.
Moon in the Steeple (anthology edited with Whitney Montgomery). Dallas: Kaleidograph, 1937.
Blood and Dust (anthology edited with Whitney Montgomery). Dallas: Kaleidograph, 1938.
Hail for Rain (poems). Dallas: Kaleidograph, 1948.

Works about Vaida Stewart Montgomery
Barns, Florence Elberta. *Texas Writers of Today*. Dallas: Tardy, 1935.

Arthur M. Sampley
North Texas State University

Whitney Montgomery (1877-1966)
poetry, anthologies

Corn Silks and Cotton Blossoms. Dallas: P. L. Turner Co., 1928.
Brown Fields and Bright Lights. Dallas: Kaleidoscope, 1930.
Bright Excalibur: A Collection of Poems Selected from Kaleidograph, A National Magazine of Poetry (edited with Vaida Stewart Montgomery). Dallas: Kaleidograph, 1933.
Hounds in the Hills. Dallas: Kaleidograph, 1934.
Merry-Go-Round (anthology ed. with Vaida Stewart Montgomery). Dallas: Kaleidograph, 1935.
Sparks Afar (anthology ed. with Vaida Stewart Montgomery). Dallas: Kaleidograph, 1936.
Moon in the Steeple (anthology ed. with Vaida Stewart Montgomery). Dallas: Kaleidograph, 1937.
Blood and Dust (anthology ed. with Vaida Stewart Montgomery). Dallas: Kaleodograph, 1938.

In addition, from 1929 to 1959, Montgomery edited, with Vaida Stewart Montgomery, *Kaleidograph: A National Magazine of Poetry.*

Arthur M. Sampley
North Texas State University

Patrick Dacus Moreland (1897-   )
poetry

Arrow Unspent. Dallas: C. C. Cockrell, 1931.
Slumber at Noon. Dallas: Kaleidograph, 1934.
Seven Songs, A Volume of Selected Poems. Garden City, New York: Doubleday, Doran, 1936.

In addition, Moreland's poems have appeared in *Harper's, Literary Digest, The New York Times, Dallas News,* and *The Lantern.*

Bobbye Wood
North Texas State University

Willie Morris (1934-   )
novel, nonfiction

The South Today: One Hundred Years after Appomattox. Ed. Willie Morris. New York: Harper and Row, 1965.
North Toward Home (autobiography). Boston: Houghton Mifflin, 1967; rpt. New York: Dell, 1970.
Good Old Boy. New York: Harper and Row, 1971.
Yazoo: Integration in a Deep-Southern Town. New York: Harper's Magazine Press, 1971.
The Last of the Southern Girls. New York: Knopf, 1973; rpt. New York: Avon, 1974.

Morris, former editor of *Harper's* and of *Texas Observer,* has published numerous articles and essays in *Commentary, Dissent, Harper's, Nation, New Republic, New Yorker, New York Times Magazine,* and *Texas Quarterly.*

Works about Willie Morris
Anon. "Spur for *Harper's,*" *Newsweek* (22 May 1967), pp. 68-69.
Anon. "Youth for *Harper's,*" *Time,* (19 May 1967), pp. 56-57.
Epstein, J. "Most Likely to Succeed," *Commentary,* (January 1968), pp. 74-77
Little, Stuart. "What Happened at Harper's," *Saturday Review,* (10 April 1971), pp. 43-47, 56.

James Cox
University of Texas, Austin

Honoré Willsie McCue Morrow (1880-1940)
novels, short stories

The Heart of the Desert. New York: A. L. Burt, 1913.
Still Jim. New York: W. Morrow, 1915.
Benefits Forgot. New York: Frederick A. Stokes, 1917.
Lydia of the Pines. New York: Frederick A. Stokes, 1917.
Mary Todd Lincoln. New York: W. Morrow, 1917; rpt. A. L. Burt, 1919.
The Enchanted Canyon. New York: Frederick A. Stokes, 1920.

The Forbidden Trail. New York: Frederick A. Stokes, 1919; rpt. A. L. Burt, 1921.

Judith of the Godless Valley. New York: Frederick A. Stokes, 1922.

The Exile of the Lariat. New York: Frederick A. Stokes, 1923.

The Devonshers. New York: Frederick A. Stokes, 1924.

The Lost Speech of Abraham Lincoln. New York: Frederick A. Stokes, 1925.

We Must March. New York: Frederick A. Stokes, 1925.

On to Oregon. New York: W. Morrow, 1926. Published in England as *The Splendid Journey: The Story of a Pioneer Boy.* London: Heinemann, 1939; 1946.

The Father of Little Women. Boston: Little, Brown, 1927.

Forever Free. New York: W. Morrow, 1927.

With Malice Toward None. New York: W. Morrow, 1928.

Splendor of God. New York: W. Morrow, 1929.

The Last Full Measure. New York: W. Morrow, 1930.

Tiger! Tiger! New York: W. Morrow, 1930. Serialized in *Good Housekeeping* (June-Sept. 1928).

Beyond the Blue Sierra. New York: W. Morrow, 1932.

Argonaut. New York: W. Morrow, 1933.

Black Daniel. New York: W. Morrow, 1933.

Ship's Monkey. New York: W. Morrow, 1933.

The Lincoln Stories of Honoré Morrow. New York: W. Morrow, 1934.

Yonder Sails the Mayflower. New York: W. Morrow, 1934.

Great Captain (The Lincoln Triology). New York: W. Morrow, 1935.

Let the King Beware. New York: W. Morrow, 1936.

Ship's Parrot. New York: W. Morrow, 1936.

Demon Daughter. New York: W. Morrow, 1939.

In addition, Morrow published twenty stories between 1923 and 1939 in such publications as *American Magazine, Bookman, Better Homes and Gardens, Delineator, Good Housekeeping,* and *Ladies Home Journal.* She was editor of *The Delineator* from 1921 to 1926.

Works about Honoré Morrow

Overton, Grant Martin. "Honoré Willsie Morrow," in *Women Who Make Our Novels.* New York: Dodd Mead, 1928.

Bobbye Wood
North Texas State University

Lena Beatrice Morton (1901-   )
poetry, nonfiction

Negro Poetry in America. Boston: The Stratford Co., 1925.
Farewell to the Public Schools—I'm Glad We Met. Boston: The Meador Press, 1952.
Man Under Stress. New York: Philosophical Library, 1960.
My First Sixty Years: Passion for Wisdom. New York: Philosophical Library, 1965.

In addition, articles and poems are published in *Harvard Summer News, American Mercury, Safety Education, Cincinnati Post and Times Star, National Poetry Anthology, American Weaver, Poetry Magazine, Classical and Contemporary Poems, Southern University Research Bulletin, Peabody Journal of Education.*

James W. Byrd
East Texas State University

Francis Sanger Mossiker (1906-   )
novels

The Queen's Necklace. New York: Simon & Schuster, 1961.
Josephine and Napoleon: The Biography of a Marriage. New York: Simon & Schuster, 1964. Rpt. London: Gollancz, 1965.
The Affair of the Poisons. New York: Knopf, 1969.
More Than A Queen: The Story of Josephine Bonaparte. New York: Knopf, 1971.

In addition to French historical novels, Mossiker writes for radio and television.

Bobbye Wood
North Texas State University

Berta Hart Nance (1883-   )
poetry

The Round Up. Albany, Texas: Privately printed, 1927.
Flute in the Distance. Dallas: Kaleidograph, 1935.
Lines from Arizona. Dallas: Kaleidograph, 1938.

In addition, Nance has uncollected poems in such periodicals as *Kaleido-graph, Contemporary Poetry, The Dallas News,* and The Year Books of the Poetry Society of Texas.

Natrelle Young
Tarleton State College

James Larry Nance (1940-   )
poetry

If This Be Real. New York: Vantage Press, 1968.
The Texas Courthouse (Illustrated by Nance, text by June Rayfield Welch). Dallas: GLA Press, 1971.

Natrelle Young
Tarleton State College

John Louw Nelson (1895-   )
novel

Rhythm for Rain. Boston: Houghton Mifflin, 1937.

Natrelle Young
Tarleton State College

Violette Newton (1912-   )
poetry

Moses In Texas. Ft. Smith, Arkansas: South and West, 1963.
The Proxy. Quanah, Texas: Nortex, 1973.

Margaret C. Sherman
North Texas State University

Lewis Nordyke (1905-1960)
nonfiction

Cattle Empire, the Fabulous Story of the 3,000,000 Acre XIT. New York: William Morrow, 1949.

The Great Roundup. New York: William Morrow, 1955.
John Wesley Hardin, Texas Gunman. New York: William Morrow, 1957.
The Truth About Texas. New York: Crowell, 1957.
Nubbin Ridge. Garden City, New York: Doubleday, 1960.
The Angels Sing. Clarendon, Texas: Clarendon Press, 1964.

In addition, Nordyke has more than twenty articles in *Southwest Review, Saturday Evening Post, Reader's Digest,* and *Collier's.*

Sr. Diane Sanders
Ursuline Academy
Kirkwood, Missouri

Stanley Noyes (1924-   )
novels, poems

No Flowers for a Clown. New York: Macmillan, 1961.
Shadowbox. New York: Macmillan, 1970.
Faces and Spirits (poems). Santa Fe: Sunstone Press, 1974.

Other works by Noyes have appeared in such publications as *Poems Southwest, Trace, New Mexico Quarterly,* and *Desert Review.*

Diane M. Dodson
North Texas State University

Hermes Nye (1908-   )
novels, nonfiction

Fortune Is a Woman. New York: Signet, 1958.
How to Be a Folksinger. New York: Oak Publications, 1965.
T. S.: A Faith for the Desperate. Taylor, Texas: Merchants Press, 1965.
Sweet Beast, I Have Gone Prowling. Dallas: Cross Timbers Press, 1972.

In addition, Nye is the author of a number of essays on folklore and popular culture. His folksongs have been recorded by Folkways Records.

James W. Lee
North Texas State University

Nelson C. Nye (1907-   )
[pseuds. Clem Colt; Drake C. Denver]
novels, non-fiction

Two Fisted Cowpoke. New York: Greenberg, 1936.
The Killer of Cibecue. New York: Greenberg, 1936.
The Waddy From Roarin' Fork. New York: Nicholson and Watson, 1937.
The Leather Slapper. New York: Greenberg, 1937.
Quick-Fire Hombre. New York: Greenberg, 1937.
The Star Packers. New York: Greenberg, 1937.
G. Stands for Gun. New York: Greenberg, 1938.
Gunsmoke [Clem Colt]. New York: Greenberg, 1938.
The Shootin' Sheriff [Clem Colt]. New York: Phoenix, 1938.
The Bandit of Bloody Run. New York: Phoenix, 1939.
The Bar Nothing Brand [Clem Colt]. New York: Phoenix, 1939.
Center-Fire Smith [Clem Colt]. New York: Phoenix, 1939.
Hair Trigger Realm [Clem Colt]. New York: Phoenix, 1939.
The Feud at Sleepy Cat [Drake C. Denver]. New York: Phoenix, 1940.
Trigger-Finger Law [Clem Colt]. New York: Phoenix, 1940.
The Five Diamond Brand [Clem Colt]. New York: Phoenix, 1941.
Pistols For Hire. New York: Macmillan, 1941.
Tinbadge [Drake C. Denver]. New York: Phoenix, 1941.
Triggers for Six [Clem Colt]. New York: Phoenix, 1941.
Wildcats of Tonto Basin [Drake C. Denver]. New York: Phoenix, 1941.
The Desert Desperadoes [Drake C. Denver]. New York: Phoenix, 1942.
Gunfighter Breed. New York: Macmillan, 1942.
Gun Quick [Drake C. Denver]. New York: Phoenix, 1942.
The Sure-Fire Kid [Clem Colt]. New York: Phoenix, 1942.
Trigger Talk [Clem Colt]. New York: Phoenix, 1942.
Rustlers' Roost [Clem Colt]. New York: Phoenix, 1943.
The Guns of Horse Prairie [Clem Colt]. New York: Phoenix, 1943.
Cartridge-Case Law. New York: Macmillan, 1944.
Fiddle-Back Ranch [Clem Colt]. New York: Phoenix, 1944.
Maverick Canyon [Clem Colt]. New York: Phoenix, 1944.
Renegade Cowboy [Clem Colt]. New York: Phoenix, 1944.
Salt River Ranny. New York: Macmillan, 1944.
Wild Horse Shorty. New York: Macmillan, 1944.
Gunslick Mountain [Clem Colt]. New York: Arcadia, 1945.
Blood of Kings. New York: Macmillan, 1946.

Breed of the Chaparral [Drake C. Denver]. New York: McBride, 1946.
Once in the Saddle [Clem Colt]. New York: Arcadia, 1946.
The Barber of Tubac. New York: Macmillan, 1947.
Coyote Song [Clem Colt]. New York: Samuel Curl, 1947.
Outstanding Modern Quarter Horse Sires. New York: Morrow, 1948.
Gunman, Gunman. Golden, Colorado: Sage Books, 1949.
Riders by Night. New York: Dodd, Mead, 1950.
Caliban's Colt. New York: Dodd, Mead, 1950.
Champions of the Quarter Tracks. New York: Coward, McCann, 1950.
Born to Trouble. New York: Dodd, Mead, 1951.
Thief River. New York: Dodd, Mead, 1951.
Desert of the Damned. New York: Dodd, Mead, 1952.
Tough Company [Clem Colt]. New York: Dodd, Mead, 1952.
Wide Loop. New York: Dodd, Mead, 1952.
Come A'Smokin'. New York: Dodd, Mead, 1953.
Strawberry Roan. New York: Dodd, Mead, 1953.
Hired Hand. New York: Dodd, Mead, 1954.
The Red Sombrero. New York: Dodd, Mead, 1954.
Smoke Talk [Clem Colt]. New York: Dodd, Mead, 1954.
The Lonely Grass. New York: Dodd, Mead, 1955.
The Parson of Gunbarrel Basin. New York: Dodd, Mead, 1955.
Quick Trigger Country [Clem Colt]. New York: Dodd, Mead, 1955.
Bandido. New York: Signet, 1957.
Maverick Marshal. New York: Signet, 1958.
The Overlanders. New York: Signet, 1958.
Horses, Women, and Guns. Hillman, 1959.
The Long Run. New York: Macmillan, 1959.
Gunfight at the OK Corral. Hillman, 1960.
The Last Bullet. Hillman, 1960.
The Wolf That Rode. New York: Macmillan, 1960.
Not Grass Alone. New York: Macmillan, 1961.
Hideout Mountain. New York: Ace Books, 1962.
Man on the Skewbald Mare. New York: Ace Books, 1962.
Bancroft's Banco. New York. Ace Books, 1963.
Death Valley Slim. New York: Ace Books, 1963.
The Kid From Lincoln County. New York: Ace Books, 1963.
The Seven Six-Gunners. New York: Ace Books, 1963.
Your Western Horse. New York: A. S. Barnes, 1963.
Frontier Scout. Vega Books, 1964.

Saddle Bow Slim. New York: Macfadden, 1965.
Born to Trouble. New York: Macfadden, 1966.
Rider on the Roan. New York: Ace Books, 1967.
Lost Mine Named Salvation. New York: Ace Books, 1968.
Desert of the Damned. New York: Tower, 1969.
Rafe. New York: Ace Books, 1969.
Gringo. New York: Ace Books, 1969.
Wolftrap. New York: Ace Books, 1969.
Death Valley Slim: The Man-Kid From Lincoln County. New York: Ace Books, 1970.
Hellbound for Ballarat. New York: Ace Books, 1970.
Texas Gun. New York: Ace Books, 1970.
Trail of Lost Skulls. New York: Ace Books, 1970.
Gunfeud at Tiedown. New York: Ace Books, 1971.
Kelly. New York: Ace Books, 1971.
Rogues Rendezvous. New York: Ace Books, 1971.
Ambush at Yum's Chimney, New York: Ace Books, 1972.
Clifton Contract. New York: Ace Books, 1972.
Gunslick Mountain. New York: Ace Books, 1972.
Iron Hand. New York: Ace Books, 1972.
The No Gun Fighter. New York: Ace Books, 1972.
The One Shot Kid. New York: Ace Books, 1972.
Ramrod Vengeance. Lancer, 1972.
The Texas Tornado. New York: Ace Books, 1972.
Treasure Trail From Tucson. New York: Ace Books, 1972.
Trouble at Quinn's Crossing. New York: Ace Books, 1972.
Speed and the Quarter Horse: A Payload of Sprinters. Caldwell, Idaho: Caxton, 1973.

James W. Lee
North Texas State University

John Woolf (Jack) O'Connor (1902-   )
novels, nonfiction

Conquest: A Novel of the Old Southwest. New York: Harper, 1930.
Boom Town: A Novel of the Southwestern Silver Boom. New York: Knopf, 1938.
Game in the Desert. New York: Derrydale Press, 1939.

Hunting in the Southwest. New York: Knopf, 1945.
Horse and Buggy West: A Boyhood on the Last Frontier. New York: Knopf, 1969.

In addition, O'Connor authored and co-authored many books on guns and hunting. He has also contributed articles on hunting to national magazines, principally to *Outdoor Life* where he has been an editor since 1939.

Carol A. Lafferty
North Texas State University

Mary Paula King O'Donnell (1909-)
novels, short stories

Peculiar Thing. Los Angeles: Anderson and Ritchie, n. d.
Quincie Bolliver. Boston: Houghton Mifflin, 1941.
Those Other People. Boston: Houghton Mifflin, 1946.
You Can Hear the Echo. New York: Simon and Schuster, 1966.

Diane Dodson
North Texas State University

Symmes Chadwick (Chad) Oliver (1928-)
novels, short stories

Mists of Dawn. Philadelphia: Winston, 1952.
Shadows in the Sun. New York: Ballantine, 1954.
Another Kind. New York: Ballantine, 1955.
The Winds of Time. Garden City, New York: Doubleday, 1957.
Unearthly Neighbors. New York: Ballantine, 1960.
The Wolf is My Brother. New York: Signet, 1967.
The Edge of Forever: Classic Anthropological Science Fiction Stories. Los Angeles: Sherbourne Press, 1971.
The Shores of Another Sea. New York: Signet, 1971.

Oliver has also published between forty-five and fifty short stories in such magazines as *Argosy, Astounding Science Fiction, Fantastic,* and *The Magazine of Fantasy and Science Fiction.*

H. W. Hall
Texas A&M University

Cothburn O'Neal (1907-   )
novels

Conquests of Tamerlane. New York: Avon, 1952.
Master of the World. New York: Crown, 1952.
The Dark Lady, New York: Crown, 1954.
The Very Young Mrs. Poe. New York: Crown, 1956.
Untold Glory. New York: Crown, 1957.
Hagar. New York: Crown, 1958.
The Gods of Our Time. New York: Crown, 1960.
PA. New York: Crown, 1962.
The Money Hunters. New York: Crown, 1966.

The Cothburn O'Neal Collection is in the Mugar Memorial Library, Boston University, Boston, Massachusetts.

Ernestine P. Sewell
University of Texas at Arlington

John Milton Oskison (1874-1947)
novels, short stories, biography, history

Wild Harvest. New York: Appleton, 1925.
Black Jack Davy. New York: Appleton, 1926.
Texas Titan: The Story of Sam Houston. Garden City, New York: Doubleday, Doran, 1929.
Brothers Three. New York: Macmillan, 1935.
Tecumseh and His Times: The Story of a Great Indian. New York: Putnam, 1938.

In addition, Oskison published over forty articles between 1900 and 1923 in such journals as *Century, Collier's, Industrial Management, McClure's, North American Review, Overland,* and *World's Work*.

Works about John Milton Oskison
Cleaveland, A. M. "Three Musketeers of Southwestern Fiction," *Overland,* 87 (December 1929), 385.
Marable, M. H. and E. Boylan. *A Handbook of Oklahoma Writers*. Norman: Univ. of Oklahoma Press, 1939.

Arney L. Strickland
Lamar University

Miguel Antonio Otero (1859-1944)
biography, history

Colonel Jose Francisco Chaves, 1833-1924 (with Paul A. F. Walter). Santa Fe: Historical Society of New Mexico, 1926.
My Life on the Frontier, 1864-1882. New York: The Press of the Pioneers, 1935.
The Real Billy the Kid, With New Light on the Lincoln County War. New York: Wilson-Erickson, 1936.
My Life on the Frontier, 1882-1897. Albuquerque, New Mexico, 1939.
My Nine Years as Governor of the Territory of New Mexico, 1897-1906. Albuquerque, New Mexico: Univ. of New Mexico Press, 1940.

Arney L. Strickland
Lamar University

Raymond Otis (1900-1938)
novels, nonfiction

Fire in the Night. New York: Farrar and Rinehart, 1934. Published in Britain as *Fire Brigade.* London: Gollancz, 1934.
Miguel of the Bright Mountain. London: Gollancz, 1936.
Little Valley. London: Cresset, 1937.

Marilyn Georgas
Lamar University

William A. Owens (1905-   )
novels, short stories, nonfiction

Swing and Turn: Texas Play-Party Games. Dallas: Tardy, 1936.
Texas Folk Songs. Dallas: Southern Methodist Univ. Press, 1950.
Slave Mutiny: The Revolt of the Schooner Amistad. New York: John Day, 1953.
Walking on Borrowed Land (novel). Indianapolis: Bobbs-Merrill, 1954.
Fever in the Earth (novel). New York: G. P. Putnam's Sons, 1958.
Pocantico Hills: 1609-1959. Tarrytown, New York: Sleepy Hollow Restorations, 1960.

Look to the River (novel). New York: Athaeneum, 1963.
This Stubbon Soil. New York: Scribner's, 1966.
Three Friends: Roy Bedichek, J. Frank Dobie, Walter Prescott Webb. Garden City, New York: Doubleday, 1969.
Tales from the Derrick Floor (with Mody C. Boatright). Garden City, New York: Doubleday, 1970.
A Season of Weathering. New York: Scribner's, 1973.

Owens has published approximately thirty-five short stories, articles, essays, and reviews in such journals as *Saturday Review, American Heritage, Southwest Review, Du Pont Magazine,* and *American Petroleum Institute Quarterly.*

Works about William A. Owens
Pilkington, William T. *William A. Owens.* Austin: Steck-Vaughn, 1968; rpt. in *My Blood's Country.* Fort Worth: Texas Christian Univ. Press, 1973.

William T. Pilkington
Tarleton State College

James Hambright Parke (1905-   )
plays

It Runs in the Family: A Mystery Comedy in Three Acts. Philadelphia: Penn Publishing, 1928.
Some Crooks Are Gentlemen: A Comedy in Three Acts. New York: Penn, c. 1928.
The Professor Crashes Through: A College Comedy in Three Acts. New York: Penn, c. 1938.

Marilyn Georgas
Lamar University

Norma Patterson (-   )
novels, short stories

Jenny; the Romance of a Nurse. New York: Farrar and Rinehart, 1930.
Gay Procession. New York: Farrar and Rinehart, 1930.

The Sun Shines Bright. New York: Farrar and Rinehart, 1932.
Drums of the Night. New York: Farrar and Rinehart, 1935.
Try and Hold Me. New York: Farrar and Rinehart, 1937.
Out of the Ground (with Crate Dalton). New York: Farrar and Rinehart, 1937.
Give Them Their Dream. New York: Farrar and Rinehart, 1938.
The Man I Love. New York: Farrar and Rinehart, 1940.
West of the Weather. New York: Farrar and Rinehart, 1941.
Love is Forever. New York: Farrar and Rinehart, 1941.
When the Lights Go Up Again. New York: Farrar and Rinehart, 1943.

In addition, Patterson published almost thirty short stories in such journals as *Good Housekeeping, Saturday Evening Post,* and *McCall's.*

Joseph Giarratano
Lamar University

George Pattullo (1879-1967)
novels, short stories, nonfiction

The Untamed. New York: D. Fitzgerald, 1911.
The Sheriff of Badger. New York: Appleton, 1912.
Fightin' Sons-of-Guns. Canada: Canadian Pacific Railway, 1917.
One Man's War: The Diary of a Leatherneck (with Joseph Rendinell). New York: Sears Pub. Co., 1928.
Tight Lines! New York: Allston and Depew, 1938.
A Good Rooster Crows Everywhere. New York: Desmond Fitzgerald, 1939.
Horrors of Moonlight. New York: Allston and Depew, 1939.
All Our Yesterdays. San Antonio: Naylor, 1948.
Always New Frontiers. New York: n.p., 1951.
Era of Infamy. San Antonio: Naylor, 1952.
The Morning After Cometh. San Antonio: Naylor, 1954.
How Silly Can We Get. San Antonio: Naylor, 1956.
Giant Afraid. San Antonio: Naylor, 1957.
Some Men in Their Time. San Antonio: Naylor, 1959.

In addition, Pattullo published numerous short stories and articles in publications such as *Collier's, Ladies Home Journal, McClure's,* and *Sunset*

374   *Southwestern American Literature*

between 1910 and 1920. Most of his uncollected stories appeared in *Saturday Evening Post* during the 1920's.

Royce G. Bass
Lamar University

James Paytiamo (-   )
novel

Flaming Arrow's People. New York: Duffield and Green, 1932.

Royce G. Bass
Lamar University

Thomas Matthews Pearce (1902-   )
nonfiction

America In The Southwest. (Ed. with Telfair Hendon). Albuquerque: Univ. of New Mexico Press, 1933.
Christopher Marlowe: Figure of the Renaissance. Albuquerque: Univ. of New Mexico Press, 1934.
Lane of the Llano (with Jim "Lane" Cook). Boston: Little, Brown, 1936.
Southwest Heritage: A Literary History with Bibliography (with Mabel Major); Rev. and enlarged. Albuquerque: Univ. of New Mexico Press, 1972. First edition (1938) and second edition, rev. and enlarged (1948), with Mabel Major and Rebecca W. Smith.
Cartoon Guide of New Mexico. New York: J. J. Augustin, 1939.
The Beloved House. Caldwell, Idaho: Caxton, 1940.
Democracy in Progress. Albuquerque: Univ. of New Mexico Press, 1943.
Southwesterners Write (with A. P. Thomason). Albuquerque: Univ. of New Mexico Press, 1947.
Signature of the Sun: Southwest Verse 1900-1950 (with Mabel Major). Albuquerque: Univ. of New Mexico Press, 1950.
New Mexico Place Names: A Geographical Dictionary (with Ina S. Cassidy and Helen S. Pearce). Albuquerque: Univ. of New Mexico Press, 1965.
Mary Hunter Austin. New York: Twayne, 1966.
Alice Corbin Henderson. Austin: Steck-Vaughn, 1969.
Music of the Spanish Folk Plays in New Mexico. Santa Fe: Museum of New Mexico, 1969.

Oliver LaFarge. New York: Twayne, 1972.
Turquoise Land, Anthology of New Mexico Poetry (ed. with Alice Briley and Jeannette Bonnette). Quanah, Texas: Nortex, 1974.

In addition, Pearce published over thirty scholarly and critical essays in *American Speech, Western Folklore, American Literature,* and *Notes and Queries.*

Charles Olson
University of New Mexico

John O. West
University of Texas at El Paso

Tom Pendleton [see Edmund Van Zandt]

Charles E. Perkins (1881-   )
novels

The Phantom Bull. Boston and New York: Houghton-Mifflin, 1932.
The Pinto Horse. New York: Devin-Adair, 1960.

Charles Olson
University of New Mexico

George Sessions Perry (1910-1956)
novels, short stories, nonfiction

Walls Rise Up. New York: Doubleday, Doran, 1939.
Hold Autumn In Your Hand. New York: Viking, 1941.
Texas: A World In Itself. New York: McGraw-Hill, 1942.
Hackberry Cavalier. New York: Viking, 1944.
Cities of America. New York: McGraw-Hill, 1947.
My Granny Van. New York: McGraw-Hill, 1949.
Families of America. New York: McGraw-Hill, 1949.
Tale of a Foolish Farmer. New York: McGraw-Hill, 1951.
The Story of Texas A and M. New York: McGraw-Hill, 1951.
The Story of Texas. Garden City, New York: Garden City Books, 1956.

In addition, Perry has approximately seventy articles published mostly by
Saturday Evening Post, but some are published in such magazines as
Country Gentleman, Esquire, New Yorker, and *Scholastic.*

Works about George Sessions Perry
Alexander, Stanley G. *George Sessions Perry.* Austin: Steck-Vaughn, 1967.

Joseph Giarratano
Lamar University

Jenny Lind Porter (1927-   )
poetry

The Lantern of Diogenes, and Other Poems. San Antonio: Naylor, 1954.
Peter Bell the Fourth. Austin: Steck, 1955.
Azle and the Attic Room. Los Angeles: W. Ritchie, 1957.
In the Still Cave of the Witch Poesy: Selected Poems. Austin: Steck, 1960.

In addition, Porter published poems in *Ladies Home Journal, Poetry Digest,
Prairie Schooner, The Personalist,* and *New York Times.*

Works about Jenny Lind Porter
Edwards, Margaret R. *Poets Laureate of Texas 1932-1966.* San Antonio:
    Naylor, 1966.
"New Voices in Poetry," *Poetry Digest,* 4 (June 1958), 10-14.

Jimmie D. Farber
Lamar University

Katherine Ann Porter (1890-   )
novels, short stories, essays, translations

Flowering Judas and Other Stories. New York: Harcourt, Brace, 1930.
Katherine Anne Porter's French Song Book. Paris: Harrison, n.d.
Hacienda. New York: Harrison, 1934.
Noon Wine. Detroit: Schuman's, 1937.
Pale Horse, Pale Rider: Three Short Novels. New York: Harcourt, Brace,
    1939. (*Old Mortality, Noon Wine,* and *Pale Horse, Pale Rider.*)
The Itching Parrot. Garden City, New York: Doubleday, Doran, 1942.

(Translation of *El Periquillo* by Jose Joaquin Fernandez de Lizardi, with an introduction by Katherine Anne Porter.)
The Leaning Tower and Other Stories. New York: Harcourt, Brace, 1944.
The Days Before. New York: Harcourt, Brace, 1952.
Ship of Fools. Boston: Little, Brown, 1962.
The Collected Stories of Katherine Anne Porter. New York: Harcourt, Brace, and World, 1965.

Works about Katherine Ann Porter
Allen, Charles A. "Katherine Anne Porter: Psychology as Art," *Southwest Review,* 41 (Summer 1956), 223-30.
———. "The Nouvelles of Katherine Anne Porter," *The University of Kansas Review,* 29 (December 1962), 87-93.
Auchincloss, Louis. *Pioneers and Caretakers: A Study of Nine American Women Novelists.* Minneapolis: Univ. of Minnesota Press, 1965. pp. 136-51.
Baker, Howard. "The Upward Path: Notes on the Work of Katherine Anne Porter," *Southern Review,* 4 (1968), 1-19.
Curley, Daniel. "Katherine Anne Porter: The Larger Plan," *Kenyon Review,* 25 (Autumn 1963), 671-95.
———. "Treasure in 'The Grave,'" *Modern Fiction Studies,* 9 (Winter 1963-64), 377-84.
Emmons, Winfred S. *Katherine Anne Porter: The Regional Stories.* Austin: Steck-Vaughn, 1967.
Gordon, Caroline. "Katherine Anne Porter and the ICM," *Harper's,* 224 (November 1964), 146-48.
Hagopian, John V. "Katherine Anne Porter: Feeling, Form, and Truth," *Four Quarters,* 12 (November 1962), 1-10.
Hartley, Lodwick. "Katherine Anne Porter," *Sewanee Review,* 48 (April 1940), 206-16.
——— and George Core, comps. *Katherine Anne Porter: A Critical Symposium.* Athens, Ga.: University of Georgia Press, 1969.
Hendrick, George. *Katherine Anne Porter.* New York: Twayne, 1965.
Herbst, Josephine. "Miss Porter and Miss Stein," *Partisan Review,* 15 (May 1948), 568-72.
Johnson, James W. "Another Look at Katherine Anne Porter," *Virginia Quarterly Review,* 36 (Autumn 1960), 598-613.
Joselyn, Sister M. "Animal Imagery in Katherine Anne Porter's Fiction,"

in *Myth and Symbol,* edited by Bernice Slote. Lincoln: Univ. of Nebraska Press, 1963.

────. " 'The Grave' as Lyrical Short Story," *Studies in Short Fiction,* 1 (Spring 1964), 216-21.

Kaplan, Charles. "The True Witness: Katherine Anne Porter," *Colorado Quarterly,* 7 (Winter 1959), 319-27.

Liberman, M. M. "The Short Story as Chapter in *Ship of Fools,*" *Criticism,* 10 (1968), 65-71.

Marshall, Margaret. "Writers in the Wilderness: Katherine Anne Porter," *The Nation,* 13 April 1940, pp. 473-75.

Mooney, Harry John, Jr. *The Fiction and Criticism of Katherine Anne Porter.* Pittsburgh: Univ. of Pittsburgh Press, 1962, 1967.

Nance, William L. "Katherine Anne Porter and Mexico," *Southwest Review,* 55 (Spring 1970), 143-53.

────. *Katherine Anne Porter and the Art of Rejection.* Chapel Hill: Univ. of North Carolina Press, 1964.

Porter, Katherine Anne. "Noon Wine: The Sources," *Yale Review,* 46 (Autumn 1956), 22-39.

Poss, S. H. "Variations on a Theme in Four Stories of Katherine Anne Porter," *Twentieth Century Literature,* 4 (April-July 1958), 21-29.

Ryan, Marjorie. "Dubliners and the Stories of Katherine Anne Porter," *American Literature,* 31 (January 1960), 464-73.

Schorer, Mark. "Biographia Literaria," *New Republic,* 10 November 1952, pp. 18-19.

Schwartz, Edward G. "The Fictions of Memory," *Southwest Review,* 45 (Summer 1960), 204-15.

────. *Katherine Anne Porter: A Critical Bibliography* (with an Introduction by Robert Penn Warren). New York: New York Public Library, 1953.

────. "The Way of Dissent: Katherine Anne Porter's Critical Position," *Western Humanities Review,* 8 (Spring 1954), 119-30.

Sylvester, William A. "Selected and Critical Bibliography of the Uncollected Works of Katherine Anne Porter," *Bulletin of Bibliography,* 19 (January 1947), 36.

Waldrip, Louise, and Shirley Ann Bauer. *A Bibliography of the Works of Katherine Anne Porter [and] A Bibliography of the Criticism of the Works of Katherine Anne Porter.* Metuchen, N. J.: Scarecrow Press, 1969.

Warren, Robert Penn. "Irony with a Center: Katherine Anne Porter," in *Selected Essays*. New York: Random House, 1958.

Westcott, Glenway. *Images of Truth: Remembrances and Criticism*. New York: Harper & Row, 1962. pp. 25-58.

————. "Katherine Anne Porter: The Making of a Novel," *Atlantic,* 209 (April 1962), 43-49.

West, Ray B., Jr. *Katherine Anne Porter*. Minneapolis: Univ. of Minnesota Press, 1963.

————. "Katherine Anne Porter and 'Historic Memory,' " *Hopkins Review,* 6 (Fall 1952), 16-27.

————. "Katherine Anne Porter: Symbol and Theme in 'Flowering Judas,' " *Accent,* 7 (Spring 1947), 182-87.

————. *The Short Story in America*. Chicago: Regnery, 1952. pp. 72-76.

Wilson, Edmund. "Katherine Anne Porter," *The New Yorker,* (30 September 1944), 64-66.

Wright, Austin McGiffert. *The American Short Story in the Twenties*. Chicago: Univ. of Chicago Press, 1961. *passim.*

Young, Vernon A. "The Art of Katherine Anne Porter," *The New Mexico Quarterly,* 15 (Autumn 1945), 326-41.

James T. F. Tanner
North Texas State University

William Sidney Porter (1862-1910)
[pseud. O. Henry]
short stories

Cabbages and Kings. New York: McClure, Phillips, 1904.

The Four Million. New York: McClure, Phillips, 1906.

Heart of the West. New York: McClure, 1907.

The Trimmed Lamp. New York: McClure, Phillips, 1907.

The Gentle Grafter, New York: McClure, 1908.

The Voice of the City. New York: McClure, 1908.

Options. New York: Harper, 1909.

Roads of Destiny. New York: Doubleday, 1909.

Strictly Business. New York: Doubleday, 1910.

Whirligigs. New York: Doubleday, 1910.

Sixes and Sevens. New York: Doubleday, 1911.

Rolling Stones. New York: Doubleday, 1912.

Waifs and Strays. New York: Doubleday, 1917.
O. Henryana. New York: Doubleday, 1920.
Letters to Lithopolis. New York: Doubleday, 1922.
Postscripts. New York: Harper, 1923.
O. Henry Encore. New York: Doubleday, 1939.
The Complete Works of O. Henry. 2 vols. New York: Doubleday, 1953.

Works about Porter
Brooks, Van Wyck. "New York: "O. Henry," *The Confident Years.* New York: Dutton, 1952.
Clarkson, Paul S. *A Bibliography of William Sydney Porter (O. Henry).* Caldwell, Idaho: Caxton, 1938.
————. "A Decomposition of Cabbages and Kings," *American Literature,* 7 (1935), 195-202.
Courtney, Luther W. "O. Henry's Case Reconsidered," *American Literature,* 14 (1943), 361-71.
Current-Garcia, Eugene. *O. Henry.* New York: Twayne, 1965.
Davis, Robert H. and Arthur B. Maurice. *The Caliph of Bagdad.* New York: Appleton, 1931.
Echols, Edward C. "O. Henry's 'Shaker of Attic Salt,' " *Classical Journal,* 43 (1948), 488-89.
Firkens, O. W. "O. Henry," *Modern Essays,* ed. Christopher Morley. New York: Harcourt, Brace, 1921.
Forman, Henry J. "O. Henry's Short Stories," *North American Review,* 187 (1908), 781-83.
Gallegly, J. S. "Backgrounds and Patterns of O. Henry's Texas Badman Stories," *Rice Institute Pamphlet,* 42 (1955), 1-32.
————. *From Alamo Plaza to Jack Harris's Saloon: O. Henry and the Southwest He Knew.* The Hague and Paris: Mouton, 1970.
Gates, William B. "O. Henry and Shakespeare," *Shakespeare Association Bulletin,* 19 (1944), 20-25.
Gohdes, Clarence. "Some Letters by O. Henry," *South Atlantic Quarterly,* 38 (1939), 31-39.
Jennings, Al. *Through the Shadows With O. Henry.* New York: H. K. Fly, 1921.
Kramer, Dale. *The Heart of O. Henry.* New York: Rinehart, 1954.
Langford, Gerald. *Alias O. Henry.* New York: Macmillan, 1957.
Leacock, Stephen. "The Amazing Genius of O. Henry," *Essays and Literary*

Studies. New York and London: John Lane, 1916.

Long, E. Hudson. *O. Henry: American Regionalist.* Austin: Steck-Vaughn, 1969.

———. "O. Henry's Christmas Stories," *Southern Literary Messenger,* 1 (1939), 795-809.

———. *O. Henry: The Man and His Work.* Philadelphia: Univ. of Pennsylvania Press, 1949.

———. "O. Henry as a Regional Artist," *Essays on American Literature in Honor of Jay B. Hubbell.* Durham: Duke Univ. Press, 1967.

———. "Social Customs in O. Henry's Texas Stories," *A Good Tale and a Bonnie Tune.* Dallas: Southern Methodist Univ. Press, 1964.

MacAdam, George. "O. Henry's Only Autobiographia," *O. Henry Papers.* New York: Doubleday, 1924.

Mais, S. P. B. "O. Henry," *From Shakespeare to O. Henry.* London: Richards, 1930.

Maltby, Frances G. *The Dimity Sweetheart.* Richmond, Virginia: Dietz, 1930.

O'Connor, Richard. *O. Henry: The Legendary Life of William S. Porter.* New York: Doubleday, 1970.

O'Quinn, Trueman. "O. Henry in Austin," *Southwestern Historical Quarterly,* 43 (1939), 143-57.

Pattee, Fred L. "O. Henry and the Handbooks," *The Development of the American Short Story.* New York: Harper. 1923.

Payne, L. W., Jr. "The Humor of O. Henry," *Texas Review,* 4 (1918), 18-37.

Pira, Gisela. "O. Henry," *Die Neueren Sprachen,* 11 (1962), 374-79.

Porter, Margaret. "My O. Henry," *Mentor,* 11 (1923), 17-20.

Quinn, Arthur H. "The Journalists," *American Fiction.* New York: Appleton-Century, 1936.

Rollins, Hyder E. "O. Henry's Texas," *Texas Review,* 4 (1919), 295-307.

———. "O. Henry's Texas Days," *Bookman,* 40 (1914), 154-65.

Samarin, Roman. "O. Henry—'A Really Remarkable Writer': On the Centennial of O. Henry's Birth," *Soviet Review,* 3 (1962), 55-58.

Shimizu, Yutaka. "Thoughts and Humor of O. Henry," *Studies in Humanities* (Doshisha University, Japan), 85 (1966), 24-50.

Smith, C. Alphonso. *O. Henry Biography.* New York: Doubleday, Page, 1916.

Travis, Edmunds. "O. Henry's Austin Years," *Bunker's Monthly,* 1 (1928), 493-508.

————. "O. Henry Enters the Shadows," *Bunker's Monthly,* 1 (1928), 669-84.
————. "The Triumph of O. Henry," *Bunker's Monthly,* 1 (1928), 839-52.
Van Doren, Carl. "O. Henry," *Texas Review,* 2 (1917), 248-59.
Williams, William W. *The Quiet Lodger of Irving Place.* New York: Dutton, 1936.

E. Hudson Long
Baylor University

Nolan Porterfield (1936-   )
novel, short stories

Trail to Marked Tree (with Roy Swank). San Antonio: Naylor, 1968.
A Way of Knowing. New York: Harper's Magazine Press, 1971.

In addition, Porterfield published stories in *Harper's* and *Sewanee Review.*

Diane Dodson
North Texas State University

Karl Postl (1793-1864)
[pseud. Charles Sealsfield]
novels, nonfiction

Note: Postl, best known under the pseudonym Charles Sealsfield, wrote numerous works about the Southwest in German. Below are listed only those works translated into English; a complete biography can be found in Heller and Leon below. [Eds.]

The Americans as They Are; Described in a Tour through the Valley of the Mississippi. London: Hurst, Chance, 1828.

Austria as It is; or, Sketches of Continental Courts, by an Eyewitness. London: Hurst, Chance, 1828.

Tokeah; or, The White Rose (An Indian Tale). 2 vols. Philadelphia: Lea and Carey, 1829; 2nd ed. Philadelphia: Lea and Blanchard, 1845.

Life in the New World; or Sketches of American Society. Translated Gustavus C. Hebbe and James Mackay. New York: J. Winchester, 1842; rpt. 1844.

The Cabin Book; or, Sketches of Life in Texas. Translated Professor C. F. Mersch. New York: J. Winchester, 1844.

North and South; or Scenes and Adventures in Mexico. Translated Joel Tyler Hendley. New York: J. Winchester, 1844.

Rambleton; A Romance of Fashionable Life in New York during the Great Speculation of 1836. Translated from the German. New York: J. Winchester, 1844; rpt. New York: William Taylor, 1946.

The Cabin Book; or, National Characteristics. Translated Sarah Powell. London: Ingram, Cooke, 1852; rpt. New York: St. John and Coffin, 1871.

The Cabin Book; or, Sketches of Life in Texas. Translated Sarah Powell. London: Ingram, Cooke, 1852.

Scenes and Adventures in Central America. Ed. Frederick Hardman. Edinburgh and London: W. Blackwood and Sons, 1852.

The Cabin Book; or, Scenes and Sketches of the Late American and Mexican War. London, n.p., 1853.

Frontier Life; or, Scenes and Adventures in the South West. Ed. Francis Hardman. New York: Miller, Orton and Mulligan, 1856; rpt. New York: Miller, Orton, 1857.

Frontier Life; or Tales of the Southwestern Border. Ed. Francis Hardman. New York: C. M. Saxton, 1859.

Adventures in Texas. Abridged from the German by F. Hardman. Edinburgh, n.p., 1860.

The United States of North America as They Are. London: John Murray, 1927; rpt. London: W. Simpkin and R. Marshall, 1928.

Works about Charles Sealsfield

Bornemann, Felix, ed. *Katalog der Charles Sealsfield.* Gedachtnisausstellung anlässlich des 100. Todestages des Dichters. Stuttgart: Kulturausschuss des Südmähr. Landschaftsrates in Verbindung mit der Charles Sealfield-Gesellschaft, 1964.

Castle, Eduard. *Das Geheimmis Des grossen Unbekannten Charles Sealsfield-Carl Postl.* Die Quellenschriften mit Einleitung, Bildnis, gegeben von Eduard Castle. Wien: Wiener Bibliophilen-Gesellschaft, 1943.

————. *Der grosse Unbekannte: Das Leben von Charles Sealsfield.* Briefe und Aktenstücke. Mit einem Vorwort von Joseph A. von Bradish. Wien: K. Werner. 1955.

————. *Der grosse Unbekannte: Das Leben von Charles Sealsfield (Karl Postl).* Wien-München: Manutiuspresse, 1952.

Conrad, Heinrich. *Charles Sealsfields Exotische Kulturromane in Neuer Auswahl und Anordnung hrsg.* München und Leipzig: G. Muller, 1917.

Faust, Albert B. *Charles Sealsfield (Carl Postl), der Dichter beider Hemisphäeren. Sein Leben und sein Werke. Mit einem vermehrten Briefanhang.* Weimar, 1897.

Heller, Otto. "Charles Sealsfield, a Forgotten Discoverer of the Valley of the Mississippi," *Missouri Historical Review,* 31 (1937), 382-401.

Heller, Otto and Theodor Leon. *Charles Sealsfield, Bibliography of His Writings.* St. Louis: Washington Univ. Studies, New Series, Language and Literature No. 8, 1939.

Jordan, E. L., ed. *America: Glorious and Chaotic Land; Charles Sealsfield Discovers the Young United States.* Englewood Cliffs, N. J.: Prentice-Hall, 1969.

Riederer, Franz. *Charles Sealsfield, Gesamtausgabe der Amerikanischen Romane.* Heraugegeben von Franz Riederer. Meersburg: F. W. Hendel Verlag, 1937.

Jimmie D. Farber
Lamar University

Jack Potter (1921-1975)
[pseud. John Moss, John Hart, P. J. Nicholson]
novels, plays, nonfiction

A Bibliography of John Dos Passos. Chicago: Normandie House, 1950; rpt. Folcroft, Pa.: Folcroft Press, 1969.

How to Win at Poker [John Moss]. Chicago: Knight Publishers, 1950; rpt. Garden City, N.Y.: Garden City Books, 1955.

The Heavy Day [John Hart]. Denmark: Privately printed, 1953; rpt. as *La Pesante Journée* (by Jack Potter). Paris: Rene Julliard, 1956.

Rat Race [P. J. Nicholson]. London: Elek Books, 1966; rpt. as *Phoenix.* Chicago: Knight Publishers, 1966.

The Governor (play). Santa Fe: Broadway Bookstore, 1968.

In addition, Potter wrote two plays, *Nothing of Value to Declare* (1973) and *Men of War* (1974), which have not been published. Other works of fiction were published in *Esperanza* and in *Les Temps Modernes.*

Durret Wagner
Chicago, Illinois

Nancy Richey Ranson (d.1972)
poetry, nonfiction

Bucking Burro, for Children from One to One Hundred. Dallas: Kaleido-
graph, 1932.
Texas Wildflower Legends. Dallas: Kaleidograph Press, 1933; 2nd ed.,
1940.
Texas Evening (poems). Dallas: Kaleidograph, 1936.
My Neighbor's Garden—And Mine. Dallas: Kaleidograph Press, 1939.

In addition, Ranson published a number of essays and uncollected poems—
several in *Sunset.*

H. L. Frissell
Lamar University

Robert Raynolds (1902-1965)
novels, play, nonfiction

Brothers In The West. New York: Harper, 1931.
Fortune. New York: William Morrow, 1935.
Boadicea (play). New York: The Poet's Press, 1941.
May Bretton. New York: G. P. Putnam's Sons, 1944.
The Obscure Enemy. New York: Margent Press, 1945.
Paquita. New York: G. P. Putnam's Sons, 1947.
The Sinner of Saint Ambrose. Indianapolis: Bobbs-Merrill, 1952.
The Quality of Quiros. Indianapolis: Bobbs-Merrill, 1955.
Far Flight of Love. New York: Pageant Press, 1957.
Choice To Love (non-fiction). New York: Harper, 1959.
In Praise of Gratitude (non-fiction). New York: Harper, 1961.
Saunders Oak. New York: Harper, 1961.
Thomas Wolfe: Memoir of a Friendship. Austin: Univ. of Texas Press,
1965.

Works about Robert Raynolds
"Interview with Robert Raynolds," *Wilson Library Bulletin,* 6 (February
1932), 398.

Mimi R. Gladstein
University of Texas at El Paso

John Rechy (1934-   )
novels, short stories

City of Night. New York: Grove, 1963.
Numbers. New York: Grove, 1967.
This Day's Death. New York: Grove, 1970.
The Vampire. New York: Grove, 1971.
The Fourth Angel. New York: Viking, 1973.

In addition to the above novels, Rechy published translations from Spanish and contributed a number of essays (usually about social problems) and short stories (often portions of his novels) to such periodicals as *Evergreen Review, Nugget, London Magazine,* and *Nation.*

Works about John Rechy
Gilman, Richard. *The Confusion of Realms.* New York: Random House, 1963. pp. 53-61.
Heifetz, Henry. "The Anti-Social Act of Writing," *Studies on the Left.* 4 (Spring 1964), 3-20.
Hicks, Granville. "The Covert Community," *Saturday Review,* (8 June 1963), pp. 23-24.
Southern, Terry. "Rechy and Gover," *Contemporary American Novelists,* ed. Harry T. Moore. Carbondale: Southern Illinois Univ. Press, 1964. pp. 222-27.

William B. Warde, Jr.
North Texas State University

Thomas Mayne Reid (1818-1883)
novels

Desert Home. Boston: Tichnor, 1852.
Rifle Rangers. New York: De Witt and Davenport, 1852.
Scalp-Hunters. Philadelphia: Lippincott, 1852.
The Boy Hunters. Boston: Tichnor, 1853.
Young Voyagers. Boston: Tichnor, 1854.
Forest Exiles. Boston: Tichnor and Fields, 1855.
Hunter's Feast. New York: De Witt and Davenport, 1855.

Quadroon. New York: De Witt, 1857.
The War Trail. New York: De Witt, 1857.
Young Yagers. Boston: Tichnor and Fields, 1857.
Bush Boys. Boston: Tichnor and Fields, 1858.
Plant Hunters. Boston: Tichnor and Fields, 1858.
The Boy Tar. Boston: Tichnor and Fields, 1859.
Odd People. New York: Harper, 1859.
Osceola, the Seminole. New York: De Witt, 1859.
Ran Away to Sea. Boston: Tichnor and Fields, 1860.
The White Chief. New York: De Witt, 1860.
Wild Life. New York: De Witt, 1860.
The Wood Rangers. New York: De Witt, 1860.
Bruin: The Grand Bear Hunt. Boston: Tichnor and Fields, 1861.
Wild Huntress. New York: De Witt, 1862.
Croquet. Boston: J. Redpath, 1863.
The Cliff Climbers. Boston: Tichnor and Fields, 1864.
The Maroon. New York: De Witt, 1864.
The Ocean Waifs. Boston: Tichnor and Fields, 1864.
The Boy Slaves. Boston: Tichnor and Fields, 1865.
Lost Lenore. London: C. H. Clarke, 1865.
The Tiger Hunters. New York: De Witt, 1865.
Afloat in the Forest. Boston: Tichnor and Fields, 1866.
The Giraffe-Hunter. Boston: Tichnor and Fields, 1866.
Headless Horseman. Boston: De Witt, 1867.
Quadrupeds: What They Are, and Where Found. London: Nelson, 1867.
Bandolero. London: Ward, Lock and Tyler, 1868.
Child Wife: A Tale of the Two Worlds. New York: Sheldon, 1868.
Helpless Hand. New York: Beadle, 1868.
The Rival Captains. New York: Munro, 1868.
White Gauntlet. New York: Carleton, 1868.
Castaways: A Story of Adventure in the Wilds of Borneo. New York: Sheldon, 1870.
The Guerilla Chief and Other Tales. London: C. H. Clarke, 1871.
Lone Ranche: A Tale of the Staked Plain. London: Chapman, 1871.
Gwen Wynn: A Romance of the Wye. London: Tinsley, 1877.
Gaspar, the Gaucho. New York: Routledge, 1879.
Queen of the Lakes: A Romance of the Mexican Valley. London: Mullan, 1880.

Finger of Fate. New York: Munro, 1885.
Land of Fire. New York: Frederick Warne, 1886.
Death Shot. New York: White and Allen, 1889.
Naturalist in Siluria. London: Sonnenschein, 1889.
Cris Rock. New York: R. Bonner, 1890.
Stories of Bold Deeds and Brave Men. New York: Ward, Lock, 1892.
The Vee-Boers. New York: Dutton, 1907.

Works about Mayne Reid
Reid, Elizabeth. *Captain Mayne Reid: His Life and Adventures.* London:
    Greening, 1900.
────. *Mayne Reid: A Memoir of His Life.* London: Ward and Downey,
    1890.

Jerry Keys
Lamar University

Eugene Manlove Rhodes (1896-1934)
novels, short stories, nonfiction

Good Men and True (novel). New York: Henry Holt, 1910. (Serialized in
    January, 1910, in the *Saturday Evening Post*.)
Bransford in Arcadia, or The Little Eohippus (novel). New York: Henry
    Holt, 1914. (Serialized as *Bransford in Arcadia* in November and Decem-
    ber, 1912, in *Saturday Evening Post*.)
The Desire of the Moth (novel). New York: Henry Holt, 1916. (Serialized
    February and March, 1916, in the *Saturday Evening Post*.)
West Is West (novel). New York: H. K. Fly, 1917.
Romances of Navaho Land (novels). New York: Grosset and Dunlap, 1920.
    (Contains four previously published novels— *Good Men and True; Brans-
    ford in Arcadia, or The Little Eohippus* changed to *Bransford of Rainbow
    Range; The Desire of the Moth;* and *West Is West*—published individ-
    ually, with *Hit the Line Hard* added to *Good Men and True* and with
    The Come On added to *The Desire of the Moth*. Four volumes.)
Say Now Shibboleth (essays). Chicago: Bookfellows, 1921.
Stepsons of Light (novel). Boston: Houghton Mifflin, 1921. (Serialized Sep-
    tember and October, 1920, in the *Saturday Evening Post*.)
Copper Streak Trail (novel). Boston: Houghton Mifflin, 1922. (Serialized as

Over, Under, Around or Through in April and May, 1917, in the *Saturday Evening Post*.)

Once in the Saddle and *Pasó Por Aquí* (novels). Boston: Houghton Mifflin, 1927. (*Once in the Saddle* serialized in April, 1925, in the *Saturday Evening Post;* and *Pasó Por Aquí* serialized in February, 1926, in the *Post*.)

Beyond the Desert (novel). Boston: Houghton Mifflin, 1934. (Originally part of *West Is West*. Serialized in expanded form as *Beyond the Desert* in May and June, 1934, in the *Saturday Evening Post*.)

Penalosa (essay). Foreword by Alice Corbin Henderson. Santa Fe: Rydal Press, 1934. (Previously published as the fourth chapter of *West Is West*.)

The Trusty Knaves (novel). Boston: Houghton Mifflin, 1934. (Serialized in April and May, 1931, in the *Saturday Evening Post*.)

The Proud Sheriff (novel). Boston: Houghton Mifflin, 1935. (Serialized in October, 1932, in the *Saturday Evening Post*.)

The Little World Waddies (bibliography, poems, and stories). Introduction by J. Frank Dobie. Chico, California: W. H. Hutchinson, 1946.

The Best Novels and Stories of Eugene Manlove Rhodes. Edited by Frank V. Dearing, with a revised version of the Dobie introduction to *The Little World Waddies*. Boston: Houghton Mifflin, 1949. (Contains four novels—*Pasó Por Aquí, Good Men and True, Bransford of Rainbow Range,* and *The Trusty Knaves;* two novelettes—*The Desire of the Moth* and *Hit the Line Hard;* four stories; a narrative; an essay; and a poem.)

Sunset Land (novels). New York: Dell, 1955. (Contains three previously published novels: *Bransford of Rainbow Range, Good Men and True,* and *The Trusty Knaves*.)

The Rhodes Reader: Stories of Virgins, Villains, and Varmints (essays and stories). Edited with an introduction by W. H. Hutchinson. Norman: Univ. of Oklahoma Press, 1957.

The Line of Least Resistance (novel). Edited with an introduction by W. H. Hutchinson. Chico, California: Hurst and Young, 1958. (Serialized in August and September, 1910, in the *Saturday Evening Post*.)

Works by Eugene Manlove Rhodes and Collaborators
The following four works by Henry Wallace Phillips are assumed by the biographer W. H. Hutchinson to be the products of collaboration with Eugene Manlove Rhodes: *Red Saunders' Pets and Other Critters* (McClure, 1906); *Mr. Scraggs* (McClure, 1906); *The Mascot of Sweet Briar Gulch* (Bobbs-Merrill, 1908); and *Trolley Folly* (Bobbs-Merrill, 1909).

Works about Eugene Manlove Rhodes

Charles, Mrs. Tom. "Recollections of Gene Rhodes," *New Mexico Magazine* (February 1953).

Cleaveland, A. M. "Three Musketeers of Southwestern Fiction," *Overland Monthly* (December 1929).

Dobie, J. Frank. "Gene Rhodes, Cowboy Novelist," *Atlantic Monthly* (June 1949).

Fife, Jim L. "Two Views of the American West," *Western American Literature,* 1 (Spring 1966), 34-43.

Gaston, Edwin W., Jr. *Eugene Manlove Rhodes: Cowboy Chronicler.* Austin: Steck-Vaughn, 1967.

Hutchinson, W. H. *A Bar Cross Man: The Life and Personal Writings of Eugene Manlove Rhodes.* Introduction by Eugene Cunningham. Norman: Univ. of Oklahoma Press, 1956. (Contains detailed bibliography.)

————. "I Pay for What I Break," *Western American Literature,* 1 (Summer 1966), 91-96.

————. "The Mythic West of W. H. D. Koerner," *The American West,* 4 (May 1967), 54-60.

————. "Virgins, Villains and Varmints," *Huntington Library Quarterly* (August 1953).

————. "The West of Eugene Manlove Rhodes," *Arizona and the West,* 9 (Autumn 1967), 211-218.

Rhodes, May Davison. *The Hired Man on Horseback: My Story of Eugene Manlove Rhodes.* With a bibliography compiled by Vincent Starret. Boston: Houghton Mifflin, 1938.

Skillman, Richard, and Jerry C. Hoke. "The Portrait of the New Mexican in the Fiction of Eugene Rhodes," *Western Review,* 6 (Spring 1969), 26-36.

Edwin W. Gaston, Jr.
Stephen F. Austin State University

Rupert Norval Richardson (1891-   )
history

The Comanche Barrier to South Plains Settlement: A Century and a Half of Savage Resistance to the Advancing White Frontier. Glendale, California: Arthur H. Clark, 1933.

The Greater Southwest: The Economic, Social, and Cultural Development of Kansas, Oklahoma, Texas, Utah, Colorado, Nevada, New Mexico, Arizona and California from the Spanish Conquest to the Twentieth Century (with Carl Coke Rister). Glendale, California: Arthur H. Clark, 1934.

Texas, the Lone Star State. New York: Prentice-Hall, 1943; 2nd ed., 1958; 3rd ed., 1970.

Adventuring with a Purpose: Life Story of Arthur Lee Wasson. San Antonio: Naylor, 1951.

The Frontier of Northwest Texas, 1846 to 1876: Advance and Defense by the Pioneer Settlers of the Cross Timbers and Prairies. Glendale, California: Arthur H. Clark, 1963.

Famous Are Thy Halls: Hardin-Simmons University As I Have Known It, With Autobiographical Sketches. Abilene: n.p., 1964.

Caddo, Texas: The Biography of a Community. Abilene: n.p., 1966.

John T. Smith
North Texas State University

Conrad Richter (1890-1968)
novels, short stories, essays

Brothers of No Kin and Other Stories. New York: Hinds, Hayden, and Eldredge, 1924.

Human Vibration (essay). New York: Dodd, Mead, 1926.

Principles in Bio-Physics (essay). Harrisburg: Good Books Corporation, 1927.

Early Americana (stories). New York: Knopf, 1936.

The Sea of Grass. New York: Knopf, 1937.

The Trees. New York: Knopf, 1940.

Tacey Cromwell. New York: Knopf, 1942.

The Free Man. New York: Knopf, 1943.

The Fields. New York: Knopf, 1946.

Always Young and Fair. New York: Knopf, 1947.

The Town. New York: Knopf, 1950.

The Light in the Forest. New York: Knopf, 1953.

The Mountain on the Desert (essay). New York: Knopf, 1955.

The Lady. New York: Knopf, 1957.

The Waters of Kronos. New York: Knopf, 1960.

A Simple Honorable Man. New York: Knopf, 1962.

The Grandfathers. New York: Knopf, 1964.

The Awakening Land (contains *The Trees, The Fields, The Town*). New York: Knopf, 1966.

A Country of Strangers. New York: Knopf, 1966.

Over the Blue Mountain (juvenile). New York: Knopf, 1967.

The Aristocrat. New York: Knopf, 1968.

Works about Conrad Richter

Barnard, Kenneth J. "Presentation of the West in Conrad Richter's Trilogy," *Northwest Ohio Quarterly,* 29 (1957), 224-34.

Barnes, Robert J. *Conrad Richter.* Austin: Steck-Vaughn, 1968.

Carpenter, Frederic I. "Conrad Richter's Pioneers: Reality and Myth," *College English,* 12 (Nov. 1950), 77-84.

Flanagan, John T. "Conrad Richter: Romancer of the Southwest," *Southwest Review,* 43 (1958), 189-96.

————. "Folklore in the Novels of Conrad Richter," *Midwest Folklore,* 2 (Spring 1952), 5-14.

Gaston, Edwin W., Jr. *Conrad Richter.* New York: Twayne, 1965.

Kohler, Dayton. "Conrad Richter: Early Americana," *College English,* 8 (Feb. 1947), 221-28.

Lahood, Marvin J. *"The Light In the Forest:* History as Fiction," *English Journal,* 55 (1966), 298-304.

————. "Richter's Early America," *University Review,* 30 (June 1964), 311-16.

Pearce, T. M. "Conrad Richter," *New Mexico Quarterly,* 20 (1950), 371-73.

Sutherland, Bruce. "Conrad Richter's Americana," *New Mexico Quarterly Review,* 15 (1945), 413-22.

Robert J. Barnes
Lamar University

Vivian Ricker (1898-   )
poetry

The Divided Heart. Norman, Oklahoma: The Transcript Press, 1971.

In addition, Ricker published poems in *The Poetry Society of Texas Yearbook* and over thirty poems in such periodicals as *The Lyric, Kaleidograph,*

Quicksilver, The Christian Science Monitor, Holland's Magazine, The Lamp, Westminster Magazine, The Ave Maria, The Christian Family, The American Bard, and *Opinion.*

Jerry Keys
Lamar University

J. C. Rickman (-   )
novel

Racing Bits. Boston: Richard G. Badger, 1926.

Numerous articles and editorials by Rickman appear in the *Marshall News,* but many freelance articles are found in various newspapers throughout the area.

Lynn W. Denton
Auburn University

Lynn Riggs (1899-1954)
poetry, plays

Big Lake. New York: Samuel French, 1927.
Knives from Syria. New York: Samuel French. 1927.
A Lantern to See By. New York: Samuel French, 1928.
Rancor. Unpublished but available from Samuel French, New York, in mimeographed form.
Sump'n Like Wings. New York: Samuel French, 1928.
The Iron Dish (poems). Garden City, New York: Doubleday, Doran, 1930.
Roadside. New York: Samuel French, 1931.
The Cherokee Night. New York: Samuel French, 1936.
Green Grow the Lilacs. New York: Samuel French, 1936.
Russet Mantle. New York: Samuel French, 1936.
The Cream in the Well. New York: Samuel French, 1947.
The Dark Encounter. New York: Samuel French, 1947.
A World Elsewhere. New York: Samuel French, 1947.
The Year of Pilár. New York: Samuel French, 1947.
Hang Onto Love. New York: Samuel French, 1948.

394   *Southwestern American Literature*

Toward the Western Sky (with Nathan Kroll; musical pageant-drama).
Cleveland: Western Reserve, 1951.

In addition, Riggs wrote a great many produced but unpublished plays. He
also published several poems not included in *The Iron Dish.*

Works about Lynn Riggs

Aughtry, Charles E. "Lynn Riggs at the University of Oklahoma," *The
Chronicles of Oklahoma,* 37 (Autumn 1959), 280-84.

Benton, Joseph. "Some Personal Remembrances about Lynn Riggs," *The
Chronicles of Oklahoma,* 34 (Autumn 1956), 296-301.

Erhard, Thomas A. *Lynn Riggs, Southwest Playwright.* Austin: Steck-
Vaughn, 1970.

Fry, Maggie Culver. "The Lynn Riggs Memorial," *Oklahoma Today,* 17
(Summer 1967), 17-18.

———. "Memories of Lynn Riggs," *Oklahoma Today,* 10 (Winter 1959-60),
6-7, 32.

Goldberg, Isaac. "Poet from Oklahoma Writing a Folk-Play," *Boston Evening Transcript,* December 6, 1930, 4, 8.

Kaho, Noel. "Green Grow the Lilacs," *American Scene* (1962), 51-53.

Kirk, Betty. "An Oklahoma Dramatist," *My Oklahoma* (n.d.), 34, 42.

Lockridge, Richard. "Lynn Riggs's Southwest," in *American Drama as Seen
by its Critics.* New York: Norton, 1934.

"Lynn Riggs, Playwright," *Theatre Arts Monthly,* 22 (July 1938), 528.

Parker, H. T. "Green Grow the Lilacs," *American Drama and its Critics.*
Chicago: Univ. of Chicago Press, 1965.

Thomas A. Erhard
New Mexico State University

Carl Coke Rister (1889-1955)
history

The Southwestern Frontier 1865-1881. Cleveland: Arthur H. Clark, 1928.

The Greater Southwest (with R. A. Richardson). Glendale, California:
Arthur H. Clark, 1934.

Southern Plainsman. Norman: Univ. of Oklahoma Press, 1938.

Border Captives. Norman: Univ. of Oklahoma Press, 1940.

Western America (with L. R. Hafen). New York: Prentice Hall, 1941; 2nd ed., 1950.

Land Hunger, David L. Payne and the Oklahoma Boomers. Norman: Univ. of Oklahoma Press, 1942.

Baptist Missions Among the Indians. Atlanta: Home Mission Board, Southern Baptist Convention, 1944.

Border Command: General Philip Sheridan in the West. Norman: Univ. of Oklahoma Press, 1944.

Robert E. Lee in Texas. Norman: Univ. of Oklahoma Press, 1946.

No Man's Land. Norman: Univ. of Oklahoma Press, 1948.

Oil: Titan of the Southwest. Norman: Univ. of Oklahoma Press, 1949.

Comanche Bondage. Glendale, California: Arthur H. Clark, 1955.

Fort Griffin, Texas. Norman: Univ. of Oklahoma Press, 1956.

Lola Beth Green
Texas Tech University

Garland Roark (1904-   )
[pseud. George Garland]
novels, short stories

Wake of the Red Witch. Boston: Little, Brown, 1946.

Fair Wind to Java. Garden City, New York: Doubleday, 1948.

Rainbow in the Royals. Garden City, New York: Doubleday, 1950.

Doubtful Valley. New York: Houghton Mifflin, 1951.

Slant of the Wild Wind. Garden City, New York: Doubleday, 1952.

The Big Dry. New York: Houghton Mifflin, 1953.

The Wreck of the Running Gale. Garden City, New York: Doubleday, 1953.

Star in the Rigging. Garden City, New York: Doubleday, 1954.

The Outlawed Banner. Garden City, New York: Doubleday, 1956.

The Cruel Cocks. Garden City, New York: Doubleday, 1957.

Captain Thomas Fenlon. New York: Julian Messner, 1958.

The Lady and the Deep Blue Sea. Garden City, New York: Doubleday, 1958.

Diamond Six, by William Fielding Smith. Ed. Garland Roark. Garden City, New York: Doubleday, 1958.

Tales of the Caribbean. Garden City, New York: Doubleday, 1959.

Should the Wind Be Fair. Garden City, New York: Doubleday, 1960.
Apache Warpath. New York: New American Library, 1961.
Witch of Manga Reva. Garden City, New York: Doubleday, 1962.
Bugles and Brass. Garden City, New York: Doubleday, 1964.
The Coin of Contraband. Garden City, New York: Doubleday, 1964.
Bay of Traitors. Garden City, New York: Doubleday, 1966.
Hellfire Jackson (with Charles Thomas). Garden City, New York: Double-
    day, 1966.
Angels in Exile. Garden City, New York: Doubleday, 1967; rpt. as *Sim-
    mer in the Sun*. New York: Cassell, 1968.
Drill a Crooked Hole. Garden City, New York: Doubleday, 1968.
Morgan's Woman. Garden City, New York: Doubleday, 1971.
Slow Wind in the West. Garden City, New York: Doubleday, 1973.

Lynn W. Denton
Auburn University

Lexie Dean Robertson (1893-1954)
poetry

Red Heels. Dallas: P. L. Turner, 1928.
I Keep a Rainbow. Dallas: C. C. Cockrell Co., 1932.
Acorn on the Roof. Dallas: Kaleidograph, 1939.
Answer in the Night. Dallas: Kaleidograph, 1948.

Work about Lexie Dean Robertson
Edwards, Margaret Royalty. *Poets Laureate of Texas 1932-1966*. San An-
    tonio: Naylor, 1966.

Arthur M. Sampley
North Texas State University

William Penn Adair Rogers (Will Rogers) (1879-1935)
humor

Rogersisms: The Cowboy Philosopher on the Peace Conference. New York:
    Harper, 1919.
Rogersisms: The Cowboy Philosopher on Prohibition. New York: Harper,
    1919.

Rogersisms: What We Laugh At. New York: Harper, 1920.

The Illiterate Digest. New York: A & C Boni, 1924.

Letters of a Self-made Diplomat to His President. New York: A & C Boni, 1927.

There's Not a Bathing Suit in Russia and Other Bare Facts. New York: A & C Boni, 1927.

Ether and Me; or, Just Relax. New York: Putnam, 1929; rpt. New York: Putnam, 1959.

Twelve Radio Talks, Delivered by Will Rogers during the Spring of 1930 through the Courtesy of E. R. Squibb & Sons. 1930.

Will Rogers Wit and Wisdom, ed. by Jack Lait. New York: Frederick A. Stokes Co., 1936.

The Autobiography of Will Rogers. (Ed. by Donald Day.) Boston: Houghton Mifflin, 1949.

How We Elect Our Presidents. (Ed. by Donald Day.) Boston: Little, Brown, 1952.

Sanity Is Where You Find It: An Affectionate History of the United States in the 20's and 30's by America's Best Loved Comedian. (Ed. by Donald Day). Boston: Houghton Mifflin, 1955.

The Will Rogers Book. (Ed. by Paula McSpadden Love.) Indianapolis: Bobbs-Merrill, 1961.

Thee and Me, or Just Relax. Stillwater: Oklahoma State Univ. Press, 1973.

Works about Will Rogers

Carr, Harry. *To Will Rogers: Vaya con Dios.* Los Angeles: Angelus Press, 1935.

Collings, Ellsworth. *The Old Home Ranch: The Will Rogers Range in the Indian Territory.* Stillwater, Okla.: Redlands Press, 1964.

Croy, Homer. *Our Will Rogers.* New York: Duell, Sloan, & Pearce, 1953.

Day, Donald. *Will Rogers.* New York: David McKay, 1962.

Grant, Doris Shannon. *Will Rogers: Immortal Cowboy.* New York: Julian Messner, 1950.

Hitch, Arthur M. *Will Rogers: Cadet. A Record of His Two Years as a Cadet at the Kemper Military School, Boonville, Missouri, Compiled from Letters from His Fellow Cadets and Interviews with Them and from School Records.* Boonville, Mo.: Kemper Military School, 1935.

Keith, Harold. *Boy's Life of Will Rogers.* New York: Crowell, 1953.

Lait, Jack. *Our Will Rogers.* New York: Greenberg, 1935.

Milsten, David R. *Appreciation of Will Rogers*. (intr. Tom Mix). San An-
   tonio: Naylor, 1935.
O'Brien, Patrick J. *Will Rogers: Ambassador of Good Will, Prince of Wit
   and Wisdom*. Philadelphia: John C. Winston, 1935.
Payne, William H. and Jake Lyons, eds. *Folks Say of Will Rogers: A Me-
   morial Anecdotage, Auspices of the Oklahoma Society of Washington,
   D.C.* New York: Putnam, 1936.
Richards, Kenneth G. *Will Rogers*. Chicago: Children's Press, 1968.
Rogers, Betty Blake. *Will Rogers: The Story of His Life Told by His Wife*.
   Garden City, New York: Garden City Publishing Co., 1943.
Trent, Spi. M. *My Cousin Will Rogers: Intimate and Untold Tales*. New
   York: Putnam's, 1938.
Van Ripper, Guernsey. *Will Rogers: Young Cowboy*. Indianapolis: Bobbs-
   Merrill, 1951; rpt. 1953; 1962.

> Elton Miles
> Sul Ross State University

Grace Ross (-   )
poetry

Divert the Interim (with Mabel Kuykendall). Dallas: Kaleidograph, 1949.
Poetry Out Where the West Begins (comp. with Mabel Kuykendall). Dallas:
   Kaleidograph, 1949.

In addition, Ross published many individual poems in magazines of verse
and regional anthologies. She and Mabel Kuykendall served for several
years as co-editors of *Quicksilver,* a quarterly devoted to the publication of
poetry.

> James W. Lee
> North Texas State University

Malcolm Harrison Ross (1895-1965)
novels, nonfiction

Deep Enough. New York: Harcourt, Brace, 1927.
Penny Dreadful. New York: Coward-McCann, 1929.

Hymn to the Sun. New York: Scribner, 1930.
Sailing the Skies; Gliding and Soaring. New York: Macmillan, 1931.
Profitable Practice in Industrial Research; Tested Principles of Research, Laboratory Organization, Administration, and Operation. Co-eds. Maurice Holland and William Sparagen. New York and London: Harper, 1932.
Machine Age in the Hills. New York: Macmillan, 1933.
Death of a Yale Man. New York and Toronto: Farrar & Rinehart, 1939.
All Manner of Men. New York: Reynal & Hitchcock, 1948.
The Man who Lived Backward. New York: Farrar, Straus, 1950.
The Cape Fear. New York: Holt, Rinehart, and Winston, 1965.

In addition, Ross has essays on labor relations and related matters in *Nation* and in various professional journals.

Works about Malcolm Harrison Ross
Corey, Herbert. "Portrait of a Man with a Mission," *Nation's Business,* 32, (February, 1944), 36-37.

T. Clinton Owen
Texas Tech University

Jane Gilmore Rushing (1925-   )
novels, short stories, nonfiction

Walnut Grove. New York: Doubleday, 1964.
Against The Moon. New York: Doubleday, 1968; rpt. as *Geh Schlafen, Mein Herz, es is Zeit.* Hamburg: Wegner, 1969.
Tamzen. New York: Doubleday, 1972.
Mary Dove: A Love Story. Garden City, New York: Doubleday, 1974. London: Hodder and Stoughton, 1974.

Several short stories by Rushing appear in *The Virginia Quarterly Review, Forum,* and *Artesian,* and several articles have been published in *The Coming West, The Texas Outlook,* and *The Writer.*

Kenneth W. Davis
Texas Tech University

David Riley Russell (1902-1964)
poetry

There Is No Night. Dallas: Kaleidograph, 1942.
Sing With Me Now. Dallas: Kaleidograph, 1945.
The Silver Fawn. Dallas: Kaleidograph, 1946.
The Incredible Flower. Dallas: Kaleidograph, 1953.

In addition, Russell had a number of uncollected poems in *Good House-keeping, Saturday Evening Post,* and the yearbooks of the Texas Poetry Society.

T. Clinton Owen
Texas Tech University

George Frederick Augustus Ruxton (1820-1848)
nonfiction

The Oregon Question. London: J. Ollivier, 1846.
Adventures in Mexico and the Rocky Mountains. London: John Murray, 1847; rpt. 1849 and 1861.
Life in the Far West. New York: Harper, 1848; Edinburgh: Blackwood, 1849.
Adventures in Mexico and the Rocky Mountains. New York: Harper, 1848; rpt. 1860.
Leben im fernen Westen. Aus dem Englischen von M. B. Lindau. Dresden: n.p., 1852.
Adventures in Mexico. Ed. Horace Kephart. New York: Outing Publishing, 1915.
In the Old West. Ed. Horace Kephart. New York: Outing Publishing, 1915.
Wildlife in the Rocky Mountains. Ed. Horace Kephart. New York: Outing Publishing, 1916; rpt. 1921.
Wildlife in the Rocky Mountains. New York: Macmillan, 1924.
Ruxton of the Rockies. Collected by Clyde and Mae Reed Porter. Ed. Le Roy Hafen. Norman: Univ. of Oklahoma Press, 1950.
Life in the Far West. Ed. Le Roy Hafen. Norman: Univ. of Oklahoma Press, 1951; rpt. 1964.
Mountain Men. Ed. Glen Rounds. New York: Holiday House, 1966.

Works about George Ruxton

DeVoto, Bernard Augustine. *Across the Wide Missouri.* Boston: Houghton-Mifflin, 1947.

Grinell, George Bird. "George Ruxton—Hunter," in *Beyond the Old Frontier; Adventures of Indian-Fighters, Hunters, and Fur-Traders.* New York: Scribner's, 1913; rpt. 1930.

Schaefer, Jack Warner. *Heroes Without Glory: Some Goodmen of the Old West.* Boston: Houghton-Mifflin, 1965.

Voelker, Frederick E. "Ruxton of the Rocky Mountains," *Bulletin of the Missouri Historical Society,* (January 1949), pp. 79-90.

Shelley Armitage
Texas Tech University

Marah Ellis Ryan (1860-1934)
[pseud. Ellis Martin]
novels, short stories

Merze. Chicago and New York: Rand McNally, 1889.

In Love's Domains. Chicago and New York: Rand McNally, 1890.

Told in the Hills. Chicago and New York: Rand McNally, 1891; rpt. New York: Grossett & Dunlap, 1918.

Squaw Eloise. Chicago and New York: Rand McNally, 1892.

A Chance Child. Chicago and New York: Rand McNally, 1896.

The Bondwoman. Chicago and New York: Rand McNally, 1899; rpt. New York: Grossett & Dunlap, 1918.

That Girl Montana. Chicago and New York: Rand McNally, 1901; rpt. New York: Grossett & Dunlap, 1918.

For the Soul of Rafael. Chicago: A. C. McClurg, 1906.

My Quaker Maid. Chicago and New York: Rand McNally, 1906.

Indian Love Letters. Chicago: A. C. McClurg, 1907.

Miss Moccasins. Chicago and New York: Rand McNally, 1912.

The Flute of the Gods. New York: F. A. Stokes, 1909; rpt. New York: Grossett & Dunlap, 1913.

Pagan Prayers. Chicago: A. C. McClurg, 1913.

The Woman of the Twilight. Chicago: A. C. McClurg, 1913.

The House of Dawn. Chicago: A. C. McClurg, 1914.

The Druid Path. Chicago: A. C. McClurg, 1917.

Flower of France. Chicago and New York: Rand McNally, 1894; rpt. New
   York: Grossett & Dunlap, 1918.
The Treasure Trail. Chicago: A. C. McClurg, 1918.
A Pagan of the Alleghanies. Chicago and New York: Rand McNally, 1891;
   rpt. New York: Grossett & Dunlap, 1920.
The Dancer of Tuluum. Chicago: A. C. McClurg, 1924.

                              Lynn W. Denton
                              Auburn University

Robert Rylee (1908-   )
novels

Deep Dark River. New York: Farrar & Rinehart, 1935.
St. George of Weldon. New York: Farrar & Rinehart, 1937.
The Ring and the Cross. New York: Knopf, 1947.

                              Lynn W. Denton
                              Auburn University

William Samelson (1928-   )
novel, biography

Gerhart Herrmann Mostar: a Critical Profile. The Hague: Mouton, 1966.
All Lie in Wait. Englewood Cliffs, New Jersey: Prentice-Hall, 1969.
The Sephardi Heritage. London: Vallentine, Mitchell, 1972.

In addition, Samelson published several textbooks; and a number of short
stories in *Jewish Forum.*

                              Zula Williams Vizard
                              San Antonio College

Arthur McCullough Sampley (1903-   )
poetry, plays

The Marriage of Francis Arden and Other One-Act Plays. Dallas: The
   South-West Press, 1933.
This is Our Time. Dallas: Kaleidograph, 1943.

Of the Strong and the Fleet. Dallas: Kaleidograph, 1947.
Furrow With Blackbirds. Dallas: Kaleidograph, 1951.
Selected Poems, 1937-1971. Denton: North Texas State Univ. Press, 1971.

In addition, Sampley published poems in such periodicals as *Antioch Review, Kenyon Review, Saturday Review,* and *Saturday Evening Post.* Critical articles have appeared in *PMLA, Modern Language Notes, College English, Shakespeare Quarterly,* and others.

Gerald A. Kirk
North Texas State University

Leonard Sanders (1929-   )
[pseud. Dan Thomas]
novels, journalism

Four-Year Hitch. New York: Ace Books, 1961.
The Wooden Horseshoe. Garden City, New York: Doubleday, 1964.
The Seed [Dan Thomas]. New York: Ballantine Books, 1963.

In addition, Sanders published numerous articles in *True* and other magazines and numerous book reviews and literary columns in the *Fort Worth Star-Telegram.*

Albert J. Griffith
Our Lady of the Lake College
San Antonio, Texas

Ross Santee (1888-1965)
novels, short stories

Men and Horses. New York: The Century Co., 1926.
Cowboy. New York: Cosmopolitan Book Corp., 1928.
The Pooch. New York: Cosmopolitan Book Corp., 1931.
The Bar X Golf Course. New York: Farrar and Rinehart, 1933.
Sleepy Black. New York: Farrar and Rinehart, 1933.
Spike: The Story of a Cowpuncher's Dog. New York: Grossett and Dunlap, 1934.
Apache Land. New York: Scribner's, 1947.
The Bubbling Spring. New York: Scribner's, 1949.

Rusty, A Cowboy of the Old West. New York: Scribner's, 1950.
Hardrock and Silver Sage. New York: Scribner's, 1952.
Lost Pony Tracks. New York: Scribner's, 1953.
Dog Days. New York: Scribner's, 1955.
The Rummy Kid Goes Home and Other Stories of the Southwest. New York: Hastings House, 1965.

For a period of thirty years, Santee contributed articles to such leading periodicals as *The American Magazine, Century Magazine,* and *Arizona Highways.*

Works about Ross Santee
Dykes, Jeff C. "Tentative Bibliographic Checklists of Western Illustrators," *American Book Collector* 15, 10, (Summer 1966).
Gerhardt, Frances. "On the Santee Trail," *Arizona Silver Belt* (10 December 1964).
Houston, Neal B. *Ross Santee.* Austin: Steck-Vaughn, 1968.
Powell, Lawrence Clark. *Heart of the Southwest.* Los Angeles: Printed for Dawson's Book Shop at the Plantin Press, 1955.
Santee, Ellis M. *Genealogy of the Santee Family.* New York: Cortland, 1899.
Weadcock, Jack F. "A Dedication to the Memory of Ross Santee 1889-1965," *Arizona and the West* (Autumn 1965).

Neal B. Houston
Stephen F. Austin State University

Dorothy Scarborough (1878-1935)
novels, short stories, poetry, folklore, nonfiction

Fugitive Verses. Waco: Baylor Univ. Press, 1912.
The Supernatural in Modern English Fiction. New York: Putnam's, 1917.
From a Southern Porch. New York: Putnam's, 1919.
The Best Psychic Stories. Ed. with preface by Joseph Lewis French. Introduction by Dorothy Scarborough. New York: Boni and Liveright, 1920.
Famous Modern Ghost Stories. Selected with an introduction by Dorothy Scarborough. New York: Putnam's 1921.

Humorous Ghost Stories. Selected and with an introduction by Dorothy
Scarborough. New York: Putnam's, 1921.
In the Land of Cotton. New York: Macmillan, 1923.
The Unfair Sex, serialized in *The Woman's Viewpoint* during 1925-26.
The Wind. New York: Harper, 1925.
On the Trail of Negro Folk-Songs. Assisted by Ola Lee Gulledge. Cam-
bridge: Harvard Univ. Press, 1925; rpt. facsimile with Foreword by
Roger D. Abrahams. Hatboro, Pa.: Folklore Associates, 1963.
Impatient Griselda. New York: Harper, 1927.
Can't Get a Redbird. New York: Harper, 1929.
The Stretch-berry Smile. Indianapolis: Bobbs-Merrill, 1932.
The Story of Cotton. New York: Harper, 1933.
Selected Short Stories of Today. Ed. with an introduction by Dorothy
Scarborough. New York: Farrar and Rinehart, 1935.
*A Song Catcher in Southern Mountains: American Folk Songs of British
Ancestry.* New York: Columbia Univ. Press, 1937.

In addition, Scarborough published approximately six stories and articles
in *Harper's, Bookman, Century,* and *MS* between 1918 and 1930.

Works about Dorothy Scarborough
Cranfill, Mabel. "Dorothy Scarborough—An Appreciation," *Baylor Bulle-
tin,* 40 (Aug. 1937), 38-45.
———. "Dorothy Scarborough," *Texas Monthly,* 4 (September 1929), 212-28.
———. "Dorothy Scarborough," *Magazine World,* 8 (October 1931), 27-28.
Leake, Grace Hillary. "Dorothy Scarborough, a Splendid Southerner,"
Holland's Magazine, 45 (February 1928), 63.

Don R. Swadley
University of Texas at Arlington

Jack Warner Schaefer (1907-   )
novels, short stories, nonfiction

Shane. Boston: Houghton Mifflin, 1949.
The Big Range. Boston: Houghton Mifflin, 1953.
The Canyon. Boston: Houghton Mifflin, 1953.
First Blood. Boston: Houghton Mifflin, 1953.

The Pioneers. Boston: Houghton Mifflin, 1954.
Out West: An Anthology of Stories. Boston: Houghton Mifflin, 1955.
Company of Cowards. Boston: Houghton Mifflin, 1957.
The Kean Land, and Other Stories. Boston: Houghton Mifflin, 1959.
Old Ramon. Boston: Houghton Mifflin, 1960.
The Great Endurance Horse Race: 600 Miles on a Single Mount, 1908, from Evanston, Wyoming, to Denver. Santa Fe: Stagecoach Press, 1963.
Monte Walsh. Boston: Houghton Mifflin, 1963.
The Plainsmen. Boston: Houghton Mifflin, 1963.
Stubby Pringle's Christmas. Boston: Houghton Mifflin, 1964.
Heroes Without Glory: Some Goodmen of the Old West. Boston: Houghton Mifflin, 1965.
Adolphe Francis Alphonse Bandelier. Santa Fe: Territorian Press, 1966.
The Collected Stories of Jack Schaefer. Boston: Houghton Mifflin, 1966.
Mavericks. Boston: Houghton Mifflin, 1967.
New Mexico. States of the Nation Series. New York: Coward-McCann, 1967.
The Short Novels of Jack Schaefer. Boston: Houghton Mifflin, 1967.

In addition, Schaefer published approximately a dozen essays in *Holiday* between 1955 and 1965; he is currently publishing some "Notes for a New Mexico Bestiary," in *New Mexico.*

Works about Jack Schaefer
Dieter, Lynn. "Behavioral Objectives in the English Classroom: A Model," *English Journal,* 59 (December 1970), 1258-1262, 1271.
Erisman, Fred. "Growing Up with the American West: the Fiction of Jack Schaefer," *Journal of Popular Culture,* 7 (Winter 1973), 710-16. Reprinted in Richard W. Etulain and Michael T. Marsden, eds., *The Popular Western.* Bowling Green: Bowling Green Univ. Popular Press, 1974, pp. 68-74.
Folsom, James K. *"Shane* and *Hud:* Two Stories in Search of a Medium," *Western Humanities Review,* 24 (Autumn 1970), 359-72.
Haslam, G. W. "Jack Schaefer's Frontier: the West as Human Testing Ground," *Rocky Mountain Review,* 4 (1967), 59-71.
Johnson, Dorothy M. "Jack Schaefer's People," in *The Short Novels of Jack Schaefer.* Boston: Houghton Mifflin, 1967. Pp. vii-x.
Mikkelsen, Robert. "The Western Writer: Jack Schaefer's Use of the Western Frontier," *Western Humanities Review.* 6 (Spring 1954), 151-55.

Nuwer, Hank. "An Interview With Jack Schaefer," *South Dakota Review,* 11 (Spring 1973), 48-58.
Scott, Winfield Townley. "Introduction. . . ," *The Collected Stories of Jack Schaefer.* Boston: Houghton Mifflin, 1966. Pp. vii-xi.
Shor, Rachel. "Jack Schaefer," *Wilson Library Bulletin,* 35 (February 1961), 471.

Fred Erisman
Texas Christian University

Ruth Garrison Scurlock (1894-   )
short stories, poetry

Voice upon the Wind. San Antonio: Naylor, 1960.
October Music. Beaumont: Blotter Press, Lamar College, 1964.
On a Summer Afternoon. Beaumont: LaBelle Press, 1968.
Two Tales Told in the Stars (stories). Baton Rouge: Blotter Press, L.S.U., 1968.

In addition, Scurlock published approximately sixty uncollected short stories in *The Coastal Cattleman* from 1937 to 1942.

Violette Newton
Beaumont, Texas

Charles Sealsfield [see Karl Postl]

Roger W. Shattuck (1923-   )
poetry, nonfiction

The Banquet Years: The Arts in France, 1885-1918. New York: Harcourt, Brace, 1958; London: Faber, 1959. Rpt. several times.
Proust's Binoculars; A Study of Memory, Time, and Recognition in A la recherche du temps perdu. New York: Random House, 1963; London: Chatto & Windus, 1964.
Half Tame, Poems. Austin: Univ. of Texas Press, 1964.

In addition, Shattuck published translations from French, editions of French authors, and critical articles in *Texas Quarterly, Yale French Studies, and Western Review.*

Judy Ponthieu
Geoffrey Grimes
Texas Tech University

Edwin (Bud) Shrake (1931-   )
novels, journalism

Blood Reckoning. New York: Bantam, 1962.
But Not For Love, Garden City, New York: Doubleday, 1964. London: Michael Joseph, 1964.
Blessed MacGill. Garden City, New York: Doubleday, 1968.
Strange Peaches. New York: Harper's Magazine Press, 1972.
Peter Arbiter. Austin: Encino, 1974.

Shrake, formerly a newspaper columnist and now an editor of *Sports Illustrated,* has published a great many articles on sports in *Sports Illustrated* and in other publications. He also wrote the screen plays for *J. W. Coop* and *Kid Blue.*

Sandra Corse
Texas Woman's University

Gene Shuford (1907-   )
poetry

The Red Bull and Other Poems. Fort Smith, Arkansas: South and West, 1964.
Selected Poems, 1931-1971. Denton: North Texas State Univ. Press, 1972.

In addition, Shuford published more than fifty poems in such journals as *Scribner's, Saturday Evening Post, New Republic, Southwest Review, New Mexico Quarterly, Arlington Quarterly,* yearbooks of the Poetry Society of Texas, and various anthologies.

Charles Ramos
Midwestern University

August Siemering (1830-1895)
nonfiction

Ein Verfehltes Leben. Cincinnati: The Cincinnati *Volkes-Blattes,* 1876.
Texas als Ziel der Auswanderung. San Antonio: Harrisburg-San Antonio
   Railroad Co., 1882; Hamburg, Germany: J. F. Richter, 1882.
The Hermit of the Cavern. Trans., adapted by May E. Francis. San An-
   tonio: Naylor, 1932.

In addition, Siemering published a number of articles, in German, in foreign language journals published in America.

James G. Cooper
South Plains College

Edgar Simmons (1921-   )
poetry

Driving to Biloxi. Baton Rouge: Louisiana State Univ. Press, 1968.

In addition, Simmons has approximately seventy-five uncollected poems in
such journals as *Atlantic Monthly, Harper's, Yale Review, Harvard Advocate, Commonweal,* and *The Nation;* and in several anthologies.

C. E. Shuford
North Texas State University

Marc Simmons (1937-   )
nonfiction

Indian and Mission Affairs in New Mexico, 1773. Translated and edited by
   Marc Simmons. Santa Fe: Stagecoach Press, 1965.
Border Comanches, Seven Spanish Colonial Documents, 1785-1819. Trans-
   lated and edited by Marc Simmons. Santa Fe: Stagecoach Press, 1967.
Two Southwesterners, Charles Lummis and Amado Chaves. Cerrillos, New
   Mexico: San Marcos Press, 1967.
Spanish Government in New Mexico. Albuquerque: Univ. of New Mexico
   Press, 1968.
Yesterday in Santa Fe, Episodes in a Turbulent History. Cerrillos, New
   Mexico: San Marcos Press, 1968.

The Fighting Settlers of Seboyeta. Cerrillos, New Mexico: San Marcos
Press, 1971.
The Little Lion of the Southwest. Chicago: Swallow Press, 1973.
Turquoise and Six Guns, The Story of Cerrillos, New Mexico. Santa Fe:
Sunstone Press, 1974.
Witchcraft in the Southwest. Flagstaff: Northland, 1974.

Durrett Wagner
Chicago, Illinois

Frank E. Simmons (1880-1952?)
short stories, history

History of Coryell County. Gatesville, Texas: *Coryell County News,* 1936.
Coryell County History Stories. Oglesby, Texas: n.p., 1948.
History of Mother Neff Memorial State Park. Gatesville, Texas: Freeman
Printing Plant, 1949.

Simmons published several stories and poems in *McGregor Mirror, Coryell County News, Cranfille's Gap Enterprise,* and *Farm and Ranch.*

Lynn W. Denton
Auburn University

Charles A. Siringo (1855-1928)
nonfiction

*A Texas Cow Boy, or Fifteen Years on the Hurricane Deck of a Spanish
Pony.* Chicago: M. Umbdenstock, 1885. Variously reprinted; most recent
is Lincoln: Univ. of Nebraska Press, 1966, with introduction by J. Frank
Dobie.
A Cowboy Detective. Chicago: W. B. Conkey Co., 1912.
Two Evil Isms: Pinkertonism and Anarchism. Chicago: Charles A. Siringo,
1915; rpt. Austin: Steck-Vaughn, 1967. (Introduction Charles Peavy)
A Lone Star Cowboy. Santa Fe: Charles Siringo, 1919.
A Song Companion of A Lone Star Cowboy. Santa Fe: Charles A. Siringo,
1919.
History of "Billy the Kid." Santa Fe: Charles A. Siringo, 1920; rpt Austin:
Steck-Vaughn, 1967.
Riata and Spurs. Boston and New York: Houghton Mifflin, 1927.

Shortened titles of Siringo's works are substituted for the long, descriptive titles Siringo gave them; they can be found in their entirety in Charles Peavy, *Charles A. Siringo.*

Works about Charles A. Siringo

Adams, Clarence Siringo. "Fair Trial at Encinoso," *True West,* 5 (March-April 1966), 32 ff.

Clark, Neil M. "Close Calls: An Interview with Charles A. Siringo," *The American Magazine,* 107 (January 1929), 38 ff.

Hess, Chester Newton. "Sagebrush Sleuth," *Cattleman,* 41 (January 1955), 36 ff.

Nolen, O. W. "Charley Siringo," *Cattleman,* 38 (December 1951), 50 ff.

Peavey, Charles D. *Charles A. Siringo: A Texas Picaro.* Austin: Steck-Vaughn, 1967.

Rhodes, Eugene M. "He'll Make A Hand," *Sunset Magazine,* 58 (June 1927), 23.

Thorp, Raymond W. "Cowboy Charley Siringo," *True West,* 12 (January-February 1965), 32 ff.

Charles D. Peavy
University of Houston

John Peter Sjolander (1851-1939)
poetry

Salt of the Earth and Sea. Dallas: P. L. Turner, 1928.

In addition, Sjolander has approximately one hundred uncollected poems in journals and newspapers.

Works about John Peter Sjolander

Bard, W. E. "John P. Sjolander," *A Book of the Year 1939.* Dallas: The Poetry Society of Texas, 1940. Pp. 36-39.

Greer, Hilton. "John P. Sjolander," *Library of Southern Literature.* Ed. E. A. Alderman and J. C. Harris. Atlanta: Martin & Hoyt, 1903-13. XI, 4833-35.

Montgomery, Vaida Stewart. *A Century with Texas Poets and Poetry.* Dallas: The Kaleidograph Press, 1934.

Richardson, T. C. "The Sage of Cedar Bayou," *Farm and Ranch,* (15 August 1934), pp. 2, 9.

————. "The Sage of Cedar Bayou," *Southwestern Historical Quarterly,* 48 (1944-45), 321-39.

Wynn, William T. *Southern Literature.* New York: Prentice-Hall, 1932.

Jack D. Wages
Texas Tech University

C. W. Smith (1940-   )
novel

Thin Men of Haddam. New York: Grossman, 1973.

Monte D. Fite
North Texas State University

Dama Margaret Smith (1893-   )
[Mrs. Charles Jerod "White Mountain" Smith, pseud. Dama Langley]
nonfiction

I Married A Ranger. Stanford: Stanford Univ. Press, 1930.
Petrified Forest National Monument. Winslow, Arizona: Winslow Daily Mail, 1930.
Hopi Girl. Stanford: Stanford Univ. Press, 1931.
Indian Tribes of the Southwest. Stanford: Stanford Univ. Press, 1933.

In addition, Smith has more than a hundred articles in such journals as *Desert, Good Housekeeping, American Girl, Catholic World, Ford, Pathways, Pathfinder, Santa Fe Magazine, Arizona Highways Magazine,* and *Trailways.*

Jack D. Wages
Texas Tech University

Charles Leland Sonnichsen (1901-   )
history, folklore

Billy King's Tombstone: The Private Life of an Arizona Boom Town. Caldwell, Idaho: Caxton, 1942.
Roy Bean: Law West of the Pecos. New York: Macmillan 1943; rpt. New York: Devin Adair, 1954; rpt. New York: Hillman, 1959.

Cowboys and Cattle Kings. Norman: Univ. of Oklahoma Press, 1950.

I'll Die Before I'll Run. New York: Harper, 1951. Rewritten and expanded. New York: Devin-Adair, 1962.

Alias Billy the Kid (with William Morrison). Albuquerque: Univ. of New Mexico Press, 1955.

Ten Texas Feuds. Albuquerque: Univ. of New Mexico Press, 1957.

The Mescalero Apaches. Norman: Univ. of Oklahoma Press, 1958.

Tularosa: Last of the Frontier West. New York: Devin-Adair, 1960.

The El Paso Salt War. El Paso: Carl Hertzog and Texas Western Press, 1961.

The Southwest in Life and Literature (anthology). New York: Devin-Adair, 1962.

Outlaw: Bill Mitchell Alias Baldy Russell, His Life and Times. Denver: Sage Books, 1965.

Pass of the North: Four Centuries on the Rio Grande. El Paso: Carl Hertzog and Texas Western Press, 1968.

The State National Since 1881: The Pioneer Bank (with Millard G. McKinney). El Paso: Texas Western Press, 1971.

Colonel Green and the Copper Skyrocket. Tucson: Univ. of Arizona Press, 1974.

San Augustin: First Cathedral Church in Arizona (with George W. Chambers). Tucson: The Arizona Historical Society, 1974.

Works about C. L. Sonnichsen

Walker, Dale L. *C. L. Sonnichsen: Grassroots Historian.* El Paso: Texas Western Press, 1972. Includes a bibliography by Bud Newman of Sonnichsen's many articles and reviews.

Joyce Roach
Keller, Texas

Terry Southern (1924-   )
novels, short stories, nonfiction

Flash and Filigree. New York: Coward, 1958.

Candy (with Mason Hoffenberg). Paris: Olympia, 1959; rpt. New York: Putnam's, 1964.

The Magic Christian. Toronto: Andre Deutsch, 1959; rpt. New York: Random House, 1960.

Red Dirt Marijuana and Other Tastes. New York: New American Library, 1968; rpt. New York: World, 1968.
Blue Movie. New York: World, 1970.

Southern has also published over fifty short stories in such magazines as *Harper's Bazaar, Esquire,* and *Evergreen Review;* written numerous critical articles for newspapers and magazines; and coauthored the screenplay of *Dr. Strangelove.*

Diane Dodson
North Texas State University

Hart Stilwell (1902-   )
novels, short stories, nonfiction

Border City. New York: Doubleday, 1945.
Hunting and Fishing in Texas. New York: Knopf, 1946.
Uncovered Wagon. New York: Doubleday, 1947.
Fishing in Mexico. New York: Knopf, 1948.
Campus Town. New York: Doubleday, 1950.
Old Soggy No. 1: The Uninhibited Story of Slats Rogers (with Slats Rogers). New York: J. Messner, 1954.
The Child Who Walks Alone: Case Studies of Rejection in the Schools (with Anne Stilwell). Austin: Univ. of Texas Press, 1972.

Stilwell is also the author of *Looking at Man's Past* (1965), juvenile literature, four short stories, and approximately forty-seven articles published in such magazines as *Outdoor Life, Field and Stream, National Common Ground, Holiday, Science Digest,* and *Collier's.*

Laura B. Kennelly
North Texas State University

Libby Stopple (1910-   )

Red Metal. Dallas: Story Book Press, 1952.
Never Touch a Lilac. San Antonio: Naylor, 1959.

Singer in the Side. Chicago: Windfall Press, 1968.
Peppermints: Poems of Childhood. Dallas: Dallas Records Publishing Co., 1970.

H. Jerome Thompson
Texas Tech University

Julia Hurd Strong (1908-   )
poetry

Postlude to Mendelssohn. Philadelphia: Dorrance, 1964.

Strong has also published poems in *Good Housekeeping, Saturday Evening Post, Christian Science Monitor, N.E.A. Journal,* and other periodicals; and in *The Golden Year: Anthology of the Poetry Society of America; Surf, Stars,* and *Stone;* Poetry Society of Texas *Yearbooks;* and other anthologies.

Arthur M. Sampley
North Texas State University

Chester Sullivan (1939-   )
novel

Alligator Gar. New York: Crown, 1973.

William T. Pilkington
Tarleton State University

Alan Swallow (1915-1966)
fiction, poetry, nonfiction

The Practice of Poetry. Albuquerque: Swallow & Critchlow, 1942.
XI Poems. Muscatine, Iowa: Prairie Press, 1943.
The Remembered Land. Prairie City, Illinois: James A. Decker, 1946.
The War Poems. New York: Fine Editions, 1948.

Two Stories. Denver: Swallow, 1953.
The Beginning Writer. Boulder: Johnson, 1954.
The Nameless Sight: Poems, 1937-56. Iowa City: Prairie Press, 1956.
An Editor's Essays of Two Decades. Seattle: Experiment Press, 1962.

Swallow also edited, in whole or part, the following magazines: *Advance Guard* (1948), *Author & Journalist* (1950-51), *Modern Verse* (1941-42), *New Mexico Quarterly Review* (1942-48), *PS* (1953-65), and *Twentieth Century Literature* (1955-66). In addition, he edited fourteen anthologies and textbooks. His uncollected short pieces can be found in North's Checklist. Perhaps the best summary of Swallow's role as book publisher is his autobiographical account, "Story of a Publisher," in *New Mexico Quarterly,* 36 (Winter 1967).

Works about Alan Swallow
Elman, R. "Publisher for Poets," *Saturday Review,* 44 (July 22, 1966), 33-34.
McConnell, Virginia. "Alan Swallow and Western Writers," *South Dakota Review,* 5 (Summer 1967), 88-97.
North, Dennis D. "A Bibliographical Checklist," *Denver Quarterly,* 2 (Spring 1967), 63-72.
Ross, Morton L. "Alan Swallow and Modern Western Poetry," *Western American Literature,* 1 (Summer 1966), 97-104.
Winters, Yvor. "Alan Swallow: 1915-1966," *Southern Review,* 3 (July 1967), 796-98.
Yueh, Norma N. "Alan Swallow, Publisher, 1915-1966," *Library Quarterly,* 39 (July 1969), 223-32.

The Dennis D. North "Bibliographical Checklist" above is part of the Memorial section of *Denver Quarterly* devoted to Alan Swallow. Included in the Spring 1967 number are thirteen tributes. Prose: Mark Harris (pp. 5-9), Gene Lundahl (pp. 33-36), Frederick Manfred (pp. 27-31), Anais Nin (pp. 11-14), Martin Robbins (pp. 37-39), Allen Tate (p. 43), and Frank Waters (pp. 16-25). Poetry: Edgar Bowers (p. 15), J. V. Cunningham (p. 44), Donald F. Drummond (p. 26), Thomas McGrath (p. 10), Alan Stephens (pp. 40-42), and Robert Penn Warren (p. 32).

Martin Bucco
Colorado State University

Alexander Edwin Sweet (1841-1901)
humor

Sketches from "Texas Siftings" (with J. Armoy Knox). New York: Texas Siftings Publishing Company, 1882.
On a Mexican Mustang through Texas from the Gulf to the Rio Grande (with J. Armoy Knox). Hartford: S. S. Scranton, 1883.
Three Dozen Good Stories from Texas Siftings (with J. Armoy Knox). New York: J. S. Ogilvie, 1887.

Works about Alexander Edwin Sweet
Miles, Elton. *Southwest Humorists*. Austin: Steck-Vaughn, 1969. pp. 13-23.
Speck, Ernest B. "Alex Sweet, Comic Journalist from Texas," *Texas Press Messenger,* 46 (May 1971), 6-8.

Ernest Speck
Sul Ross State University

Rosemary Taylor (1899-   )
novels

Chicken Every Sunday: My Life with Mother's Boarders. New York: Mc-Graw-Hill, 1943.
Ridin' the Rainbow: Father's Life in Tucson. New York: McGraw-Hill, 1944.
Bar Nothing Ranch. New York: McGraw-Hill, 1947.
Come Clean, My Love. New York: Crowell, 1949.
Harem Scar'em. New York: Crowell, 1951.
Ghost Town Bonanza. New York: Crowell, 1954.
Broadway in a Barn. New York: Crowell, 1957.
Looking Up. New York: Putnam, 1959.

Elton Miles
Sul Ross State University

Ross McLaury Taylor (1909-   )
novels

Brazos. Indianapolis, New York: Bobbs-Merrill, 1938.
The Saddle and the Plow. Indianapolis, New York: Bobbs-Merrill, 1942.

The Fabric of Fiction (Anthology of short stories with Douglas Bement). New York: Harcourt, Brace, 1943.
We Were There on the Chisholm Trail. New York: Grosset and Dunlap, 1957.
We Were There on the Santa Fe Trail. New York: Grosset and Dunlap, 1960.

Billie Phillips
San Antonio College

Marshall Terry (1931-   )
novels, short stories, literary criticism

Old Liberty. New York: Viking, 1961. London: Jonathan Cape, 1961. Reissued as *Don't Blow Your Cool.* New York: Paperback Library, 1967.
Tom Northway. New York: Harcourt, Brace and World, 1968.

In addition, Terry has five stories in *Southwest Review* and several articles and book reviews in that journal and in *S-CMLA Bulletin.*

Margaret Hartley
Southern Methodist University

Dan Thomas [see Leonard Sanders]

Mack Thomas (1928-   )
novels, short stories

Gumbo. New York: Grove Press, 1965.
Total Beast. New York: Simon and Schuster, 1970.

In addition, Thomas has a few stories in *Evergreen Review* and *Saturday Evening Post.*

Sandra Corse
Texas Woman's University

John William Thomason, Jr. (1893-1944)
novels, short stories, nonfiction

Fix Bayonets! New York: Scribner, 1926; rpt. 1970.

Marines and Others. New York: Scribner, 1929.
Jeb Stuart. New York: Scribner, 1930. Rpt. 1934, 1958.
Salt Winds and Gobi Dust. New York: Scribner, 1934.
Adventures of General Marbot. Edited and illustrated by Thomason. New York: Scribner, 1935.
Gone to Texas. New York: Scribner, 1937; rpt. New York: Avon, 1954.
Lone Star Preacher. New York: Scribner, 1941.
And a Few Marines. New York: Scribner, 1943; rpt. 1958.
A Thomason Sketchbook: Drawings. Austin: Univ. of Texas Press, 1969. Edited with a foreword by Arnold Rosenfeld.

In addition, Thomason published many stories in *Scribner's* and *Saturday Evening Post.*

Works about John W. Thomason
Norwood, W. D., Jr. *John W. Thomason, Jr.* Austin: Steck-Vaughn, 1969.
Perkins, Maxwell. *Editor to Author.* New York: Scribner, 1950.
Willock, Roger. *Lone Star Marine: A Biography of the Late Colonel John W. Thomason, Jr., U.S.M.C.* Princeton: Roger Willock, 1961.

> Arlene E. Kyle
> North Texas State University

Nathan Howard (Jack) Thorp (1867-1940)
cowboy songs, tales

Songs of the Cowboys (23 ballads). Estancia, New Mexico: Author, 1908; rev. and expanded edition (101 songs), Boston: Houghton Mifflin, 1921.
Tales of the Chuck Wagon. Santa Fe: New Mexican Publishing Co., 1926.
Pardner of the Wind (autobiography with Neil McCullough Clark). Caldwell, Idaho: Caxton, 1945.

In addition, Thorp has several uncollected songs, poems, and tales in *Cattleman, New Mexico Magazine,* and *Poetry.*

Works about Jack Thorp
Dobie, J. Frank. "Early Mustangers and Their Methods," *The Cattleman,* 38 (September 1951), 41.

420   *Southwestern American Literature*

————. "In a Pit with a Grizzly," *Frontier Times,* Winter 1959-1960, pp. 20-21, 52.
————. "Jack Thorp's Horse Stories," *The Cattleman,* 32 (October 1945), 108-9.
Fife, Austin E. and Alta S. Fife, eds. *Songs of the Cowboys.* New York: Potter, 1966.

Ann Carpenter
Angelo State University

Zoe Agnes Stratton Tilghman (1880-   )
novels

The Dugout. Oklahoma City: Harlow, 1925.
Outlaw Days. Oklahoma City: Harlow, 1926.
Prairie Winds. Oklahoma City: Harlow, 1930.
Quanah, the Eagle of the Comanches. Oklahoma City: Harlow, 1938.
Marshal of the Last Frontier. Glendale, California: A. H. Clark, 1949.
Spotlight. San Antonio: Naylor, 1960.

Patricia Lee Ashmore
North Texas State University

Lon Tinkle (1906-   )
history, biography

13 Days to Glory: The Siege of the Alamo. New York: McGraw-Hill, 1958.
Story of Oklahoma. New York: Random House, 1962.
Valiant Few: Crisis at the Alamo. New York: Macmillan, 1964.
Key to Dallas. Philadelphia: Lippincott, 1965.
J. Frank Dobie: The Makings of an Ample Mind. Austin: Encino Press, 1968.
Mr. Dee: A Biography of Everette Lee De Golyer. Boston: Little, Brown, 1970.

E. Hudson Long
Baylor University

Frank X. Tolbert (1910-   )
nonfiction, journalism

Neiman-Marcus, Texas. New York: Holt, 1953.
Bigamy Jones. New York: Holt, 1954.
The Staked Plain. New York: Harper, 1958.
The Day of San Jacinto. New York: McGraw-Hill, 1959.
An Informal History of Texas. New York: Harper, 1961.
Dick Dowling at Sabine Pass. New York: McGraw-Hill,
A Bowl of Red. New York: Doubleday, 1966.

In addition, Tolbert published hundreds of articles and short stories in *Collier's, Saturday Evening Post, Sports Illustrated, Library Journal,* and *Motor Trend.* He has been a columnist for the *Dallas News* since 1946.

Jan Epton Seale
McAllan, Texas

Bess Truitt (1884-   )
novel

Thistle Down and Prairie Rose. Kansas City: Burton, 1941.

Patricia Lee Ashmore
North Texas State University

Steven Turner (1923-   )
novels, short stories, play, literary criticism

A Measure of Dust (novel). New York: Simon and Schuster, 1970.
George Milburn (criticism). Austin: Steck-Vaughn, 1970.

Turner has written a short story and a play, "Three Golden Monkeys" (unpublished but produced by an amateur theatrical group in 1967 at the University of Texas at Arlington).

Works about Steven Turner
Anon. "An Interview with Novelist Steven Turner," *Prism Magazine,* 1 (December 1970), 24-27.

James Cox
Denton, Texas

Wilbur Coleman Tuttle (1883-   )
novels

Henry the Sheriff. New York: Grosset & Dunlap, 1936.
The Keeper of Red Horse Pass. Cleveland, New York: World, 1937.
Straws In the Wind. Boston: Houghton Mifflin, 1948.
Renegade Sheriff. New York: Bouregy & Curl, 1953.
Mission River Justice. New York: Avalon, 1955.
Outlaw Empire. New York: Thomas Bouregy, 1960.

Patricia Lee Ashmore
North Texas State University

Ruth Murray Underhill (1884-   )
nonfiction

The Papago Indians of Arizona and Their Relatives the Pima. Ed. Willard
W. Beatty. Washington: Bureau of Indian Affairs, 1941.
Pueblo Crafts. Washington: Bureau of Indian Affairs, 1944.
First Came the Family. New York: Morrow, 1958.
Red Man's America: A History of Indians in the United States. Chicago:
Univ. of Chicago Press, 1963.
Red Man's Religion: Beliefs and Practices of the Indians North of Mexico.
Chicago: Univ. of Chicago Press, 1965.
Indians of the Southwest. Garden City: Doubleday, 1966.
The Navajos. Norman: Univ. of Oklahoma Press, 1967.
Papago Indian Religion. New York: AMS Press, 1969.
*Singing for Power: The Song Magic of the Papago Indians of Southern
Arizona.* Berkeley: Univ. of California Press, 1969.
Social Organization of the Papago Indians. New York: AMS Press, 1969.

Underhill also contributed several articles on American Indian culture to
American Anthropology and *Arizona Quarterly,* and a section on Indian
religion to *The North American Indian* (New York: Macmillan, 1970).

Works about Ruth M. Underhill
Parshalles, Eve. *Kashmir Bridge-Women.* New York: Oxford Univ. Press,
1965.

Sondra Sugarman
San Antonio, Texas

Eleanor Graham Vance (1908-   )
poetry, juveniles, essays

Christmas in Old England (operetta). USA: Silver Burdett, 1938.
For These Moments (poems). Brattleboro, Vermont: S. Daye, 1939.
A Musical Calendar. USA: Silver Burdett, 1940.
Canciones Pan-Americanas. USA: Silver Burdett, 1942.
Store in Your Heart (poems). New York: Bookman Associates, 1950.
It Happens Every Day (poems). Francestown, New Hampshire: Golden
    Quill, 1962.
Jonathan. Chicago: Follett, 1966.

Vance has also written nine juvenile books and numerous essays, poems,
articles, and stories published in such periodicals as *Good Housekeeping,
Saturday Evening Post, New Yorker, Ladies Home Journal, Saturday Review, Parents', New York Times, New York Herald Tribune,* and children's
magazines.

Linda J. Strauss
North Texas State University

Frank Everson Vandiver (1925-   )
history, biography

Confederate Blockade-Running Through Bermuda, 1861-1865. Austin:
    Univ. of Texas Press, 1947.
The Civil War Diary of General Josiah Gorgas, by Josiah Gorgas. (Ed.
    Frank Vandiver). Alabama: Univ. of Alabama Press, 1947.
Ploughshares into Swords: Josiah Gorgas and Confederate Ordnance. Aus-
    tin: Univ. of Texas Press, 1952.
Rebel Brass: The Confederate Command System. Baton Rouge: Louisiana
    State Univ. Press, 1952.
Proceedings of the Congress of the Confederate States of America. (Ed.
    Frank Vandiver). Virginia Historical Society, 1953-1959.
Mighty Stonewall. New York: McGraw-Hill, 1957.
Narrative of Military Operations, by Joseph E. Johnston. (Ed. Frank Van-
    diver). Bloomington: Indiana Univ. Press, 1959.
War Memoirs, by Jubal A. Early. (Ed. Frank Vandiver). Bloomington:
    Indiana Univ. Press, 1960.

Fields of Glory, an Illustrated Narrative of American Land Warfare. (With
William H. Nelson). New York: Dutton, 1960.
Jubal's Raid: General Early's Famous Attack on Washington. New York:
McGraw-Hill, 1960.
Basic History of the Confederacy. Princeton: Van Nostrand, 1962.
John J. Pershing. Morristown, N. J.: Silver Burdett, 1967.
Their Tattered Flags: The Epic of the Confederacy. New York: Harper's
Magazine Press, 1970.

Bessie M. Pearce
San Antonio College

Edmund van Zandt (1916-1972)
[pseud. Tom Pendleton]
novels

Deep Test [Edmund Van Zandt]. Serialized in *Collier's,* 1953.
The Iron Orchard. New York: McGraw-Hill, 1966.
Hodak. New York: McGraw-Hill, 1969.
The Seventh Girl: A Romantic Tale of Civil War Texas. New York:
McGraw-Hill, 1970.

James T. F. Tanner
North Texas State University

R. G. Vliet (1929-   )
short stories, poetry

Events and Celebrations. New York: Viking Press, 1966.
Man with the Big Mouth. Santa Cruz: Kayak Press, 1970.
Rockspring. New York: Viking, 1974.

In addition to the volumes of poetry listed above, Vliet has two stories and
approximately thirty uncollected poems in such journals as *Hudson Review,
Kayak, Texas Quarterly,* and *Accent.*

Sondra Sugarman
San Antonio, Texas

Edward S. Wallace (1897-1964)
nonfiction

General William Jenkins Worth, Monterey's Forgotten Hero. Dallas: Southern Methodist Univ. Press, 1953.
The Story of the U.S. Cavalry (with Major General John K. Herr). Boston: Little, Brown, 1953.
The Great Reconnaissance. Soldiers, Artists, and Scientists on the Frontier 1848-1861. Boston: Little, Brown, 1955.
Destiny and Glory. New York: Coward-McCann, 1957.

In addition, Wallace has a number of articles in such journals as *American Heritage* and *Southwestern Historical Quarterly.*

Ben E. Pingenot
Eagle Pass, Texas

Lew Wallace (1827-1905)
novels, nonfiction

The Fair God, Or the Last of the 'Tzins. Boston: J. R. Osgood, 1873.
Ben-Hur: A Tale of Christ. New York: Harper, 1880. Reprinted in part as *The First Christmas,* New York: n.p., 1902.
The Life of Benjamin Harrison. Philadelphia: Hubbard, 1888.
The Boyhood of Christ. New York: Harper, 1889.
The Prince of India. New York: Harper, 1893.
The Wooing of Malkatoon, and Commodus, a Poem (1889). New York: Harper, 1898.
Lew Wallace, An Autobiography. New York: Harper, 1906.
Our English Cousin. MS (1875?). Lew Wallace, Jr., Collection.
An American Duchess. MS (1901?). Lew Wallace, Jr., Collection

Wallace published four articles, one each in *Youth's Companion* (Feb. 2, 1893), *Harper's Weekly* (Aug. 19, 1893), *Century* (Sept. 1901), and *North American Review* (Dec. 1901).

Works about Lew Wallace
Armstrong, W. P. "General Lew Wallace: Indiana Lawyer Who Found Fame as an Author," *American Bar Association Journal,* 34 (April 1948), 283-86.

426   *Southwestern American Literature*

Banta, R. E., ed. "Lew Wallace, An Autobiography," *Hoosier Caravan,* Indiana: Indiana Univ. Press, 1951. pp. 296-330.

Barber, A. W., ed. *Benevolent Raid of General Lew Wallace.* Washington, D. C.: Privately printed, 1914.

Cunliffe, J. W., and A. H. Thorndike, eds. "Lew Wallace," in *Warner Library.* USA: US Publishing Association, 1917. Vol. 25.

Field, E. M. "Christ of Ben-Hur," *Humanities Review,* 93 (Jan. 1927), 449-51.

Forbes, John D. "Lew Wallace, Romantic," *Indiana Magazine of History,* 44 (1949), 385-92.

Harkins, E. F. "The Literary Creed of Lew Wallace," in *Famous Authors.* USA: Page, 1901. pp. 59-74.

Horwood, W. P. "Ben-Hur," *Classical Journal,* October 1930, pp. 39-40.

Howard, O. O. "Lew Wallace, An Autobiography," *North American Review,* 173 (Dec. 21, 1906), 1294-99.

Krout, M. H. "Personal Reminiscences of Lew Wallace," *Harper's Weekly* (18 March 1905), pp. 406-09.

Lamont, H. "The Winner in the Chariot Race," *Nation* (Feb. 23, 1905), 48.

McKee, Irving. *"Ben-Hur" Wallace: The Life of General Lew Wallace.* Berkeley: Univ. of California Press, 1947.

———. "The Early Life of Lew Wallace," *Indiana Magazine of History,* 37 (1941), 205-16.

McMillen, W. "Century of Lew Wallace and a Half Century of *Ben-Hur,*" *Mentor,* 15 (May 1947), 33-5.

Mott, Frank Luther. *Golden Multitudes.* New York: Macmillan Co., 1947.

Nicholson, Meredith. "Was Lew Wallace 'An Oriental with Medieval Tastes'?" *Review of Reviews,* 31 (April 1905), 480-81.

Price, R. "Teacher's Part in *Ben-Hur,*" *Primary Education-Popular Education,* 44 (April 1927), 613.

Riley, J. W. "General Lew Wallace," *Collier's Weekly* (March 4, 1905), 17.

Russo, Dorothy and T. L. Sullivan. *Bibliographical Studies of Seven Authors of Crawfordsville, Indiana.* Indiana: Indiana Historical Society, 1952. pp. 305-416.

Schaaf, M. E. *Lew Wallace, Boy Writer.* New York: Bobbs Merrill, 1962.

Schnell, E. A. "General Lew Wallace and *Ben-Hur,*" *Methodist Review,* 65 (c. 1902-06), 729.

Swift, L. "Literary Work of Lew Wallace," *Book Buyer,* 21 (Sept. 1900), 93.

Tarkington, B. "Lew Wallace," in *There Were Giants in the Land.* New York: Rinehart, 1942. pp. 75-82.

Ticknor, C., ed. *Glimpses of Authors.* Boston: Houghton, 1922.

Towne, Jackson E. "Lew Wallace's *Ben-Hur,*" *New Mexico Historical Review,* 36 (1961), 62-66.

Whittlesey, C. "General Lew Wallace at Shiloh," *Magazine of Western History,* 2 (c. 1885), 213.

Young, William. *Lew Wallace's Ben-Hur.* New York: n.p., 1899.

Linda J. Strauss
North Texas State University

Frank Waters (1902-   )
novels, nonfiction

Fever Pitch (novel). New York: Liveright, 1930.

The Wild Earth's Nobility (novel). New York: Liveright, 1935.

Below Grass Roots (novel). New York: Liveright, 1937.

Midas of the Rockies: Biography of Winfield Scott Stratton. New York: Covici-Friede, 1937; rpt. Denver: Swallow, 1954; Chicago: Swallow Press, 1973.

The Dust Within the Rock (novel). New York: Liveright, 1940.

People of the Valley (novel). New York: Farrar & Rinehart, 1941; rpt. Denver: Swallow, 1956.

The Man Who Killed the Deer (novel). New York: Farrar & Rinehart, 1942; rpt. Denver: Swallow, 1954.

River Lady (novel). New York: Farrar & Rinehart, 1942.

The Colorado. New York: Farrar & Rinehart, 1946.

The Yogi of Cockroach Court (novel). New York: Rinehart, 1947; rpt. Chicago: Swallow Press, 1973.

Diamond Head (novel). NewYork: Farrar & Straus, 1948.

Masked Gods: Navaho and Pueblo Ceremonialism. Albuquerque: Univ. of New Mexico Press, 1950; rpt. Denver: Swallow, 1962.

The Earp Brothers of Tombstone. New York: Clarkson Potter, 1960.

The Sketches of Leon Gaspard. Los Angeles: Southwest Museum, 1962.

Book of the Hopi. New York: Viking, 1963.

Leon Gaspard. Flagstaff: Northland Press, 1964.

Mysticism and Witchcraft. Fort Collins, Colorado State Univ., 1966.

The Woman at Otowi Crossing (novel). Denver: Swallow, 1966.

Pumpkin Seed Point: Being Within the Hopi. Chicago: Swallow Press, 1969.

428   *Southwestern American Literature*

Pike's Peak: A Family Saga (novel). Chicago: Swallow Press, 1971. A one-volume revised edition of trilogy: *The Wild Earth's Nobility, Below Grass Roots, The Dust Within the Rock.*
First ABC. New York: Watts, 1971.
To Possess the Land: A Biography of Arthur Rochford Manby. Chicago: Swallow Press, 1973.

In addition, Waters has a number of shorter pieces in such journals as *Holiday, Yale Review, Southwest Review, New Mexico Quarterly Review,* and *Western American Literature.*

Works about Frank Waters
Bucco, Martin. *Frank Waters.* Austin: Steck-Vaughn, 1969.
Lyon, Thomas J. "An Ignored Meaning of the West," *Western American Literature,* 3 (Summer 1968), 103-13.
————. *Frank Waters.* New York: Twayne, 1973.
Milton, John R. "The Land as Form in Frank Waters and William Eastlake," *Kansas Quarterly,* 2 (Spring 1970), 104-08.
————, ed. *Conversations with Frank Waters.* Chicago: Swallow Press, 1972.
Pilkington, William T. "Character and Landscape: Frank Waters' Colorado Trilogy," *Western American Literature,* 3 (Fall 1967), 183-93; rpt. in *My Blood's Country.* Ft. Worth: Texas Christian Univ. Press, 1973.
Young, Vernon. "Frank Waters: Problems of the Regional Imperative," *New Mexico Quarterly Review,* 19 (Autumn 1949), 353-72.

Martin Bucco
Colorado State University

John Cherry Watson (1909-   )
novel, short stories

The Red Dress. New York: Harper, 1949; rpt., New York: Pocket Books, 1950.
Between 1946 and 1954, Watson published ten short stories in *Atlantic Monthly, Collier's, Esquire, Harper's, Southwest Review,* and *Today's Woman.*

Vetal Flores
Angelo State University

Winston Weathers (1926-   )
short stories, poetry, nonfiction

The Strategy of Style (with Otis Winchester). New York: McGraw-Hill, 1967.

The Archetype and the Psyche: Essays in World Literature. Tulsa: Univ. of Tulsa Monograph Series, 1968.

Par Lagerkvist: A Critical Essay. Grand Rapids: Erdman, 1968.

The Prevalent Forms of Prose (with Otis Winchester). Boston: Houghton Mifflin, 1968.

Copy and Compose (with Otis Winchester). Englewood Cliffs: Prentice-Hall, 1969.

William Blake's "The Tyger": A Casebook. Columbus: Merrill, 1969.

The Attitudes of Rhetoric (with Otis Winchester). Englewood Cliffs: Prentice-Hall, 1970.

Indian and White; Sixteen Ecologues. Lincoln: Univ. of Nebraska Press, 1970.

The Lonesome Game: Thirteen Stories. New York: David Lewis, 1970.

Messages From the Asylum. Tulsa: Joseph Nichols, 1970.

The Island: A Quadricinium. Tulsa: Joseph Nichols, 1974.

In addition, Weathers has published six radio plays as well as dozens of critical essays, stories, and poems in such periodicals as *Arizona Quarterly, North American Review, Texas Quarterly, Commonweal,* and *Southwest Review.*

Helen Lang Leath
North Texas State University

Walter Prescott Webb (1888-1963)
history

The Great Plains. Boston: Ginn, 1931.

The Texas Rangers: A Century of Frontier Defense. Boston: Houghton Mifflin, 1935. Rpt. with Introduction by Lyndon B. Johnson, Austin: Univ. of Texas Press, 1965.

Divided We Stand: The Crisis of a Frontierless Democracy. New York: Farrar and Rinehart, 1937. Rev., Austin: Acorn Press, 1944. Rev. and abridged, Manchaca, Texas: Chapparal Press, 1947. Rev., Austin: The University Co-op, 1964.

The Great Frontier. Boston: Houghton Mifflin, 1952. Rpt. with Introduction by Arnold Toynbee, 1964.

The Handbook of Texas. Ed. by Walter P. Webb and others. 2 vols. Austin: Texas State Historical Association, 1952.

More Water for Texas: The Problem and the Plan. Austin: Univ. of Texas Press, 1954.

The Story of the Texas Rangers. New York: Grosset and Dunlap, 1957.

An Honest Preface and Other Essays. Boston: Houghton Mifflin, 1959.

Flat Top: A Story of Modern Ranching. El Paso: Carl Hertzog, 1960.

History as High Adventure. Edited with Introduction by E. C. Barksdale. Austin: Pemberton Press, 1969.

Talks on Texas Books: A Collection of Book Reviews. Compiled and edited with Introduction by Llerena Friend. Austin: Texas State Historical Association, 1970.

In addition, Webb was co-author of nine secondary school textbooks and more than a hundred essays and reviews in learned journals, popular magazines, and newspapers.

Works about W. P. Webb

Barraclough, G., "Metropolis and Macrocosm," *Past and Present,* 5 (May 1954), 77-93.

Billington, Ray A. "Frederick Jackson Turner and Walter Prescott Webb: Frontier Historians," *Essays on The American West, The Walter Prescott Webb Memorial Lectures: III,* ed. by Harold M. Hollingsworth and Sandra L. Myres, Austin: Univ. of Texas Press, 1969. pp. 89-114.

Brown, Lyle C. "Tribute to a Texan, Walter Prescott Webb," *West Texas Historical Association Year Book,* 39 (1963), 93-105.

Caughey, John W. "A Criticism of the Critique of Webb's *The Great Plains,"* *Mississippi Valley Historical Review,* 27 (December 1940), 442-44.

Dugger, Ronnie, ed., *Three Men in Texas: Bedichek, Webb, and Dobie.* Austin: Univ. of Texas Press, 1967.

Frantz, Joe B. "Walter Prescott Webb: 'He'll Do to Ride the River With,' " An Appreciative Introduction to *An Honest Preface and other Essays,* by Walter Prescott Webb. Boston: Houghton Mifflin, 1959.

———. "Walter Prescott Webb: The Life of a Texan," *Texas Libraries,* 25 (Fall 1963), 77-82.

———. "Bibliography: Walter Prescott Webb," *Texas Libraries,* 25 (Fall 1963), 82-87.

————. "Walter Prescott Webb: No Slave of Whistle, Clock or Bell," *Prairie Schooner*, 38 (Spring 1964), 45-47.

————. "Walter Prescott Webb," *The American West*, 1 (Winter 1964), 40-43.

Friend, Llerena B. "W. P. Webb's Texas Rangers," *Southwestern Historical Quarterly*, 74 (January 1971), 293-323.

Jacobs, Wilbur R., John W. Caughey, and Joe B. Frantz. *Turner, Bolton, and Webb: Three Historians of the American Frontier*. Seattle: Univ. of Washington Press, 1965.

Lea, Tom, Arnold Toynbee, C. Vann Woodward, John Fischer, J. Frank Dobie, J. Alton Burdine, Logan Wilson, Clarence Ayres and W. Gordon Whaley. "A Man, His Land and His Work: Walter Prescott Webb," *The Graduate Journal*, 6 (Winter 1964), 32-61.

Lewis, Archibald R., and Thomas F. McGann, eds. *The New World Looks at Its History*. Austin: Univ. of Texas Press, 1963.

Malin, James C. *The Grassland of North America: Prolegomena to Its History*. Lawrence, Kansas: Privately printed, 1947.

————. *On the Nature of History: Essays About History and Dissidence*. Ann Arbor: Edwards, 1954.

Morris, Margaret F., comp. "Walter Prescott Webb, 1888-1963: A Bibliography," in *Essays on the American Civil War, The Walter Prescott Webb Memorial Lectures: I*, ed. by William F. Holmes and Harold M. Hollingsworth. Austin: Univ. of Texas Press, 1968. pp. 88-107.

Owens, William A. *Three Friends: Roy Bedichek, J. Frank Dobie, Walter Prescott Webb*. Garden City: Doubleday, 1969.

Parker, Edith H. "William Graham Sumner and the Frontier," *Southwest Review*, 41 (Autumn 1956), 357-65.

Parker, Franklin. "Walter Prescott Webb, 1888-1963: Western Historian," *Journal of the West*, 2 (July 1963), 362-64.

Rundell, Walter, Jr. "Walter Prescott Webb: Product of Environment," *Arizona and the West*, 5 (Spring 1963), 1-28.

————. *Walter Prescott Webb*. Austin: Steck-Vaughn, 1971.

————. "Webb to Bolton," *Western Historical Quarterly*, 2 (April 1971), 229-31.

Shannon, Fred A. *An Appraisal of Walter Prescott Webb's The Great Plains: A Study in Institutions and Environment*. New York: Social Science Research Council, 1940.

Stevens, Harry R. "Cross Section and Frontier," *South Atlantic Quarterly*, 52 (July 1953), 445-63.

Vandiver, Frank E. "Walter Prescott Webb: Teacher," *Southwest Review,* 48 (Autumn 1963), 377-79.

Wish, Harvey. *The American Historian.* New York: Oxford Univ. Press, 1960. pp. 150, 204-05, 208.

Young, Sister Anne Marie. "Walter Prescott Webb," *Texas Quarterly,* 11 (Spring 1968), 70-79.

Walter Rundell, Jr.
University of Maryland

Charles Wilkins Webber (1819-1856)
[pseud. C. W. Eimi]
novels, short stories

Adventures, or Wild Life on the Texan Frontier, by a Kentuckian [C. W. Eimi]. Published in *The New World,* March-July 1844.

Old Hicks the Guide, or Adventures . . . in Search of a Gold Mine. New York: Harper, 1848.

The Gold Mines of the Gila. New York: DeWitt & Davenport, 1849.

The Romance of Natural History, or Wild Scenes and Wild Hunters. Philadelphia: J. W. Bradley, 1851.

The Hunter-Naturalist, or Wild Scenes and Wild Hunters! Philadelphia: Lippincott and Grambo, 1852.

The Prairie Scout, or Agatone the Renegade. New York: DeWitt & Davenport, 1852.

The Texan Virago; Or the Tailor of Gotham and Other Tales. Philadelphia: Lippincott and Grambo, 1852.

The Wild Girl of Nebraska. Philadelphia: Lippincott and Grambo, 1852.

Adventures with the Texas Rifle Rangers. London: n.p., 1853.

The Romance of the Forest and Prairie Life. London: H. Vizetelly, 1853.

Shot in the Eye. London: n.p., 1853.

Tales of the Southern Border. Philadelphia: Lippincott and Grambo, 1853.

Yieger's Cabinet: Spiritual Vampirism: The History of Etherial Softdown and Her Friends of the "New Light." London: H. Vizetelly, 1853.

Wild Scenes and Song Birds. New York: J. C. Riker, 1854.

"Sam," or the History of Mystery. Cincinnati: A. M. Rulison, 1855.

History and Revolutionary Incidents of the Early Settlers of the United States. Philadelphia: D. Rulison, 1859.

In addition, Webber published numerous articles and stories in such publications as *Democratic Review, Graham's American Monthly, Godey's Lady's Book, Literary World,* and others. He was also editor and joint proprietor of the *American Review,* later called the *American Whig Review.*

Works about Charles W. Webber
Hawthorne, Nathaniel. Review of *Hunter-Naturalist,* reprinted in *New England Quarterly,* 9 (Sept. 1936), 508-09.

Linda J. Strauss
North Texas State University

Robert S. Weddle (1921-   )
history

The San Saba Mission: Spanish Pivot in Texas. Austin: Univ. of Texas Press, 1964.
San Juan Bautista: Gateway to Spanish Texas. Austin: Univ. of Texas Press, 1968.
Wilderness Manhunt, The Spanish Search for La Salle. Austin: Univ. of Texas Press, 1973.
Plow-Horse Cavalry. Austin: Madrona, 1974.

In addition, Weddle has essays in such journals as *Southwest Heritage, Southwestern Historical Quarterly,* and *Texas Military History.*

Ben E. Pingnot
Eagle Pass, Texas

John Edward Weems (1924-   )
nonfiction

A Weekend in September. New York: Holt, 1957.
The Fate of the Maine, New York: Holt, 1958.
Race for the Pole. New York: Holt, 1960.
Peary: The Explorer and the Man. Boston: Houghton Mifflin, 1967.
Men Without Countries: Three Adventurers of the Early Southwest. Boston: Houghton Mifflin, 1969.

A Dream of Empire: Human History of the Republic of Texas, 1836-1846.
New York: Simon and Schuster, 1971.
To Conquer a Peace: The War Between the United States and Mexico.
New York: Doubleday, 1974.

E. Hudson Long
Baylor University

Paul Iselin Wellman (1898-1966)
novels, nonfiction

Death on the Prairie (history). New York: Macmillan, 1934.
Death in the Desert (history). New York: Macmillan, 1935.
Jubal Troop. New York: Grossett and Dunlap, 1939.
The Trampling Herd (history). Philadelphia: Lippincott, 1939.
Broncho Apache. New York: Grosset and Dunlap, 1942.
The Bowl of Brass. Philadelphia: Lippincott, 1944.
The Walls of Jericho. Philadelphia: Lippincott, 1947.
The Chain. Garden City: Doubleday, 1949.
The Iron Mistress. Garden City: Doubleday, 1951.
The Comancheros, Garden City: Doubleday, 1952.
The Female. Garden City: Doubleday, 1953.
Glory, God and Gold: Mainstream of America Series. Ed. Lewis Gannett.
    Garden City: Doubleday, 1954.
Jericho's Daughters. Garden City: Doubleday, 1956.
Gold in California (juvenile). Los Angeles: North Star, 1958.
Ride the Red Earth. Garden City: Doubleday, 1958.
The Fiery Flower. Garden City: Doubelday, 1959.
Indian Wars and Warriors: East (juvenile). Los Angeles: North Star, 1959.
Indian Wars and Warriors: West (juvenile). Los Angeles: North Star, 1959.
Portage Bay (memoirs). Garden City: Doubleday, 1959.
Stuart Symington (biography). Garden City: Doubleday, 1959.
A Dynasty of Western Outlaws (history). Garden City: Doubleday, 1961.
Magnificent Destiny. Garden City: Doubleday, 1962.
Race to the Golden Spike (juvenile). Los Angeles: North Star, 1962.
The Greatest Cattle Drive (juvenile). Los Angeles: North Star, 1964.
Spawn of Evil (history). Garden City: Doubleday, 1964.

In addition, Wellman has a number of journalistic articles in *Saturday Evening Post, Field and Stream,* and *Saturday Review.*

Gordon Cole
Southwest Texas State University

Green Peyton Wertenbaker (1907-   )
[pseuds. Green Peyton, Peyton Green]
nonfiction

Black Cabin. Boston: Houghton Mifflin, 1933.
Rain on the Mountain. Boston: Houghton Mifflin, 1934.
San Antonio, City in the Sun. New York: McGraw-Hill, 1946.
For God and Texas; The Life of P. B. Hill. New York: McGraw-Hill, 1947.
America's Heartland, The Southwest. Norman: Univ. of Oklahoma Press, 1948.
5000 Miles Towards Tokyo. Norman: Univ. of Oklahoma Press, 1955.
The Face of Texas; A Survey in Words and Pictures. New York: Crowell, 1961.

Sam G. Terry
Appalachian State University

David Westheimer (1917-   )
[pseud. Z. Z. Smith]
novels, short stories, play

Summer on the Water. New York: Macmillan, 1948.
Long Bright Days. London: Wingate, 1950.
The Magic Fallacy. New York: Macmillan, 1950. Also adapted as three-act play entitled *Day Into Night.*
Watching Out for Dulie [Z. Z. Smith]. New York: Dodd, Mead, 1960.
A Very Private Island. New York: New American Library, 1962.
J. P. Miller's Days of Wine and Roses (novel based on Miller's screenplay). New York: Bantam, 1963.
This Time Next Year. New York: New American Library, 1963.
Von Ryan's Express. Garden City: Doubleday, 1964.
My Sweet Charlie (play). Garden City: Doubleday, 1965.
Song of the Young Sentry. Boston: Little, Brown, 1968.

436   *Southwestern American Literature*

Lighter Than a Feather. Boston: Little, Brown, 1971.
Downfall. New York: Bantam, 1972.
Over the Edge. Boston: Little, Brown, 1972.
Going Public. New York: Mason & Lipscomb, 1973.
The Olmec Head. Boston: Little, Brown, 1973.

In addition, Westheimer has published stories in *American Mercury* (1947) and *Good Housekeeping* (1949), and an article in *Writer* (1967).

Linda J. Strauss
North Texas State University

John Weston (1932-   )
novels, short stories

Jolly. New York: David McKay, 1965.
The Telling. New York: McKay, 1966.
Hail, Hero! New York: McKay, 1968.
Goat Songs. New York: Atheneum, 1971.

William T. Pilkington
Tarleton State University

Elizabeth Lee Wheaton (-   )
poetry, nonfiction

Mr. George's Joint. New York: Dutton, 1941.
Texas City Remembers. San Antonio: Naylor, 1948.

Wheaton has published articles and poems in educational magazines such as *Grade Teacher, The Instructor,* and *Texas Outlook.*

Jan Epton Seale
McAllen, Texas

Thomas Bacon Whitbread (1931-   )
short stories, poetry, nonfiction

Four Infinitives (poems). New York: Harper & Row, 1958.
The Later Poems of Wallace Stevens. Cambridge: Harvard Univ. Press, 1959.

Seven Contemporary Authors: Essays on Cozzens, and Others. Edited with Introduction by Whitbread. Austin: Univ. of Texas Press, 1966.

In addition, Whitbread has approximately fifty uncollected poems and a few stories in such journals as *Approach, Carleton Miscellany, Minnesota Review, Chicago Review, Paris Review,* and *Southwest Review.*

Billie Phillips
San Antonio College

Stewart Edward White (1873-1946)
novels, short stories, nonfiction

Conjuror's House: A Romance of the Free Forest. New York: McClure, Phillips, 1903. Rpt. as *The Call of the North: Being a Dramatized Version of Conjuror's House.* New York: Grosset and Dunlap, 1903.
Camp and Trail. Garden City: Doubleday, Doran, 1907.
Silent Places. Garden City: Doubleday, Doran, 1909.
Rules of the Game. Garden City: Doubleday, Doran, 1910.
Adventures of Bobby Orde. Garden City: Doubleday, Doran, 1911.
Cabin. Garden City: Doubleday, Doran, 1911.
Land of Footprints. Garden City: Doubleday, Doran, 1912.
African Camp Fires. Garden City: Doubleday, Doran, 1913.
Gold. Garden City: Doubleday, Doran, 1913.
Gray Dawn. Garden City: Doubleday, Doran, 1915.
The Rediscovered Country. Garden City: Doubleday, Doran, 1915.
Leopard Woman. Garden City: Doubleday, Doran, 1916.
The Forty-Niners: A Chronicle of the California Trail and El Dorado. New Haven: Yale Univ. Press, 1918.
Simba. Garden City: Doubleday, Doran, 1918.
Daniel Boone, Wilderness Scout. Garden City: Doubleday, Page, 1920.
The Forest. Garden City: Doubleday, Page, 1920.
Killer. Garden City: Doubleday, Doran, 1920.
Mystery (with S. H. Adams). Garden City: Doubleday, Doran, 1920.
Rose Dawn. Garden City: Doubleday, Doran, 1920.
On Tiptoe. Garden City: Doubleday, Doran, 1922.
The Magic Forest, New York: Macmillan, 1923.
Glory Hole. Garden City: Doubleday, Doran, 1924.

Credo. Garden City: Doubleday, Doran, 1925.
The Pass. Garden City: Doubleday, Doran, 1925.
Skookum-Chuck. Garden City: Doubleday, Doran, 1925.
Lions in the Path. Garden City: Doubleday, Doran, 1926.
Claim Jumpers. Garden City: Doubleday, Doran, 1928.
The Mountains. Garden City: Doubleday, Doran, 1928.
Riverman. Garden City: Doubleday, Doran, 1928.
Secret Harbour. New York: Grosset and Dunlap, 1928.
The Westerners. Garden City: Doubleday, Doran, 1928.
Why Be a Mud-Turtle? Garden City: Doubleday, Doran, 1928.
Back of Beyond. New York: Grosset and Dunlap, 1929.
Dog Days: Other Times, Other Dogs (autobiography). Garden City: Doubleday, Doran, 1930.
Arizona Nights. Garden City: Sun Dial Press, 1931.
The Shepper-Newfounder. Garden City: Doubleday, Doran, 1931.
The Long Rifle. Garden City: Doubleday, Doran, 1932.
Folded Hills. Garden City: Doubleday, Doran, 1934.
Pole Star (with Harry De Vighne). Garden City: Doubleday, Doran, 1935.
Ranchero. Garden City: Doubleday, Doran, 1935.
Betty Book. New York: Dutton, 1937.
Across the Unknown (with H. A. White). New York: Dutton, 1939.
Unobstructed Universe. New York: Dutton, 1940.
Wild Geese Calling. Garden City: Doubleday, Doran, 1940.
The Road I Know. New York: Dutton, 1942.
Stampede. Garden City: Doubleday, Doran, 1942.
Anchors to Windward. New York: Dutton, 1943.
Speaking for Myself. Garden City: Doubleday, Doran, 1943.
Stars Are Still There. New York: Dutton, 1946.
With Folded Wings, New York: Dutton, 1947.
Job of Living. New York: Dutton, 1948.

Works about Stewart Edward White
Baldwin, Charles C. *The Men Who Make Our Novels.* Freeport, New York: Dodd, Mead, 1924.
Overton, Grant. *When Winter Comes to Main Street.* New York: George H. Doran, 1922.

Robert G. Cowser
University of Tennessee at Martin

Frederic Will (1928-   )
poetry

Mosaic and Other Poems. University Park: Pennsylvania State Univ. Press, 1959.

A Wedge of Words. Austin: Univ. of Texas Press, 1962.

Planets. Francestown, New York: Golden Quill Press, 1967.

In addition, Will has approximately twenty-five uncollected poems in such journals as *Poetry, Tri-Quarterly, Kayak,* and *Antioch Review.* He is also the author of several volumes of scholarly and critical essays.

C. E. Shuford
North Texas State University

George Guion Williams (1902-   )
novels, nonfiction

Creative Writing for Advanced College Classes. New York: Harper, 1935. Rev., 1954.

Readings for Creative Writers. New York: Harper, 1938.

The Blind Bull. New York: Abelard-Schuman, 1952.

British Poems of the Nineteenth Century. Houston, Texas: Privately printed, 1957.

Some of My Best Friends are Professors: A Critical Commentary on Higher Education. New York: Abelard-Schuman, 1958.

Geological Factors in the Distribution of American Birds. Evolutionary Aspects of Migration. Two Lida Scott Brown Lectures in Ornithology given at the University of California, Los Angeles, on July 22 and July 25, 1958. Berkeley: Univ. of California Press, 1965.

A New View of Chaucer. Durham: Duke Univ. Press, 1965.

Guide to Literary London. London: B. T. Batsford, 1973.

In addition, Williams published some forty essays on literature and on ornithology between 1927 and 1967.

Works about George Guion Williams

" 'The Man of Letters In a World of Science,' " *Rice University Sallyport,* 22 (December 1965), 1, 4.

Fred Erisman
Texas Christian University

Augusta Jane Evans Wilson (1835-1909)
novels, short stories, nonfiction

Inez: A Tale of the Alamo. New York: Harper, 1855.

Beulah. New York: Derby & Jackson, 1859.

Macaria; or, Altars of Sacrifice. Richmond: West & Johnson, 1864; New York: John Bradburn, 1864.

St. Elmo. New York: G. W. Carleton & Co.; London: S. Low, Son & Co., 1867.

Vashti; or, "Until Death Us Do Part." New York: G. W. Carleton & Co.; London: S. Low, Son & Co., 1869.

Infelice. New York: G. W. Carleton & Co.; London: S. Low, Son & Co., 1876.

At the Mercy of Tiberius. New York: G. W. Dillingham Co., 1887.

A Speckled Bird. New York: G. W. Dillingham Co., 1902.

Devota. New York: G. W. Dillingham Co., 1907; new edition 1913 with biographical reminiscences by Thomas C. DeLeon.

Works about Augusta Jane Evans Wilson

Brewton. W. W. "St. Elmo and St. Twelmo," *Saturday Review of Literature,* 5 (June 22, 1929), 1123-24.

Calkins, Ernest E. "St. Elmo: or, Named for a Best Seller," *Saturday Review of Literature,* 21 (December 16, 1939), 3-4, 14-17.

Cowie, Alexander. "Augusta Jane Evans Wilson," in *The Rise of the American Novel.* New York: American Book Company, 1948. pp. 430-34.

Davidson, James W. *The Living Writers of the South.* New York: G. W. Carleton & Co., 1869.

Derby, J. C. *Fifty Years Among Authors, Books and Publishers.* New York: G. W. Carleton & Co., 1884.

Fidler, William P. *Augusta Evans Wilson, 1835-1909, A Biography.* University: Univ. of Alabama Press, 1951.

———. "Augusta Evans Wilson as Confederate Propagandist," *Alabama Review,* 2 (January 1949). 32-44.

Forrest, Mary. *Women of the South Distinguished in Literature.* New York: Derby & Jackson, 1960.

Holliday, Carl. "Augusta Evans Wilson," in *A History of Southern Literature.* New York: Neale Publishing Co., 1906. pp. 281-86.

Hubbell, Jay B. "Augusta Jane Evans Wilson," in *The South in American Literature, 1607-1900.* Durham: Duke Univ. Press, 1954. pp. 610-16.

Manly, Louise. "Augusta Evans Wilson: 1835-1909." in *Library of Southern Literature,* ed. E. A. Alderman and J. C. Harris. Atlanta: Martin & Hoyt, 1910, XIII, 5842.

Maurice, Arthur B. "Best Sellers of Yesterday: I—Augusta Jane Evans' *St. Elmo," Bookman,* 31 (March 1910), 35.

Pickett, La Salle C. "The 'Mother' of 'St. Elmo,' " in *Literary Hearthstones of Dixie.* Philadelphia: Lippincott, 1912. pp. 283-305.

Rutherford, Mildred Lewis. "Augusta Evans (Mrs. Wilson)," in *The South in History and Literature; A Hand-Book of Southern Authors From the Settlement of Jamestown, 1607, to Living Writers.* Atlanta: The Franklin-Turner Co., 1907. pp. 568-72.

David B. Kesterson
North Texas State University

John Walter Wilson (1920-   )
novel, short stories

High John, the Conqueror. New York: Macmillan, 1948.

In addition, Wilson published eight stories in *Southwest Review, New Mexico Quarterly Review,* and *Prairie Schooner* between 1940 and 1955.

George C. Greenlee
North Texas State University

Marvin Davis Winsett (1902-   )
poetry

Winding Stairway. Dallas: Wilkinson, 1953.
April Always. Dallas: Wilkinson, 1956.
Remembered Earth. San Antonio: Naylor, 1962.

Poems in *Kaleidograph, Quicksilver, Poet Lore, American Bard,* and other periodicals; and in *The Spring Anthology, From Sea to Sea in Song Anthology, The Singing Muse Anthology, The Guild Anthology,* and other anthologies.

442   *Southwestern American Literature*

Works about Marvin Davis Winsett
Edwards, Margaret Royalty. *Poets Laureate of Texas 1932-1966.* San Antonio: Naylor, 1966.

> Arthur M. Sampley
> North Texas State University

Clee Woods (1893-   )
[pseud. Lee Forest]
novels, short stories, nonfiction

Riders of the Sierra Madre. New York: Macaulay, 1935.
Buckaroo Clan of Montana. New York: Macaulay, 1936.
Raiders of Lost River. New York: Macaulay, 1937.
Rebels Rendezvous [Lee Forest]. New York: D. Appleton-Century, 1937.

In addition, Clee Woods has written many short stories and novelettes for Western magazines (many under his pseudonym). His story "Sky Hoofs" was made into a 1925 movie starring Jack Hoxie.

> James W. Lee
> North Texas State University

Kathleen Witherspoon (-   )
plays

Jute. Southwest Review, 16 (April 1931), 385-436.
Three Southwestern Plays. Dallas: *Southwest Review,* 1942.

> George C. Greenlee
> North Texas State University

Douglas Woolf (1922-   )
novels, short stories

Fade Out. New York: Grove Press, 1959. Rpt. London: Weidenfeld, 1968.
Wall to Wall. New York: Grove Press, 1961.
Ya! [and] John Juan. New York: Harper & Row, 1971.

In addition, Woolf has published over a dozen stories in such periodicals as *Evergreen Review, Southwest Review,* and *Prairie Schooner.*

George C. Greenlee
North Texas State University

Harold Bell Wright (1872-1944)
novels, short stories, poetry, nonfiction

That Printer of Udell's: A Story of the Middle West. Chicago: Book Supply Co., 1903. Rpt., 1911.
The Shepherd of the Hills. Chicago: Book Supply Co., 1907.
The Calling of Dan Matthews. Chicago: Book Supply Co., 1909.
The Uncrowned King. Chicago: Book Supply Co., 1910.
The Winning of Barbara Worth. Chicago: Book Supply Co., 1911.
Their Yesterdays. Chicago: Book Supply Co., 1912.
The Eyes of the World. Chicago: Book Supply Co., 1914.
When a Man's a Man. Chicago: Book Supply Co., 1916.
The Re-Creation of Brian Kent. Chicago: Book Supply Co., 1919.
Helen of the Old House. New York: Appleton, 1921.
The Mine With the Iron Door. New York: Appleton, 1923.
A Son of His Father. New York: Appleton, 1925.
God and the Groceryman. New York: Appleton, 1927.
Long Ago Told (Huh-Kew ah-Kah) Legends of the Papago Indians. New York: Appleton, 1929.
Exit. New York: Appleton, 1930.
Ma Cinderella. New York: Harper, 1932.
The Devil's Highway. New York: Appleton, 1932.
To My Sons. New York: Harper, 1934.
The Man Who Went Away. New York: Harper, 1942.

In addition, Wright published eight stories, articles, and poems between 1912 and 1932 in *American Magazine, Good Housekeeping, Ladies Home Journal,* and *Pictorial Review.*

Works about Harold Bell Wright
Baldwin, Charles C. "Harold Bell Wright," *The Men Who Make Our Novels.* New York: Dodd, Mead, 1924. pp. 601-12.

Boynton, H. W. "Some American Novelists and the Lame Art," *Dial,* Dec. 9, 1915, pp. 548-49.

————. "A Word on 'The Genteel Critic,' " *Dial,* Oct. 14, 1915, pp. 303-06.

Cooper, F. T. "The Popularity of Harold Bell Wright," *Bookman,* 40 (January 1915), 498-500.

Hastings, M. "Fiction is Stranger Than Truth," *New Republic,* July 21, 1940, pp. 227-28.

Hawthorne, Hildegarde. "The Wright American," *The Bookman Anthology of Essays,* ed. John Farrar. New York: Doran, 1923.

Kenamore, Clair. "A Curiosity in Best-Seller Technique," *Bookman,* 44 (July 1918), 538-44.

MacMullen, M. "Love's Old Sweetish Song," *Harper's,* 195 (October 1947), 371-80.

Millard, Bailey. "The Personality of Harold Bell Wright," *Bookman,* 44 (January 1917), 463-69.

Mott, Frank L. "Harold Bell Wright," *Golden Multitudes: The Story of Best Sellers in the United States.* New York: Macmillan, 1947. pp. 225-33.

Patrick, A. "Getting Into Six Figures," *Bookman,* 61 (August 1925), 673-77.

"Portrait by Amero," *Independent,* Dec. 5, 1925, pp. 14-21.

Randall, Dale B. J. "The 'Seer' and 'Seen' Themes in 'Gatsby' and Some of Their Parallels in Eliot and Wright," *Twentieth Century Literature,* 10 (July 1964), 51-63.

Reynolds, Elsbery W. *Harold Bell Wright: A Biography Intimate and Authoritative.* Chicago: Book Supply Co., 1916.

Tinsley, Henry G. "Sketch," *Sunset,* 41 (December 1918), 46-47.

Numerous articles on Harold Bell Wright and his works, especially *The Shepherd of the Hills,* appeared in early Springfield, Mo., newspapers and several Ozark publications. Many of these items are available (as is the rare Elsbery W. Reynolds biography of Wright) in the Springfield, Mo., Public Library.

David B. Kesterson
North Texas State University

Fay Yauger (1902-   )
poetry

Planter's Charm. Dallas: Kaleidograph, 1935.

In addition, Yauger has published poems in *Literary Digest, Texas Poets.* and the *Yearbook* of the Texas Poetry Society.

Eleanor James
Texas Woman's University

Ramsey Yelvington (1913-1973)
short stories, plays

The Roaring Kleinschmids (Texas hill country sketches). Boerne, Texas: Highland Press, 1950.

A Cloud of Witnesses (drama of the Alamo). Austin: Univ. of Texas Press, 1959.

Dramatic Images for the Church (nine plays; three choral readings). Waco: Baylor Theatre, 1959.

Charles B. Martin
North Texas State University